PART TWO

(SOLSTICE)

The Dragonslayer

Volume Four:
The Dragonslayer

Jeff Smith

Cartoon Books
Columbus, Ohio

THIS BOOK IS
FOR
IRENE KILTY
FOR INSPIRING
HER GRANDSON'S
IMAGINATION

BONE Volume Four: The Dragonslayer copyright © 1997 by Jeff Smith.

Acknowledgements:
The Harvestar Family Crest designed by Charles Vess
Cover art by Jeff Smith and Drew

For information write:
Cartoon Books
P.O. Box 16973
Columbus, OH 43216
or
ask@boneville.com

Hardcover ISBN: 1-888963-01-8
Softcover ISBN: 1-888963-00-X

10 9 8 7 6

Printed in Canada

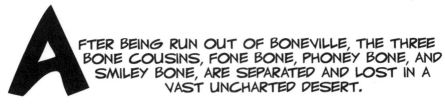

AFTER BEING RUN OUT OF BONEVILLE, THE THREE BONE COUSINS, FONE BONE, PHONEY BONE, AND SMILEY BONE, ARE SEPARATED AND LOST IN A VAST UNCHARTED DESERT.

ONE BY ONE, THEY FIND THEIR WAY INTO A DEEP, FORESTED VALLEY FILLED WITH WONDERFUL AND TERRIFYING CREATURES. . .

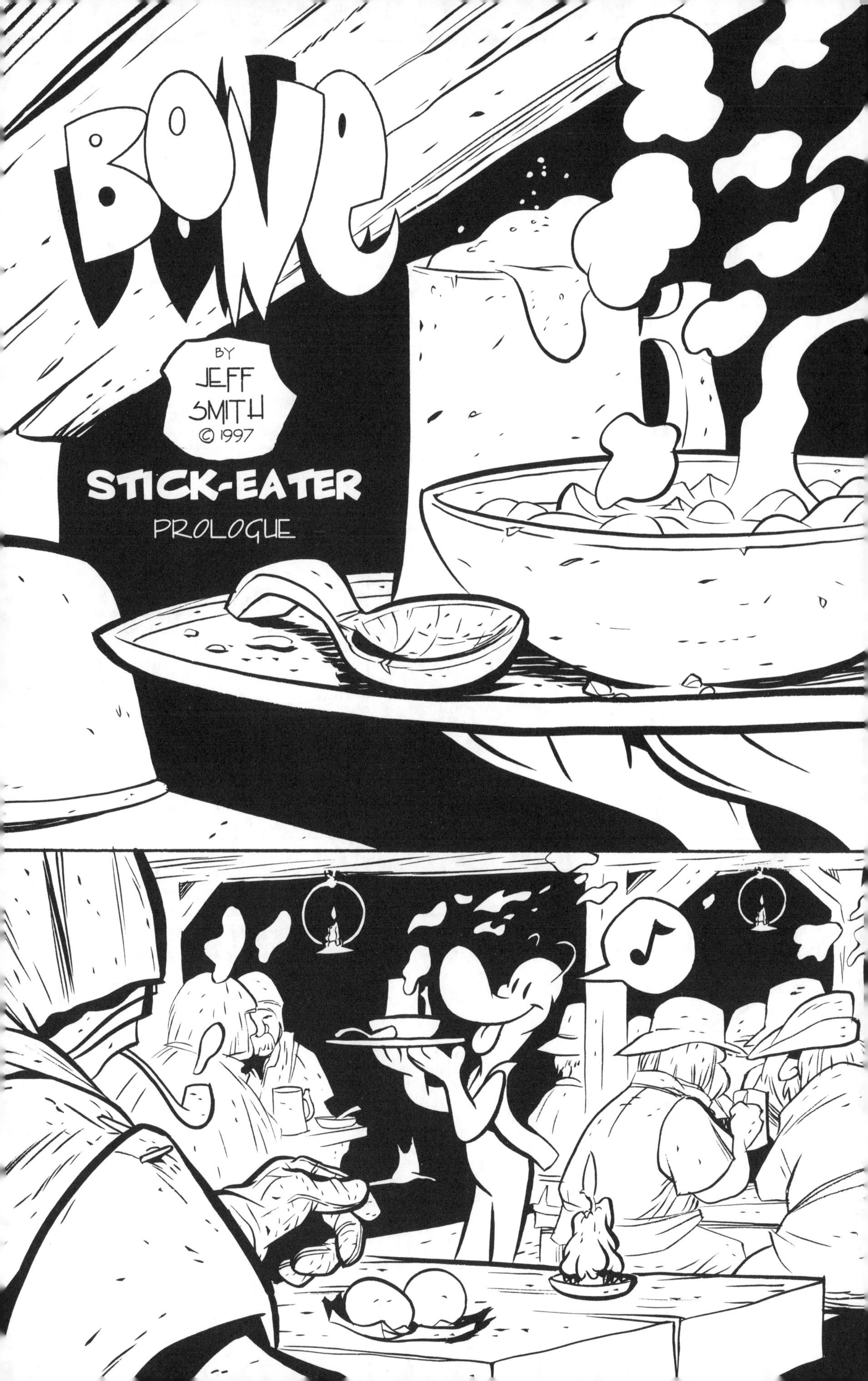
BONE
BY
JEFF
SMITH
© 1997
STICK-EATER
PROLOGUE
♪

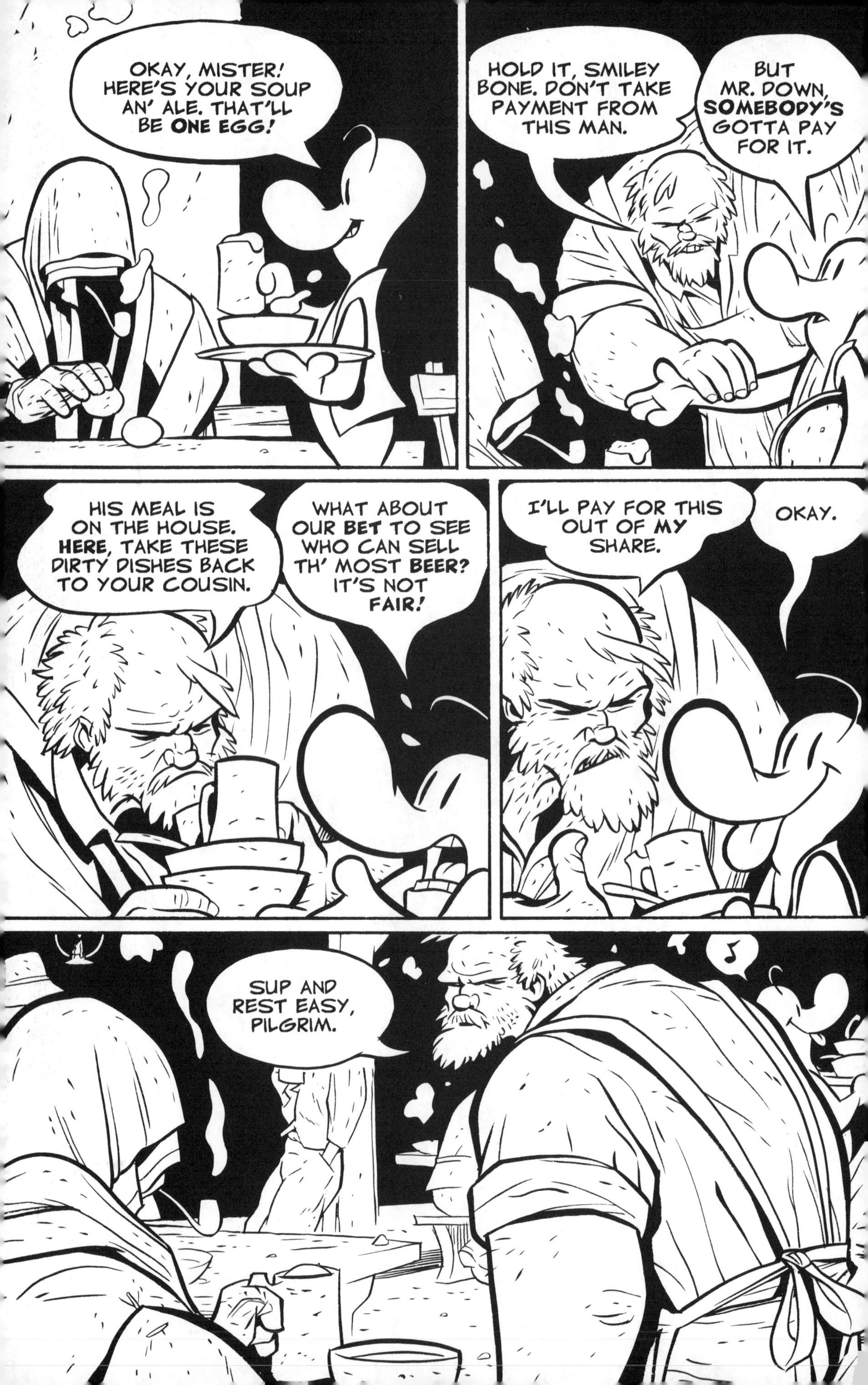
OKAY, MISTER! HERE'S YOUR SOUP AN' ALE. THAT'LL BE ONE EGG!
HOLD IT, SMILEY BONE. DON'T TAKE PAYMENT FROM THIS MAN.
BUT MR. DOWN, SOMEBODY'S GOTTA PAY FOR IT.
HIS MEAL IS ON THE HOUSE. HERE, TAKE THESE DIRTY DISHES BACK TO YOUR COUSIN.
WHAT ABOUT OUR BET TO SEE WHO CAN SELL TH' MOST BEER? IT'S NOT FAIR!
I'LL PAY FOR THIS OUT OF MY SHARE.
OKAY.
SUP AND REST EASY, PILGRIM.

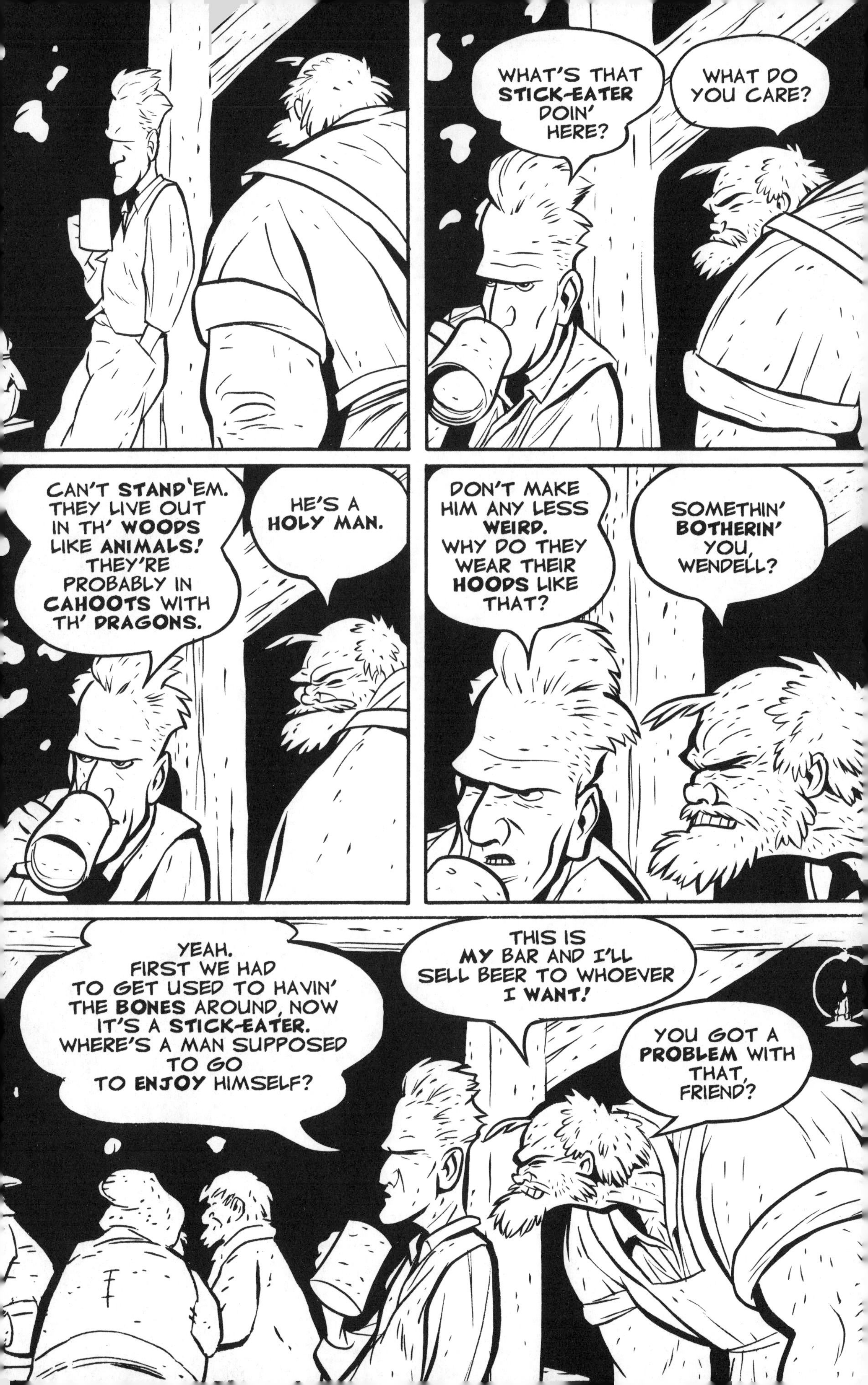
WHAT'S THAT STICK-EATER DOIN' HERE?
WHAT DO YOU CARE?
CAN'T STAND'EM. THEY LIVE OUT IN TH' WOODS LIKE ANIMALS! THEY'RE PROBABLY IN CAHOOTS WITH TH' DRAGONS.
HE'S A HOLY MAN.
DON'T MAKE HIM ANY LESS WEIRD. WHY DO THEY WEAR THEIR HOODS LIKE THAT?
SOMETHIN' BOTHERIN' YOU, WENDELL?
YEAH. FIRST WE HAD TO GET USED TO HAVIN' THE BONES AROUND, NOW IT'S A STICK-EATER. WHERE'S A MAN SUPPOSED TO GO TO ENJOY HIMSELF?
THIS IS MY BAR AND I'LL SELL BEER TO WHOEVER I WANT!
YOU GOT A PROBLEM WITH THAT, FRIEND?

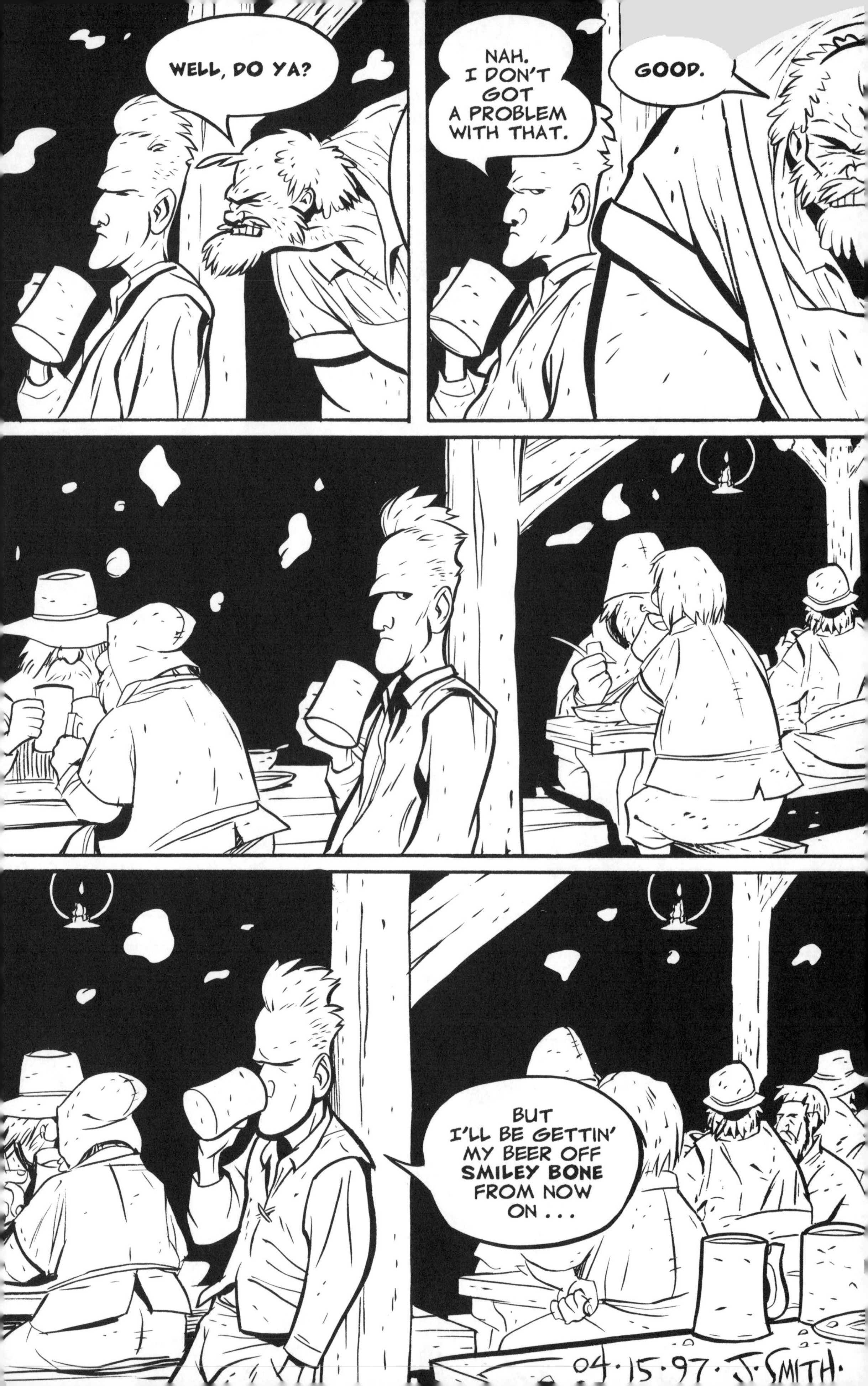
WELL, DO YA?
NAH. I DON'T GOT A PROBLEM WITH THAT.
GOOD.
BUT I'LL BE GETTIN' MY BEER OFF SMILEY BONE FROM NOW ON . . .
04·15·97· J·SMITH·

THE DRAGONSLAYER

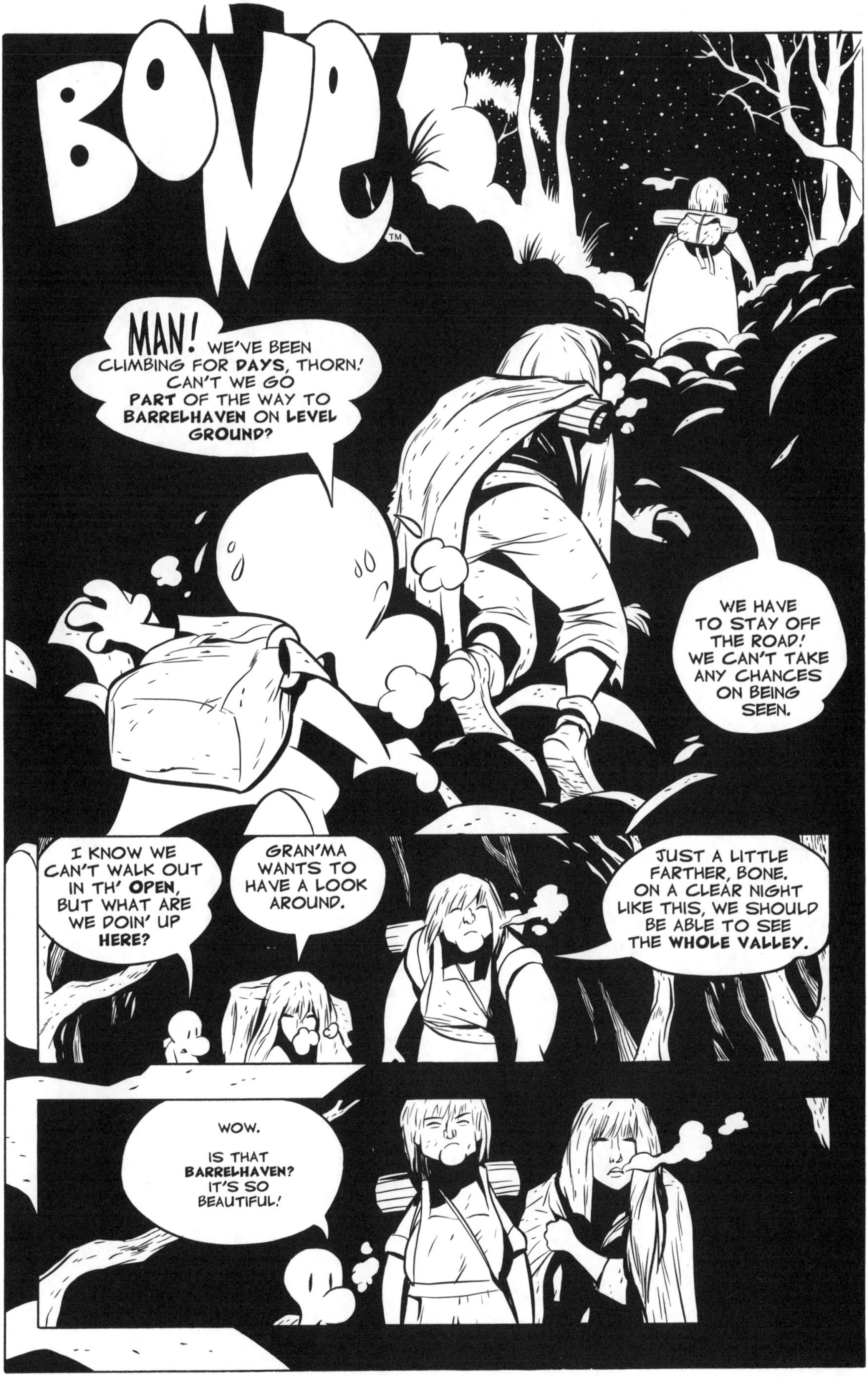
BONE™
MAN! WE'VE BEEN CLIMBING FOR DAYS, THORN! CAN'T WE GO PART OF THE WAY TO BARRELHAVEN ON LEVEL GROUND?
WE HAVE TO STAY OFF THE ROAD! WE CAN'T TAKE ANY CHANCES ON BEING SEEN.
I KNOW WE CAN'T WALK OUT IN TH' OPEN, BUT WHAT ARE WE DOIN' UP HERE?
GRAN'MA WANTS TO HAVE A LOOK AROUND.
JUST A LITTLE FARTHER, BONE. ON A CLEAR NIGHT LIKE THIS, WE SHOULD BE ABLE TO SEE THE WHOLE VALLEY.
WOW.
IS THAT BARRELHAVEN? IT'S SO BEAUTIFUL!

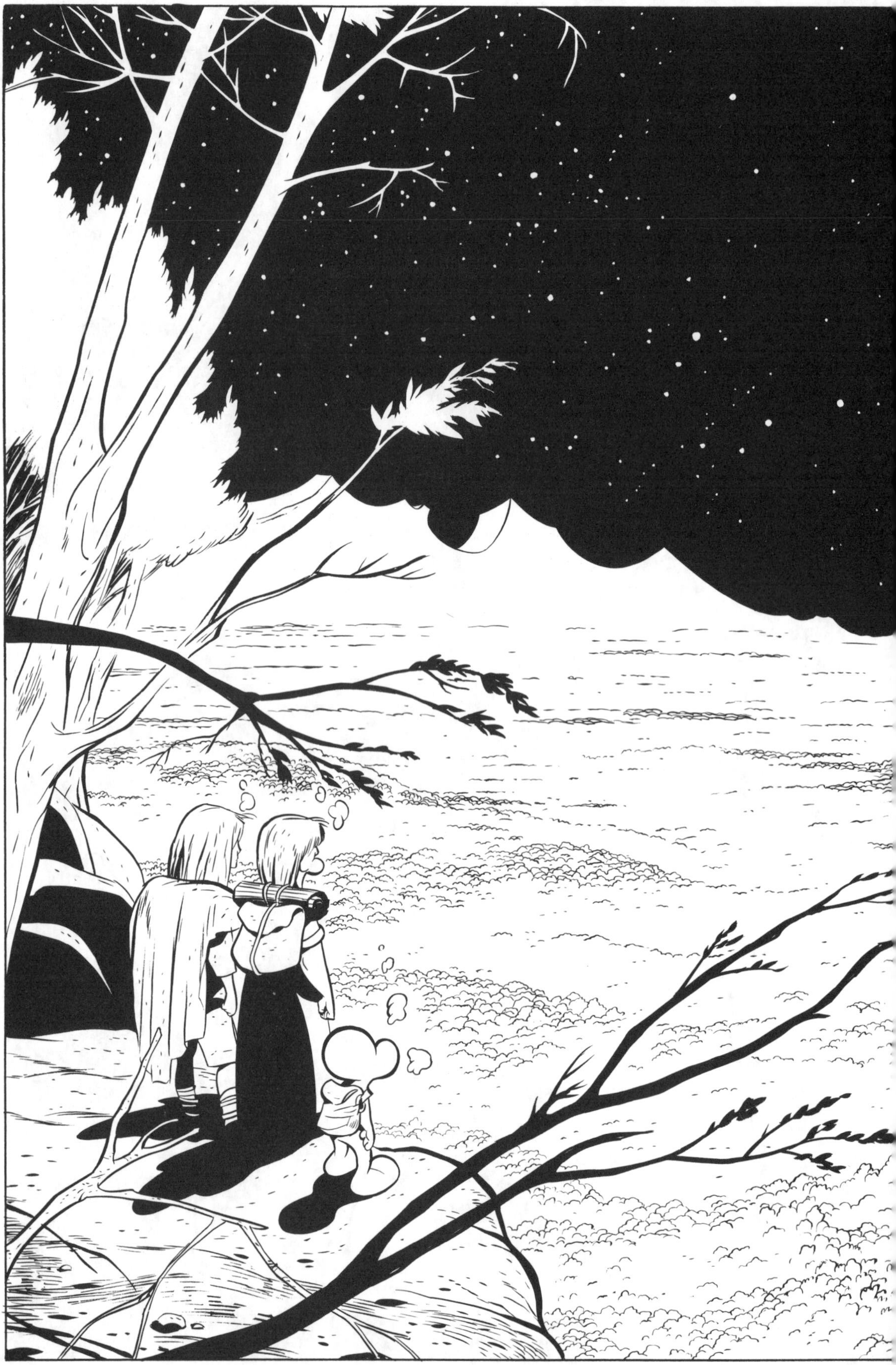

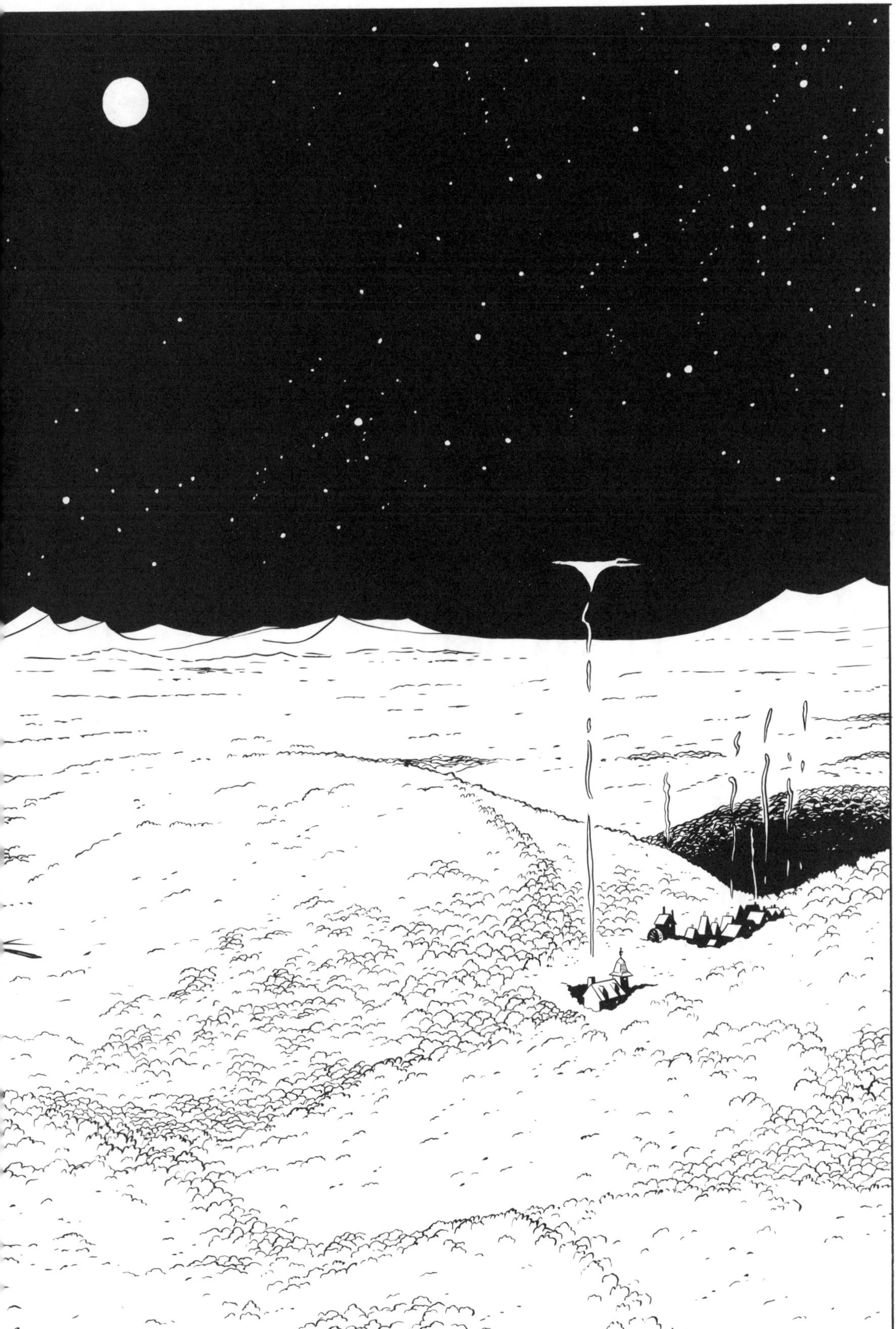

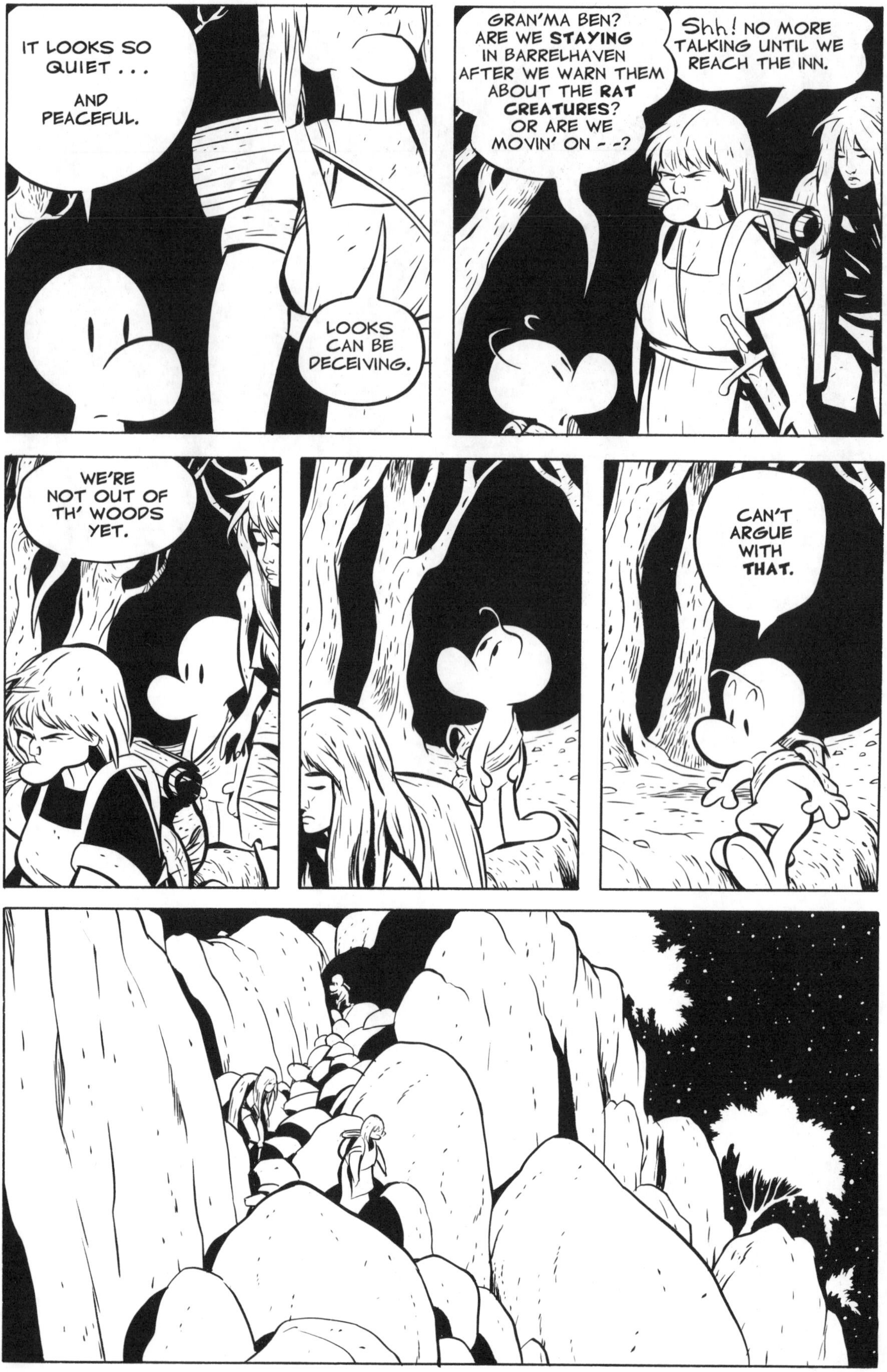
IT LOOKS SO QUIET . . .
AND PEACEFUL.
LOOKS CAN BE DECEIVING.
GRAN'MA BEN? ARE WE **STAYING** IN BARRELHAVEN AFTER WE WARN THEM ABOUT THE **RAT CREATURES**? OR ARE WE MOVIN' ON - -?
Shh! NO MORE TALKING UNTIL WE REACH THE INN.
WE'RE NOT OUT OF TH' WOODS YET.
CAN'T ARGUE WITH **THAT**.

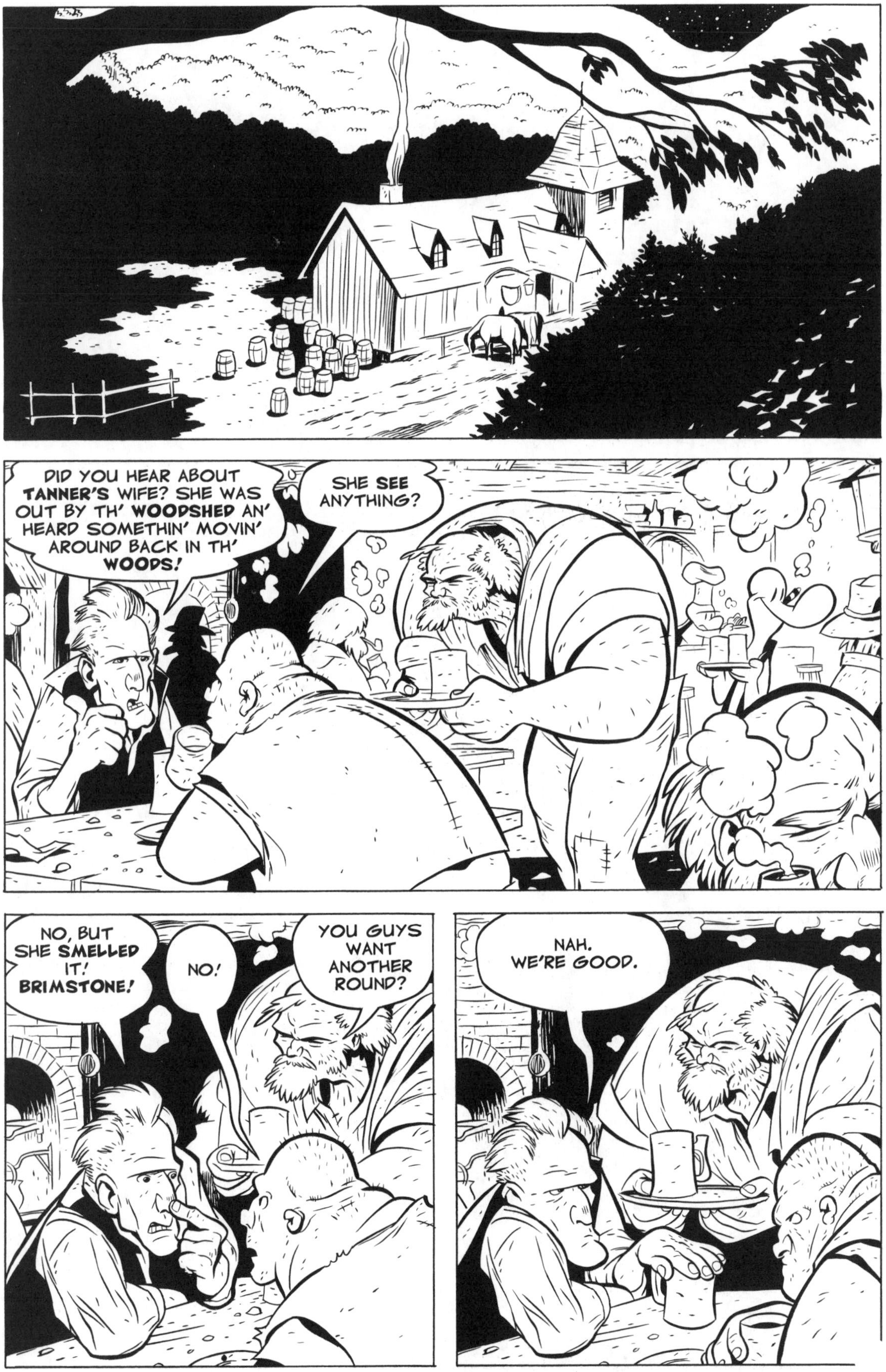
DID YOU HEAR ABOUT TANNER'S WIFE? SHE WAS OUT BY TH' WOODSHED AN' HEARD SOMETHIN' MOVIN' AROUND BACK IN TH' WOODS!
SHE SEE ANYTHING?
NO, BUT SHE SMELLED IT! BRIMSTONE!
NO!
YOU GUYS WANT ANOTHER ROUND?
NAH. WE'RE GOOD.

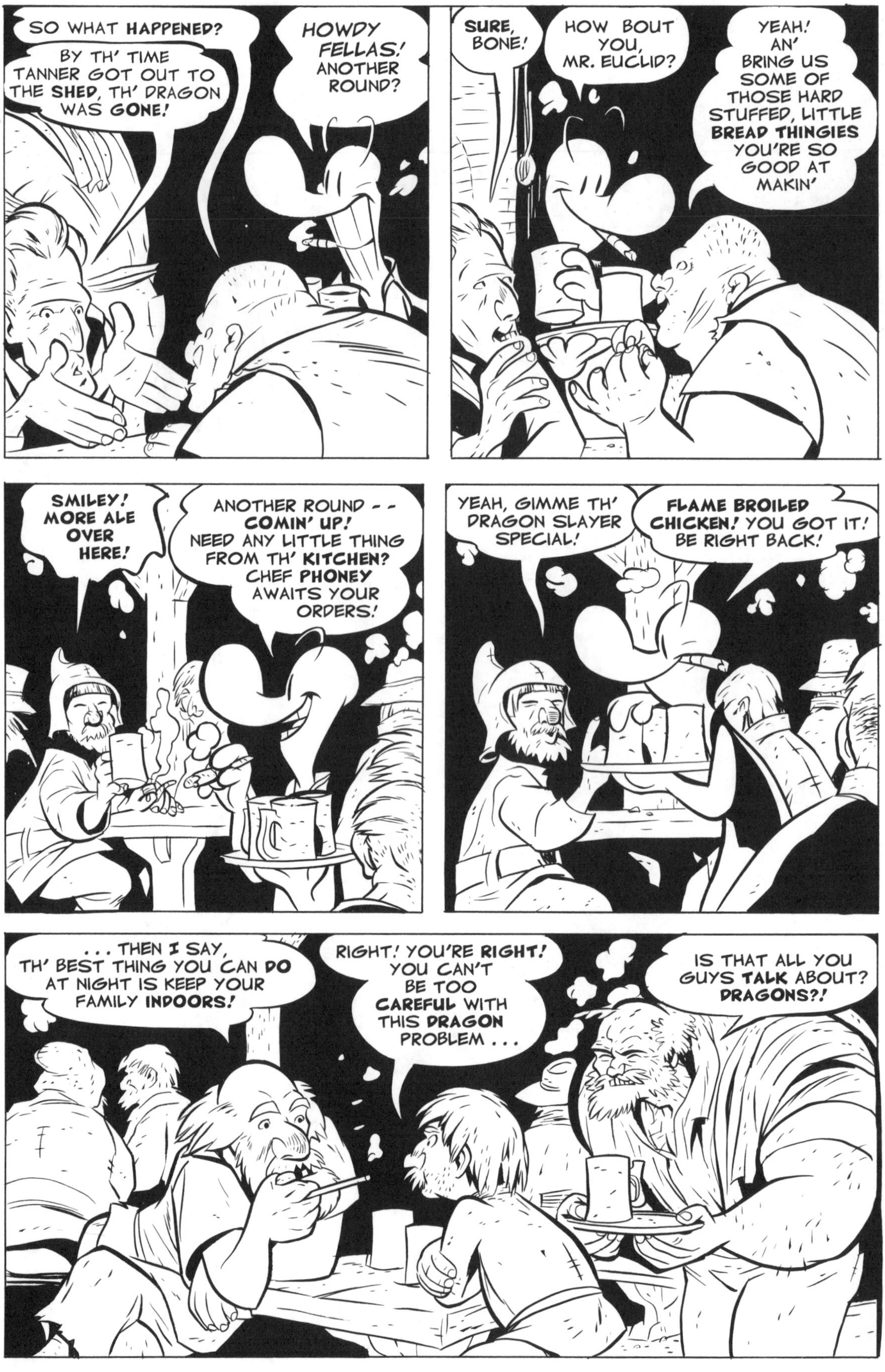
SO WHAT HAPPENED?
BY TH' TIME TANNER GOT OUT TO THE SHED, TH' DRAGON WAS GONE!
HOWDY FELLAS! ANOTHER ROUND?
SURE, BONE!
HOW BOUT YOU, MR. EUCLID?
YEAH! AN' BRING US SOME OF THOSE HARD STUFFED, LITTLE BREAD THINGIES YOU'RE SO GOOD AT MAKIN'
SMILEY! MORE ALE OVER HERE!
ANOTHER ROUND - - COMIN' UP! NEED ANY LITTLE THING FROM TH' KITCHEN? CHEF PHONEY AWAITS YOUR ORDERS!
YEAH, GIMME TH' DRAGON SLAYER SPECIAL!
FLAME BROILED CHICKEN! YOU GOT IT! BE RIGHT BACK!
. . . THEN I SAY, TH' BEST THING YOU CAN DO AT NIGHT IS KEEP YOUR FAMILY INDOORS!
RIGHT! YOU'RE RIGHT! YOU CAN'T BE TOO CAREFUL WITH THIS DRAGON PROBLEM . . .
IS THAT ALL YOU GUYS TALK ABOUT? DRAGONS?!

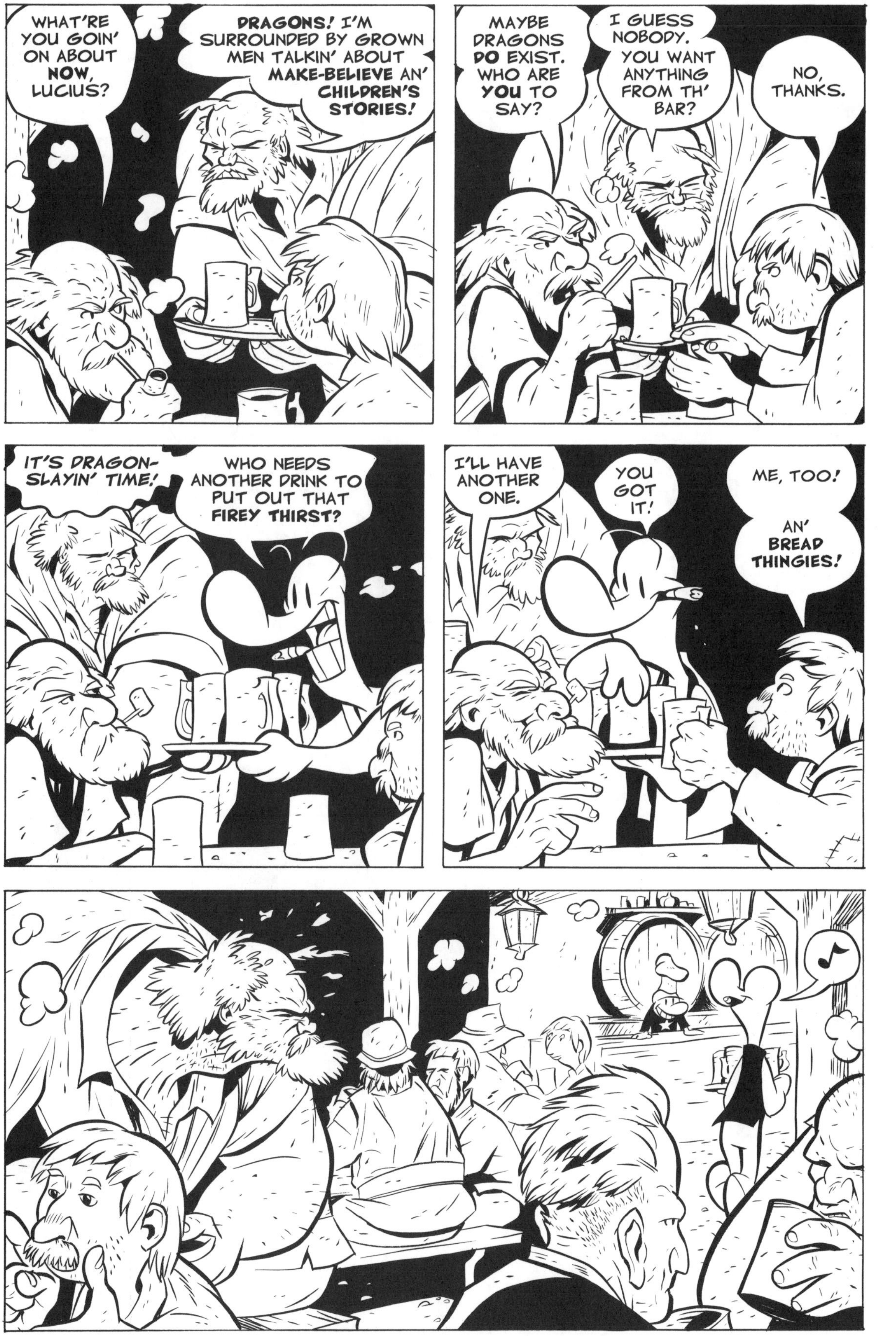
WHAT'RE YOU GOIN' ON ABOUT **NOW**, LUCIUS?
DRAGONS! I'M SURROUNDED BY GROWN MEN TALKIN' ABOUT **MAKE-BELIEVE** AN' **CHILDREN'S STORIES!**
MAYBE DRAGONS **DO** EXIST. WHO ARE **YOU** TO SAY?
I GUESS NOBODY. YOU WANT ANYTHING FROM TH' BAR?
NO, THANKS.
IT'S DRAGON-SLAYIN' TIME!
WHO NEEDS ANOTHER DRINK TO PUT OUT THAT **FIREY THIRST?**
I'LL HAVE ANOTHER ONE.
YOU GOT IT!
ME, TOO!
AN' **BREAD THINGIES!**

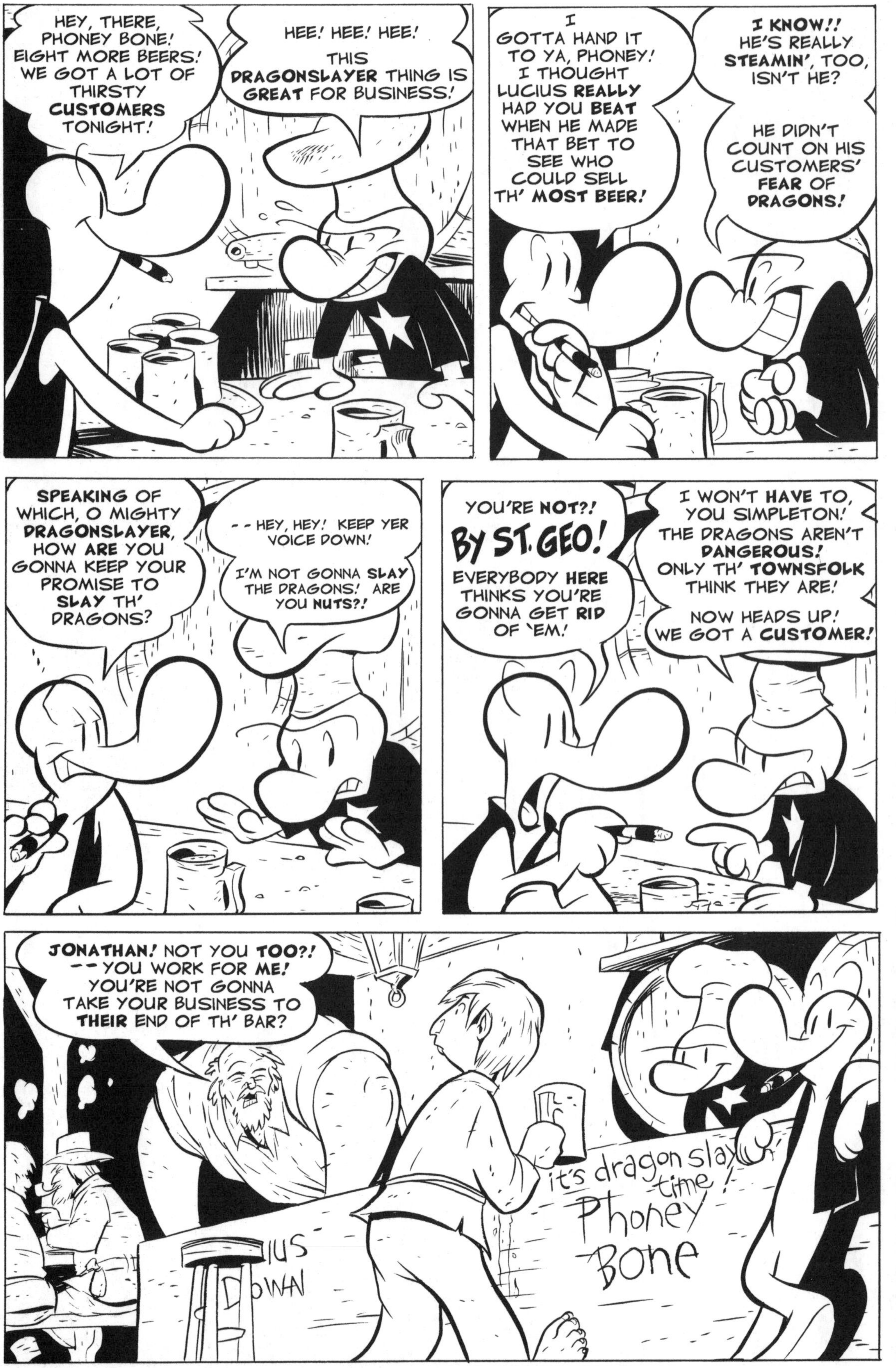
HEY, THERE, PHONEY BONE! EIGHT MORE BEERS! WE GOT A LOT OF THIRSTY CUSTOMERS TONIGHT!
HEE! HEE! HEE! THIS DRAGONSLAYER THING IS GREAT FOR BUSINESS!
I GOTTA HAND IT TO YA, PHONEY! I THOUGHT LUCIUS REALLY HAD YOU BEAT WHEN HE MADE THAT BET TO SEE WHO COULD SELL TH' MOST BEER!
I KNOW!! HE'S REALLY STEAMIN', TOO, ISN'T HE?
HE DIDN'T COUNT ON HIS CUSTOMERS' FEAR OF DRAGONS!
SPEAKING OF WHICH, O MIGHTY DRAGONSLAYER, HOW ARE YOU GONNA KEEP YOUR PROMISE TO SLAY TH' DRAGONS?
-- HEY, HEY! KEEP YER VOICE DOWN!
I'M NOT GONNA SLAY THE DRAGONS! ARE YOU NUTS?!
YOU'RE NOT?!
BY ST. GEO!
EVERYBODY HERE THINKS YOU'RE GONNA GET RID OF 'EM!
I WON'T HAVE TO, YOU SIMPLETON! THE DRAGONS AREN'T DANGEROUS! ONLY TH' TOWNSFOLK THINK THEY ARE!
NOW HEADS UP! WE GOT A CUSTOMER!
JONATHAN! NOT YOU TOO?! -- YOU WORK FOR ME! YOU'RE NOT GONNA TAKE YOUR BUSINESS TO THEIR END OF TH' BAR?
it's dragon slay time! Phoney Bone

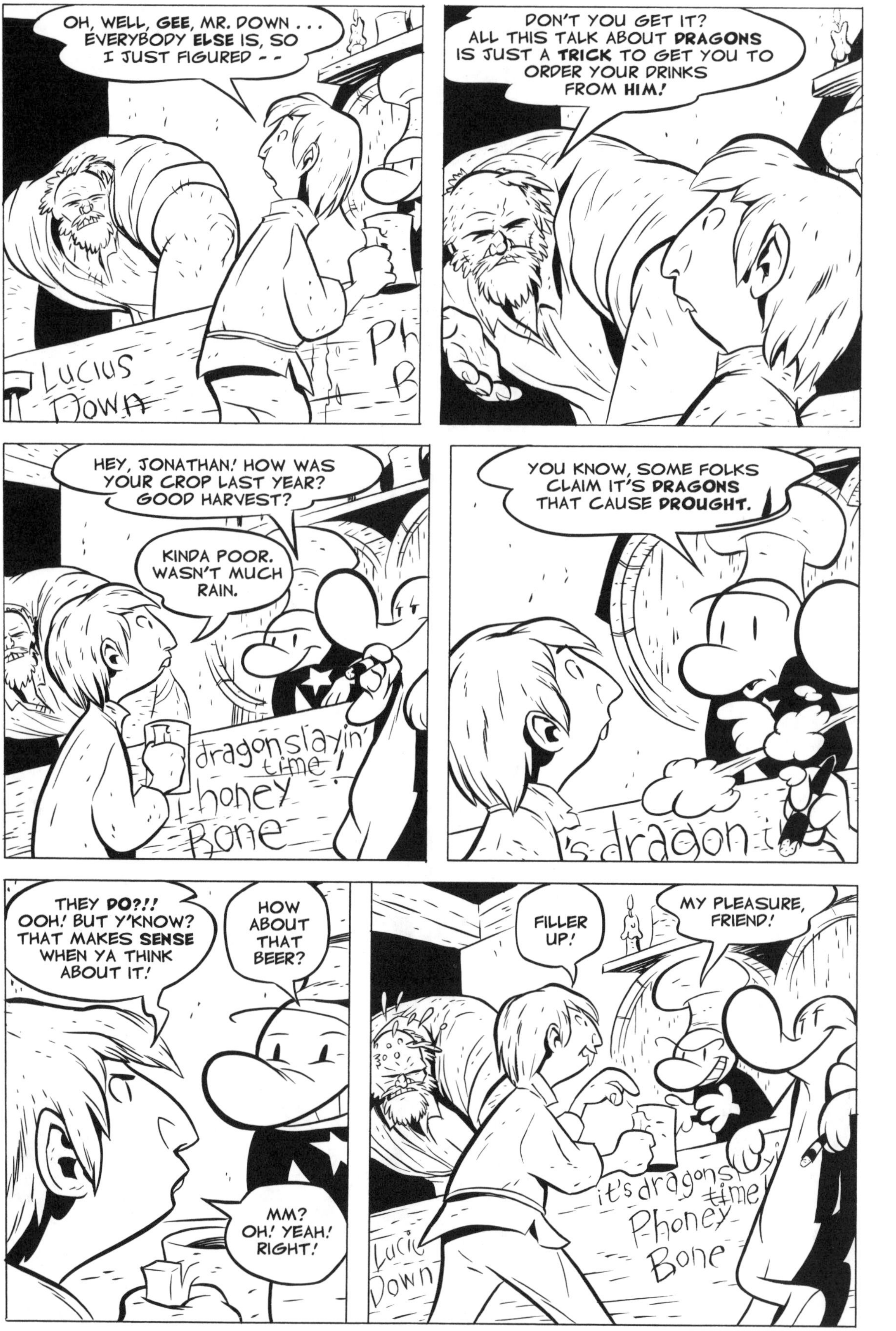
OH, WELL, GEE, MR. DOWN . . . EVERYBODY ELSE IS, SO I JUST FIGURED - -
Lucius Down
DON'T YOU GET IT? ALL THIS TALK ABOUT DRAGONS IS JUST A TRICK TO GET YOU TO ORDER YOUR DRINKS FROM HIM!
HEY, JONATHAN! HOW WAS YOUR CROP LAST YEAR? GOOD HARVEST?
KINDA POOR. WASN'T MUCH RAIN.
dragonslayin' time! Phoney Bone
YOU KNOW, SOME FOLKS CLAIM IT'S DRAGONS THAT CAUSE DROUGHT.
THEY DO?!! OOH! BUT Y'KNOW? THAT MAKES SENSE WHEN YA THINK ABOUT IT!
HOW ABOUT THAT BEER?
MM? OH! YEAH! RIGHT!
FILLER UP!
MY PLEASURE, FRIEND!
it's dragonslayin' time! Phoney Bone
Lucius Down

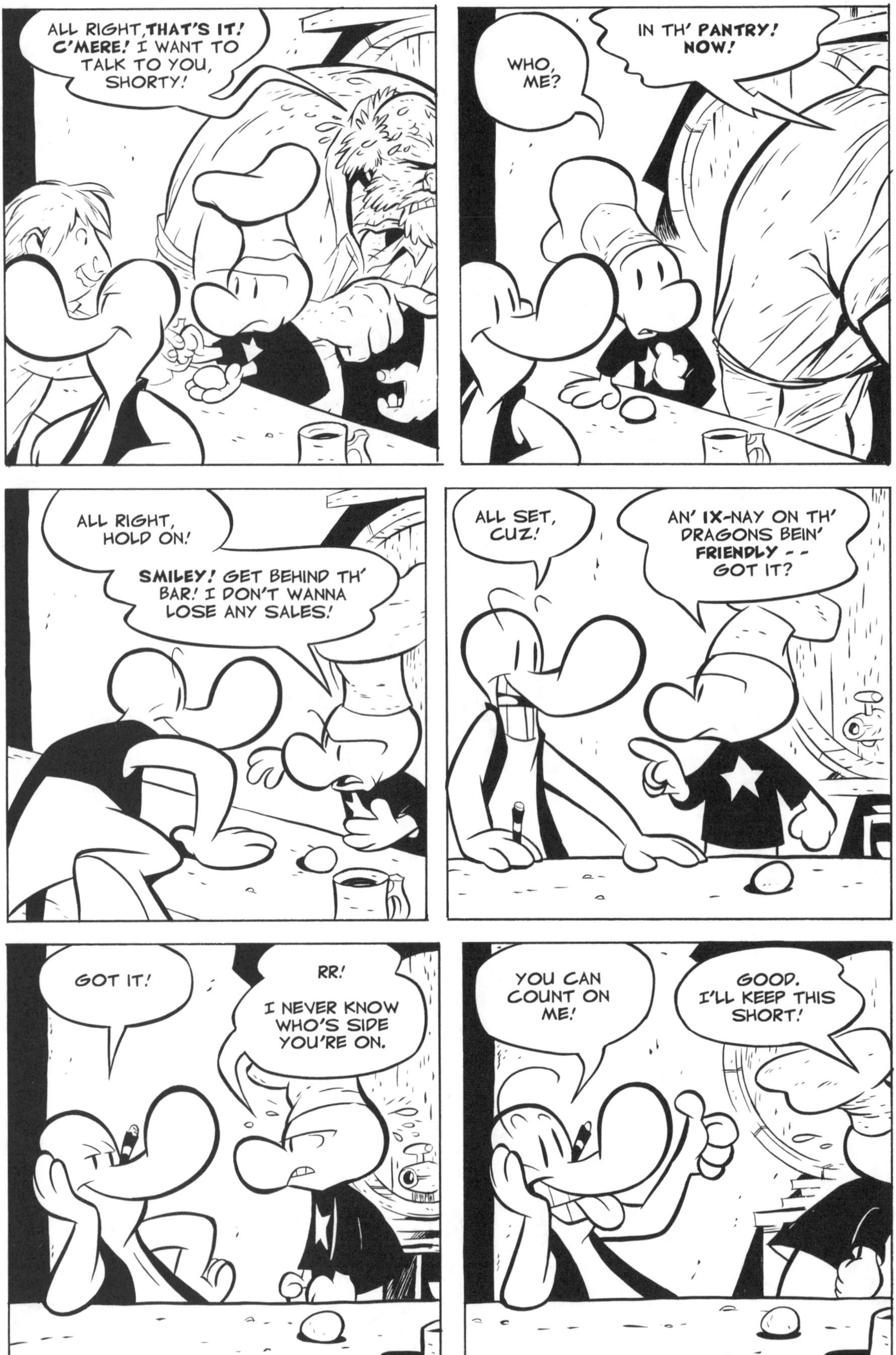
ALL RIGHT, THAT'S IT! C'MERE! I WANT TO TALK TO YOU, SHORTY!
WHO, ME?
IN TH' PANTRY! NOW!
ALL RIGHT, HOLD ON!
SMILEY! GET BEHIND TH' BAR! I DON'T WANNA LOSE ANY SALES!
ALL SET, CUZ!
AN' IX-NAY ON TH' DRAGONS BEIN' FRIENDLY -- GOT IT?
GOT IT!
RR!
I NEVER KNOW WHO'S SIDE YOU'RE ON.
YOU CAN COUNT ON ME!
GOOD. I'LL KEEP THIS SHORT!

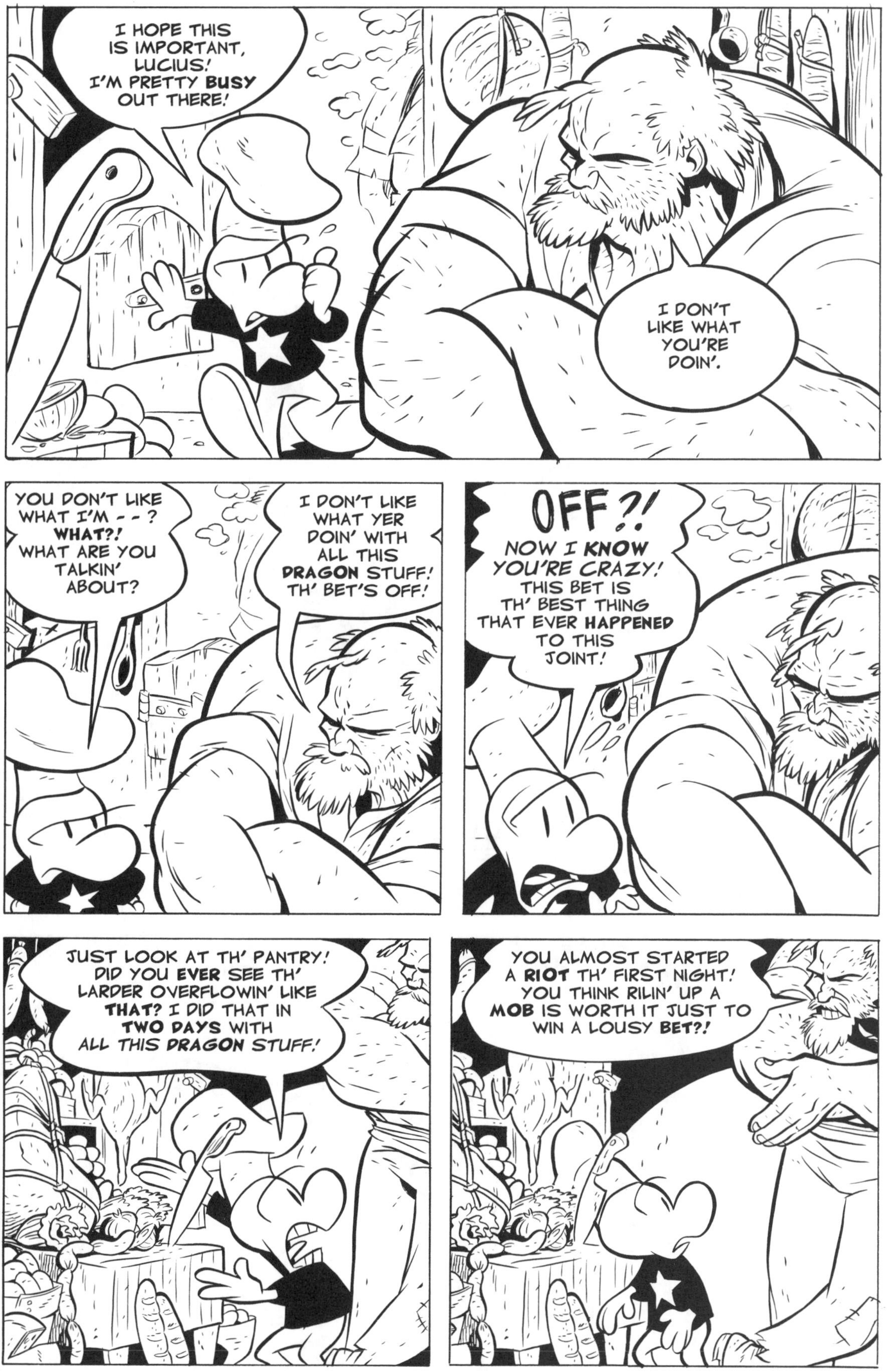

I HOPE THIS IS IMPORTANT, LUCIUS! I'M PRETTY BUSY OUT THERE!
I DON'T LIKE WHAT YOU'RE DOIN'.
YOU DON'T LIKE WHAT I'M - - ? WHAT?! WHAT ARE YOU TALKIN' ABOUT?
I DON'T LIKE WHAT YER DOIN' WITH ALL THIS DRAGON STUFF! TH' BET'S OFF!
OFF?!
NOW I KNOW YOU'RE CRAZY! THIS BET IS TH' BEST THING THAT EVER HAPPENED TO THIS JOINT!
JUST LOOK AT TH' PANTRY! DID YOU EVER SEE TH' LARDER OVERFLOWIN' LIKE THAT? I DID THAT IN TWO DAYS WITH ALL THIS DRAGON STUFF!
YOU ALMOST STARTED A RIOT TH' FIRST NIGHT! YOU THINK RILIN' UP A MOB IS WORTH IT JUST TO WIN A LOUSY BET?!

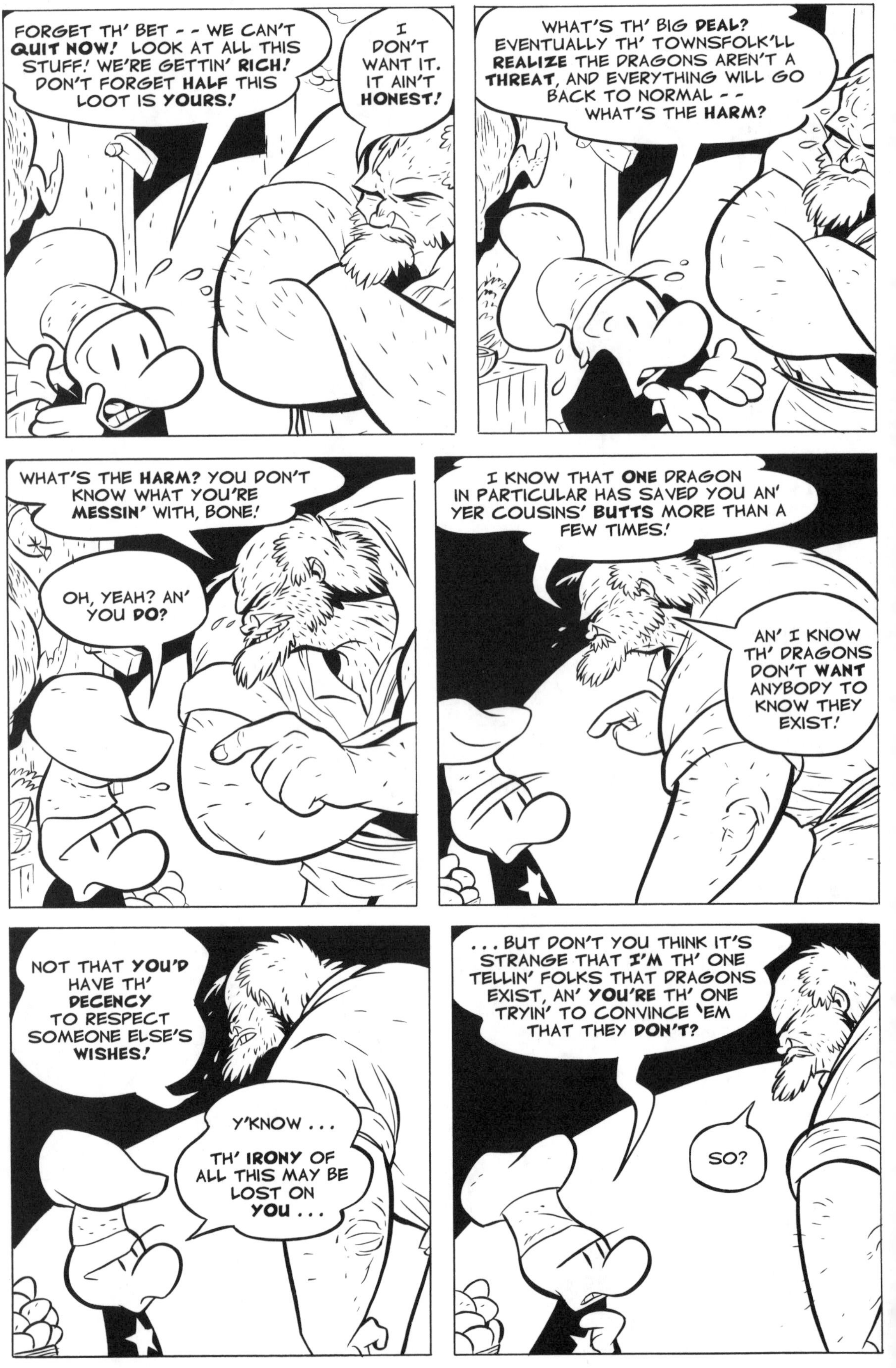
FORGET TH' BET - - WE CAN'T QUIT NOW! LOOK AT ALL THIS STUFF! WE'RE GETTIN' RICH! DON'T FORGET HALF THIS LOOT IS YOURS!
I DON'T WANT IT. IT AIN'T HONEST!
WHAT'S TH' BIG DEAL? EVENTUALLY TH' TOWNSFOLK'LL REALIZE THE DRAGONS AREN'T A THREAT, AND EVERYTHING WILL GO BACK TO NORMAL - - WHAT'S THE HARM?
WHAT'S THE HARM? YOU DON'T KNOW WHAT YOU'RE MESSIN' WITH, BONE!
OH, YEAH? AN' YOU DO?
I KNOW THAT ONE DRAGON IN PARTICULAR HAS SAVED YOU AN' YER COUSINS' BUTTS MORE THAN A FEW TIMES!
AN' I KNOW TH' DRAGONS DON'T WANT ANYBODY TO KNOW THEY EXIST!
NOT THAT YOU'D HAVE TH' DECENCY TO RESPECT SOMEONE ELSE'S WISHES!
Y'KNOW . . .
TH' IRONY OF ALL THIS MAY BE LOST ON YOU . . .
. . . BUT DON'T YOU THINK IT'S STRANGE THAT I'M TH' ONE TELLIN' FOLKS THAT DRAGONS EXIST, AN' YOU'RE TH' ONE TRYIN' TO CONVINCE 'EM THAT THEY DON'T?
SO?

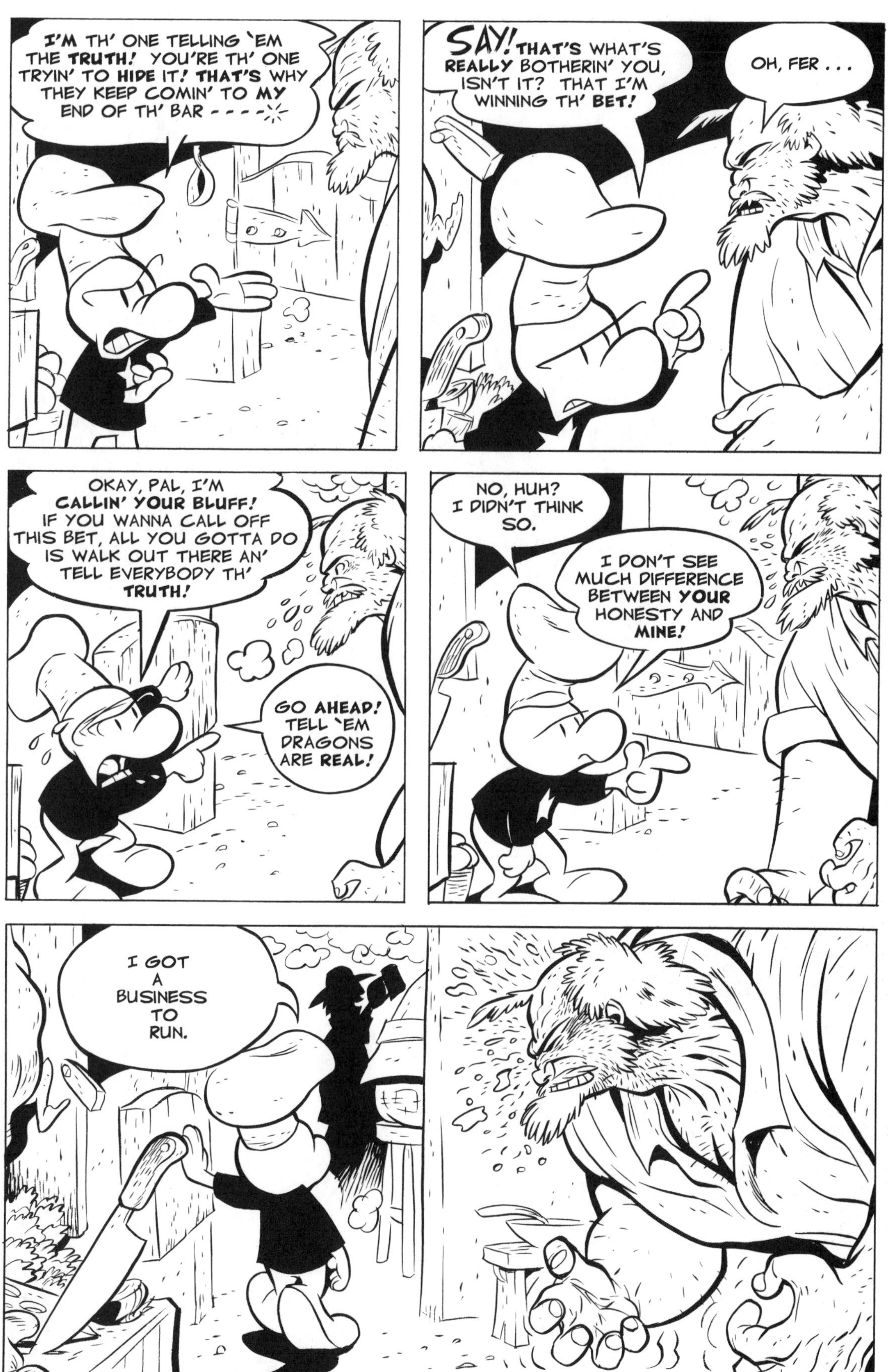

I'M TH' ONE TELLING 'EM THE TRUTH! YOU'RE TH' ONE TRYIN' TO HIDE IT! THAT'S WHY THEY KEEP COMIN' TO MY END OF TH' BAR - - - -
SAY! THAT'S WHAT'S REALLY BOTHERIN' YOU, ISN'T IT? THAT I'M WINNING TH' BET!
OH, FER . . .
OKAY, PAL, I'M CALLIN' YOUR BLUFF! IF YOU WANNA CALL OFF THIS BET, ALL YOU GOTTA DO IS WALK OUT THERE AN' TELL EVERYBODY TH' TRUTH!
GO AHEAD! TELL 'EM DRAGONS ARE REAL!
NO, HUH? I DIDN'T THINK SO.
I DON'T SEE MUCH DIFFERENCE BETWEEN YOUR HONESTY AND MINE!
I GOT A BUSINESS TO RUN.

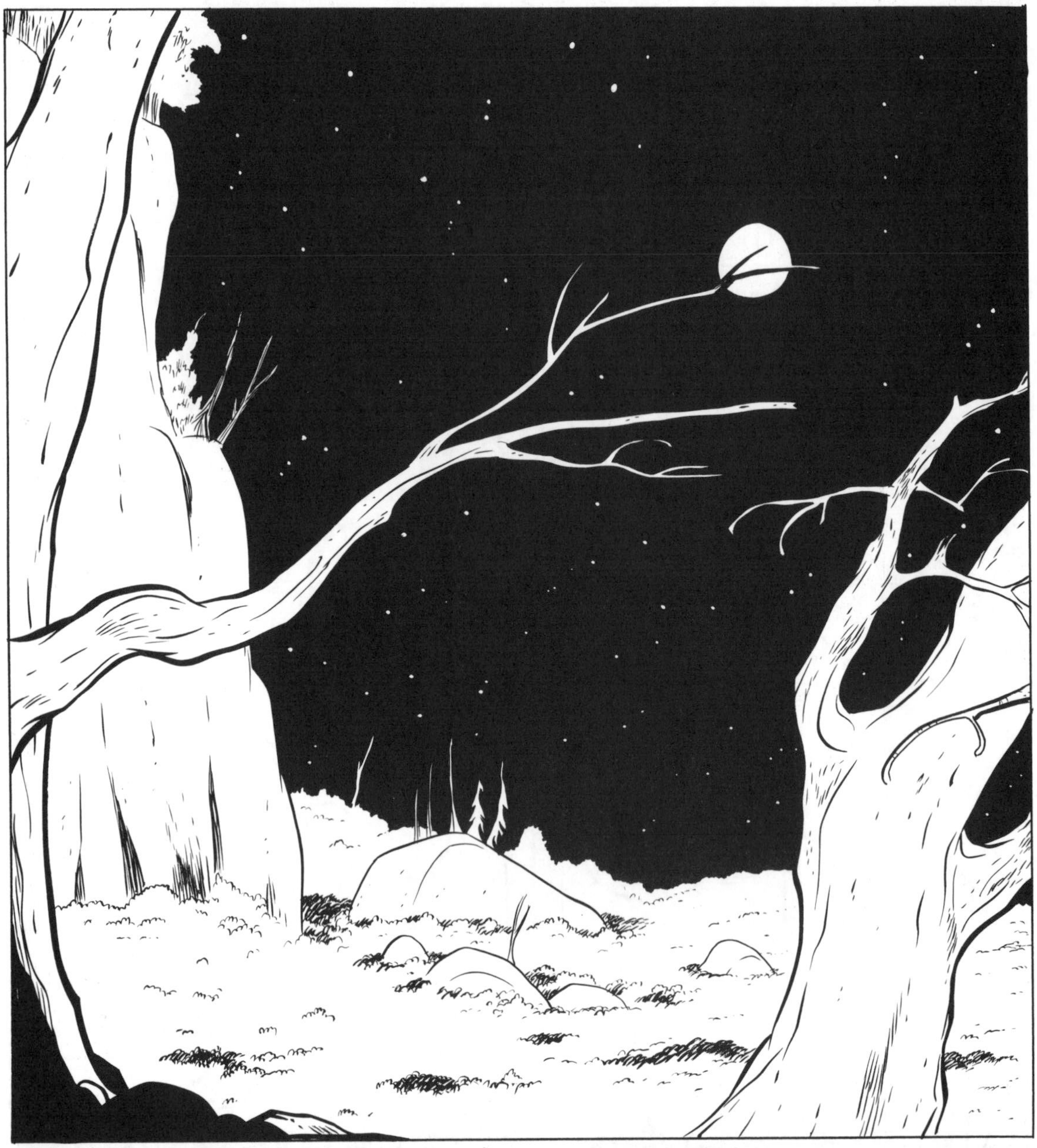
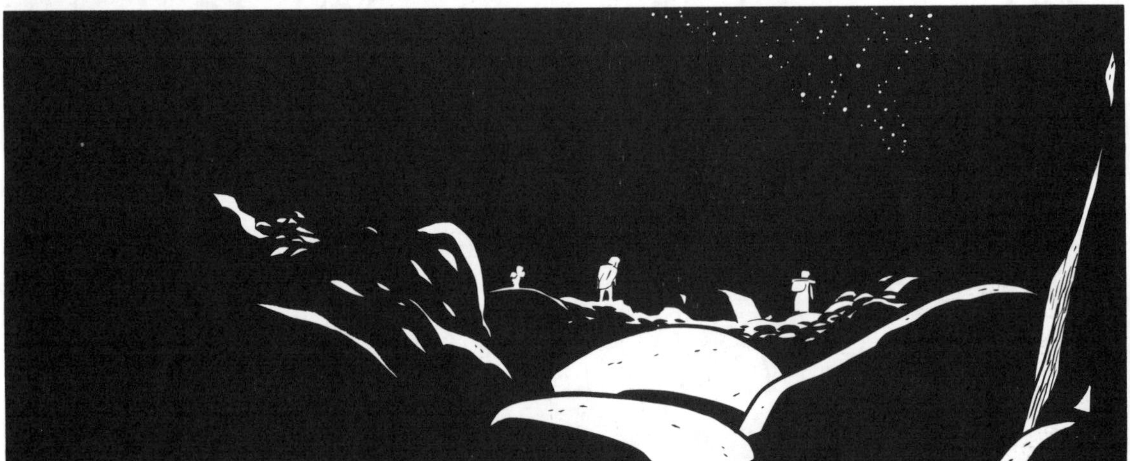

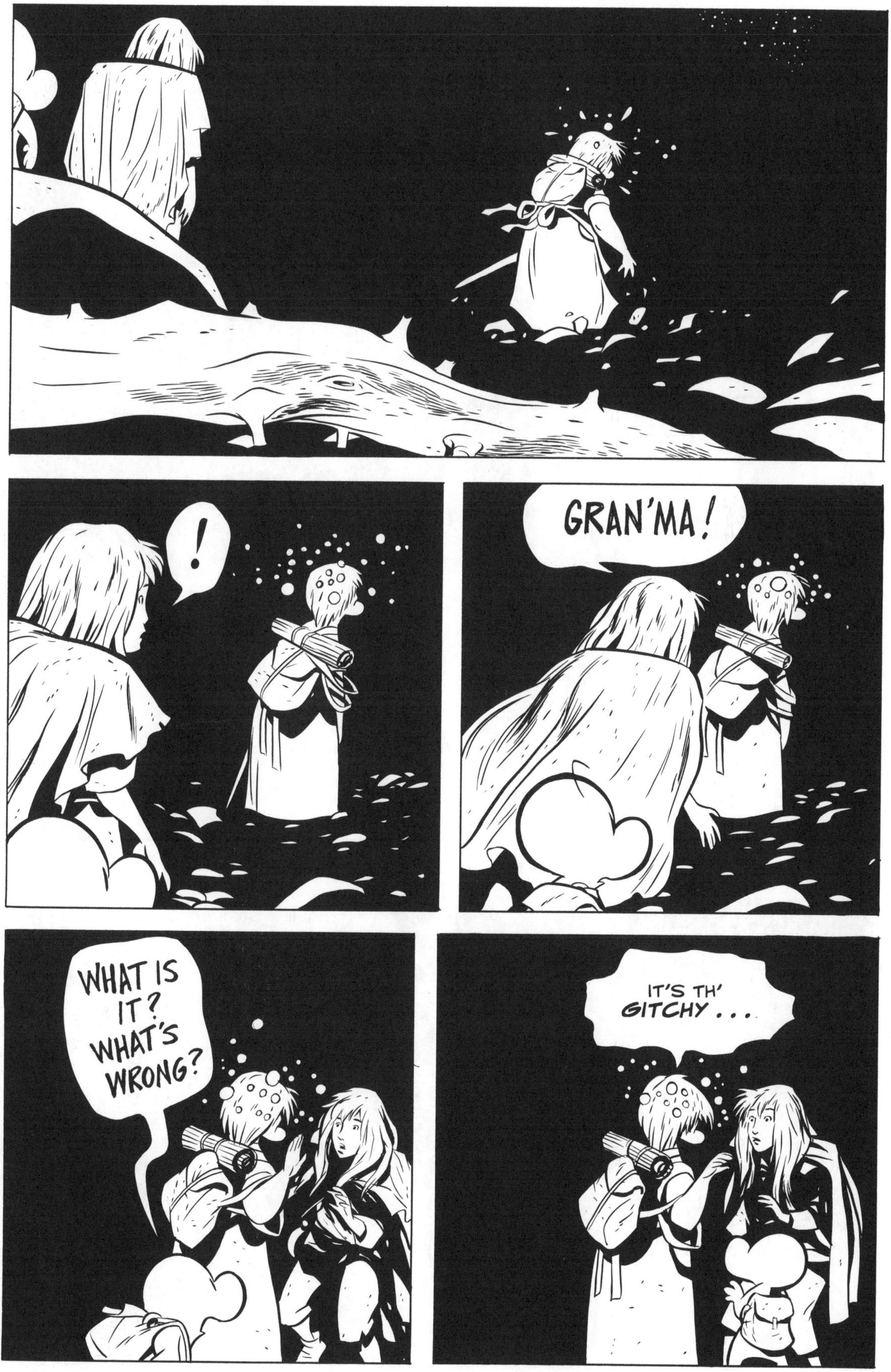
!
GRAN'MA!
WHAT IS IT? WHAT'S WRONG?
IT'S TH' GITCHY . . .

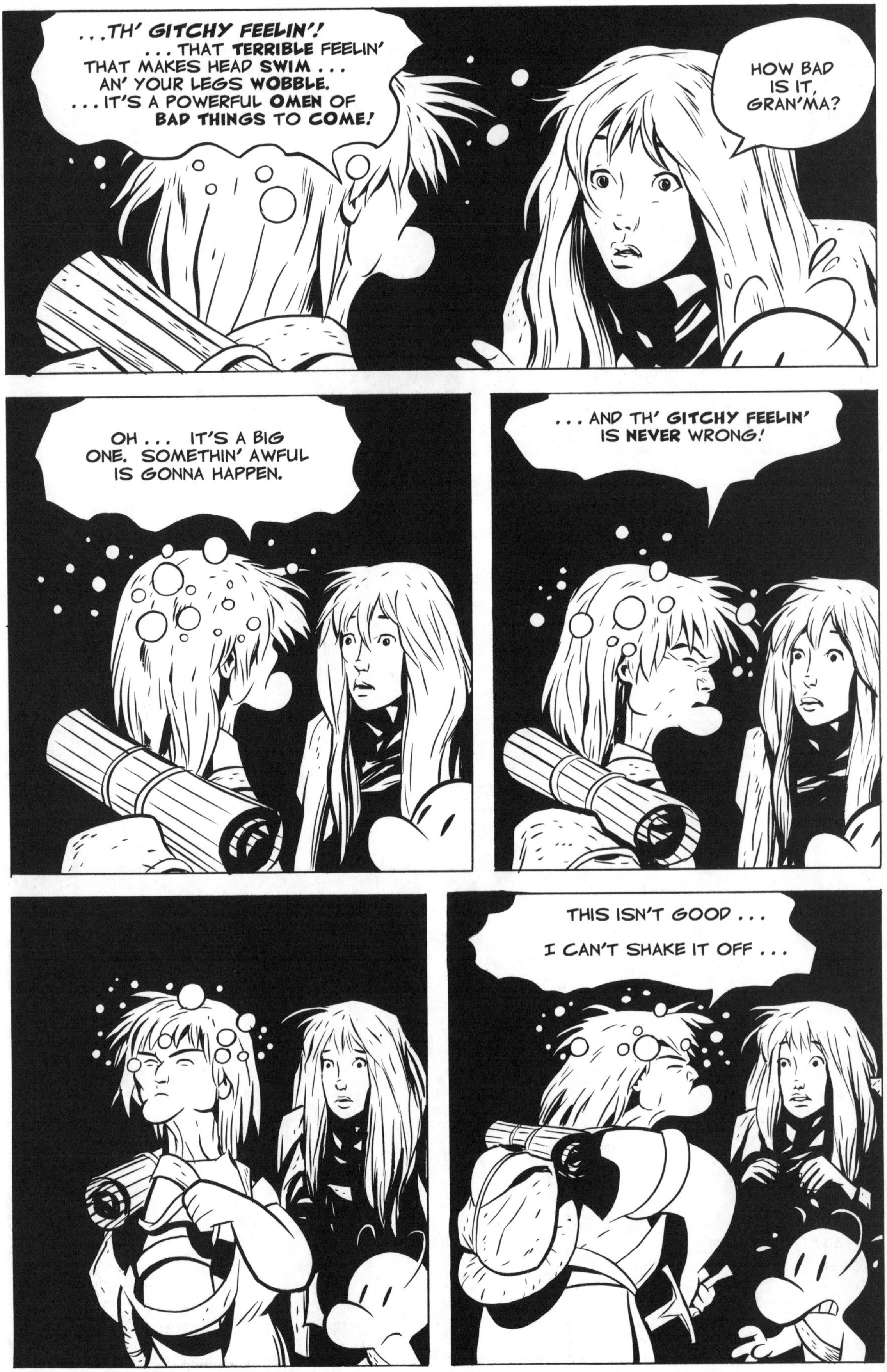
...TH' GITCHY FEELIN'! ...THAT TERRIBLE FEELIN' THAT MAKES HEAD SWIM... AN' YOUR LEGS WOBBLE. ...IT'S A POWERFUL OMEN OF BAD THINGS TO COME!
HOW BAD IS IT, GRAN'MA?
OH... IT'S A BIG ONE. SOMETHIN' AWFUL IS GONNA HAPPEN.
...AND TH' GITCHY FEELIN' IS NEVER WRONG!
THIS ISN'T GOOD...
I CAN'T SHAKE IT OFF...

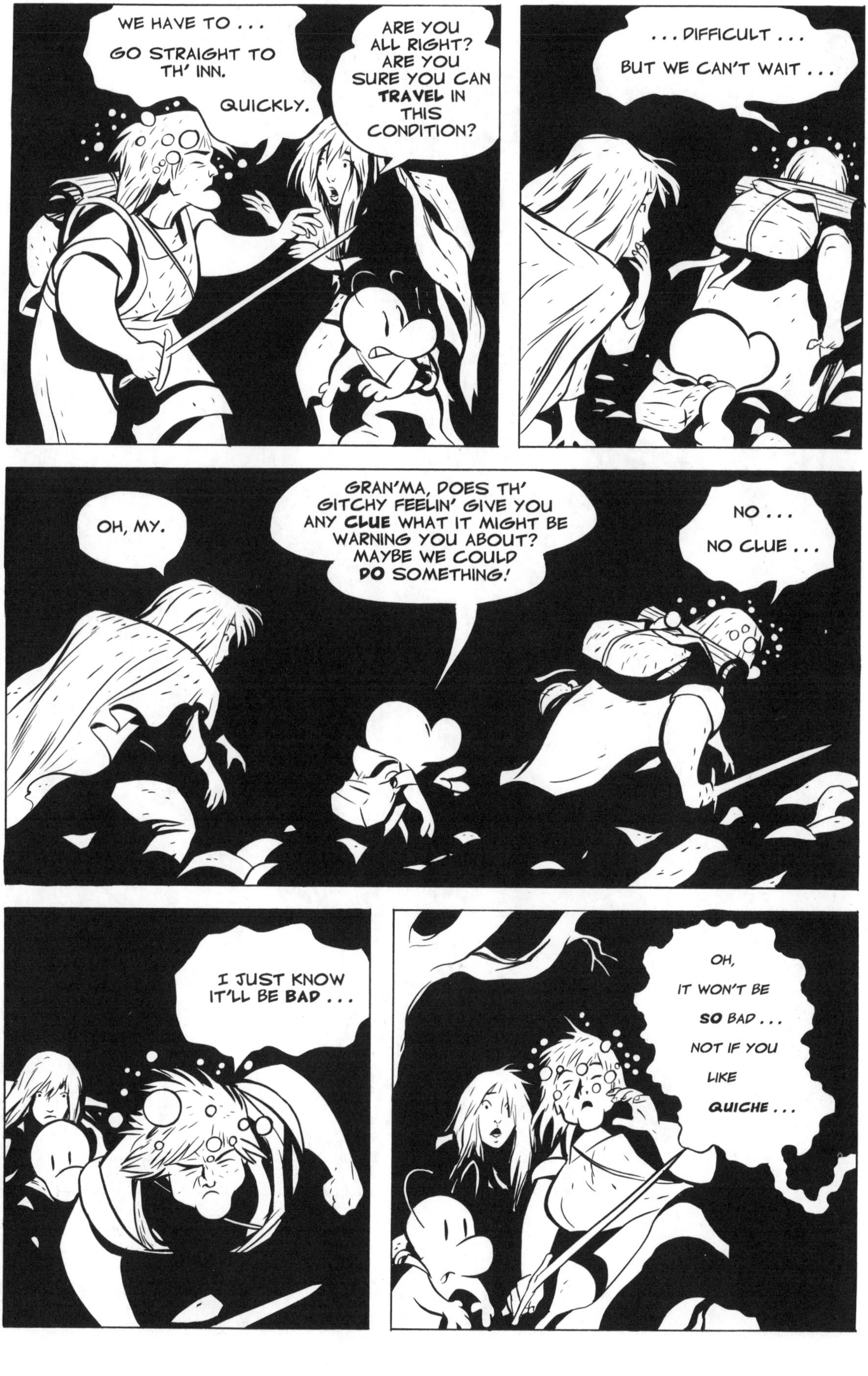
WE HAVE TO . . . GO STRAIGHT TO TH' INN. QUICKLY.
ARE YOU ALL RIGHT? ARE YOU SURE YOU CAN TRAVEL IN THIS CONDITION?
. . . DIFFICULT . . . BUT WE CAN'T WAIT . . .
OH, MY.
GRAN'MA, DOES TH' GITCHY FEELIN' GIVE YOU ANY CLUE WHAT IT MIGHT BE WARNING YOU ABOUT? MAYBE WE COULD DO SOMETHING!
NO . . . NO CLUE . . .
I JUST KNOW IT'LL BE BAD . . .
OH, IT WON'T BE SO BAD . . . NOT IF YOU LIKE QUICHE . . .

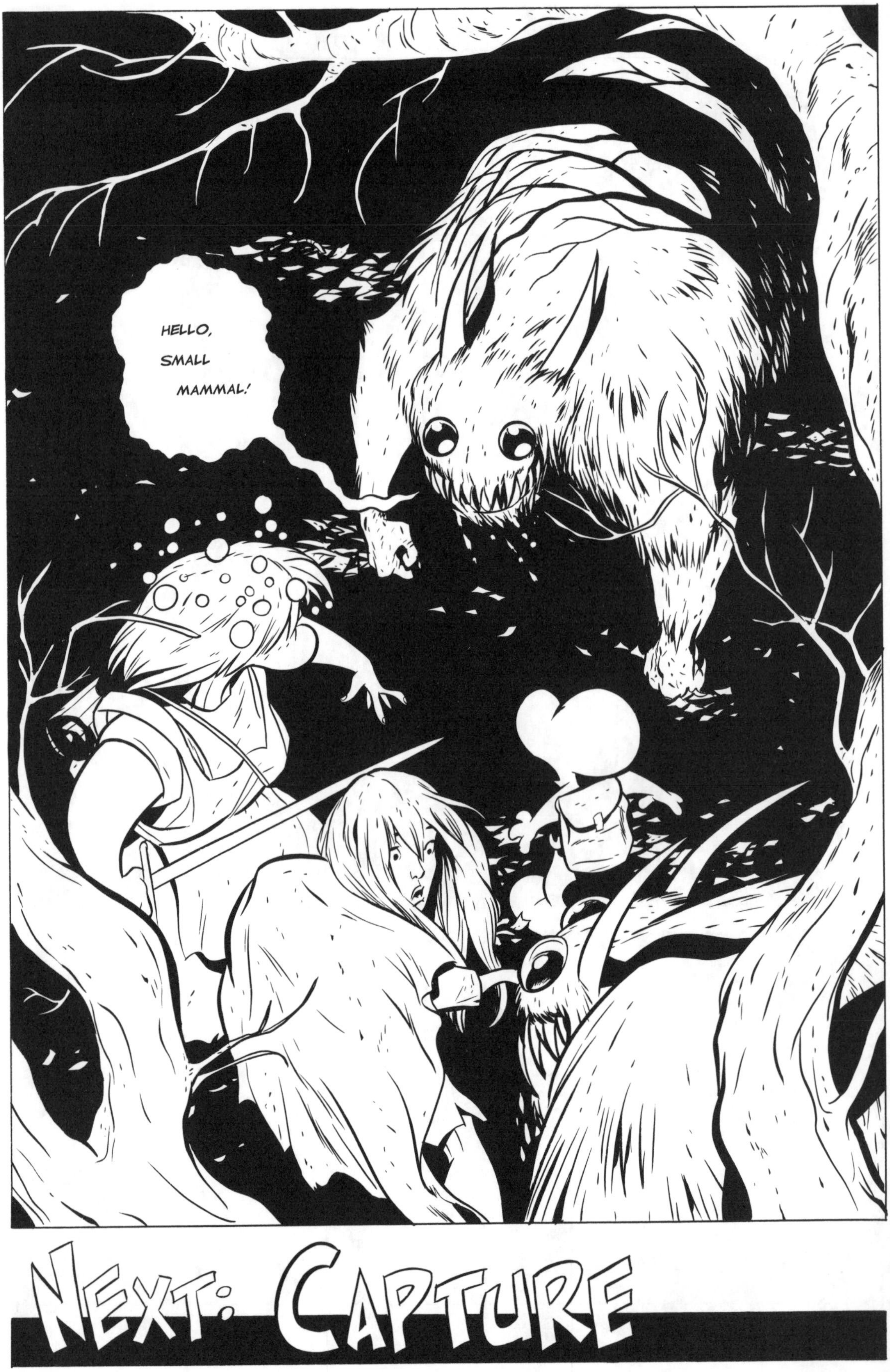
HELLO, SMALL MAMMAL!

NEXT: CAPTURE

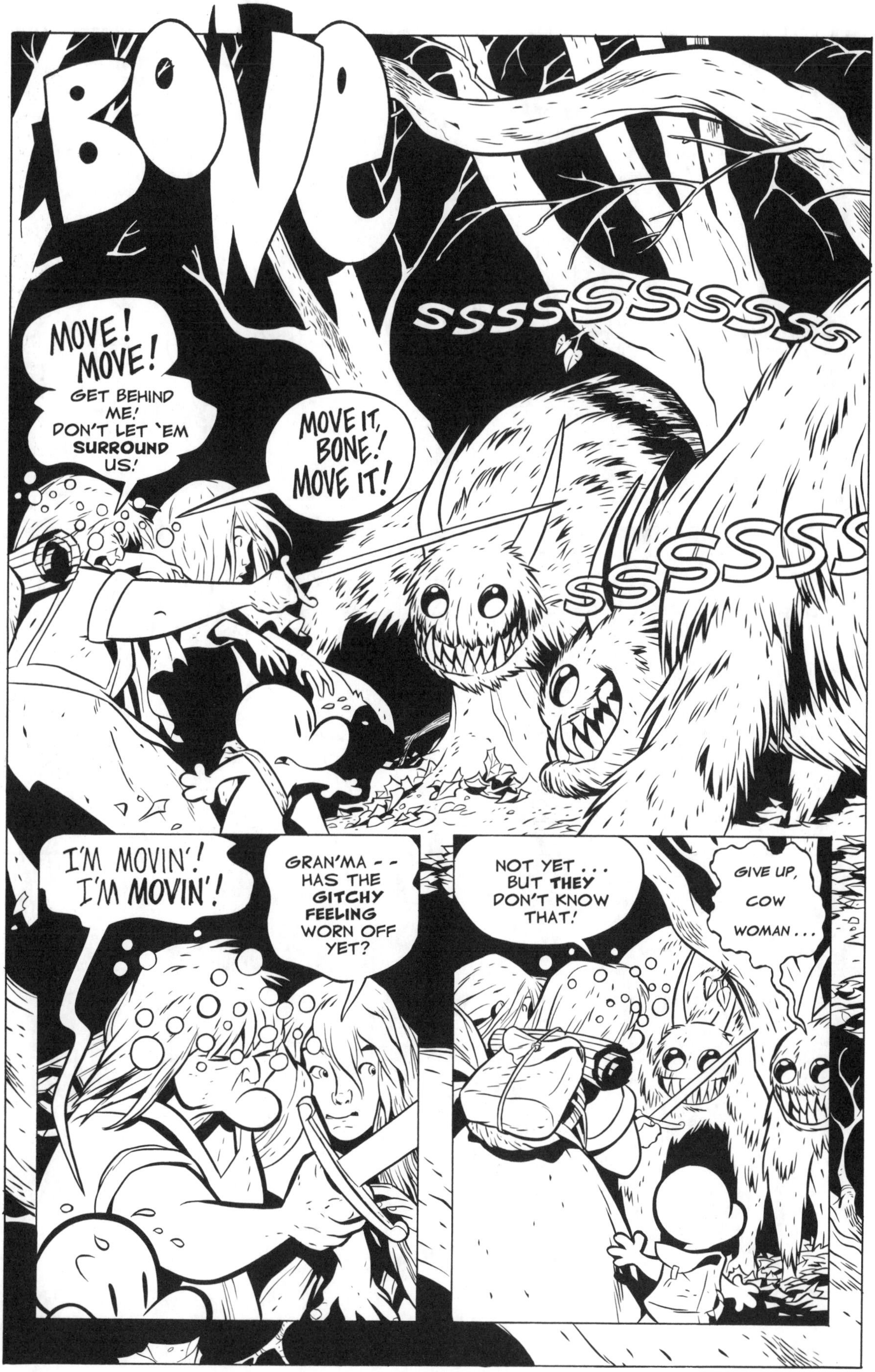
BONE
SSSSSSSSSSSSS
MOVE! MOVE! GET BEHIND ME! DON'T LET `EM SURROUND US!
MOVE IT, BONE! MOVE IT!
SSSSSSSS
I'M MOVIN'! I'M MOVIN'!
GRAN'MA -- HAS THE GITCHY FEELING WORN OFF YET?
NOT YET... BUT THEY DON'T KNOW THAT!
GIVE UP, COW WOMAN...

YOUR TIRED OLD FRAME CAN DO NOTHING TO STOP US...

PUT DOWN THAT BLADE AND WE WILL GIVE YOU A **SWIFT** DEATH...

OUR BELLIES ARE EMPTY AND OUR PATIENCE IS SHORT... SUBMIT TO US AND WE WILL MAKE OF YOU A GREAT **QUICHE!**

AGAIN WITH THE **QUICHE?!** WHAT KIND OF SELF-RESPECTING **MONSTER** WOULD EAT A **DAINTY PASTRY DISH?!** **STEW** IS WHAT WE WILL MAKE OF THEIR BONES!

DON'T GET **GREEDY** ON ME! THERE'S **THREE** OF THEM! I JUST WANT THE LITTLE ONE FOR MY **QUICHE!**

IT HAS NOTHING TO **DO** WITH GREED! IT'S A MATTER OF **PRINCIPLE!** MONSTERS DO **NOT** EAT QUICHE!

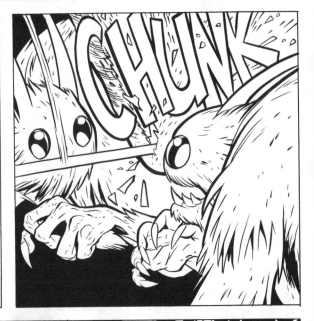

CHUNK

DID I HIT ONE?

NO. YOU MISSED.

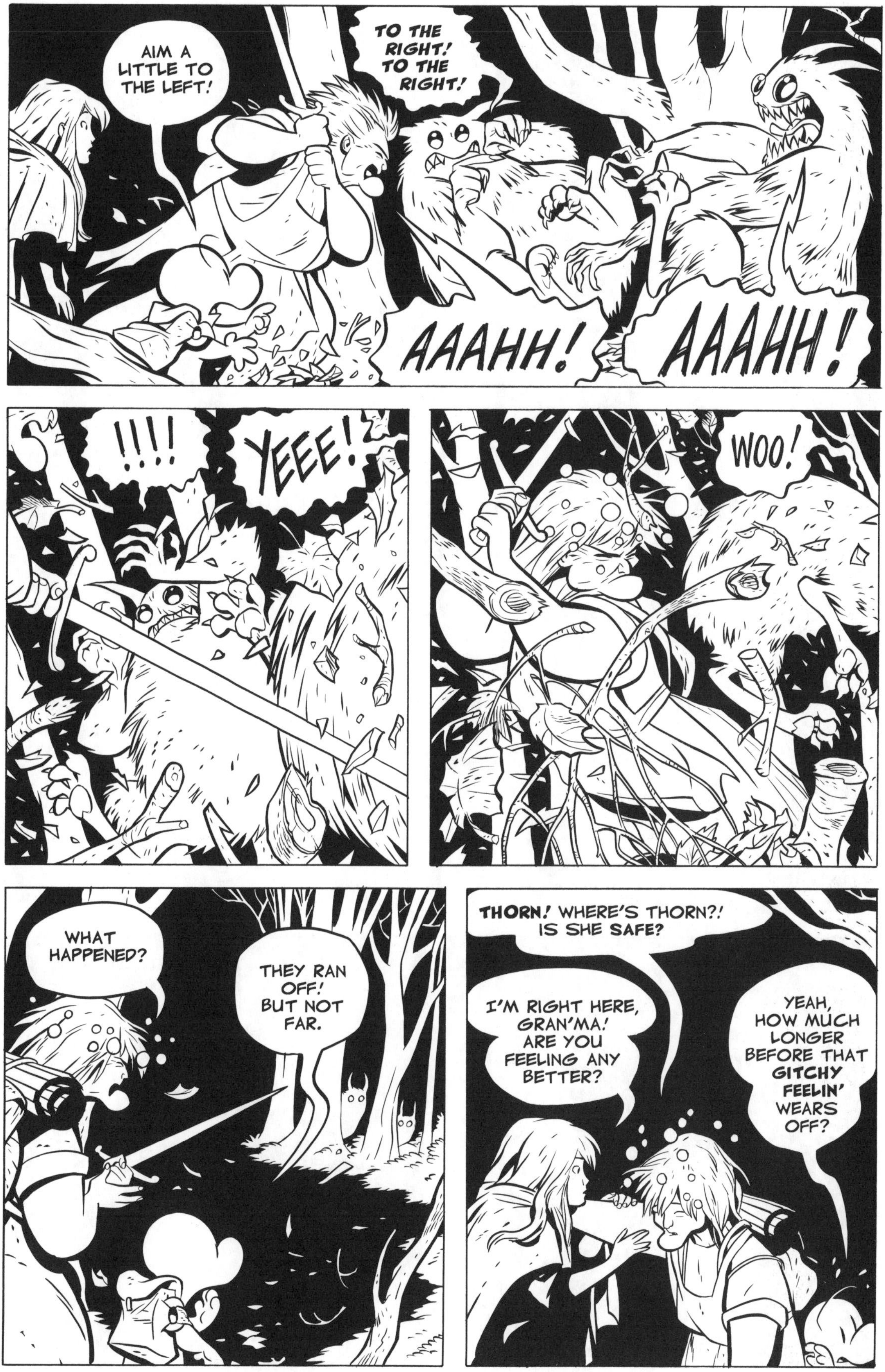
AIM A LITTLE TO THE LEFT!
TO THE RIGHT! TO THE RIGHT!
AAAHH!
AAAHH!
!!!!
YEEE!
WOO!
WHAT HAPPENED?
THEY RAN OFF! BUT NOT FAR.
THORN! WHERE'S THORN?! IS SHE SAFE?
I'M RIGHT HERE, GRAN'MA! ARE YOU FEELING ANY BETTER?
YEAH, HOW MUCH LONGER BEFORE THAT GITCHY FEELIN' WEARS OFF?

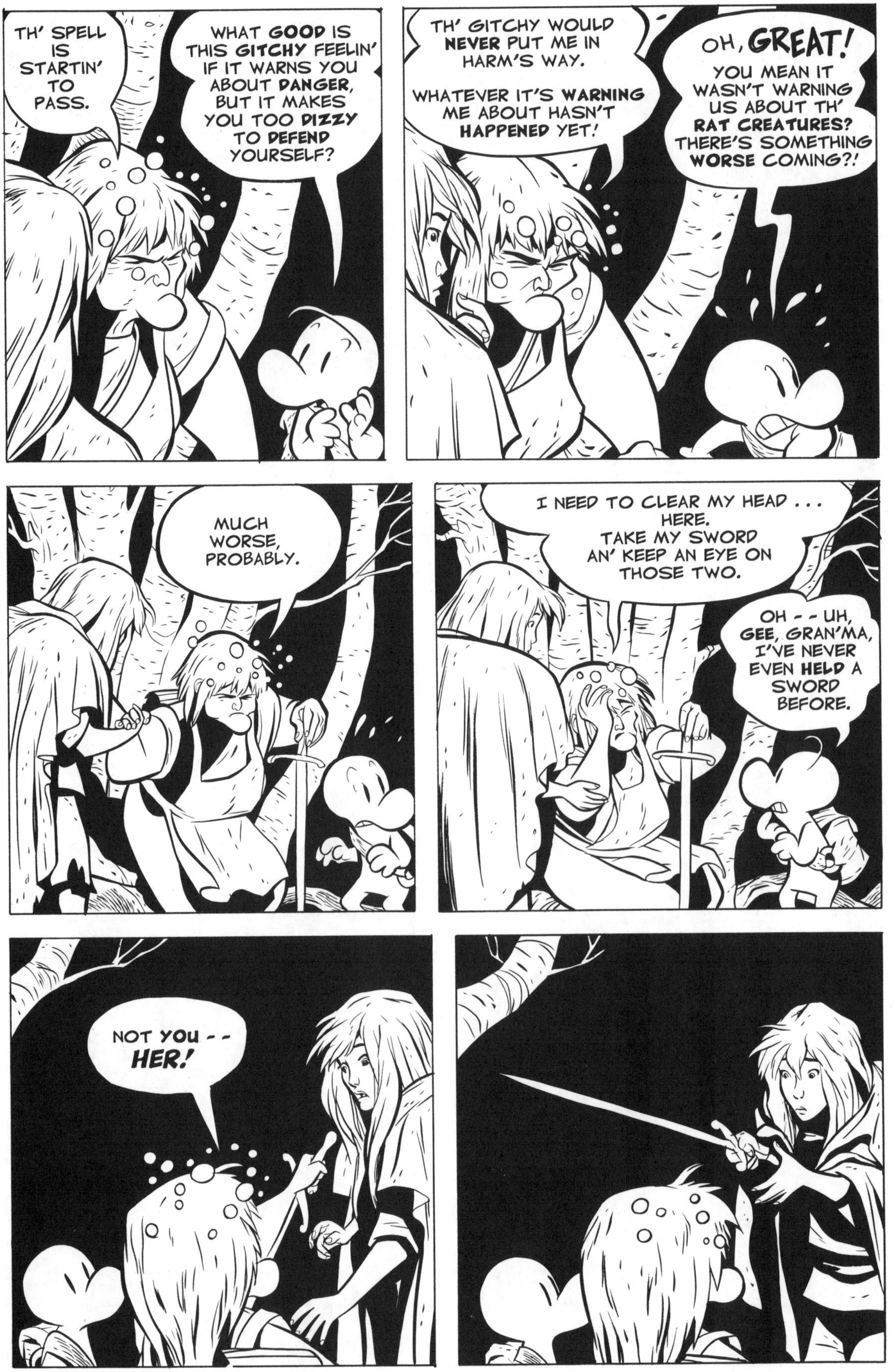
TH' SPELL IS STARTIN' TO PASS.
WHAT GOOD IS THIS GITCHY FEELIN' IF IT WARNS YOU ABOUT DANGER, BUT IT MAKES YOU TOO DIZZY TO DEFEND YOURSELF?
TH' GITCHY WOULD NEVER PUT ME IN HARM'S WAY.
WHATEVER IT'S WARNING ME ABOUT HASN'T HAPPENED YET!
OH, GREAT!
YOU MEAN IT WASN'T WARNING US ABOUT TH' RAT CREATURES? THERE'S SOMETHING WORSE COMING?!
MUCH WORSE, PROBABLY.
I NEED TO CLEAR MY HEAD . . . HERE. TAKE MY SWORD AN' KEEP AN EYE ON THOSE TWO.
OH - - UH, GEE, GRAN'MA, I'VE NEVER EVEN HELD A SWORD BEFORE.
NOT YOU - - HER!

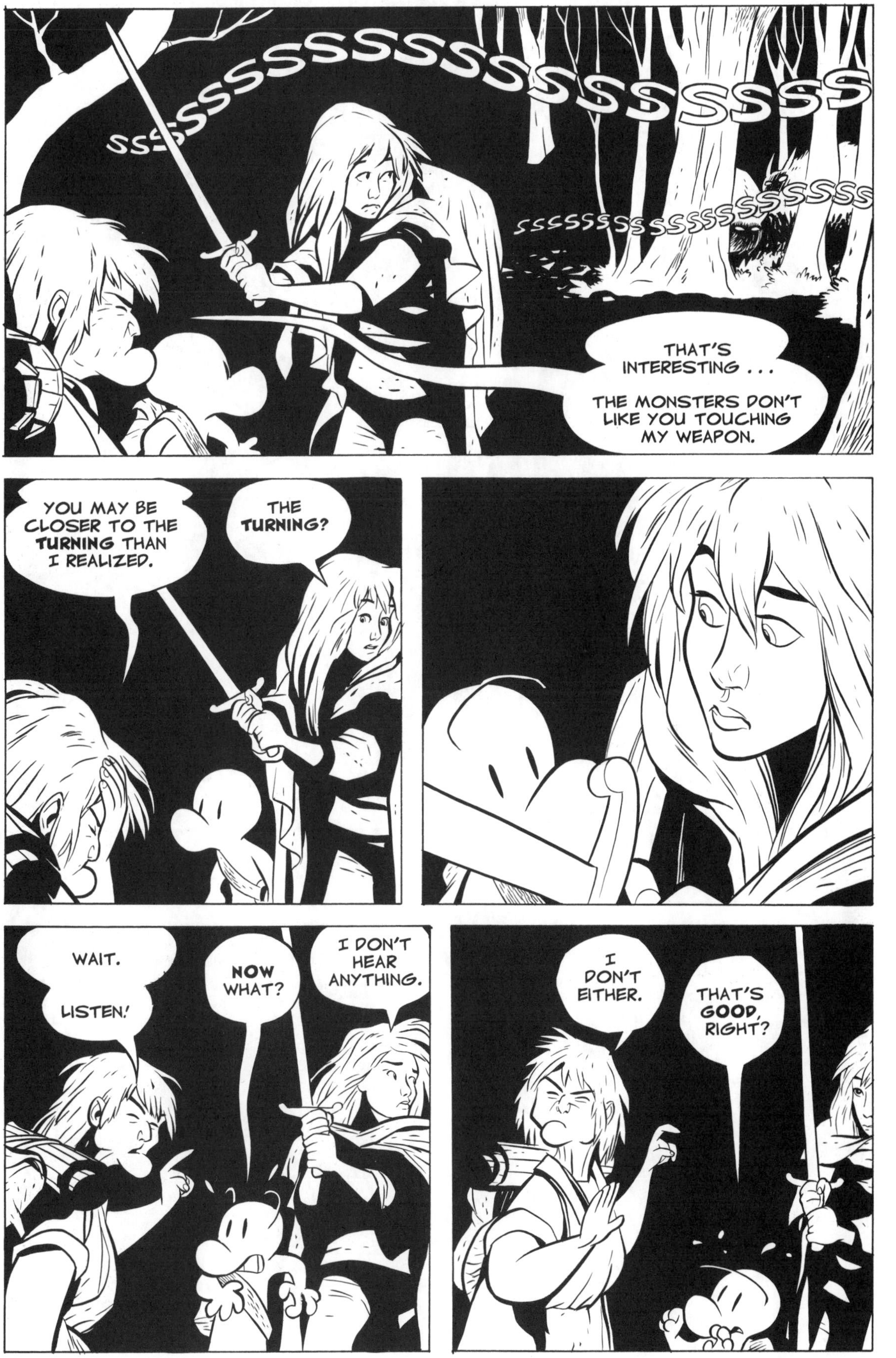

SSSSSSSSSSSSSSSSSSSSSSS
SSSSSSSSSSSSSSSSSSSSSSS
THAT'S INTERESTING . . .
THE MONSTERS DON'T LIKE YOU TOUCHING MY WEAPON.
YOU MAY BE CLOSER TO THE **TURNING** THAN I REALIZED.
THE **TURNING**?
WAIT.
LISTEN!
NOW WHAT?
I DON'T HEAR ANYTHING.
I DON'T EITHER.
THAT'S **GOOD**, RIGHT?

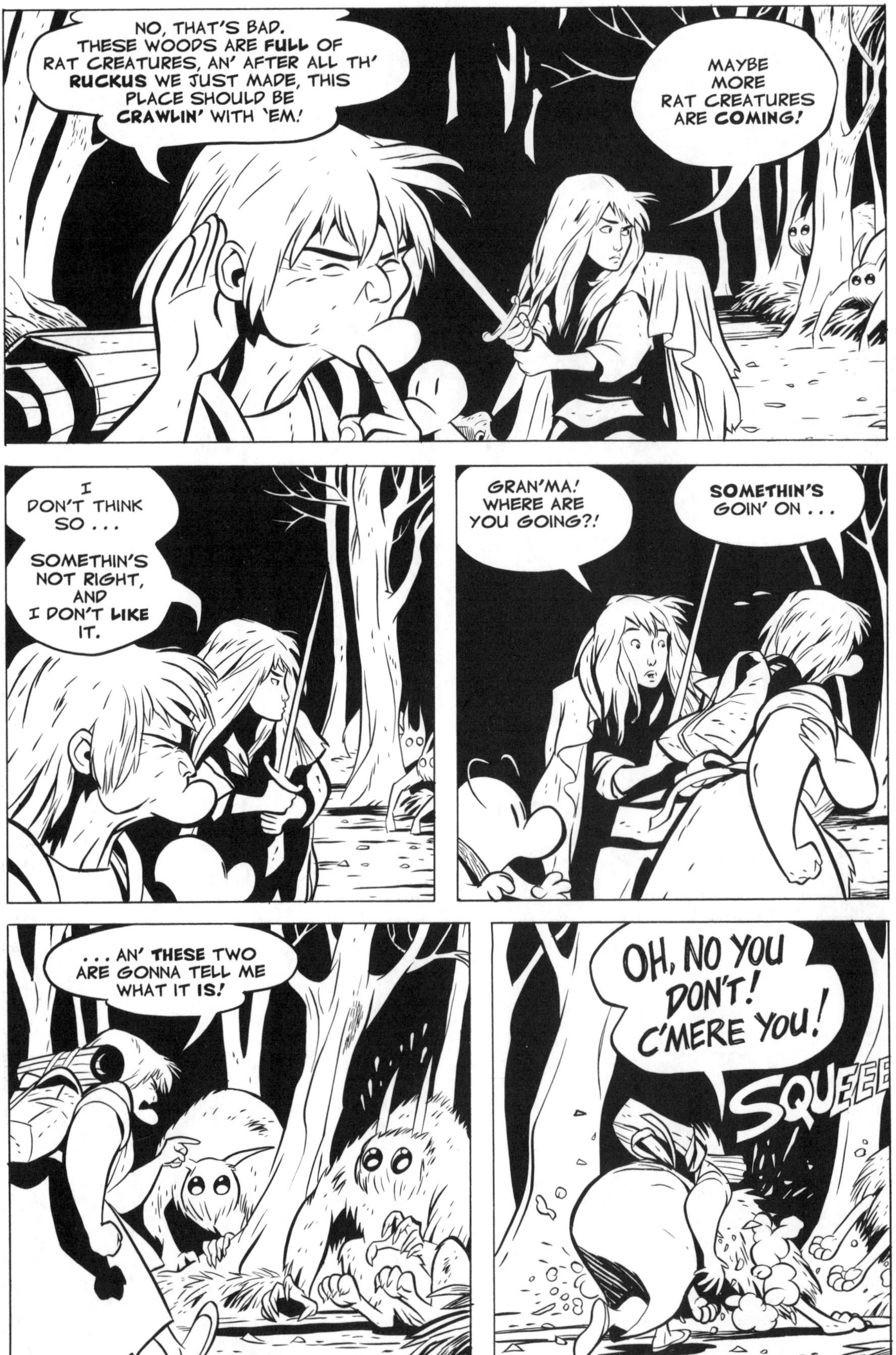
NO, THAT'S BAD. THESE WOODS ARE FULL OF RAT CREATURES, AN' AFTER ALL TH' RUCKUS WE JUST MADE, THIS PLACE SHOULD BE CRAWLIN' WITH 'EM!
MAYBE MORE RAT CREATURES ARE COMING!
I DON'T THINK SO . . .
SOMETHIN'S NOT RIGHT, AND I DON'T LIKE IT.
GRAN'MA! WHERE ARE YOU GOING?!
SOMETHIN'S GOIN' ON . . .
. . . AN' THESE TWO ARE GONNA TELL ME WHAT IT IS!
OH, NO YOU DON'T! C'MERE YOU!
SQUEEE

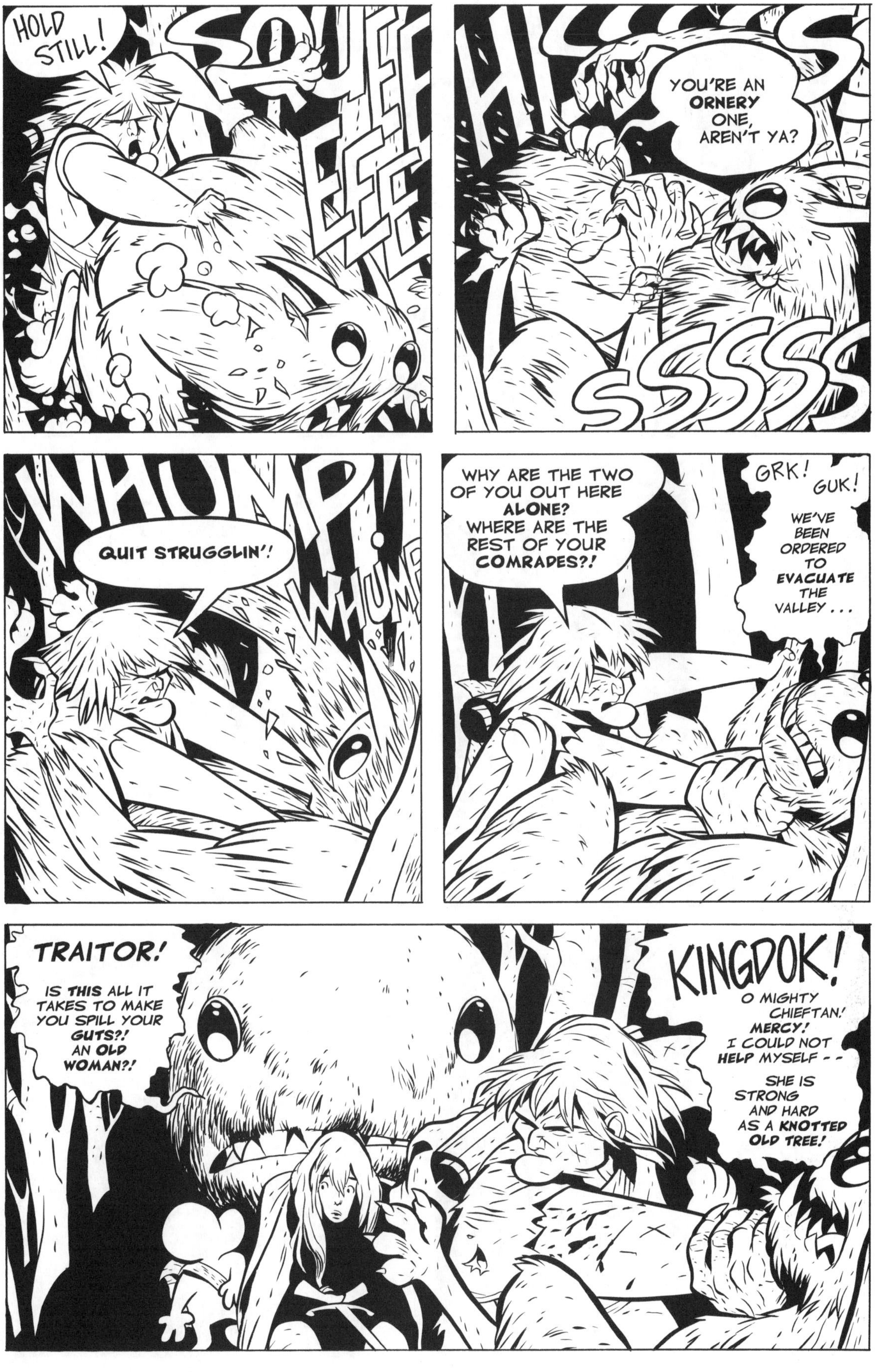
HOLD STILL!
SQUEEEEE
HISSSSSSSS
YOU'RE AN ORNERY ONE, AREN'T YA?
SSSSS
WHUMP!
QUIT STRUGGLIN'!
WHUMP
WHY ARE THE TWO OF YOU OUT HERE ALONE? WHERE ARE THE REST OF YOUR COMRADES?!
GRK!
GUK!
WE'VE BEEN ORDERED TO EVACUATE THE VALLEY . . .
TRAITOR!
IS THIS ALL IT TAKES TO MAKE YOU SPILL YOUR GUTS?! AN OLD WOMAN?!
KINGDOK!
O MIGHTY CHIEFTAN! MERCY! I COULD NOT HELP MYSELF - -
SHE IS STRONG AND HARD AS A KNOTTED OLD TREE!

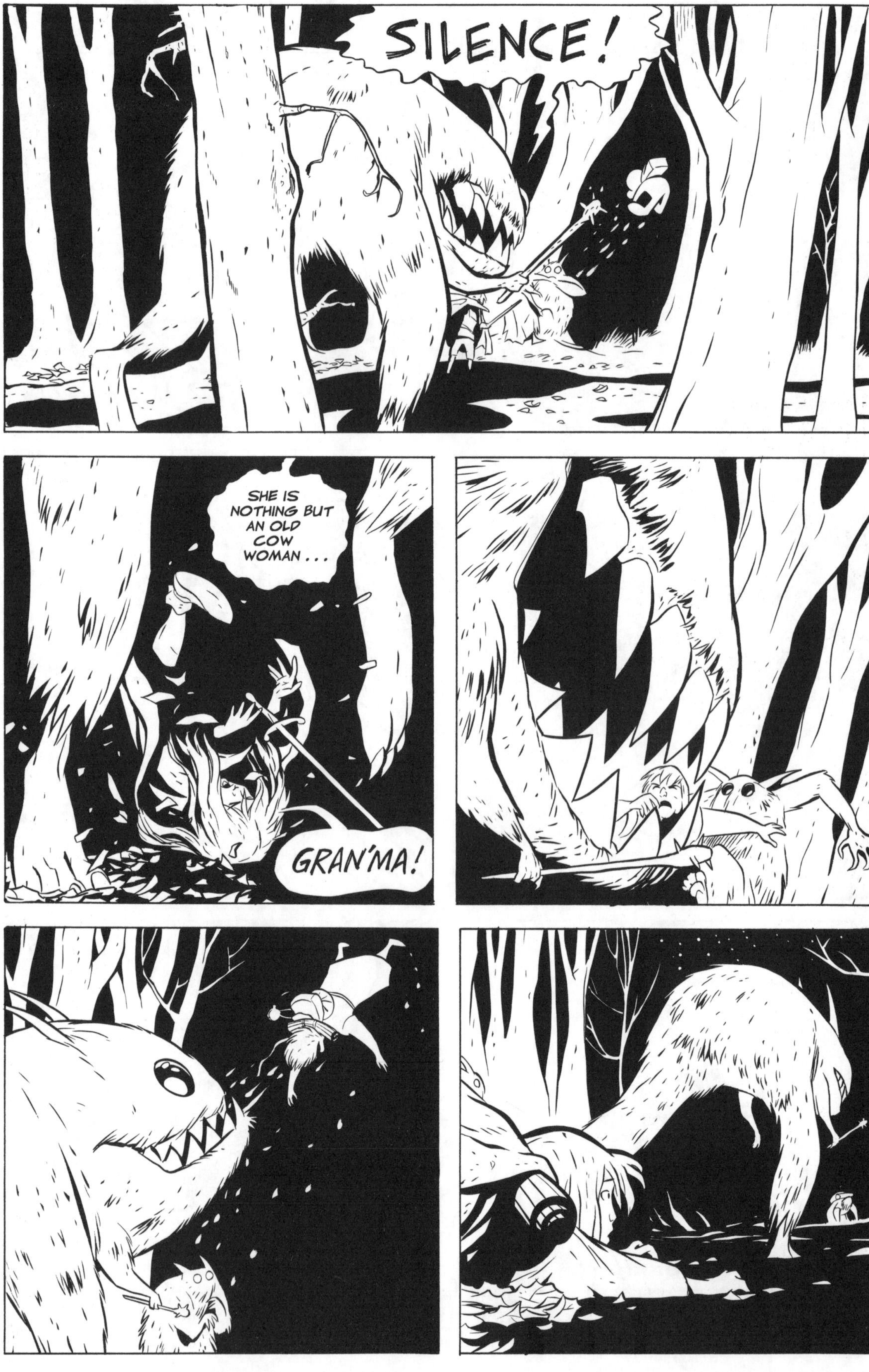
SILENCE!
SHE IS NOTHING BUT AN OLD COW WOMAN . . .
GRAN'MA!

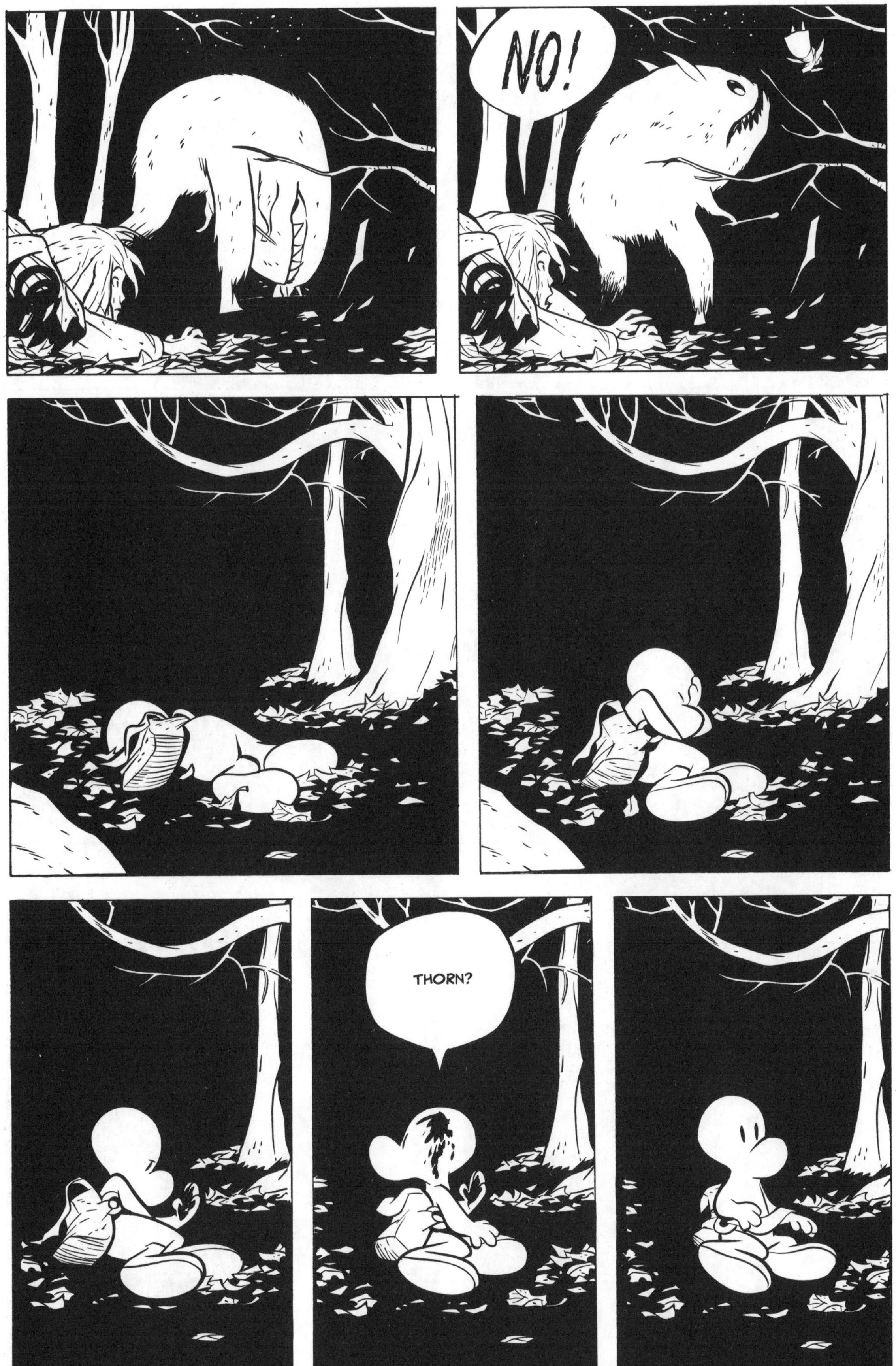
NO!
THORN?

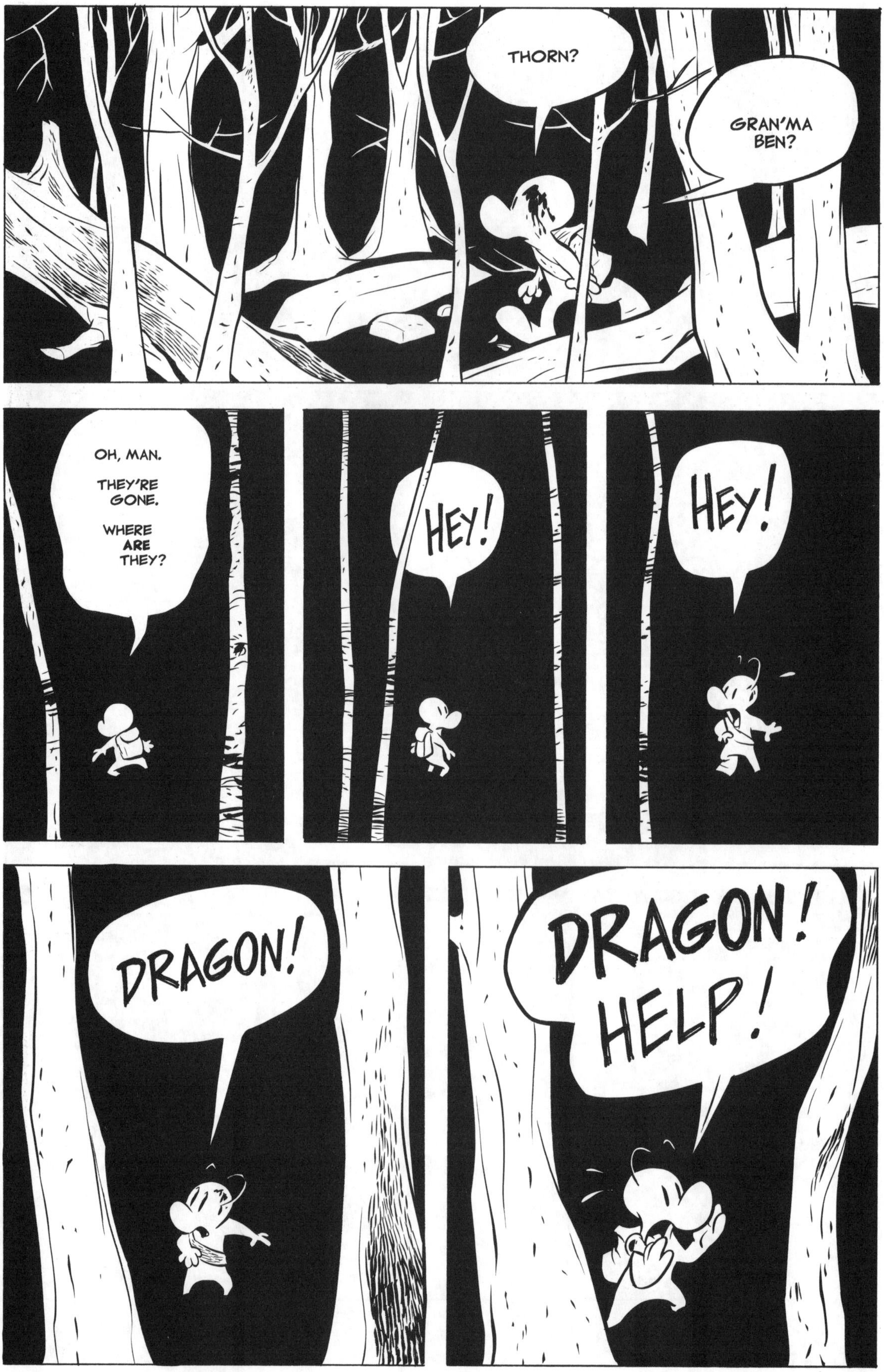
THORN?
GRAN'MA BEN?
OH, MAN.
THEY'RE GONE.
WHERE **ARE** THEY?
HEY!
HEY!
DRAGON!
DRAGON! HELP!

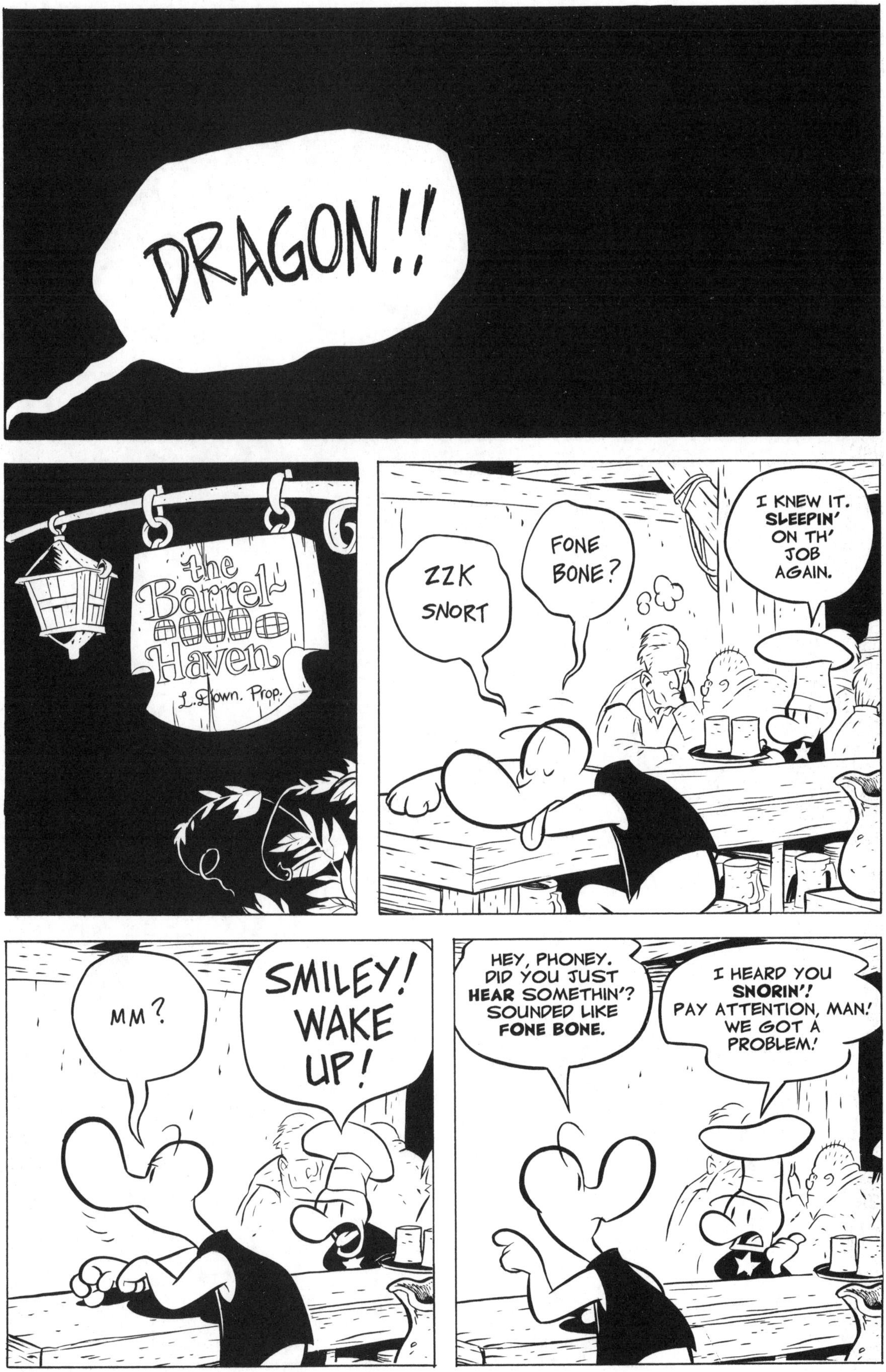
DRAGON!!
the Barrel Haven
L. Down. Prop.
ZZK SNORT
FONE BONE?
I KNEW IT. SLEEPIN' ON TH' JOB AGAIN.
MM?
SMILEY! WAKE UP!
HEY, PHONEY. DID YOU JUST HEAR SOMETHIN'? SOUNDED LIKE FONE BONE.
I HEARD YOU SNORIN'! PAY ATTENTION, MAN! WE GOT A PROBLEM!

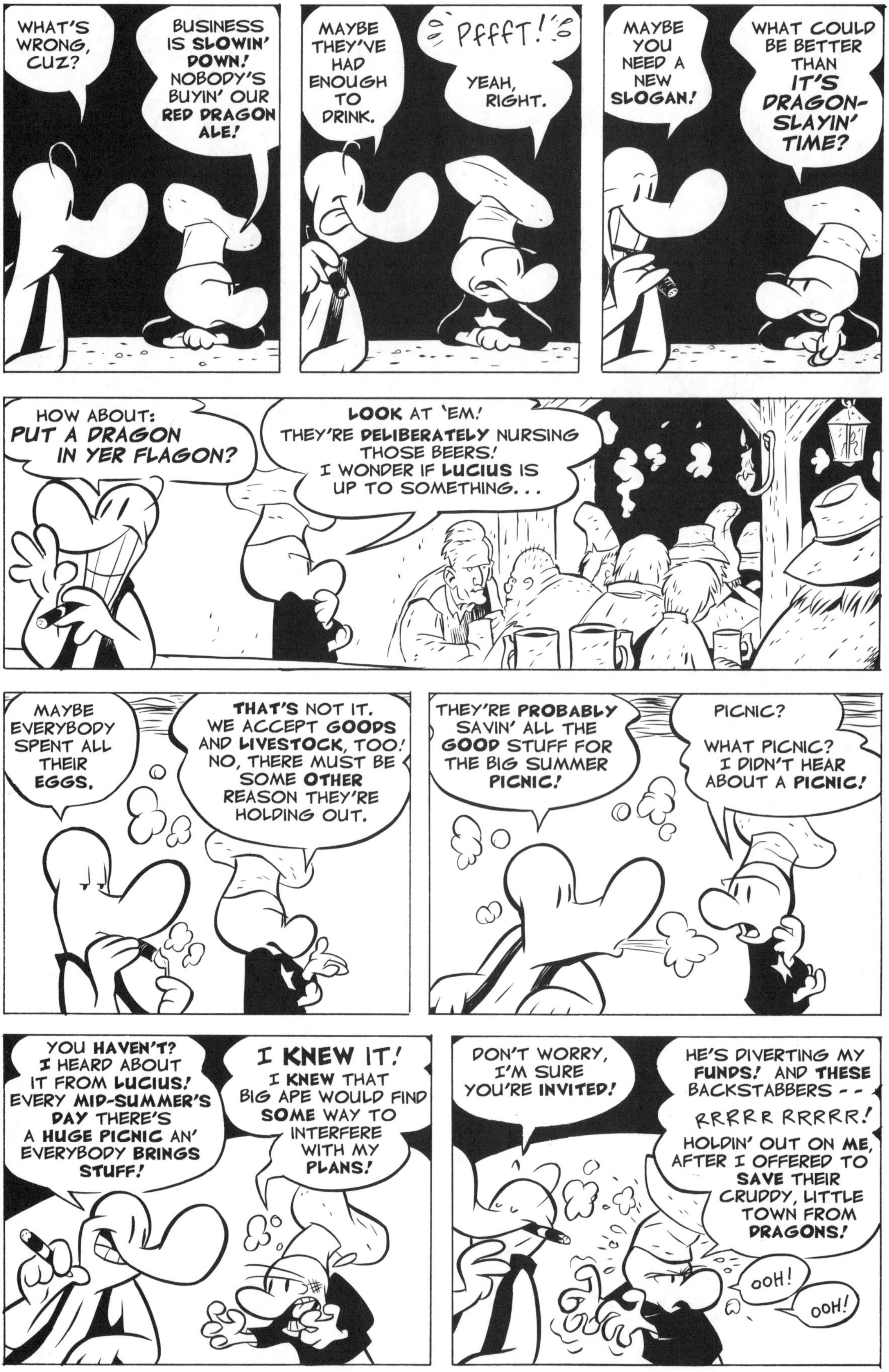
WHAT'S WRONG, CUZ?
BUSINESS IS SLOWIN' DOWN! NOBODY'S BUYIN' OUR RED DRAGON ALE!
MAYBE THEY'VE HAD ENOUGH TO DRINK.
PFFFT!
YEAH, RIGHT.
MAYBE YOU NEED A NEW SLOGAN!
WHAT COULD BE BETTER THAN IT'S DRAGON-SLAYIN' TIME?
HOW ABOUT: PUT A DRAGON IN YER FLAGON?
LOOK AT 'EM! THEY'RE DELIBERATELY NURSING THOSE BEERS! I WONDER IF LUCIUS IS UP TO SOMETHING...
MAYBE EVERYBODY SPENT ALL THEIR EGGS.
THAT'S NOT IT. WE ACCEPT GOODS AND LIVESTOCK, TOO! NO, THERE MUST BE SOME OTHER REASON THEY'RE HOLDING OUT.
THEY'RE PROBABLY SAVIN' ALL THE GOOD STUFF FOR THE BIG SUMMER PICNIC!
PICNIC? WHAT PICNIC? I DIDN'T HEAR ABOUT A PICNIC!
YOU HAVEN'T? I HEARD ABOUT IT FROM LUCIUS! EVERY MID-SUMMER'S DAY THERE'S A HUGE PICNIC AN' EVERYBODY BRINGS STUFF!
I KNEW IT! I KNEW THAT BIG APE WOULD FIND SOME WAY TO INTERFERE WITH MY PLANS!
DON'T WORRY, I'M SURE YOU'RE INVITED!
HE'S DIVERTING MY FUNDS! AND THESE BACKSTABBERS --
RRRRR RRRRR!
HOLDIN' OUT ON ME, AFTER I OFFERED TO SAVE THEIR CRUDDY, LITTLE TOWN FROM DRAGONS!
OOH!
OOH!

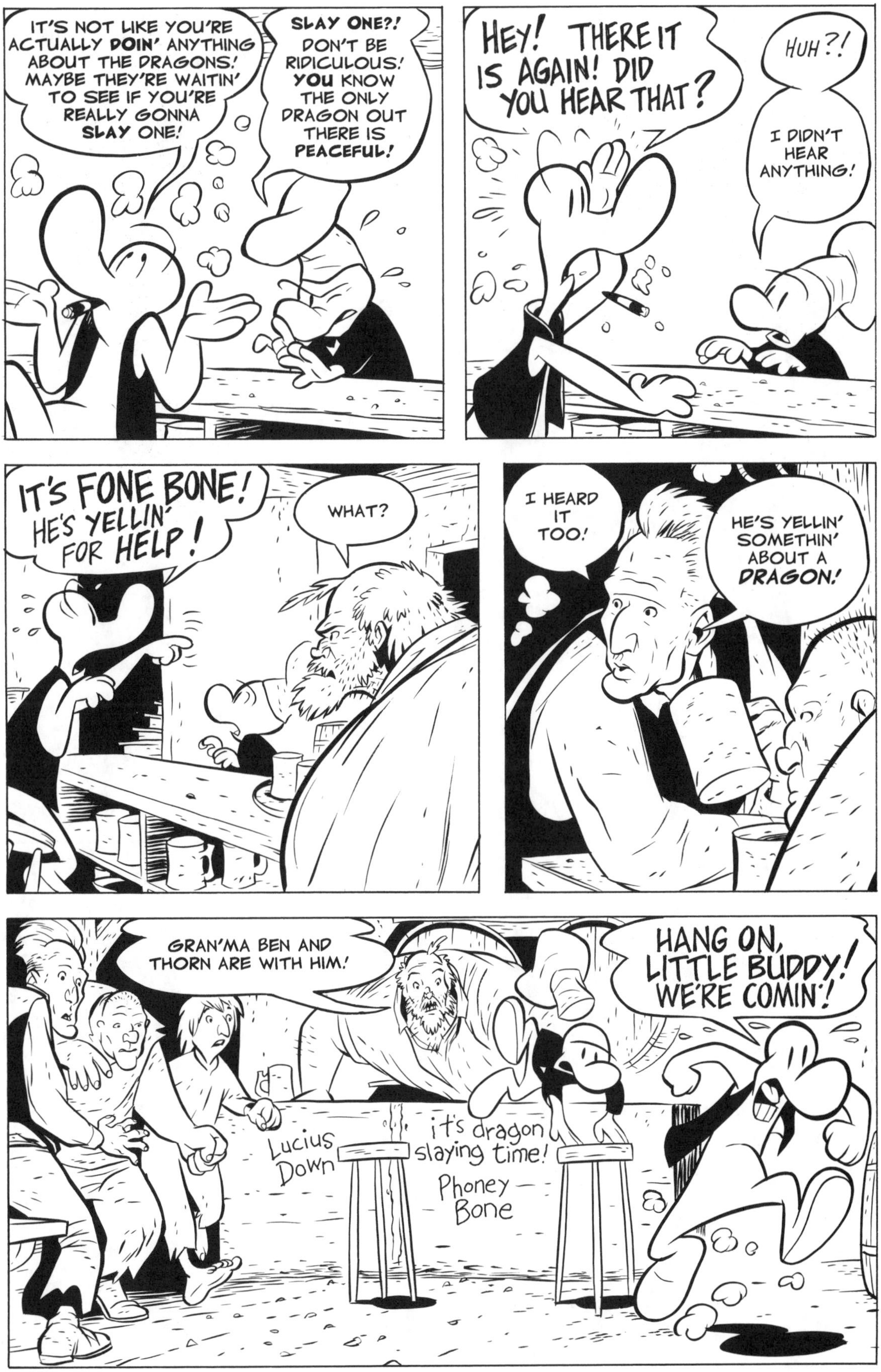
IT'S NOT LIKE YOU'RE ACTUALLY DOIN' ANYTHING ABOUT THE DRAGONS! MAYBE THEY'RE WAITIN' TO SEE IF YOU'RE REALLY GONNA SLAY ONE!
SLAY ONE?! DON'T BE RIDICULOUS! YOU KNOW THE ONLY DRAGON OUT THERE IS PEACEFUL!
HEY! THERE IT IS AGAIN! DID YOU HEAR THAT?
HUH?!
I DIDN'T HEAR ANYTHING!
IT'S FONE BONE! HE'S YELLIN' FOR HELP!
WHAT?
I HEARD IT TOO!
HE'S YELLIN' SOMETHIN' ABOUT A DRAGON!
GRAN'MA BEN AND THORN ARE WITH HIM!
HANG ON, LITTLE BUDDY! WE'RE COMIN'!
Lucius Down
it's dragon slaying time! Phoney Bone

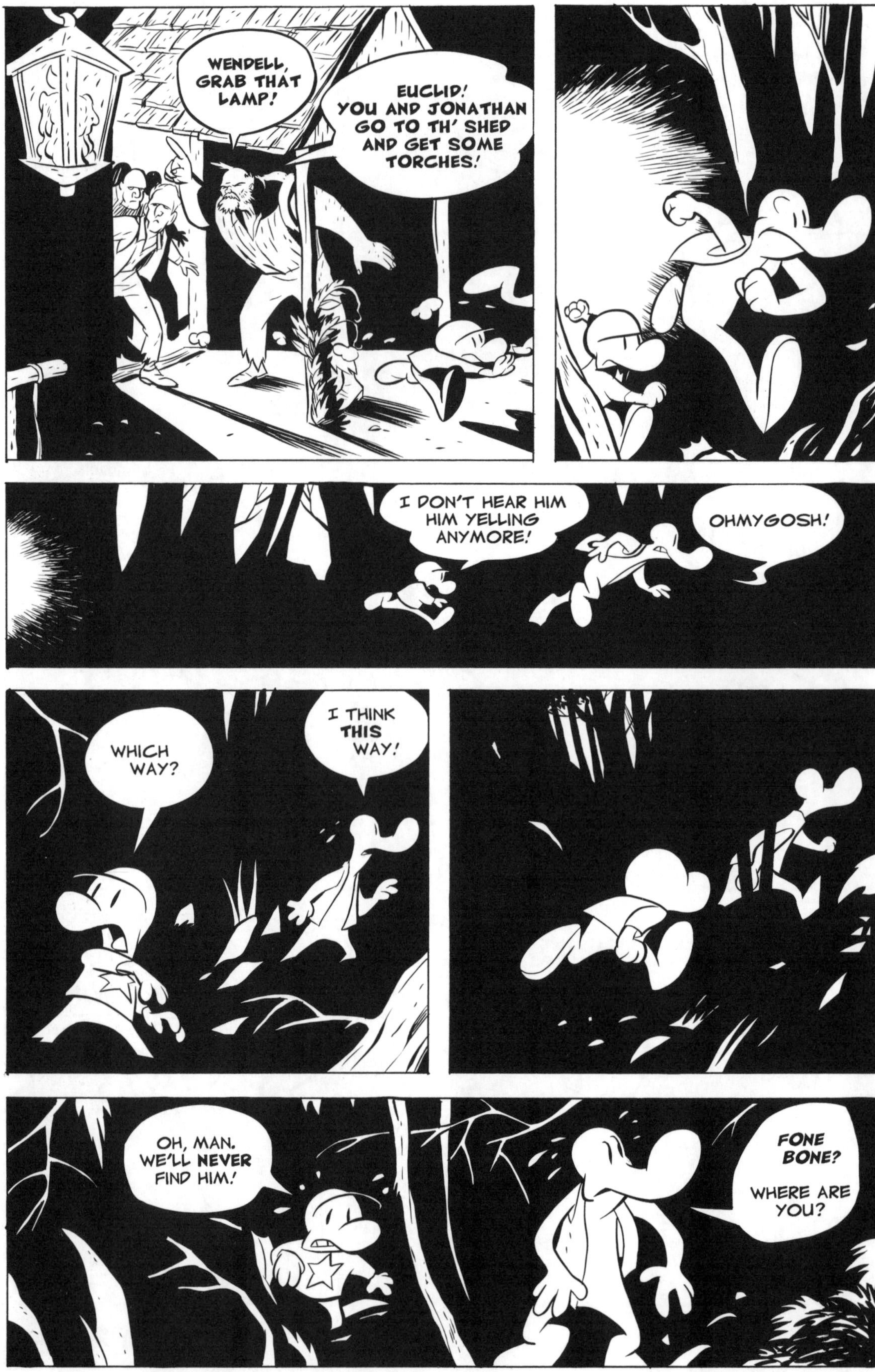
WENDELL, GRAB THAT LAMP!
EUCLID! YOU AND JONATHAN GO TO TH' SHED AND GET SOME TORCHES!
I DON'T HEAR HIM HIM YELLING ANYMORE!
OHMYGOSH!
WHICH WAY?
I THINK THIS WAY!
OH, MAN. WE'LL NEVER FIND HIM!
FONE BONE?
WHERE ARE YOU?

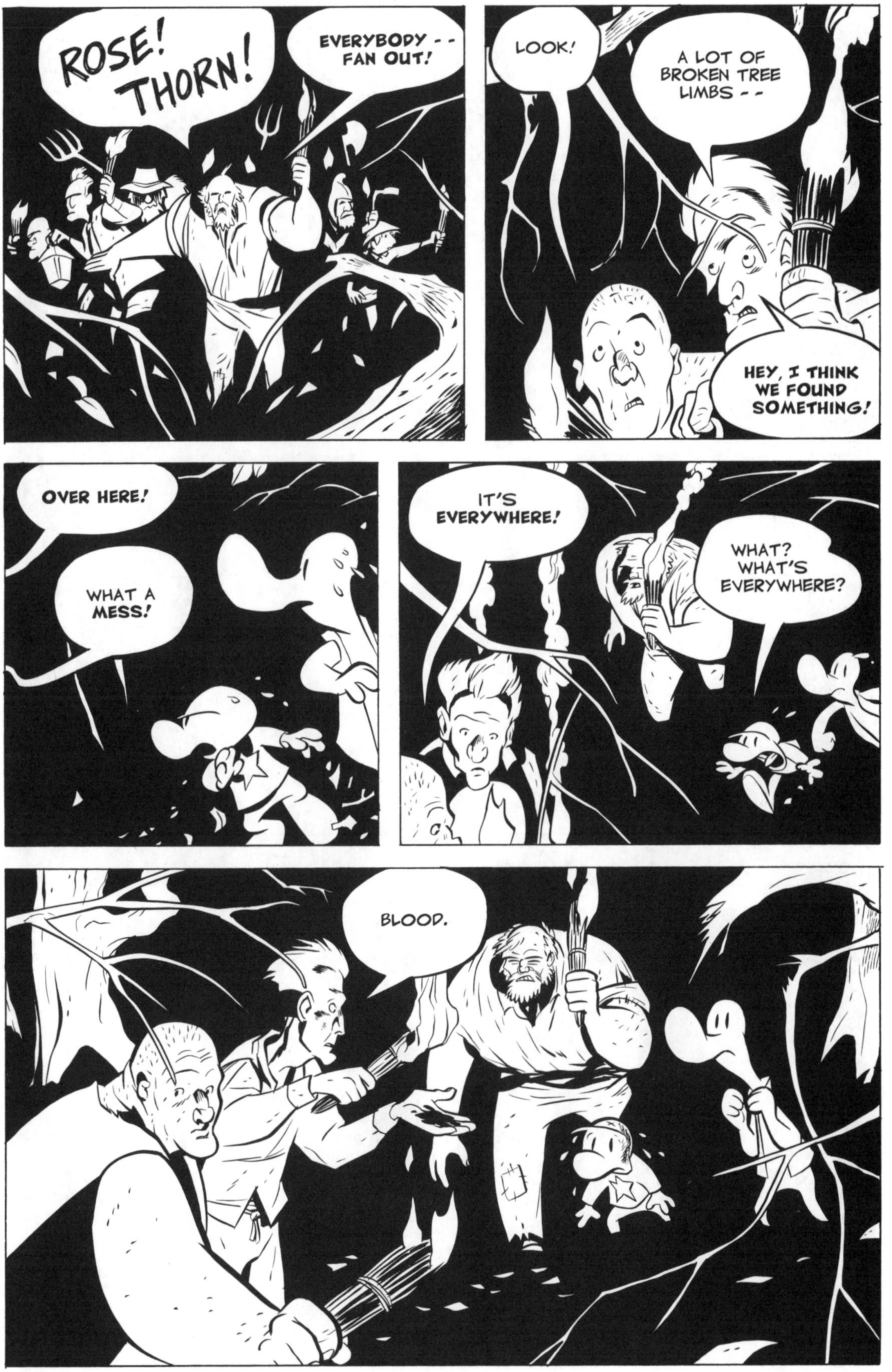
ROSE! THORN!
EVERYBODY - - FAN OUT!
LOOK!
A LOT OF BROKEN TREE LIMBS - -
HEY, I THINK WE FOUND SOMETHING!
OVER HERE!
WHAT A MESS!
IT'S EVERYWHERE!
WHAT? WHAT'S EVERYWHERE?
BLOOD.

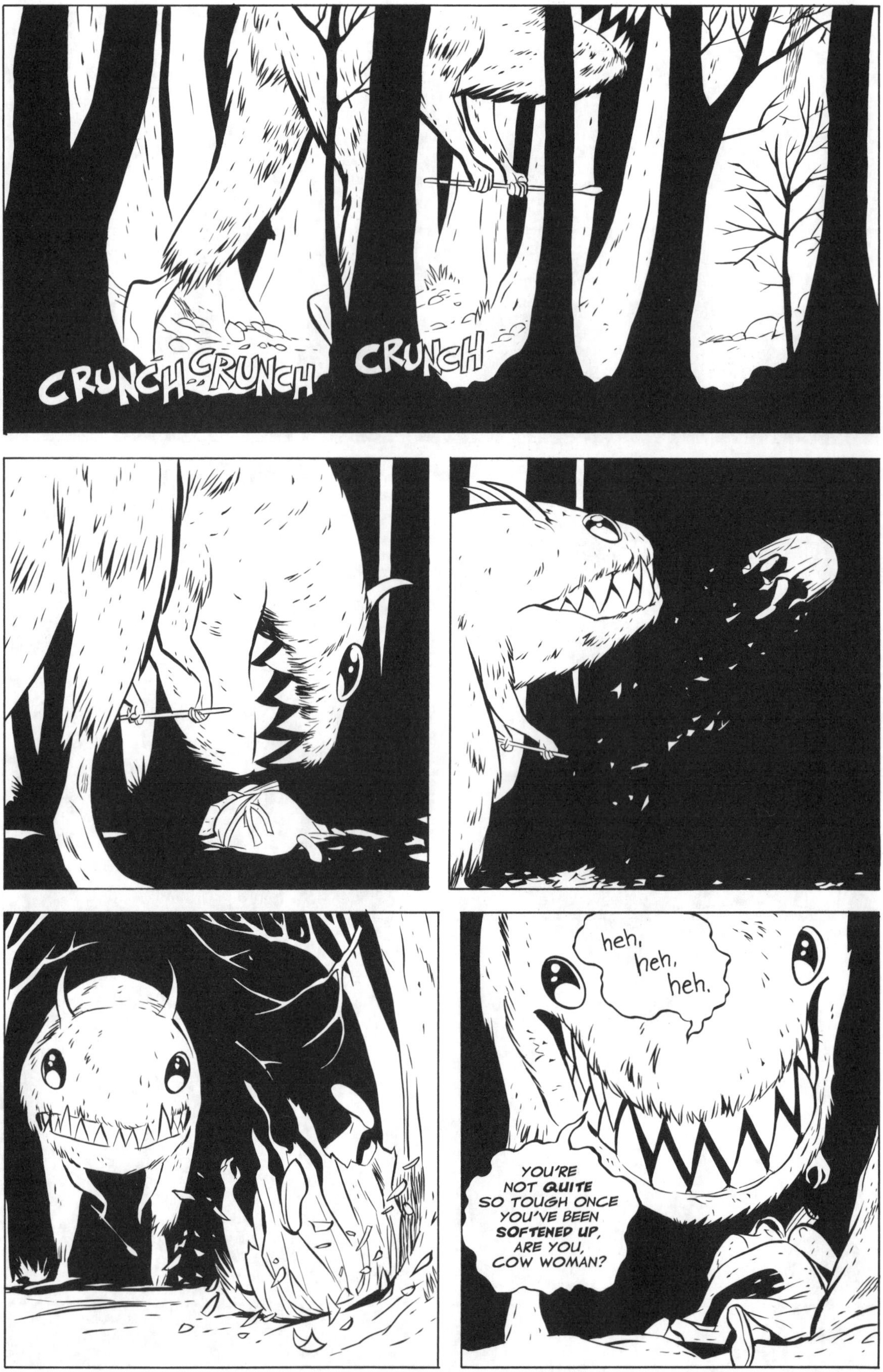
CRUNCH CRUNCH CRUNCH
heh, heh, heh.
YOU'RE NOT QUITE SO TOUGH ONCE YOU'VE BEEN SOFTENED UP, ARE YOU, COW WOMAN?

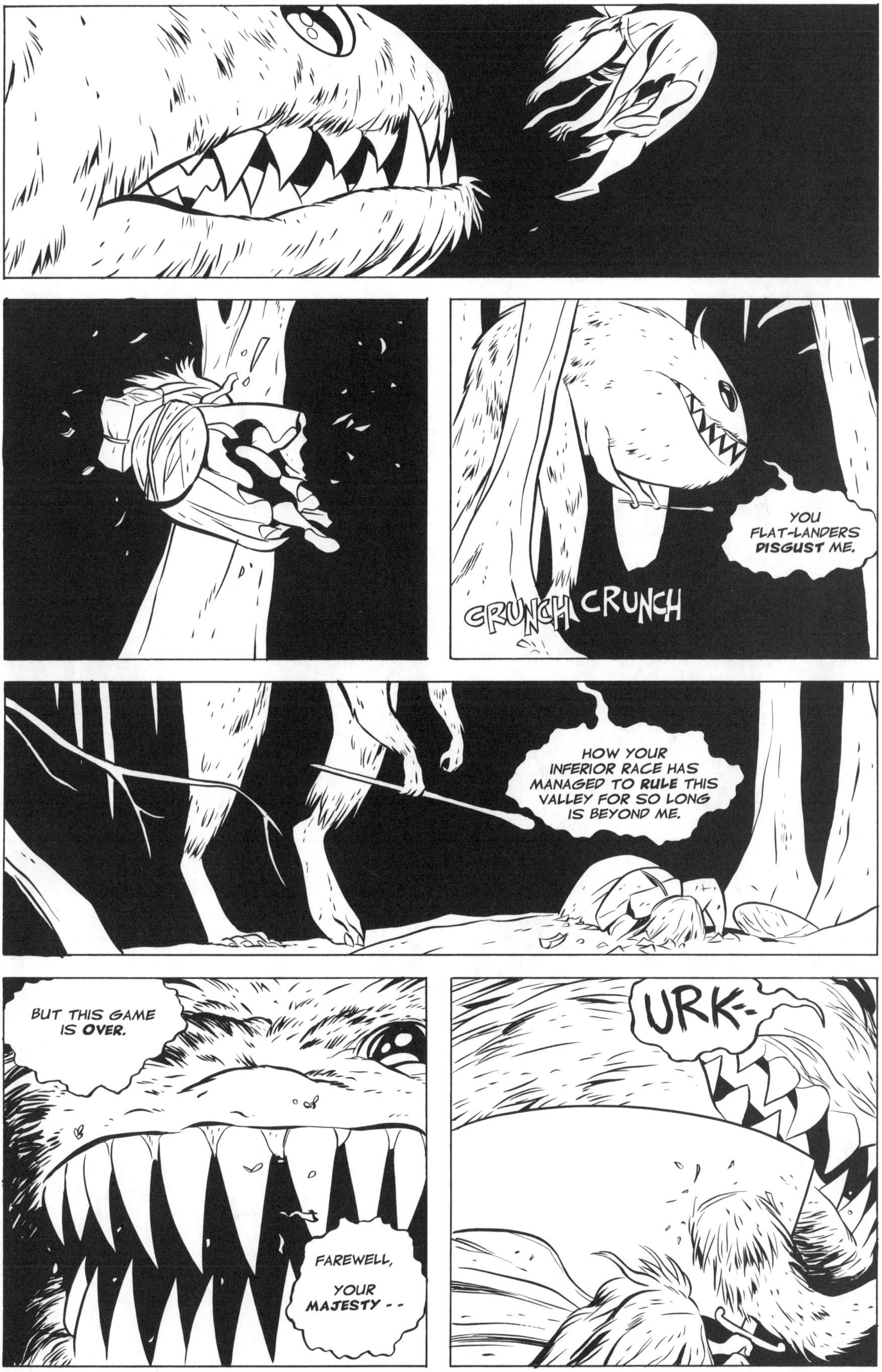
YOU FLAT-LANDERS DISGUST ME.
CRUNCH CRUNCH
HOW YOUR INFERIOR RACE HAS MANAGED TO RULE THIS VALLEY FOR SO LONG IS BEYOND ME.
BUT THIS GAME IS OVER.
FAREWELL, YOUR MAJESTY - -
URK-

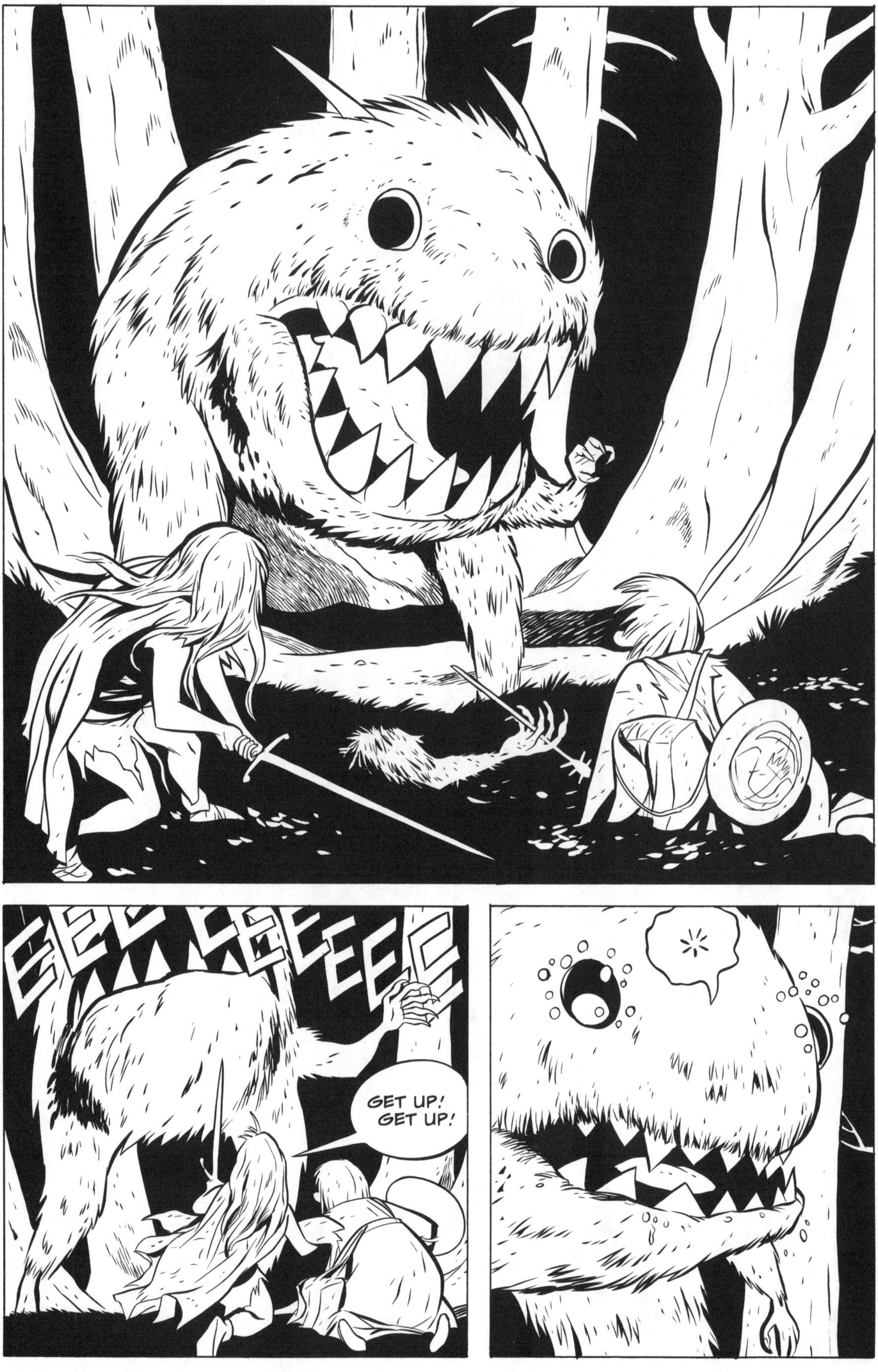
GET UP!
GET UP!

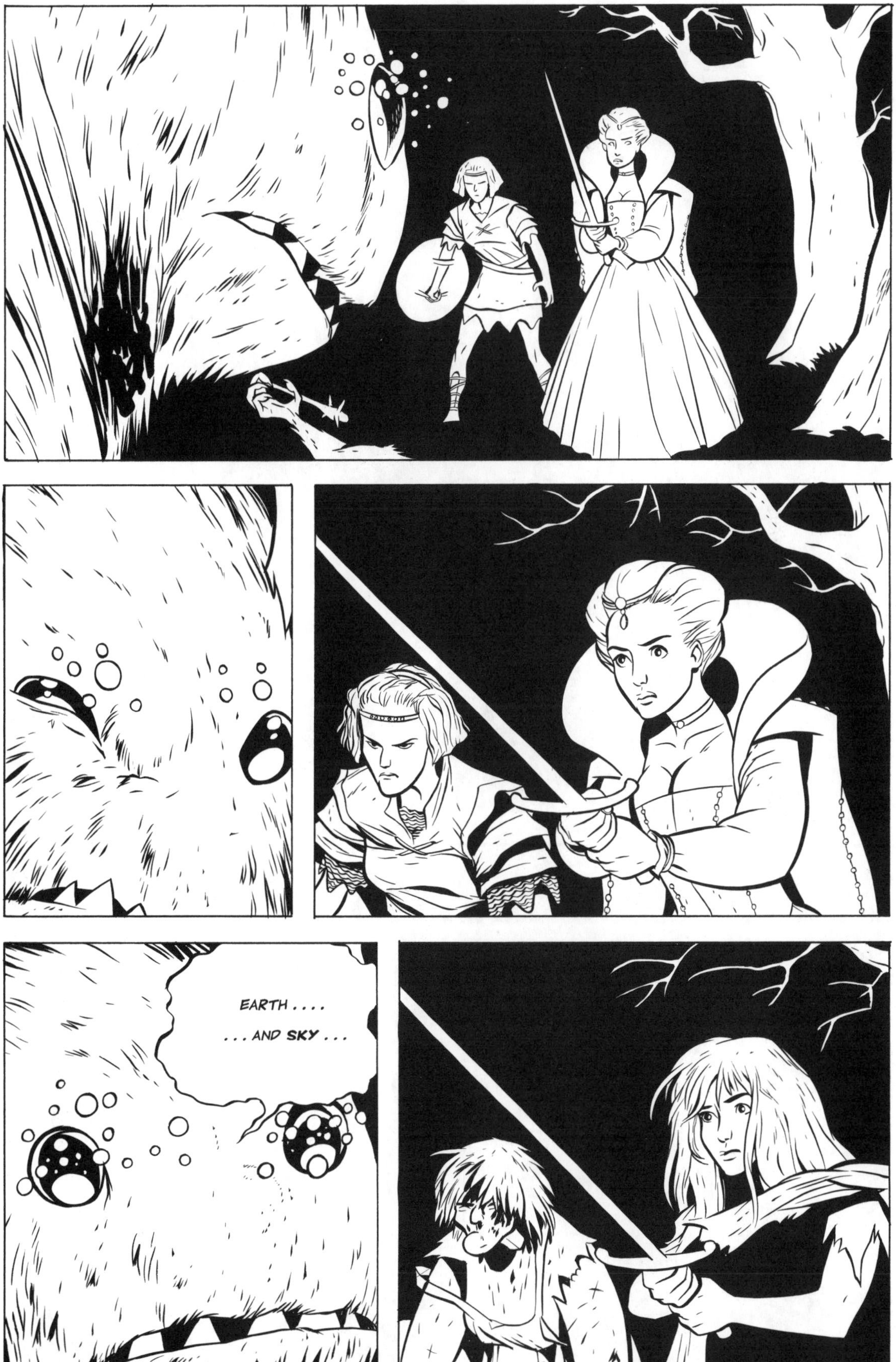
EARTH . . . .
. . . AND SKY . . .

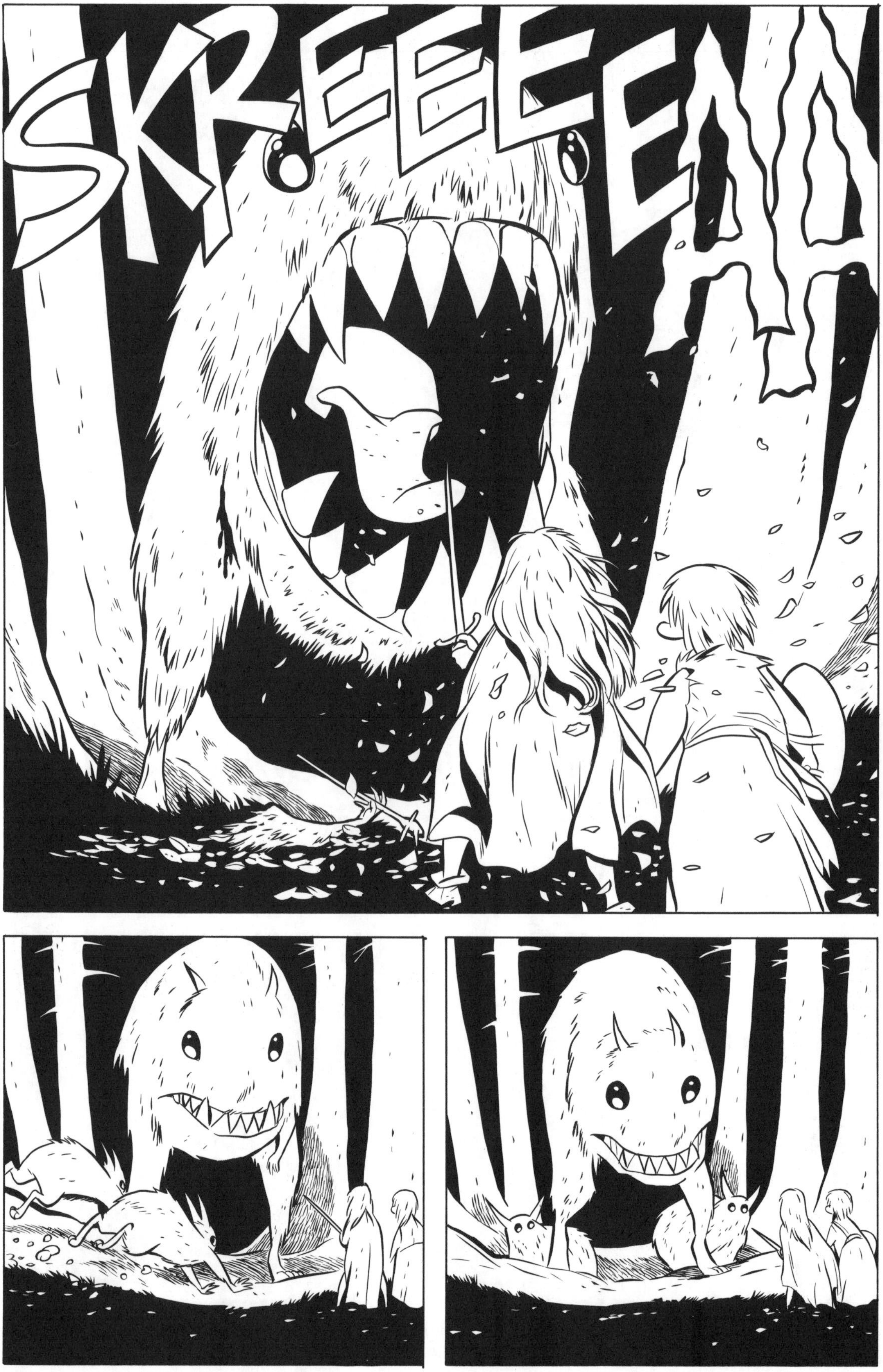
SKREEEEAAA

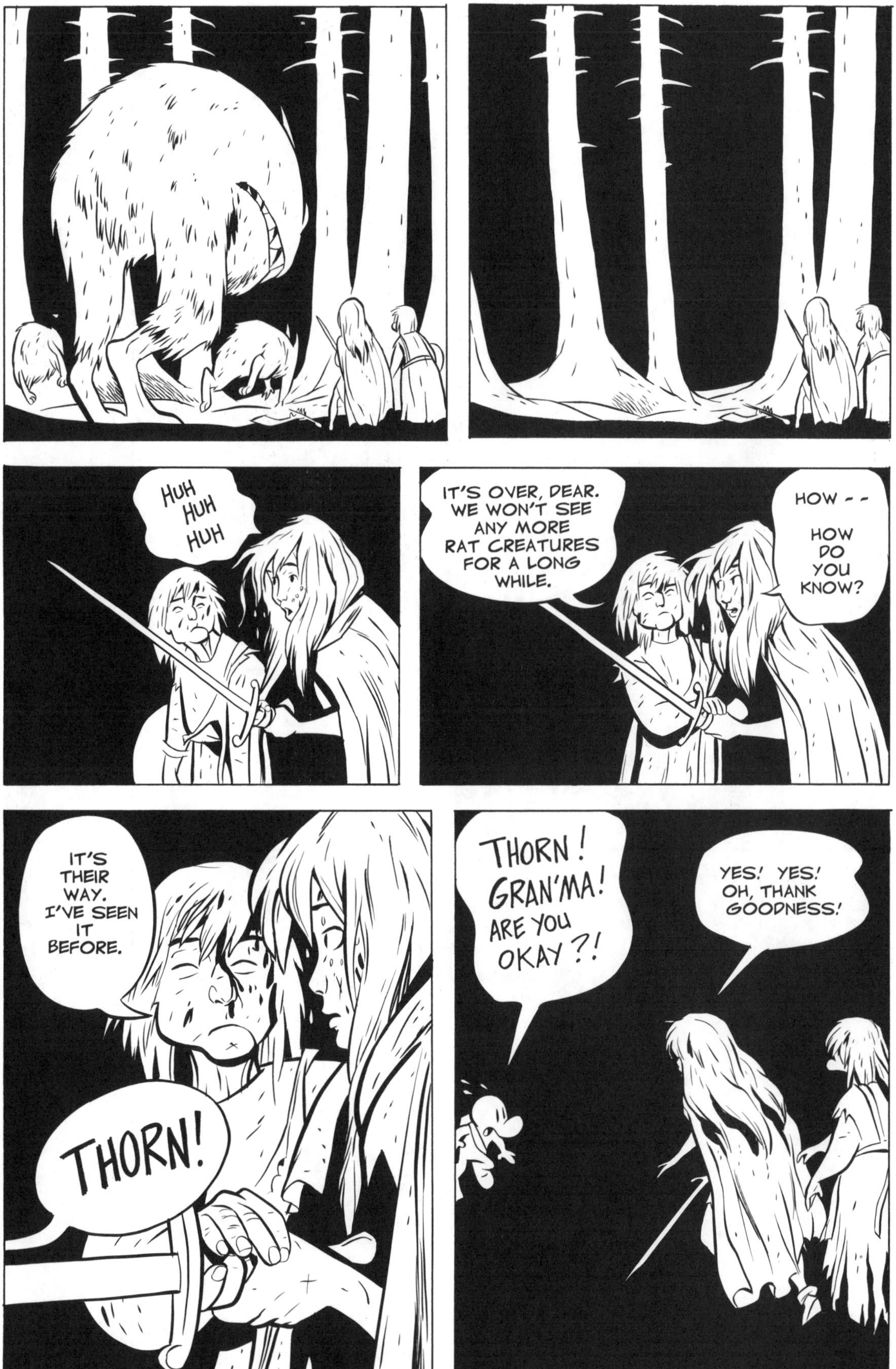
HUH HUH HUH
IT'S OVER, DEAR. WE WON'T SEE ANY MORE RAT CREATURES FOR A LONG WHILE.
HOW - - HOW DO YOU KNOW?
IT'S THEIR WAY. I'VE SEEN IT BEFORE.
THORN!
THORN! GRAN'MA! ARE YOU OKAY ?!
YES! YES! OH, THANK GOODNESS!

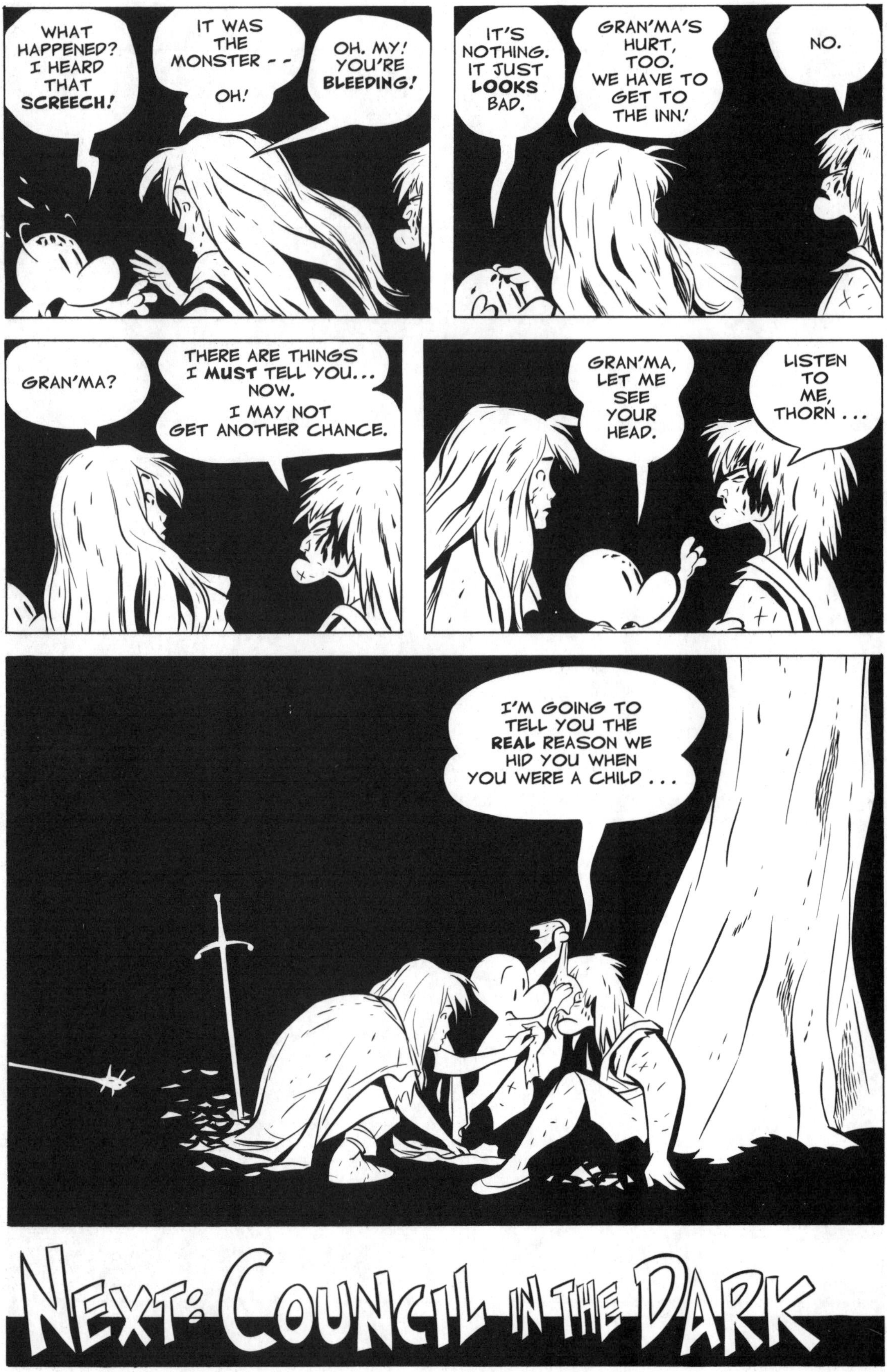
WHAT HAPPENED? I HEARD THAT SCREECH!
IT WAS THE MONSTER - - OH!
OH. MY! YOU'RE BLEEDING!
IT'S NOTHING. IT JUST LOOKS BAD.
GRAN'MA'S HURT, TOO. WE HAVE TO GET TO THE INN!
NO.
GRAN'MA?
THERE ARE THINGS I MUST TELL YOU... NOW. I MAY NOT GET ANOTHER CHANCE.
GRAN'MA, LET ME SEE YOUR HEAD.
LISTEN TO ME, THORN...
I'M GOING TO TELL YOU THE REAL REASON WE HID YOU WHEN YOU WERE A CHILD...
NEXT: COUNCIL IN THE DARK

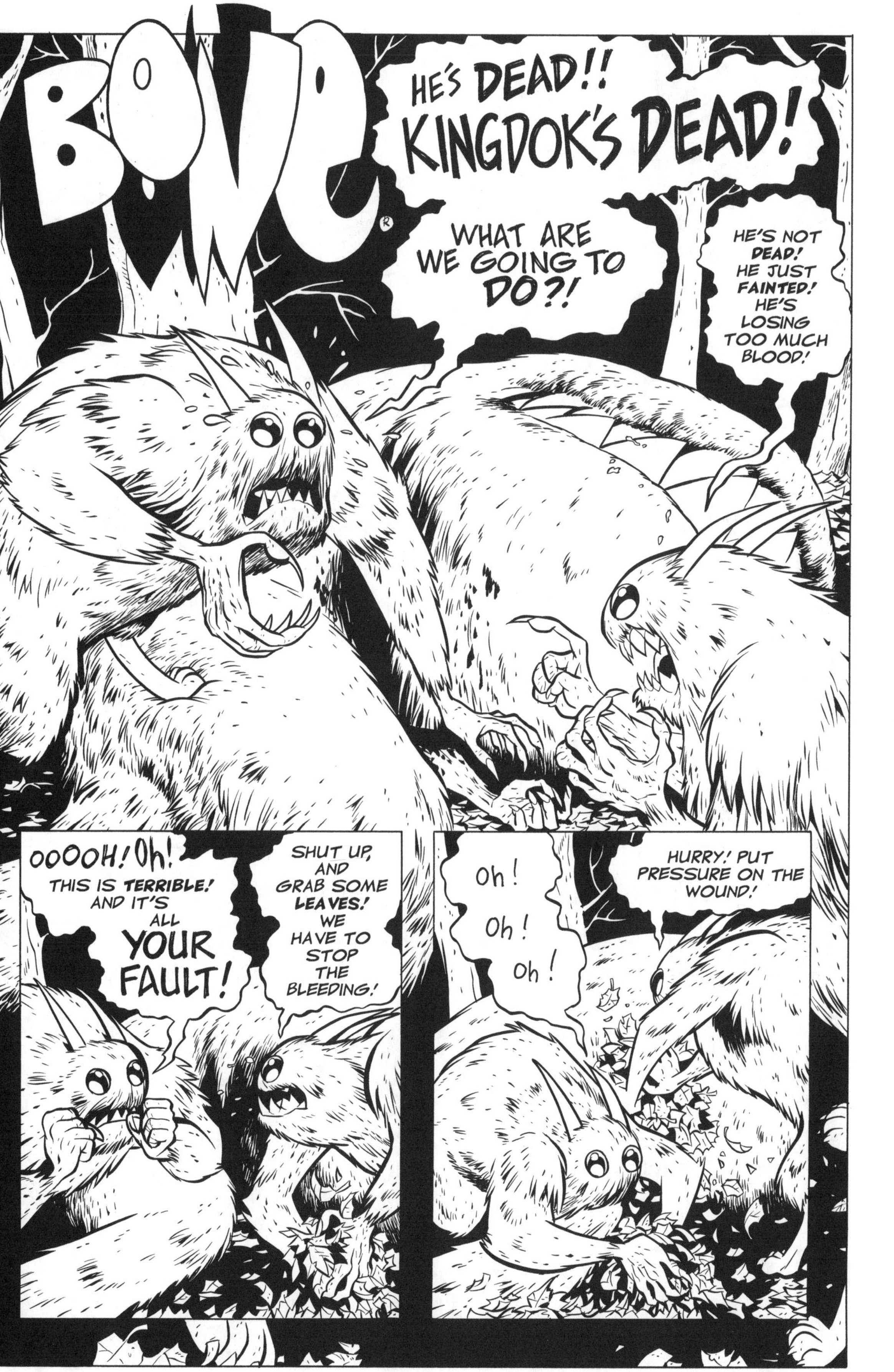
BONE®
HE'S DEAD!! KINGDOK'S DEAD!
WHAT ARE WE GOING TO DO?!
HE'S NOT DEAD! HE JUST FAINTED! HE'S LOSING TOO MUCH BLOOD!
OOOOH! Oh! THIS IS TERRIBLE! AND IT'S ALL YOUR FAULT!
SHUT UP, AND GRAB SOME LEAVES! WE HAVE TO STOP THE BLEEDING!
Oh! Oh! Oh!
HURRY! PUT PRESSURE ON THE WOUND!

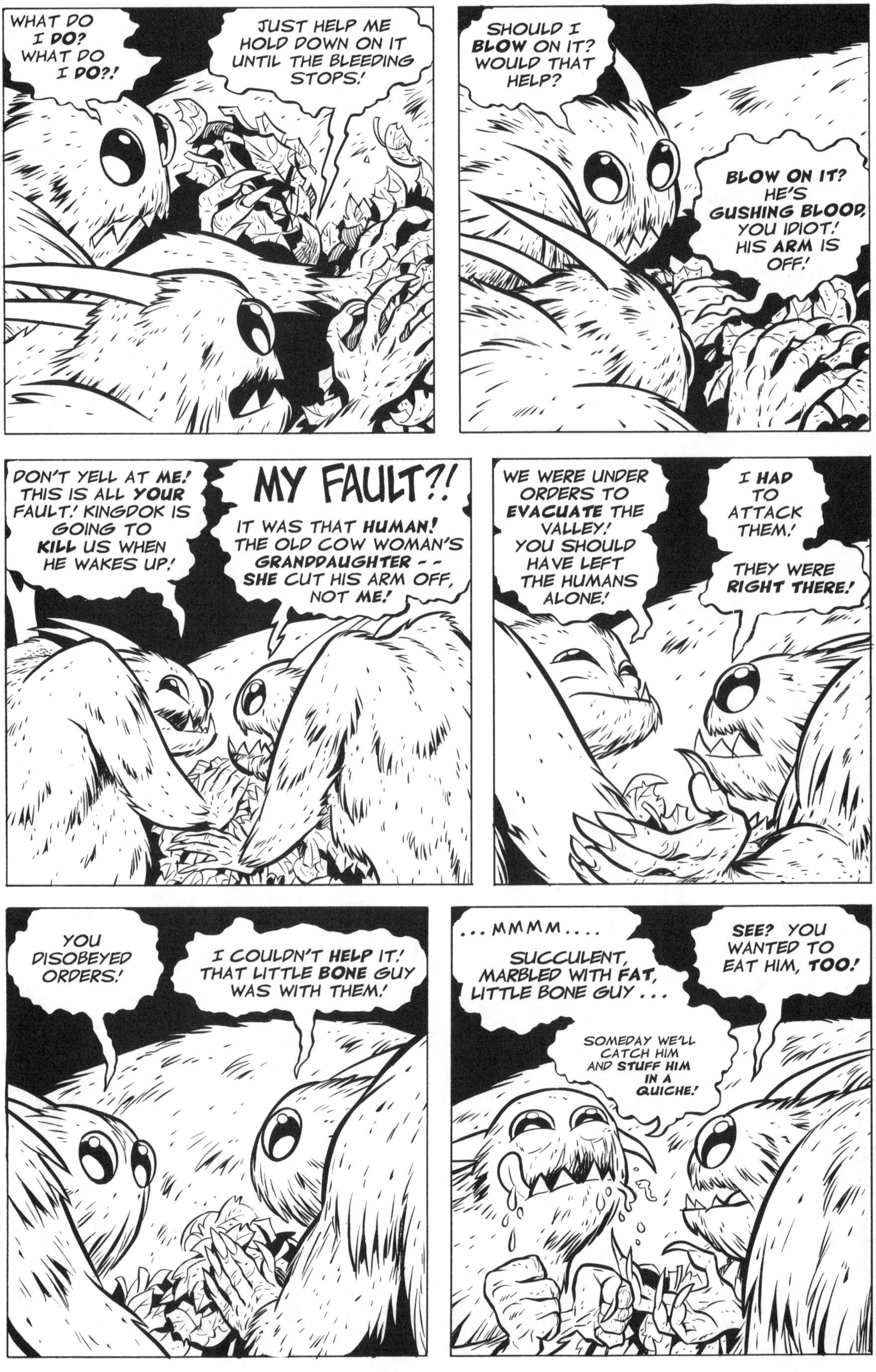
WHAT DO I DO? WHAT DO I DO?!
JUST HELP ME HOLD DOWN ON IT UNTIL THE BLEEDING STOPS!
SHOULD I BLOW ON IT? WOULD THAT HELP?
BLOW ON IT? HE'S GUSHING BLOOD, YOU IDIOT! HIS ARM IS OFF!
DON'T YELL AT ME! THIS IS ALL YOUR FAULT! KINGDOK IS GOING TO KILL US WHEN HE WAKES UP!
MY FAULT?!
IT WAS THAT HUMAN! THE OLD COW WOMAN'S GRANDDAUGHTER - - SHE CUT HIS ARM OFF, NOT ME!
WE WERE UNDER ORDERS TO EVACUATE THE VALLEY! YOU SHOULD HAVE LEFT THE HUMANS ALONE!
I HAD TO ATTACK THEM!
THEY WERE RIGHT THERE!
YOU DISOBEYED ORDERS!
I COULDN'T HELP IT! THAT LITTLE BONE GUY WAS WITH THEM!
. . . MMMM . . . .
SUCCULENT, MARBLED WITH FAT, LITTLE BONE GUY . . .
SEE? YOU WANTED TO EAT HIM, TOO!
SOMEDAY WE'LL CATCH HIM AND STUFF HIM IN A QUICHE!

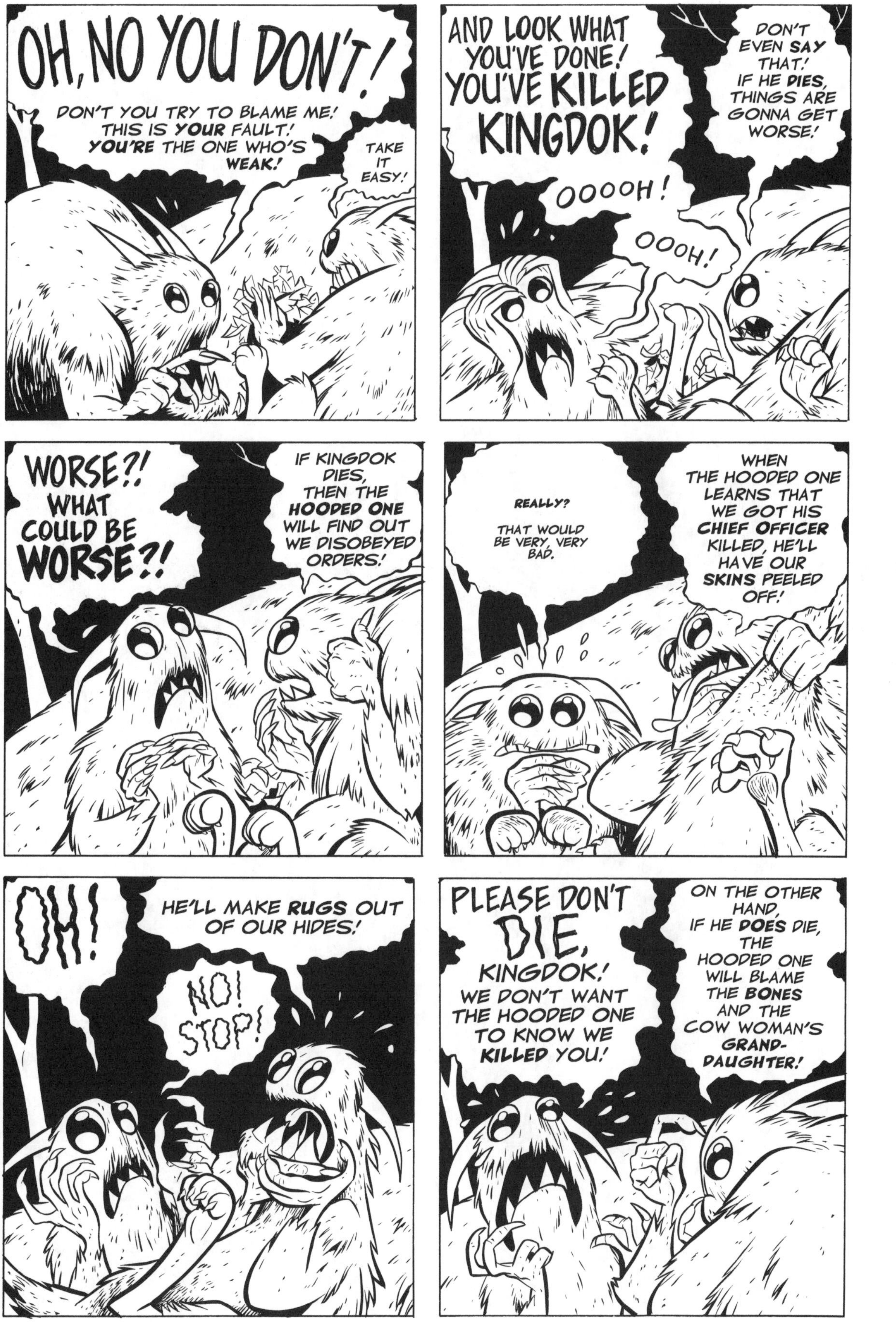
OH, NO YOU DON'T!
DON'T YOU TRY TO BLAME ME! THIS IS YOUR FAULT! YOU'RE THE ONE WHO'S WEAK!
TAKE IT EASY!
AND LOOK WHAT YOU'VE DONE! YOU'VE KILLED KINGDOK!
DON'T EVEN SAY THAT! IF HE DIES, THINGS ARE GONNA GET WORSE!
OOOOH!
OOOH!
WORSE?! WHAT COULD BE WORSE?!
IF KINGDOK DIES, THEN THE HOODED ONE WILL FIND OUT WE DISOBEYED ORDERS!
REALLY?
THAT WOULD BE VERY, VERY BAD.
WHEN THE HOODED ONE LEARNS THAT WE GOT HIS CHIEF OFFICER KILLED, HE'LL HAVE OUR SKINS PEELED OFF!
OH!
HE'LL MAKE RUGS OUT OF OUR HIDES!
NO! STOP!
PLEASE DON'T DIE, KINGDOK! WE DON'T WANT THE HOODED ONE TO KNOW WE KILLED YOU!
ON THE OTHER HAND, IF HE DOES DIE, THE HOODED ONE WILL BLAME THE BONES AND THE COW WOMAN'S GRAND-DAUGHTER!

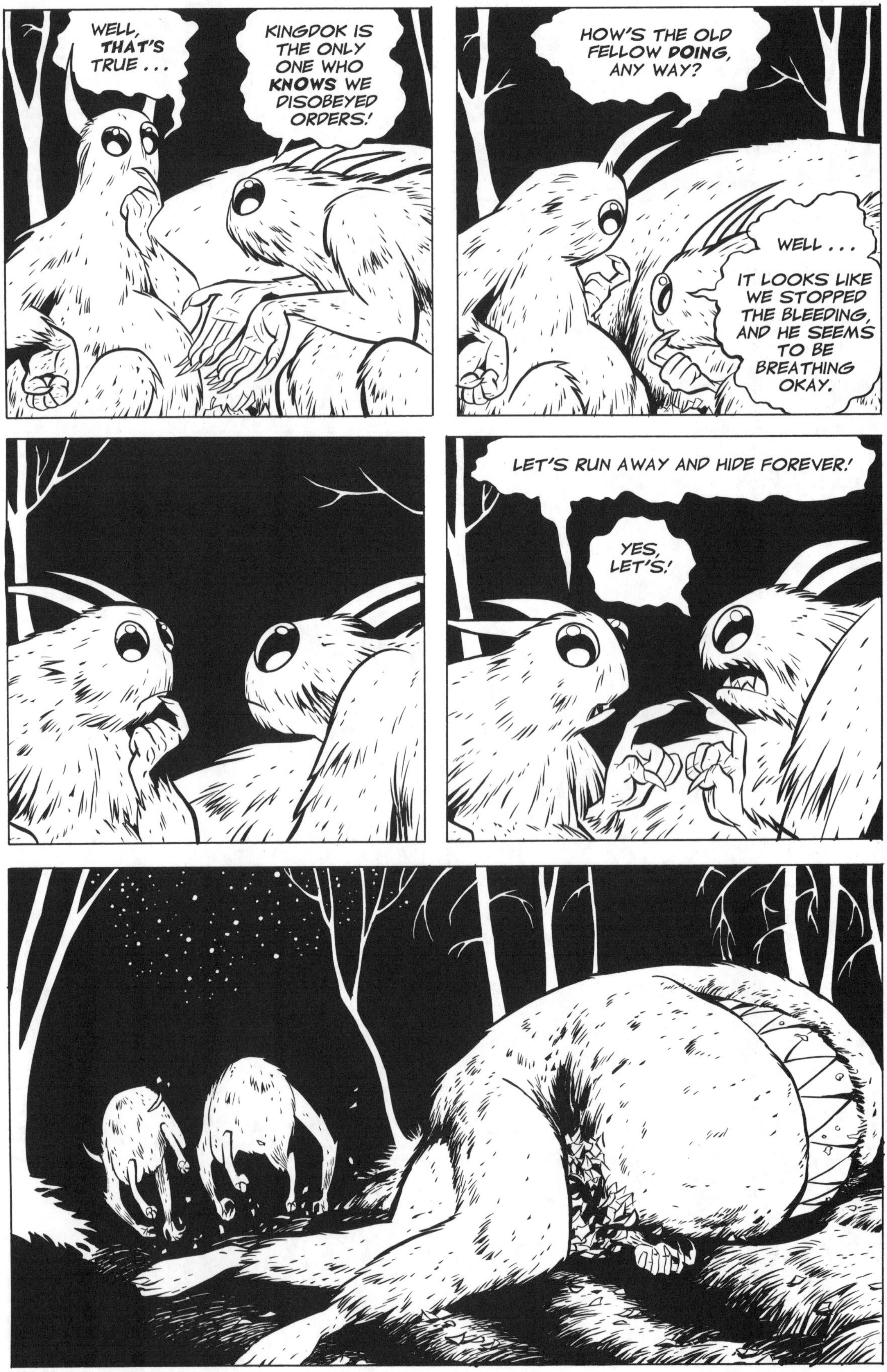
WELL, **THAT'S** TRUE . . .
KINGDOK IS THE ONLY ONE WHO **KNOWS** WE DISOBEYED ORDERS!
HOW'S THE OLD FELLOW **DOING**, ANY WAY?
WELL . . .
IT LOOKS LIKE WE STOPPED THE BLEEDING, AND HE SEEMS TO BE BREATHING OKAY.
LET'S RUN AWAY AND HIDE FOREVER!
YES, LET'S!

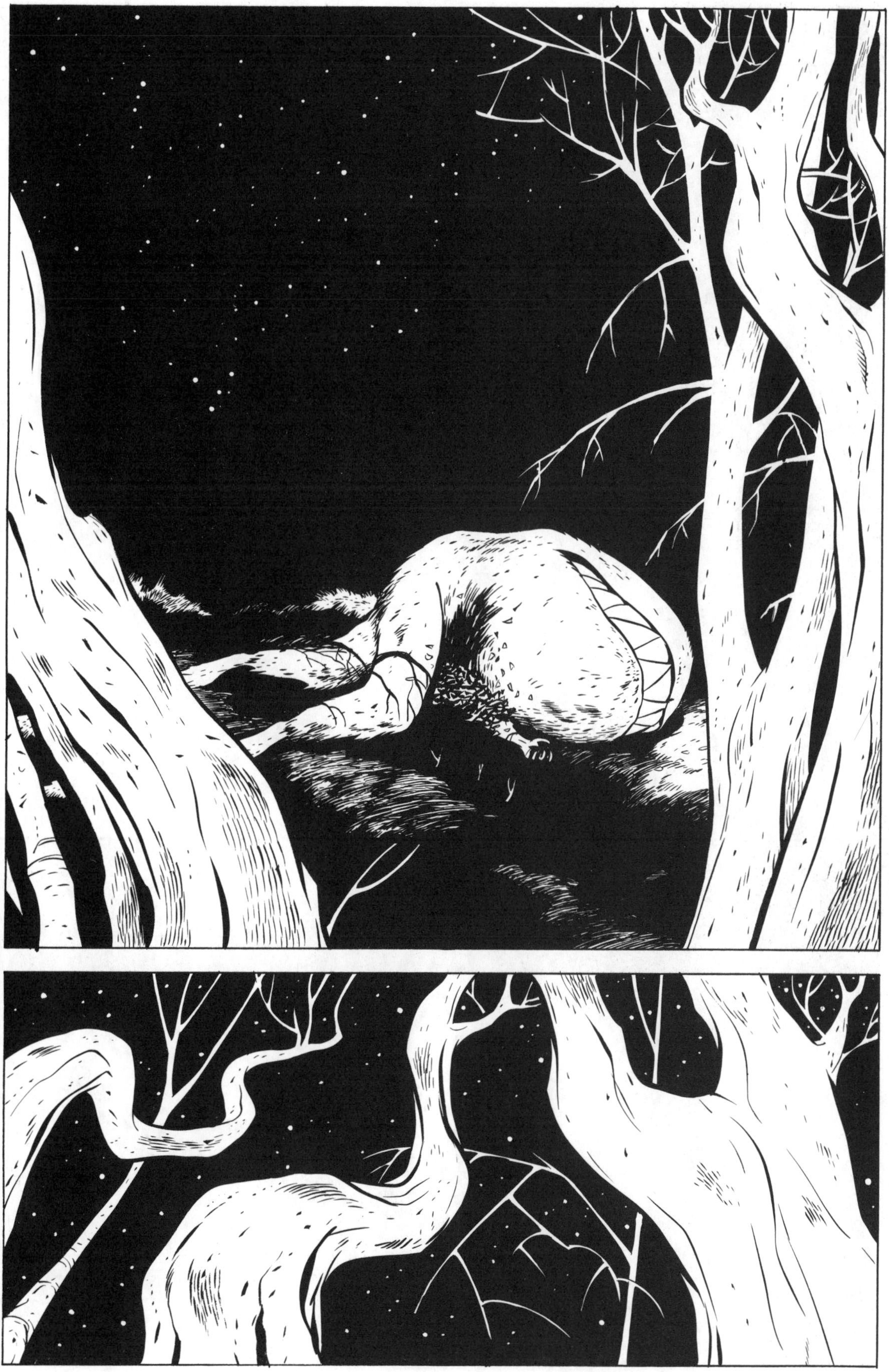

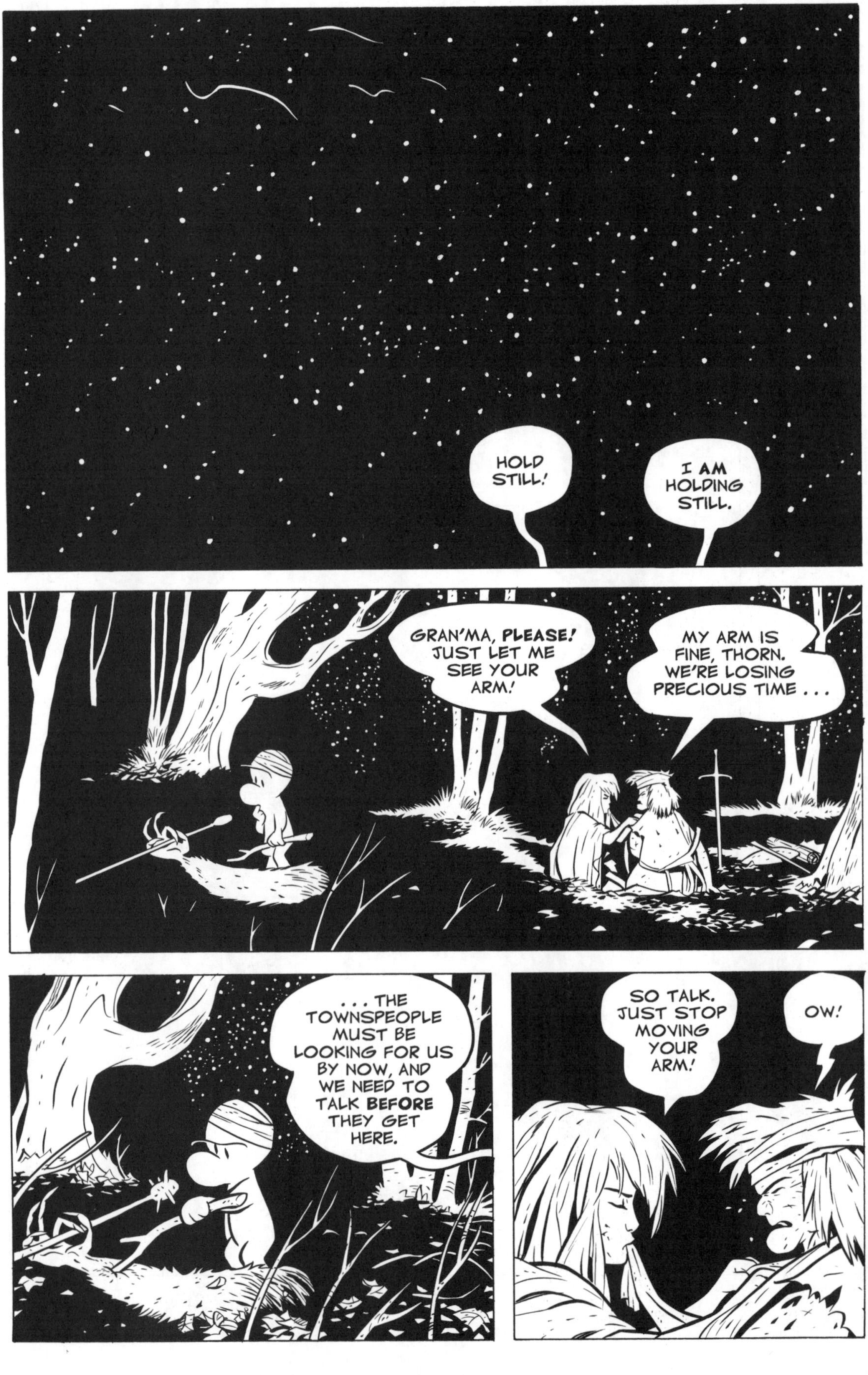
HOLD STILL!
I AM HOLDING STILL.
GRAN'MA, PLEASE! JUST LET ME SEE YOUR ARM!
MY ARM IS FINE, THORN. WE'RE LOSING PRECIOUS TIME . . .
. . . THE TOWNSPEOPLE MUST BE LOOKING FOR US BY NOW, AND WE NEED TO TALK BEFORE THEY GET HERE.
SO TALK. JUST STOP MOVING YOUR ARM!
OW!

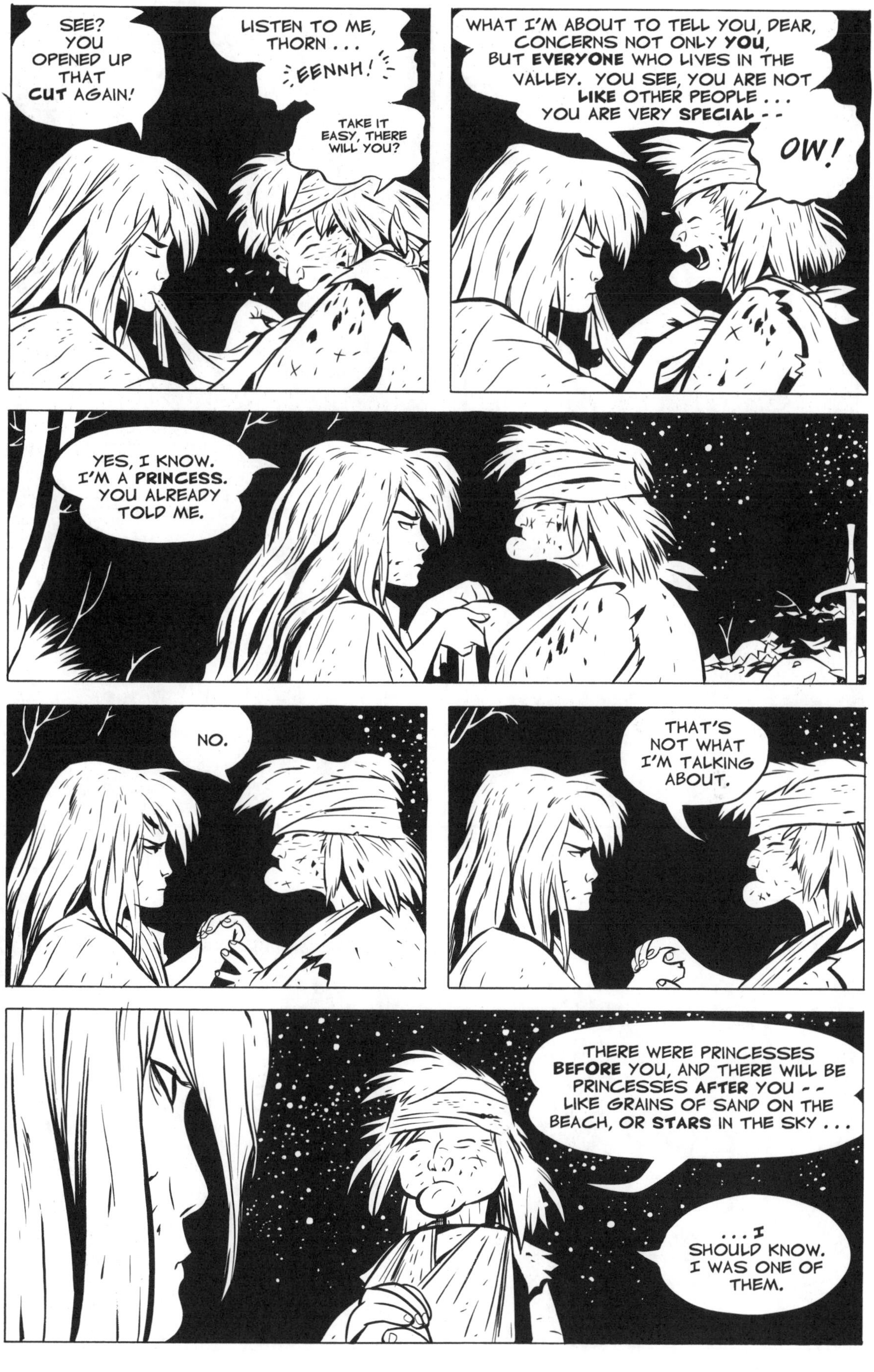
SEE? YOU OPENED UP THAT CUT AGAIN!
LISTEN TO ME, THORN . . .
EENNH!
TAKE IT EASY, THERE WILL YOU?
WHAT I'M ABOUT TO TELL YOU, DEAR, CONCERNS NOT ONLY YOU, BUT EVERYONE WHO LIVES IN THE VALLEY. YOU SEE, YOU ARE NOT LIKE OTHER PEOPLE . . . YOU ARE VERY SPECIAL - -
OW!
YES, I KNOW. I'M A PRINCESS. YOU ALREADY TOLD ME.
NO.
THAT'S NOT WHAT I'M TALKING ABOUT.
THERE WERE PRINCESSES BEFORE YOU, AND THERE WILL BE PRINCESSES AFTER YOU - - LIKE GRAINS OF SAND ON THE BEACH, OR STARS IN THE SKY . . .
. . . I SHOULD KNOW. I WAS ONE OF THEM.

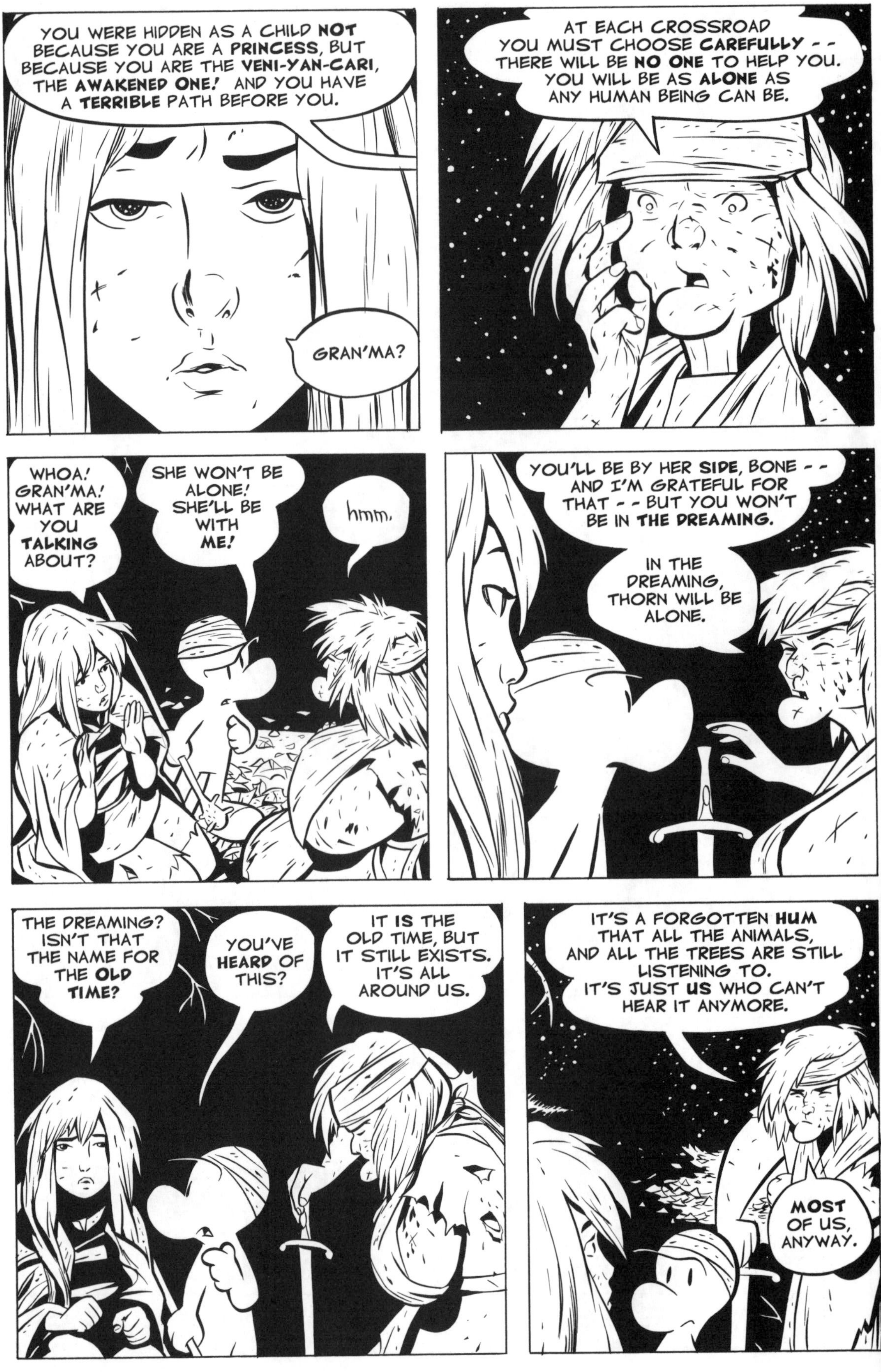

YOU WERE HIDDEN AS A CHILD NOT BECAUSE YOU ARE A PRINCESS, BUT BECAUSE YOU ARE THE VENI-YAN-CARI, THE AWAKENED ONE! AND YOU HAVE A TERRIBLE PATH BEFORE YOU.
GRAN'MA?
AT EACH CROSSROAD YOU MUST CHOOSE CAREFULLY -- THERE WILL BE NO ONE TO HELP YOU. YOU WILL BE AS ALONE AS ANY HUMAN BEING CAN BE.
WHOA! GRAN'MA! WHAT ARE YOU TALKING ABOUT?
SHE WON'T BE ALONE! SHE'LL BE WITH ME!
hmm.
YOU'LL BE BY HER SIDE, BONE -- AND I'M GRATEFUL FOR THAT -- BUT YOU WON'T BE IN THE DREAMING.
IN THE DREAMING, THORN WILL BE ALONE.
THE DREAMING? ISN'T THAT THE NAME FOR THE OLD TIME?
YOU'VE HEARD OF THIS?
IT IS THE OLD TIME, BUT IT STILL EXISTS. IT'S ALL AROUND US.
IT'S A FORGOTTEN HUM THAT ALL THE ANIMALS, AND ALL THE TREES ARE STILL LISTENING TO. IT'S JUST US WHO CAN'T HEAR IT ANYMORE.
MOST OF US, ANYWAY.

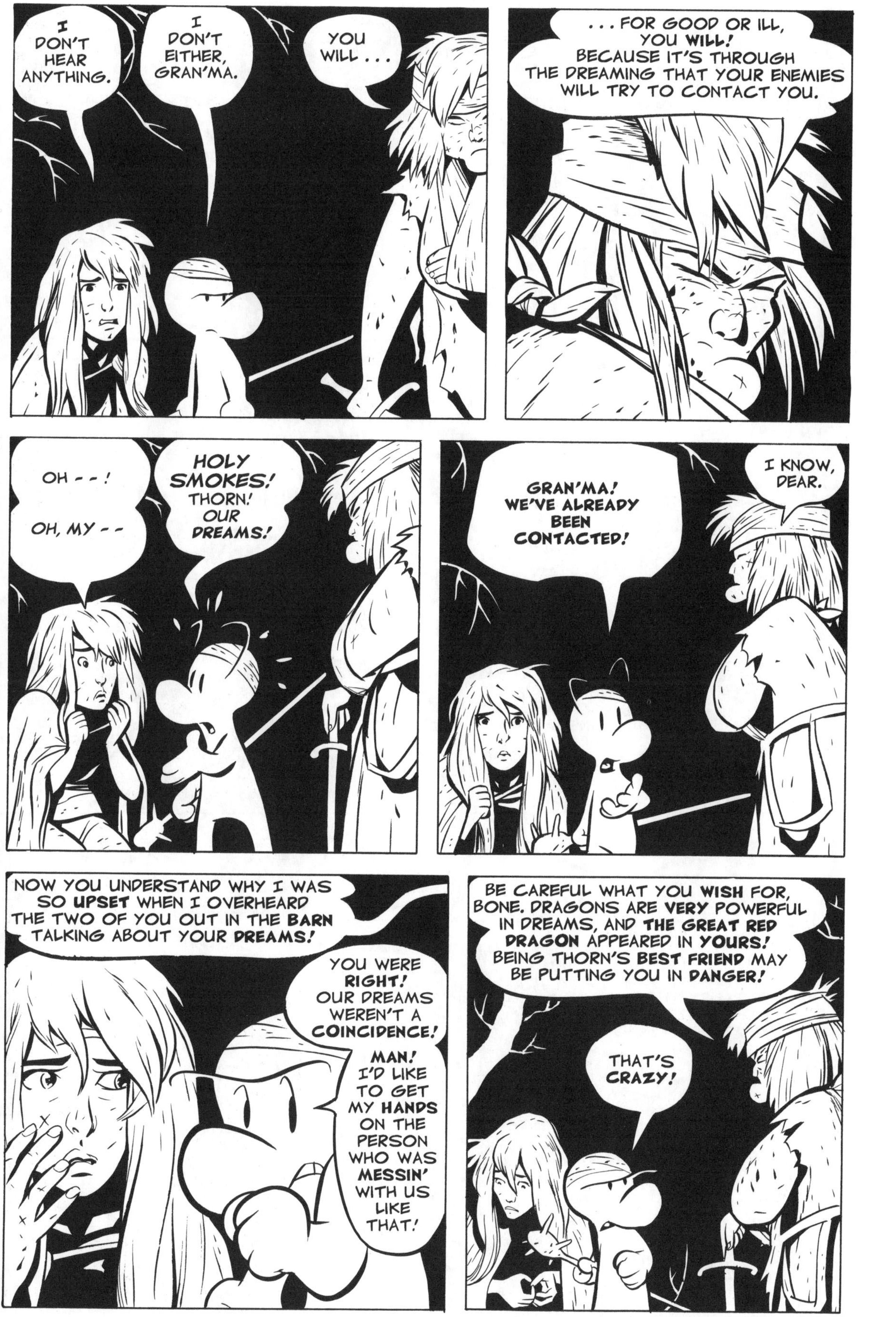
I DON'T HEAR ANYTHING.
I DON'T EITHER, GRAN'MA.
YOU WILL . . .
. . . FOR GOOD OR ILL, YOU WILL! BECAUSE IT'S THROUGH THE DREAMING THAT YOUR ENEMIES WILL TRY TO CONTACT YOU.
OH - - ! OH, MY - -
HOLY SMOKES! THORN! OUR DREAMS!
GRAN'MA! WE'VE ALREADY BEEN CONTACTED!
I KNOW, DEAR.
NOW YOU UNDERSTAND WHY I WAS SO UPSET WHEN I OVERHEARD THE TWO OF YOU OUT IN THE BARN TALKING ABOUT YOUR DREAMS!
YOU WERE RIGHT! OUR DREAMS WEREN'T A COINCIDENCE!
MAN! I'D LIKE TO GET MY HANDS ON THE PERSON WHO WAS MESSIN' WITH US LIKE THAT!
BE CAREFUL WHAT YOU WISH FOR, BONE. DRAGONS ARE VERY POWERFUL IN DREAMS, AND THE GREAT RED DRAGON APPEARED IN YOURS! BEING THORN'S BEST FRIEND MAY BE PUTTING YOU IN DANGER!
THAT'S CRAZY!

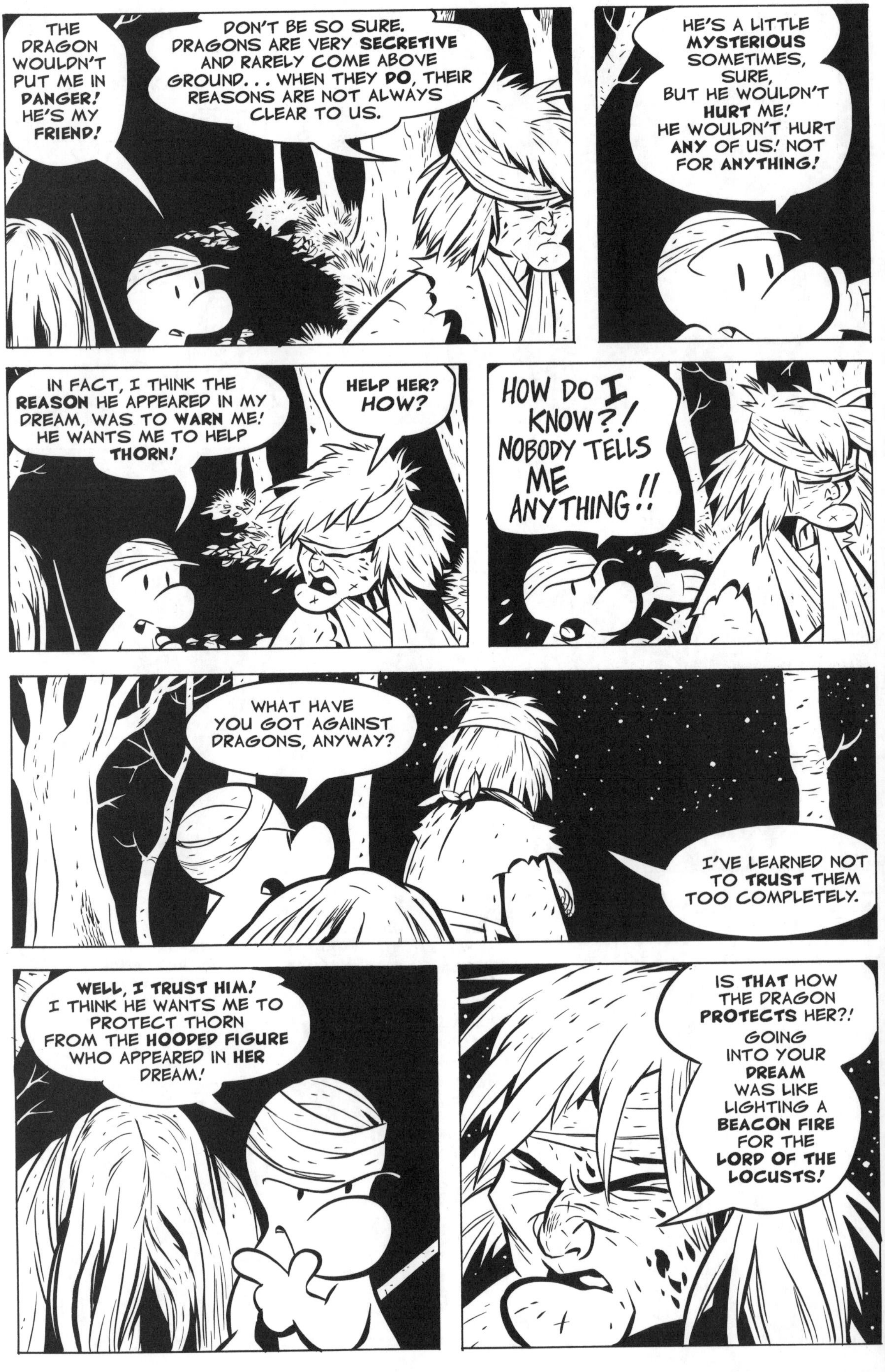

THE DRAGON WOULDN'T PUT ME IN DANGER! HE'S MY FRIEND!
DON'T BE SO SURE. DRAGONS ARE VERY SECRETIVE AND RARELY COME ABOVE GROUND. . . WHEN THEY DO, THEIR REASONS ARE NOT ALWAYS CLEAR TO US.
HE'S A LITTLE MYSTERIOUS SOMETIMES, SURE, BUT HE WOULDN'T HURT ME! HE WOULDN'T HURT ANY OF US! NOT FOR ANYTHING!
IN FACT, I THINK THE REASON HE APPEARED IN MY DREAM, WAS TO WARN ME! HE WANTS ME TO HELP THORN!
HELP HER? HOW?
HOW DO I KNOW?! NOBODY TELLS ME ANYTHING!!
WHAT HAVE YOU GOT AGAINST DRAGONS, ANYWAY?
I'VE LEARNED NOT TO TRUST THEM TOO COMPLETELY.
WELL, I TRUST HIM! I THINK HE WANTS ME TO PROTECT THORN FROM THE HOODED FIGURE WHO APPEARED IN HER DREAM!
IS THAT HOW THE DRAGON PROTECTS HER?! GOING INTO YOUR DREAM WAS LIKE LIGHTING A BEACON FIRE FOR THE LORD OF THE LOCUSTS!

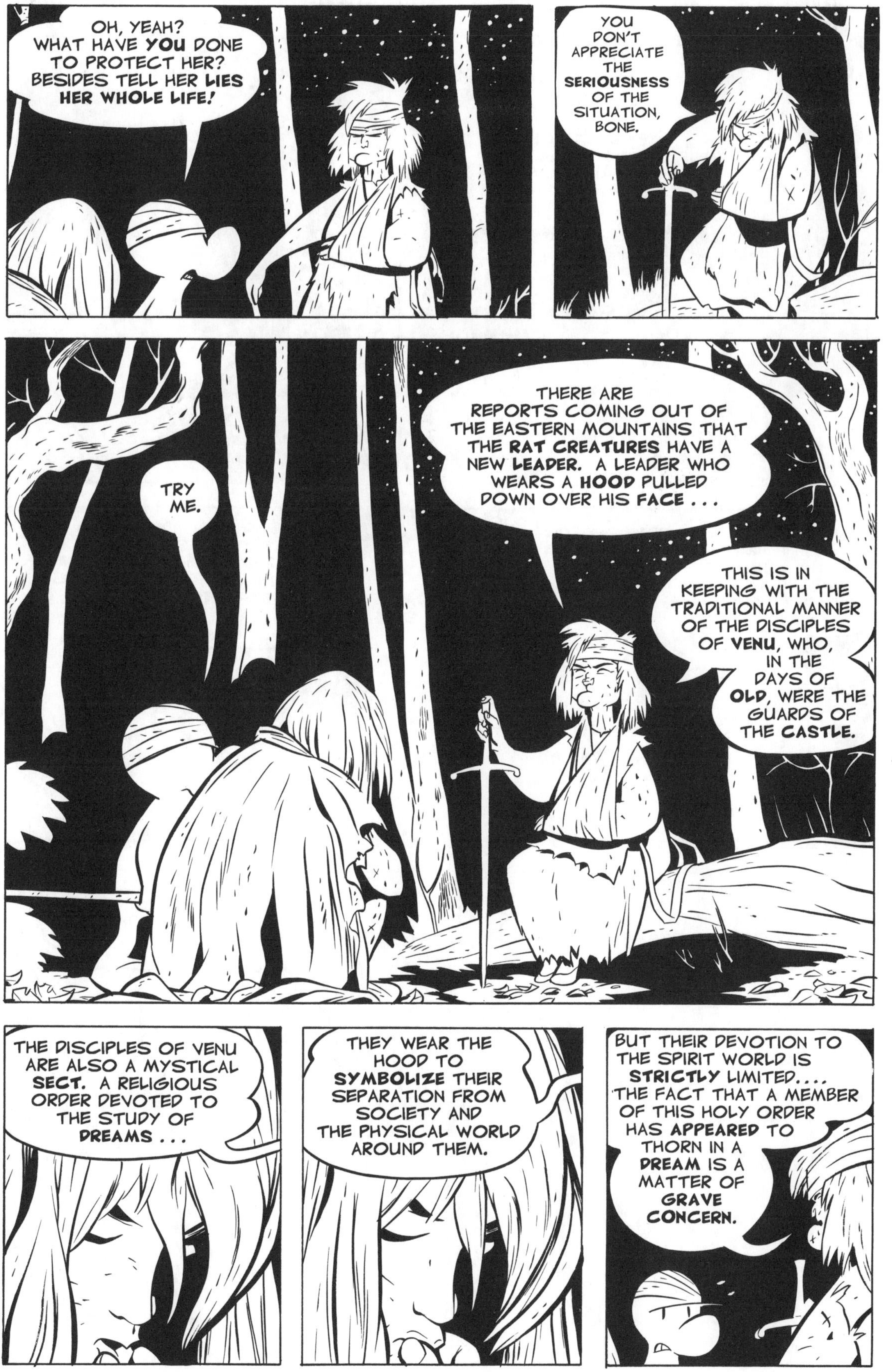
OH, YEAH? WHAT HAVE YOU DONE TO PROTECT HER? BESIDES TELL HER LIES HER WHOLE LIFE!
YOU DON'T APPRECIATE THE SERIOUSNESS OF THE SITUATION, BONE.
TRY ME.
THERE ARE REPORTS COMING OUT OF THE EASTERN MOUNTAINS THAT THE RAT CREATURES HAVE A NEW LEADER. A LEADER WHO WEARS A HOOD PULLED DOWN OVER HIS FACE . . .
THIS IS IN KEEPING WITH THE TRADITIONAL MANNER OF THE DISCIPLES OF VENU, WHO, IN THE DAYS OF OLD, WERE THE GUARDS OF THE CASTLE.
THE DISCIPLES OF VENU ARE ALSO A MYSTICAL SECT. A RELIGIOUS ORDER DEVOTED TO THE STUDY OF DREAMS . . .
THEY WEAR THE HOOD TO SYMBOLIZE THEIR SEPARATION FROM SOCIETY AND THE PHYSICAL WORLD AROUND THEM.
BUT THEIR DEVOTION TO THE SPIRIT WORLD IS STRICTLY LIMITED. . . . THE FACT THAT A MEMBER OF THIS HOLY ORDER HAS APPEARED TO THORN IN A DREAM IS A MATTER OF GRAVE CONCERN.

WHY?

ACCORDING TO THEIR BELIEFS, A **VISITATION** CAN ONLY BE ACCOMPLISHED IN **TWO WAYS.**

ONE IS WITH THE HELP OF THE DRAGONS -- WHICH IS **FORBIDDEN** BY THE **TREATY** --

THE ONLY OTHER WAY IT CAN BE DONE IS BY THE POWER OF **THE LORD OF THE LOCUSTS.**

THIS IS NO ORDINARY **HOLY MAN** APPEARING IN THORN'S DREAMS . . .

WHOEVER THIS HOODED PERSON IS . . . IF HE IS USING THE **POWER** OF THE LORD OF THE LOCUSTS . . . THEN HE MAY VERY WELL **BECOME** THE LOCUST KING ON EARTH.

WHOA.

THAT DOESN'T SOUND GOOD.

I'VE KNOWN FOR A **LONG TIME** THAT THE RAT CREATURES HAD A NEW LEADER -- BUT I NEVER **IMAGINED** THAT HE WAS POSSESSED BY THE SPIRIT OF THE ANCIENT LORD **HIMSELF.**

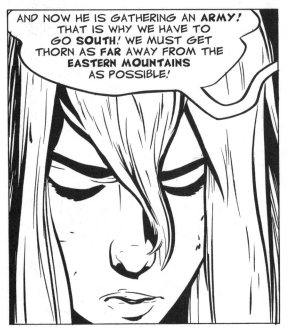

AND NOW HE IS GATHERING AN **ARMY!** THAT IS WHY WE HAVE TO GO **SOUTH!** WE MUST GET THORN AS **FAR** AWAY FROM THE **EASTERN MOUNTAINS** AS POSSIBLE!

OUR ONLY HOPE NOW IS TO GET HER INTO THE HANDS OF THE PEOPLE OF **ATHEIA** --

I'M NOT GOING ANYWHERE.

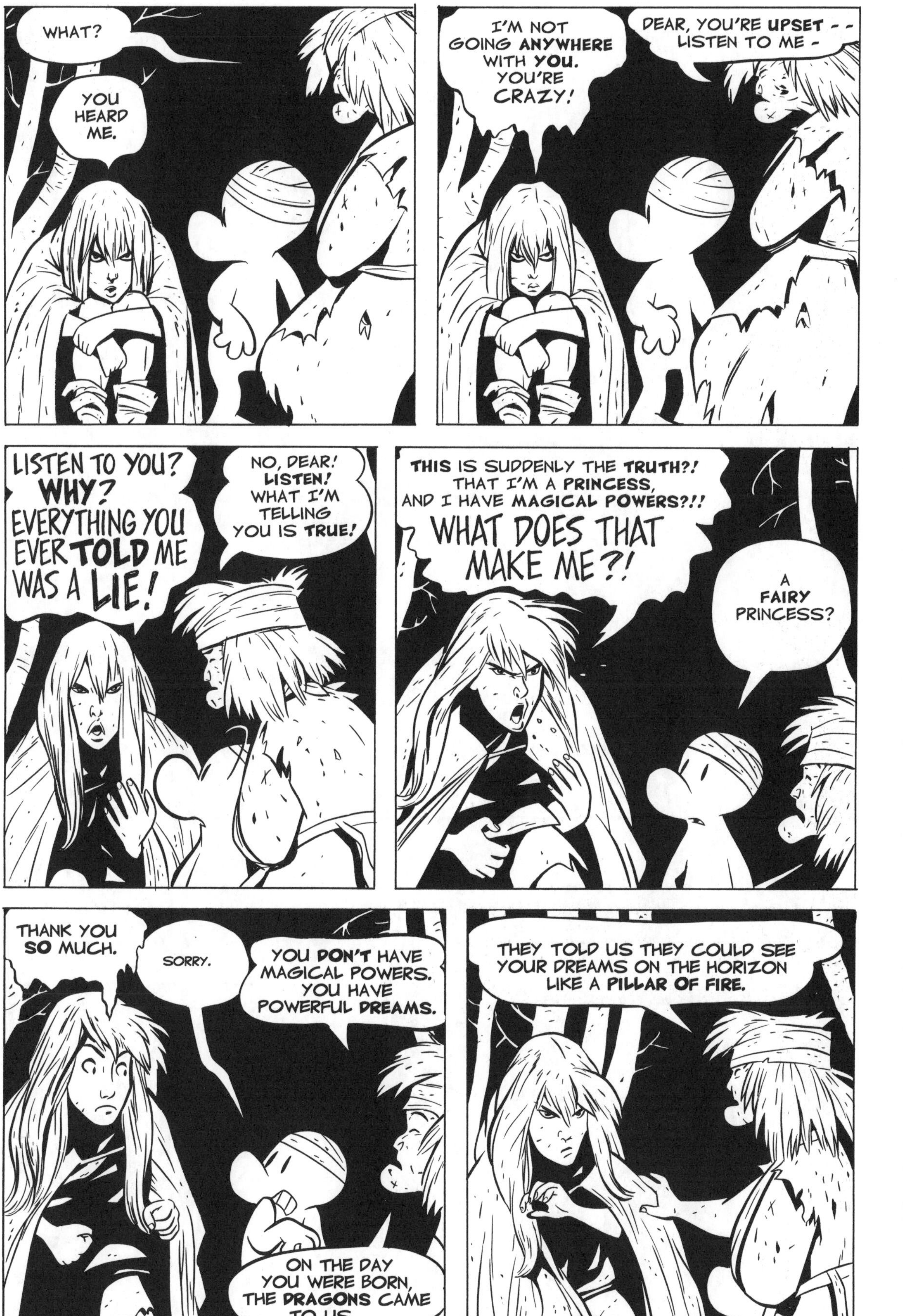
WHAT?
YOU HEARD ME.
I'M NOT GOING ANYWHERE WITH YOU. YOU'RE CRAZY!
DEAR, YOU'RE UPSET - - LISTEN TO ME -
LISTEN TO YOU? WHY? EVERYTHING YOU EVER TOLD ME WAS A LIE!
NO, DEAR! LISTEN! WHAT I'M TELLING YOU IS TRUE!
THIS IS SUDDENLY THE TRUTH?! THAT I'M A PRINCESS, AND I HAVE MAGICAL POWERS?!!
WHAT DOES THAT MAKE ME?!
A FAIRY PRINCESS?
THANK YOU SO MUCH.
SORRY.
YOU DON'T HAVE MAGICAL POWERS. YOU HAVE POWERFUL DREAMS.
ON THE DAY YOU WERE BORN, THE DRAGONS CAME TO US . . .
THEY TOLD US THEY COULD SEE YOUR DREAMS ON THE HORIZON LIKE A PILLAR OF FIRE.

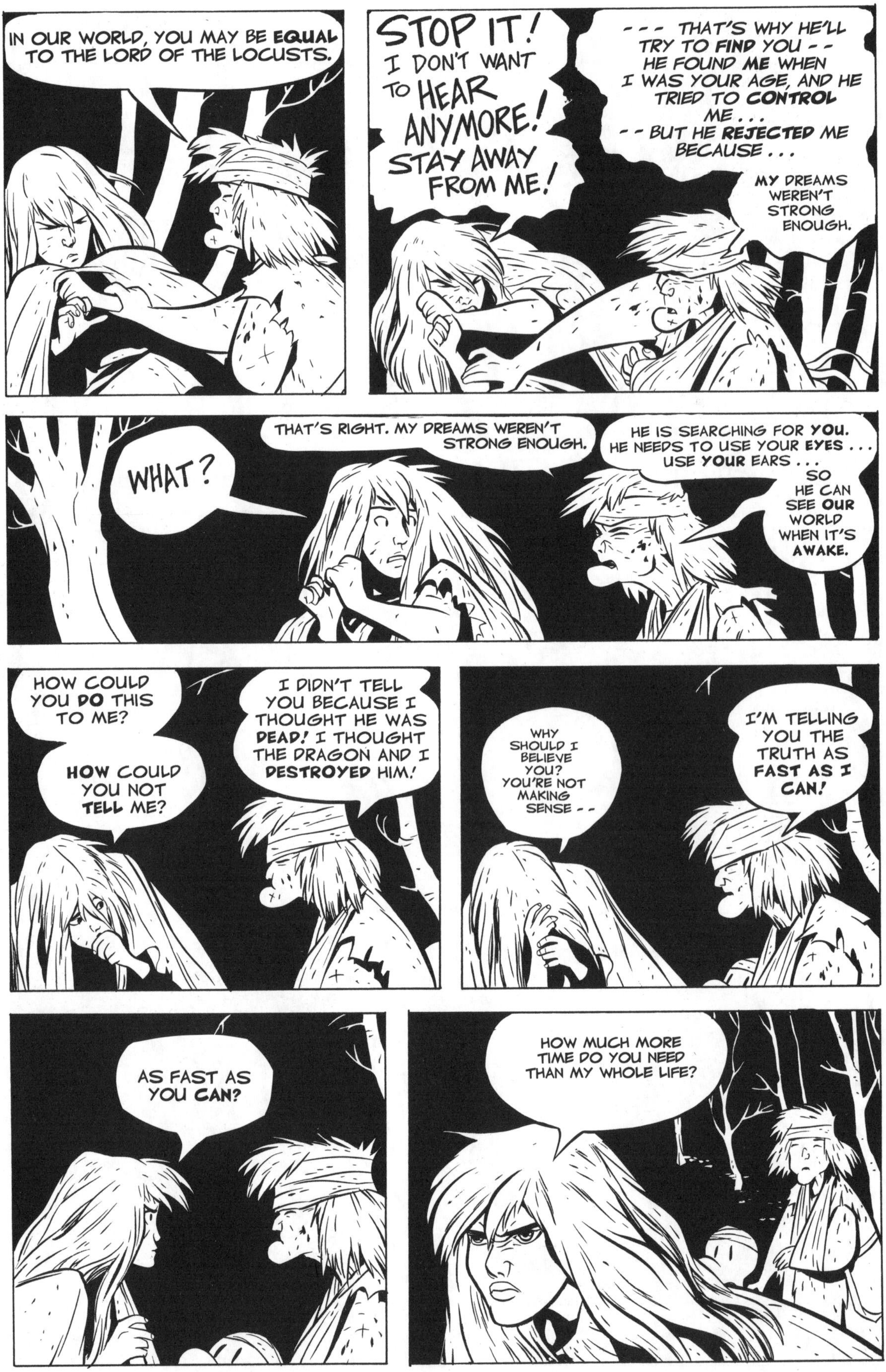
IN OUR WORLD, YOU MAY BE **EQUAL** TO THE LORD OF THE LOCUSTS.
STOP IT! I DON'T WANT TO HEAR ANYMORE! STAY AWAY FROM ME!
- - - THAT'S WHY HE'LL TRY TO **FIND** YOU - - HE FOUND **ME** WHEN I WAS YOUR AGE, AND HE TRIED TO **CONTROL** ME . . .
- - BUT HE **REJECTED** ME BECAUSE . . .
MY DREAMS WEREN'T STRONG ENOUGH.
WHAT?
THAT'S RIGHT. MY DREAMS WEREN'T STRONG ENOUGH.
HE IS SEARCHING FOR **YOU**. HE NEEDS TO USE YOUR **EYES** . . . USE **YOUR** EARS . . .
SO HE CAN SEE **OUR** WORLD WHEN IT'S **AWAKE**.
HOW COULD YOU **DO** THIS TO ME?
HOW COULD YOU NOT **TELL** ME?
I DIDN'T TELL YOU BECAUSE I THOUGHT HE WAS **DEAD!** I THOUGHT THE DRAGON AND I **DESTROYED** HIM!
WHY SHOULD I BELIEVE YOU? YOU'RE NOT MAKING SENSE - -
I'M TELLING YOU THE TRUTH AS **FAST AS I CAN!**
AS FAST AS YOU **CAN?**
HOW MUCH MORE TIME DO YOU NEED THAN MY WHOLE LIFE?

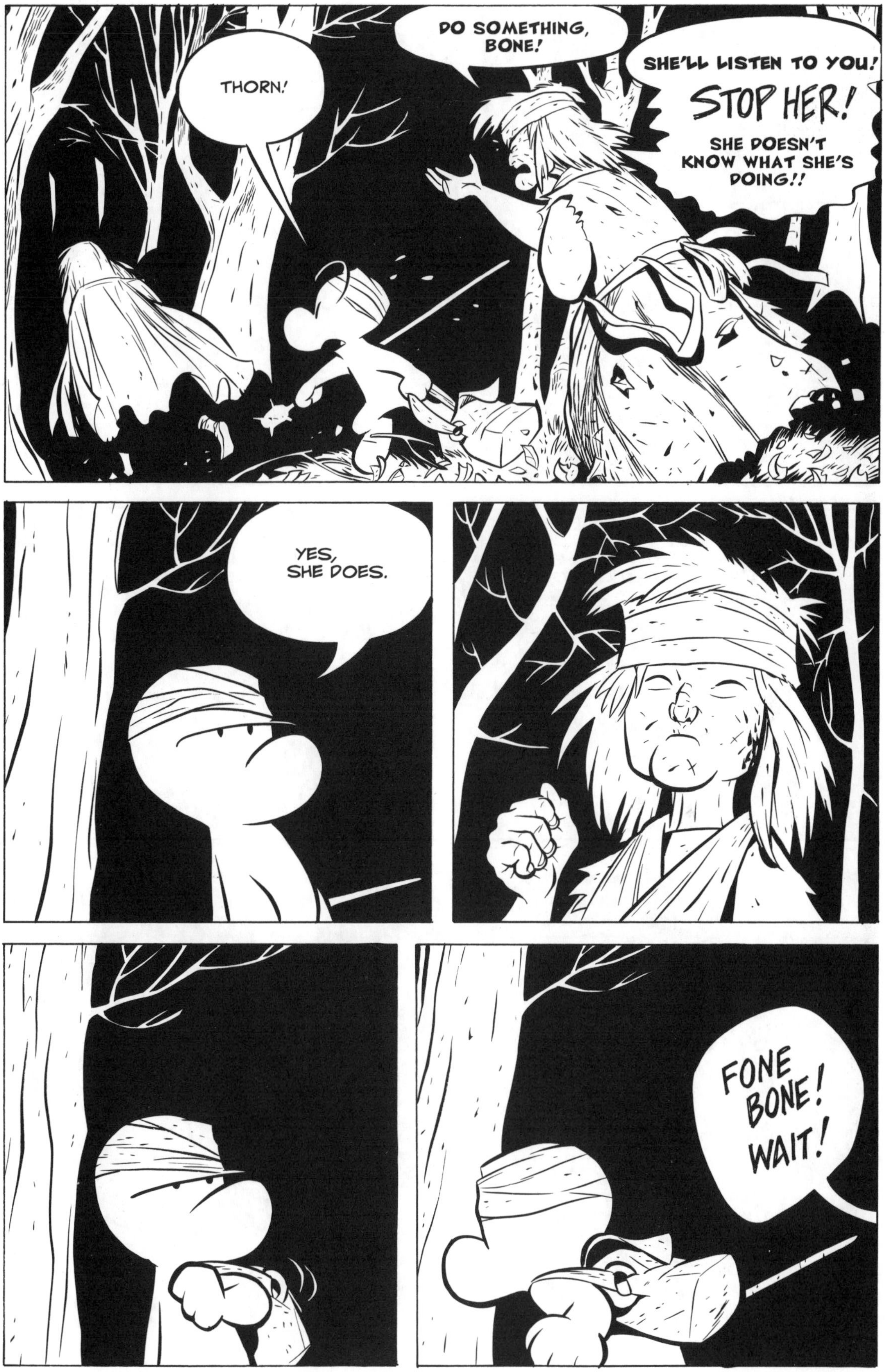
THORN!
DO SOMETHING, BONE!
SHE'LL LISTEN TO YOU!
STOP HER!
SHE DOESN'T KNOW WHAT SHE'S DOING!!
YES, SHE DOES.
FONE BONE! WAIT!

YOU'RE RIGHT.

YOU'RE **BOTH** RIGHT.

HERE. TAKE THIS SWORD WITH YOU.

NOW, GO! **QUICK**, BEFORE YOU **LOSE** HER. GET THORN BACK TO THE **BARRELHAVEN TAVERN** IN ONE PIECE. I'M COUNTING ON YOU, BONE!

WHAT ARE **YOU** GOING TO DO?

DON'T WORRY ABOUT ME. YOU GO SEE **LUCIUS DOWN!** BE SURE AND TELL HIM THAT THE **RAT CREATURES** HAVE **EVACUATED** THE VALLEY...

AND TAKE THIS . . .

SHOW IT TO LUCIUS. **HE'LL** KNOW WHAT TO DO.

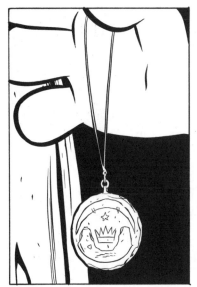

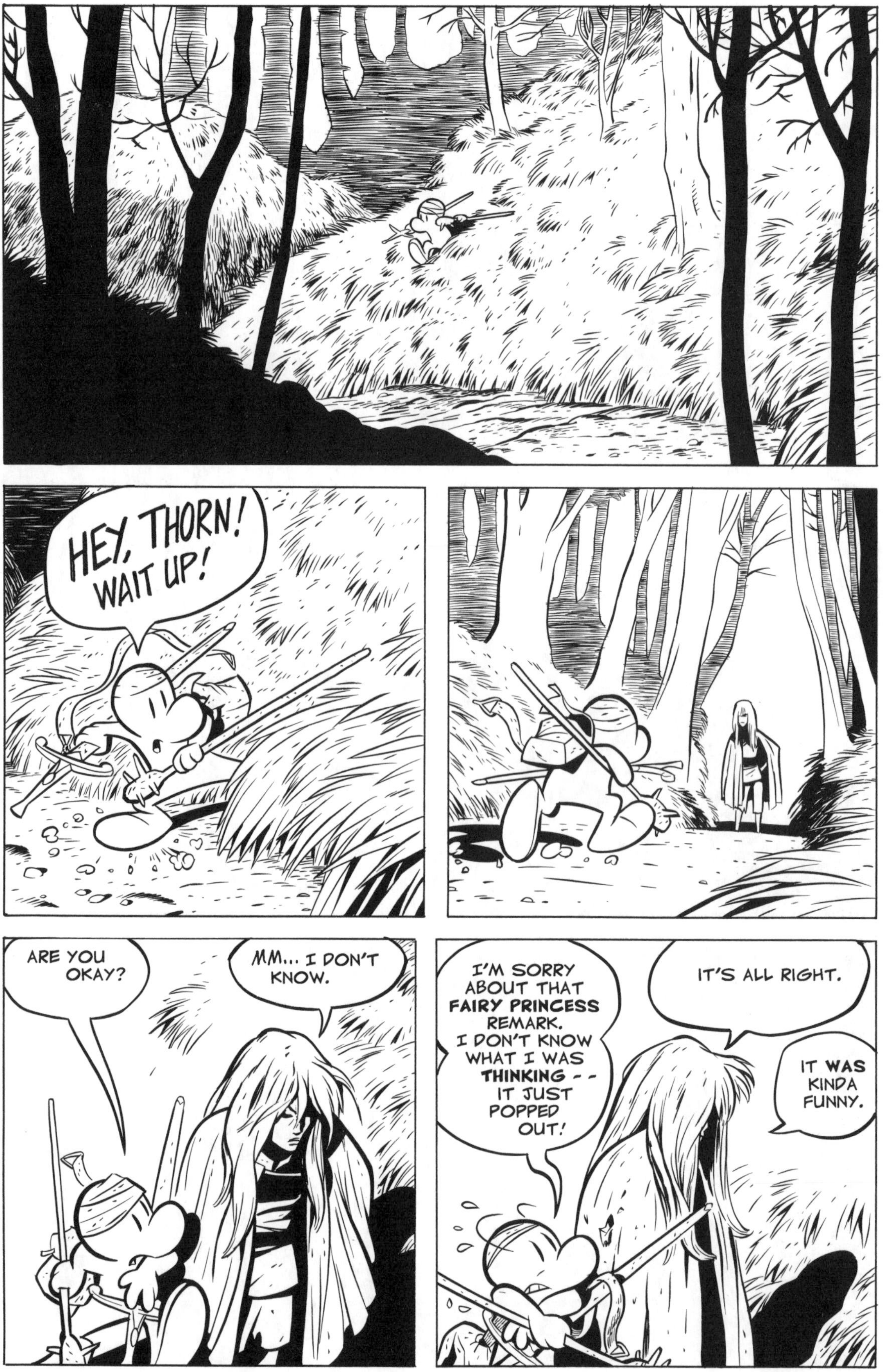
HEY, THORN! WAIT UP!
ARE YOU OKAY?
MM... I DON'T KNOW.
I'M SORRY ABOUT THAT FAIRY PRINCESS REMARK. I DON'T KNOW WHAT I WAS THINKING -- IT JUST POPPED OUT!
IT'S ALL RIGHT.
IT WAS KINDA FUNNY.

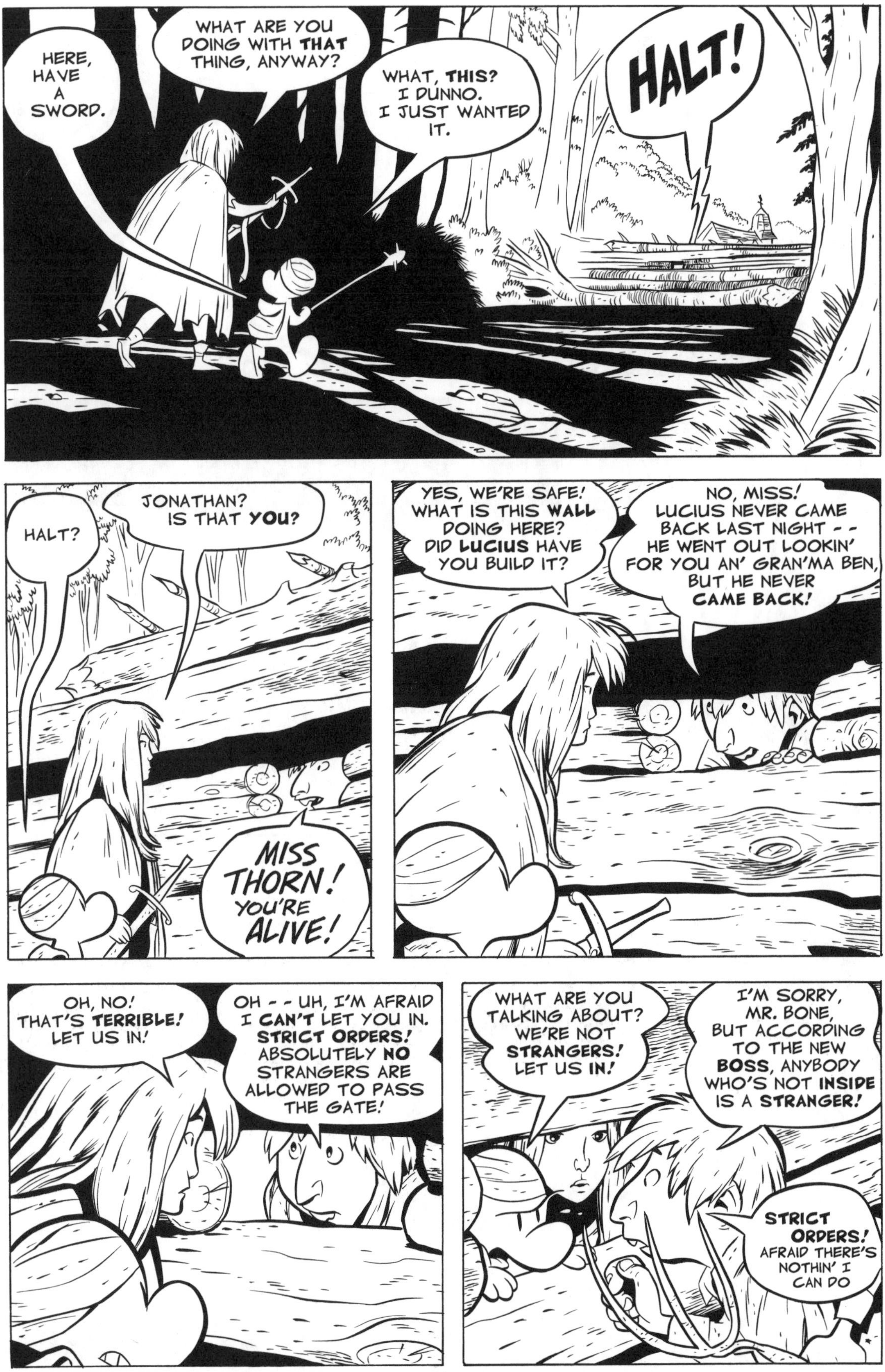
HERE, HAVE A SWORD.
WHAT ARE YOU DOING WITH THAT THING, ANYWAY?
WHAT, THIS? I DUNNO. I JUST WANTED IT.
HALT!
HALT?
JONATHAN? IS THAT YOU?
MISS THORN! YOU'RE ALIVE!
YES, WE'RE SAFE! WHAT IS THIS WALL DOING HERE? DID LUCIUS HAVE YOU BUILD IT?
NO, MISS! LUCIUS NEVER CAME BACK LAST NIGHT - - HE WENT OUT LOOKIN' FOR YOU AN' GRAN'MA BEN, BUT HE NEVER CAME BACK!
OH, NO! THAT'S TERRIBLE! LET US IN!
OH - - UH, I'M AFRAID I CAN'T LET YOU IN. STRICT ORDERS! ABSOLUTELY NO STRANGERS ARE ALLOWED TO PASS THE GATE!
WHAT ARE YOU TALKING ABOUT? WE'RE NOT STRANGERS! LET US IN!
I'M SORRY, MR. BONE, BUT ACCORDING TO THE NEW BOSS, ANYBODY WHO'S NOT INSIDE IS A STRANGER!
STRICT ORDERS! AFRAID THERE'S NOTHIN' I CAN DO

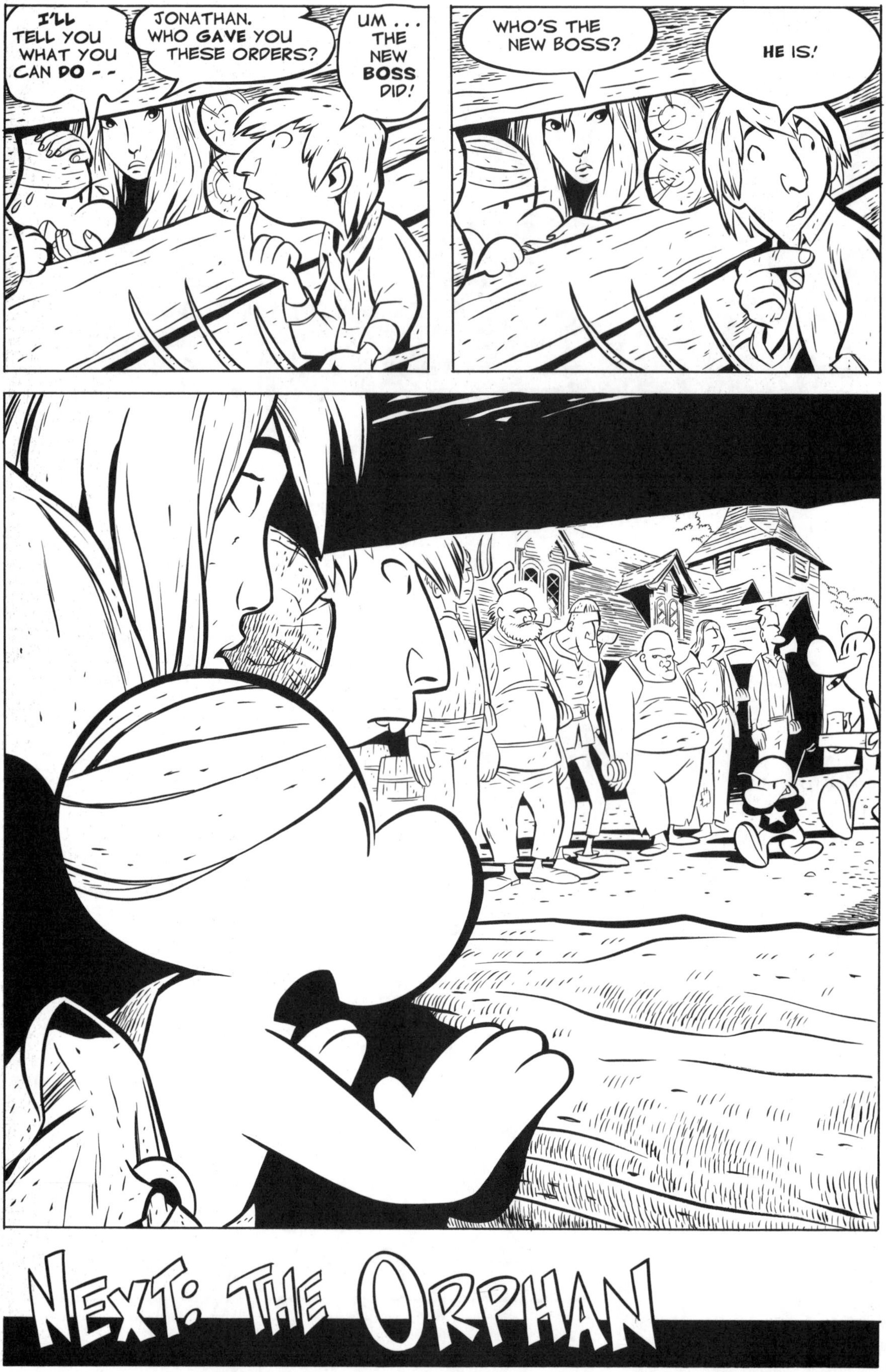
I'LL TELL YOU WHAT YOU CAN DO - -
JONATHAN. WHO GAVE YOU THESE ORDERS?
UM . . . THE NEW BOSS DID!
WHO'S THE NEW BOSS?
HE IS!
NEXT: THE ORPHAN

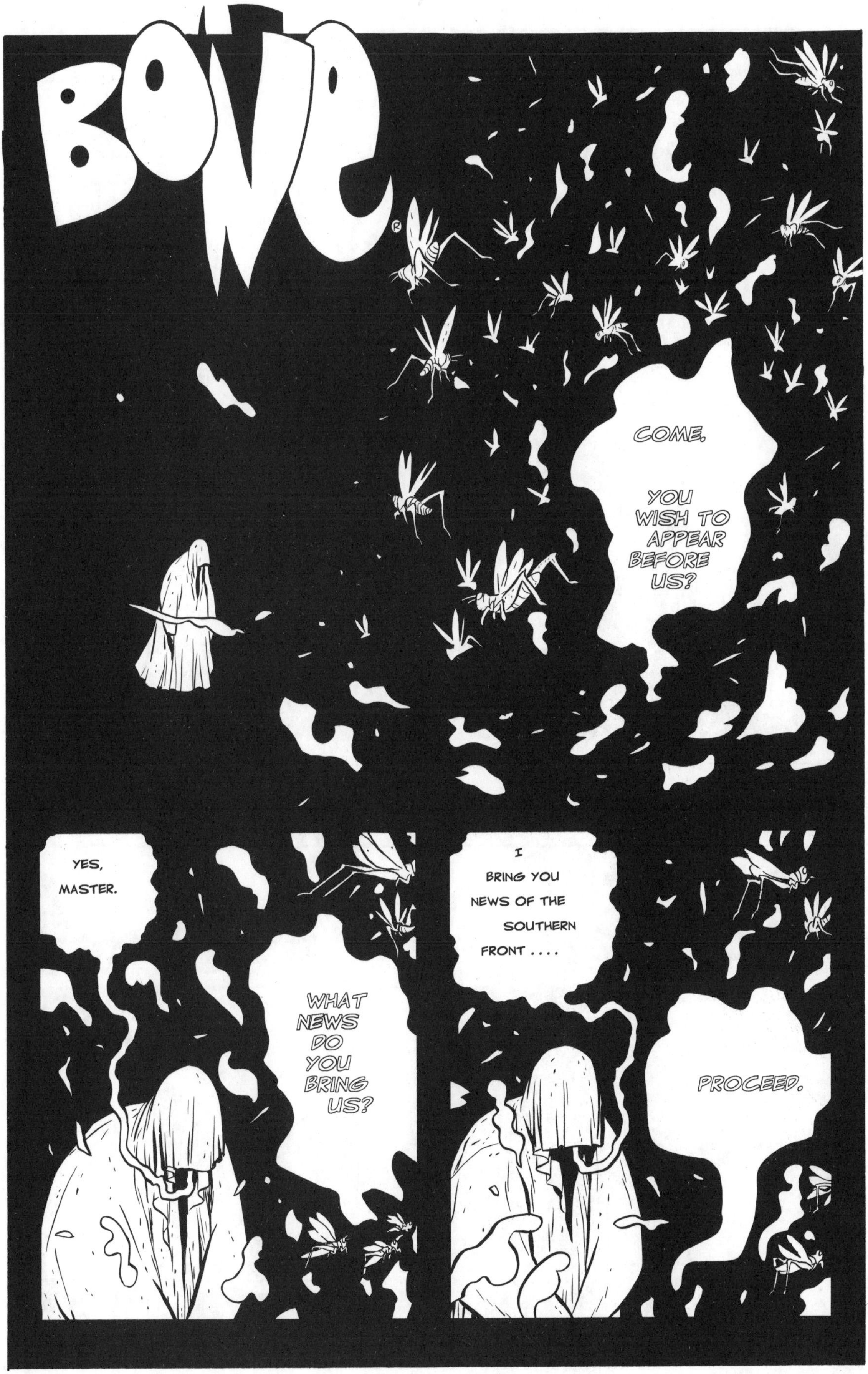
BONE®
COME.
YOU WISH TO APPEAR BEFORE US?
YES, MASTER.
WHAT NEWS DO YOU BRING US?
I BRING YOU NEWS OF THE SOUTHERN FRONT . . . .
PROCEED.

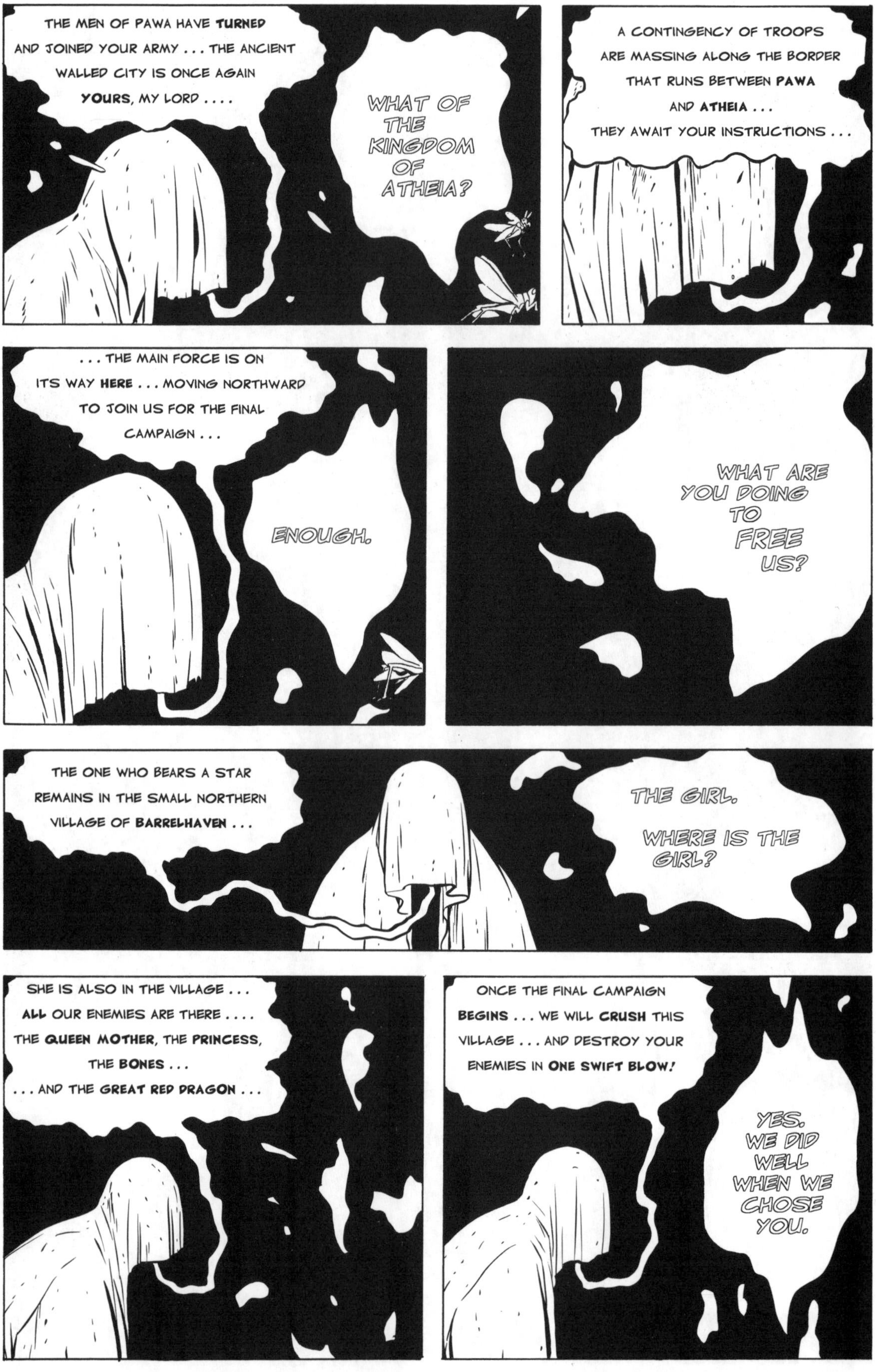
THE MEN OF PAWA HAVE TURNED AND JOINED YOUR ARMY . . . THE ANCIENT WALLED CITY IS ONCE AGAIN YOURS, MY LORD . . . .
WHAT OF THE KINGDOM OF ATHEIA?
A CONTINGENCY OF TROOPS ARE MASSING ALONG THE BORDER THAT RUNS BETWEEN PAWA AND ATHEIA . . . THEY AWAIT YOUR INSTRUCTIONS . . .
. . . THE MAIN FORCE IS ON ITS WAY HERE . . . MOVING NORTHWARD TO JOIN US FOR THE FINAL CAMPAIGN . . .
ENOUGH.
WHAT ARE YOU DOING TO FREE US?
THE ONE WHO BEARS A STAR REMAINS IN THE SMALL NORTHERN VILLAGE OF BARRELHAVEN . . .
THE GIRL.
WHERE IS THE GIRL?
SHE IS ALSO IN THE VILLAGE . . . ALL OUR ENEMIES ARE THERE . . . . THE QUEEN MOTHER, THE PRINCESS, THE BONES . . . . . . AND THE GREAT RED DRAGON . . .
ONCE THE FINAL CAMPAIGN BEGINS . . . WE WILL CRUSH THIS VILLAGE . . . AND DESTROY YOUR ENEMIES IN ONE SWIFT BLOW!
YES. WE DID WELL WHEN WE CHOSE YOU.

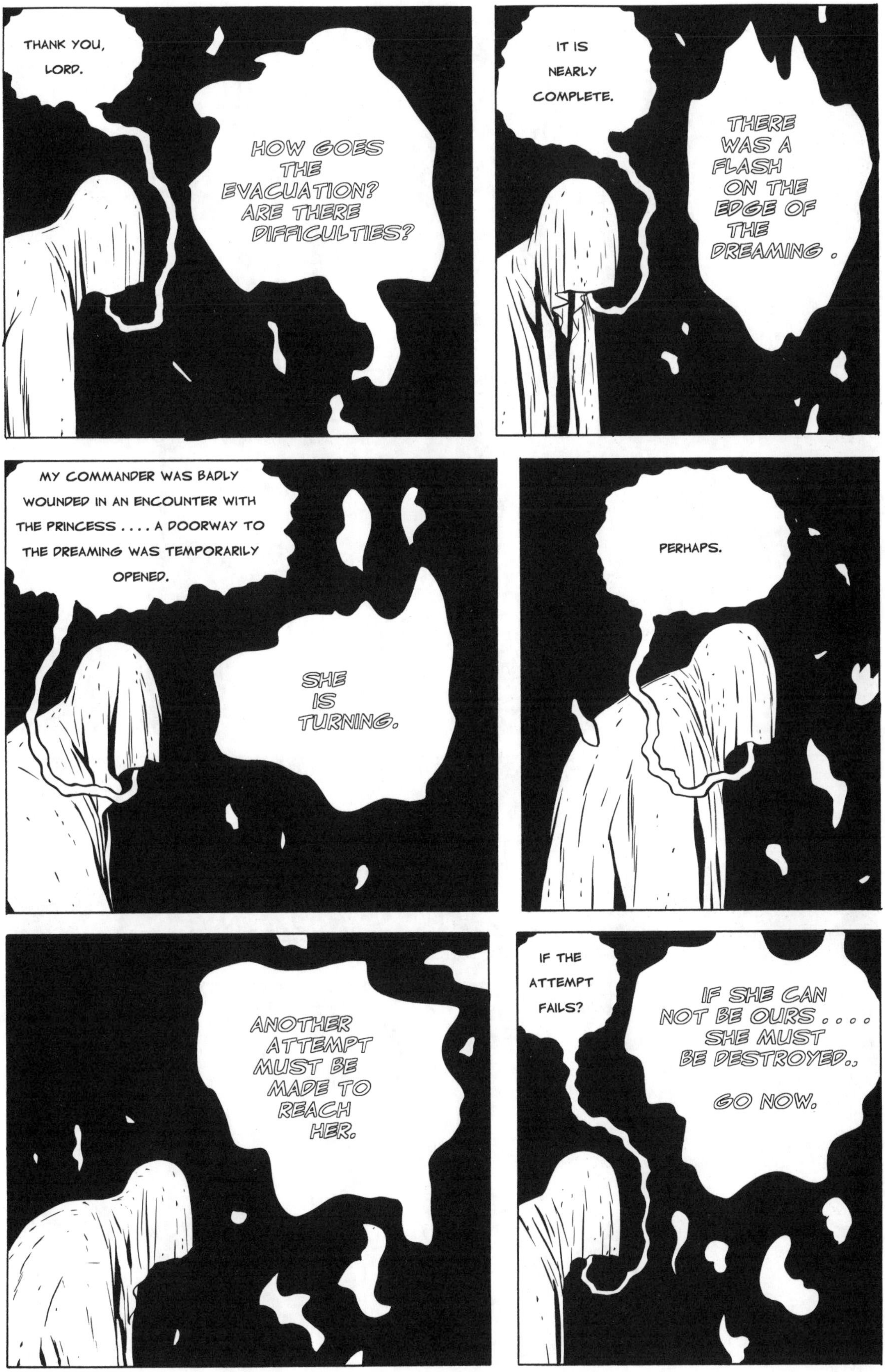
THANK YOU, LORD.
HOW GOES THE EVACUATION? ARE THERE DIFFICULTIES?
IT IS NEARLY COMPLETE.
THERE WAS A FLASH ON THE EDGE OF THE DREAMING .
MY COMMANDER WAS BADLY WOUNDED IN AN ENCOUNTER WITH THE PRINCESS . . . . A DOORWAY TO THE DREAMING WAS TEMPORARILY OPENED.
SHE IS TURNING.
PERHAPS.
ANOTHER ATTEMPT MUST BE MADE TO REACH HER.
IF THE ATTEMPT FAILS?
IF SHE CAN NOT BE OURS . . . . SHE MUST BE DESTROYED..
GO NOW.

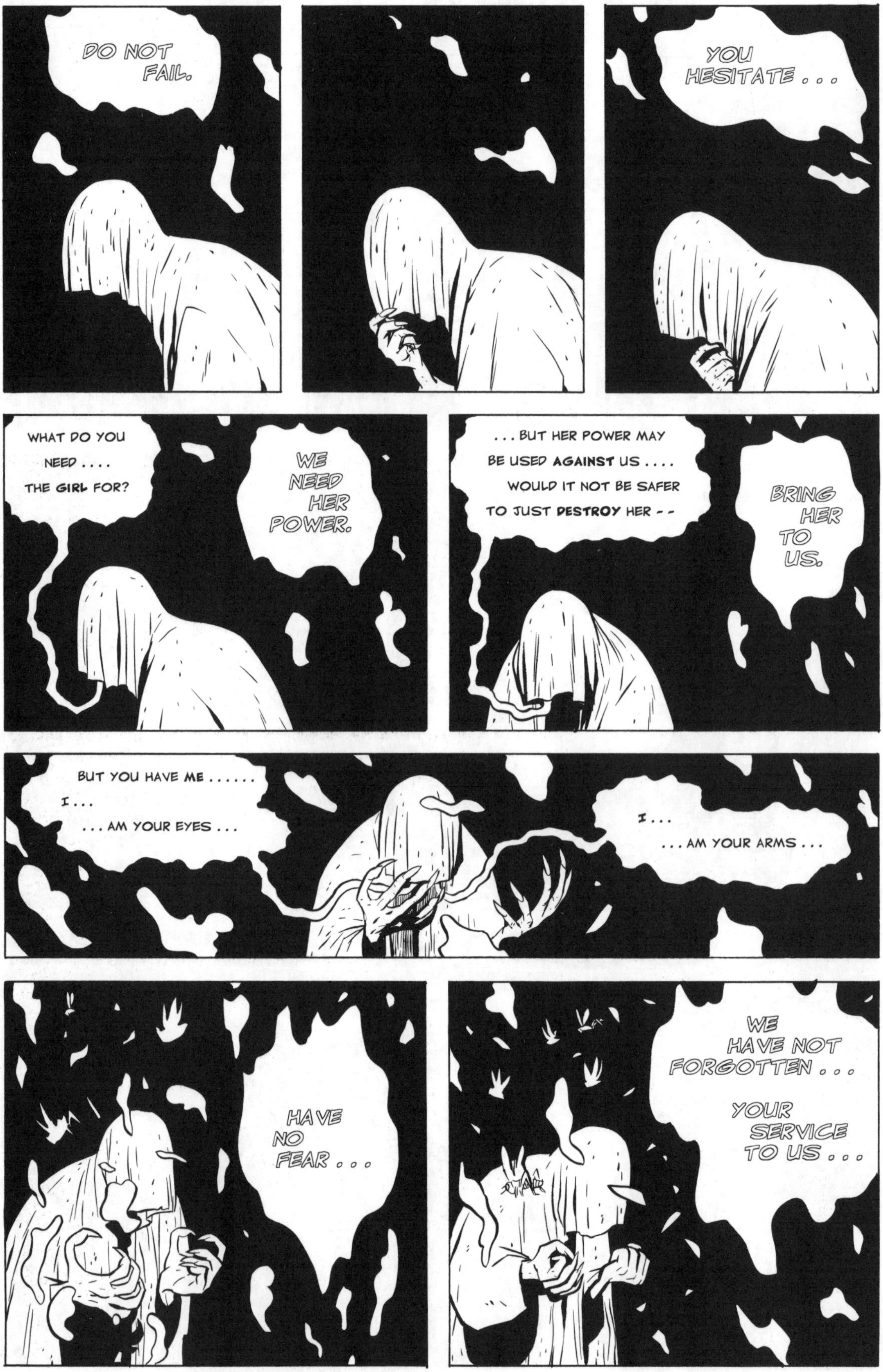
DO NOT FAIL.
YOU HESITATE . . .
WHAT DO YOU NEED . . . . THE GIRL FOR?
WE NEED HER POWER.
. . . BUT HER POWER MAY BE USED AGAINST US . . . . WOULD IT NOT BE SAFER TO JUST DESTROY HER - -
BRING HER TO US.
BUT YOU HAVE ME . . . . . . I . . . . . . AM YOUR EYES . . .
I . . . . . . AM YOUR ARMS . . .
HAVE NO FEAR . . .
WE HAVE NOT FORGOTTEN . . .
YOUR SERVICE TO US . . .

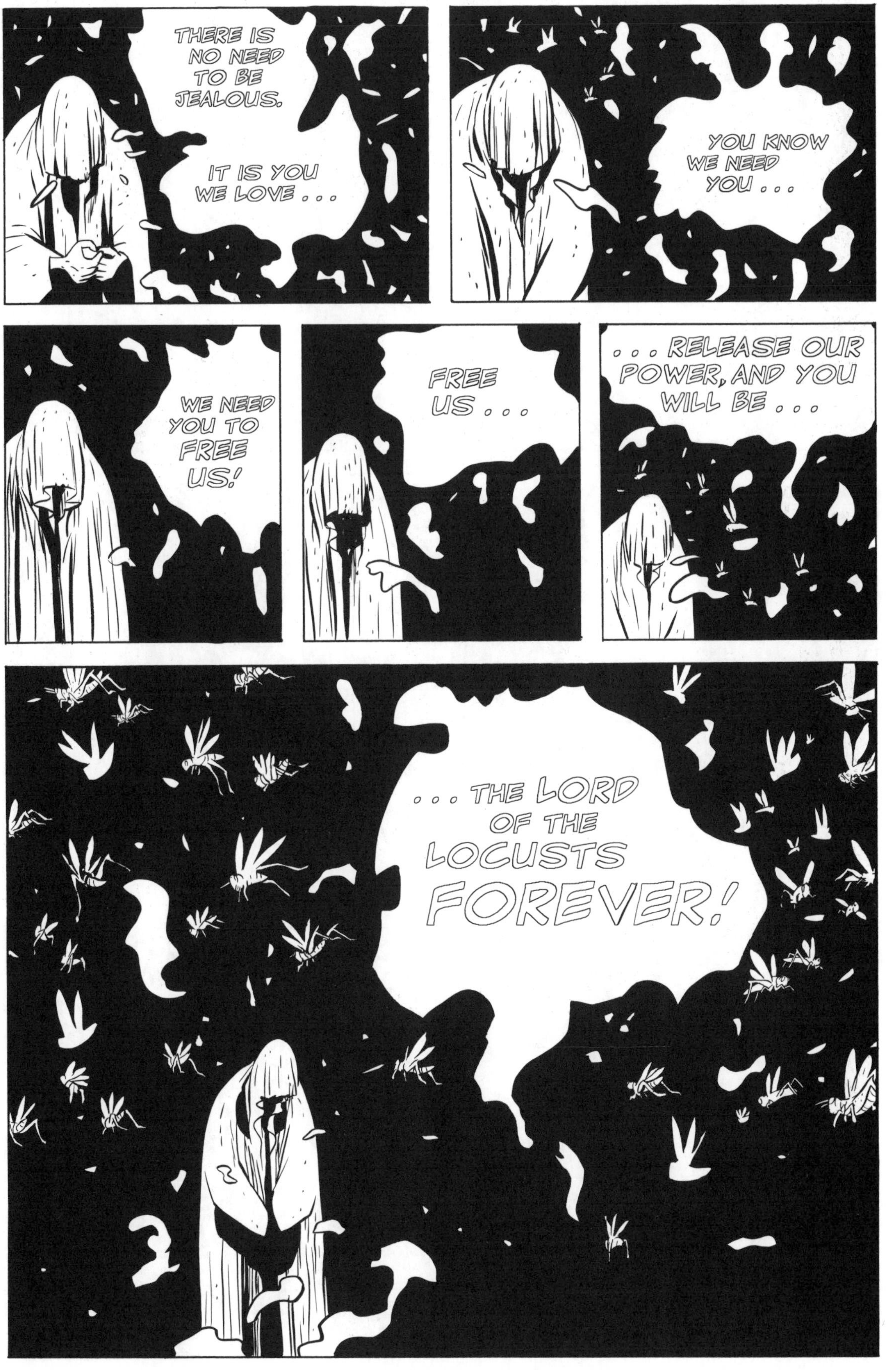
THERE IS NO NEED TO BE JEALOUS.
IT IS YOU WE LOVE . . .
YOU KNOW WE NEED YOU . . .
WE NEED YOU TO FREE US!
FREE US . . .
. . . RELEASE OUR POWER, AND YOU WILL BE . . .
. . . THE LORD OF THE LOCUSTS FOREVER!

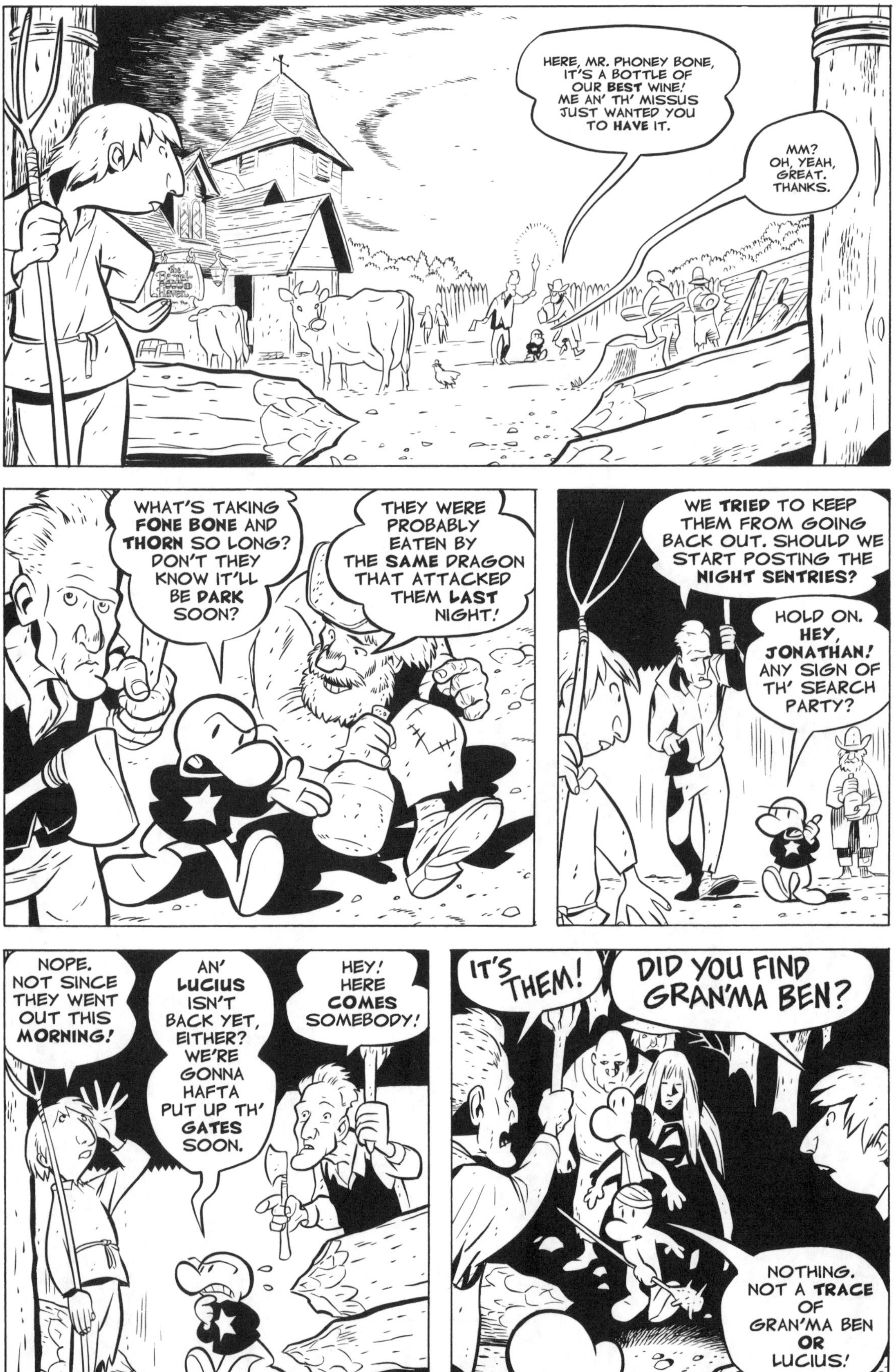

HERE, MR. PHONEY BONE, IT'S A BOTTLE OF OUR BEST WINE! ME AN' TH' MISSUS JUST WANTED YOU TO HAVE IT.
MM? OH, YEAH, GREAT. THANKS.
WHAT'S TAKING FONE BONE AND THORN SO LONG? DON'T THEY KNOW IT'LL BE DARK SOON?
THEY WERE PROBABLY EATEN BY THE SAME DRAGON THAT ATTACKED THEM LAST NIGHT!
WE TRIED TO KEEP THEM FROM GOING BACK OUT. SHOULD WE START POSTING THE NIGHT SENTRIES?
HOLD ON. HEY, JONATHAN! ANY SIGN OF TH' SEARCH PARTY?
NOPE. NOT SINCE THEY WENT OUT THIS MORNING!
AN' LUCIUS ISN'T BACK YET, EITHER? WE'RE GONNA HAFTA PUT UP TH' GATES SOON.
HEY! HERE COMES SOMEBODY!
IT'S THEM!
DID YOU FIND GRAN'MA BEN?
NOTHING. NOT A TRACE OF GRAN'MA BEN OR LUCIUS!

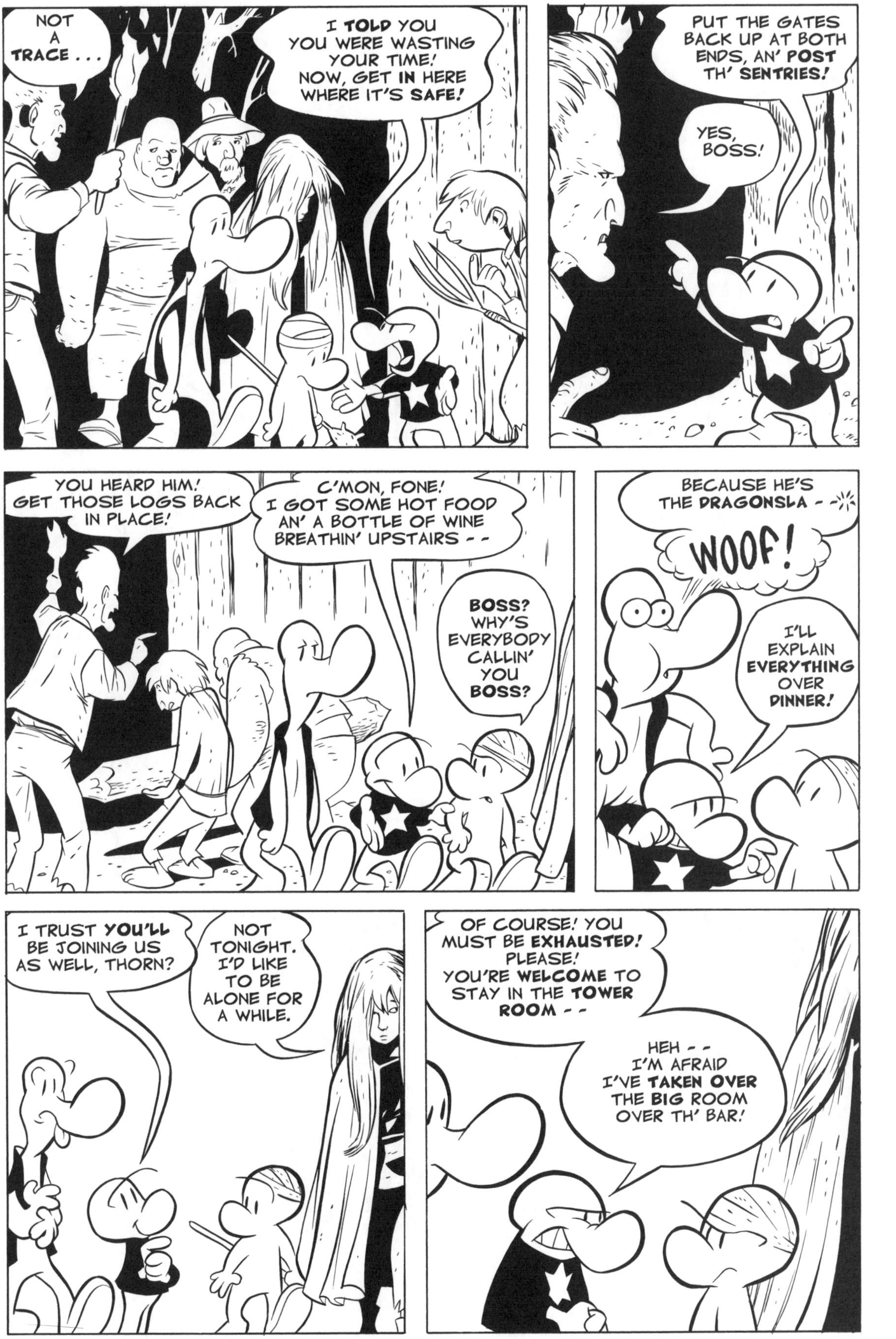
NOT A TRACE . . .
I TOLD YOU YOU WERE WASTING YOUR TIME! NOW, GET IN HERE WHERE IT'S SAFE!
PUT THE GATES BACK UP AT BOTH ENDS, AN' POST TH' SENTRIES!
YES, BOSS!
YOU HEARD HIM! GET THOSE LOGS BACK IN PLACE!
C'MON, FONE! I GOT SOME HOT FOOD AN' A BOTTLE OF WINE BREATHIN' UPSTAIRS - -
BOSS? WHY'S EVERYBODY CALLIN' YOU BOSS?
BECAUSE HE'S THE DRAGONSLA - -
WOOF!
I'LL EXPLAIN EVERYTHING OVER DINNER!
I TRUST YOU'LL BE JOINING US AS WELL, THORN?
NOT TONIGHT. I'D LIKE TO BE ALONE FOR A WHILE.
OF COURSE! YOU MUST BE EXHAUSTED! PLEASE! YOU'RE WELCOME TO STAY IN THE TOWER ROOM - -
HEH - - I'M AFRAID I'VE TAKEN OVER THE BIG ROOM OVER TH' BAR!

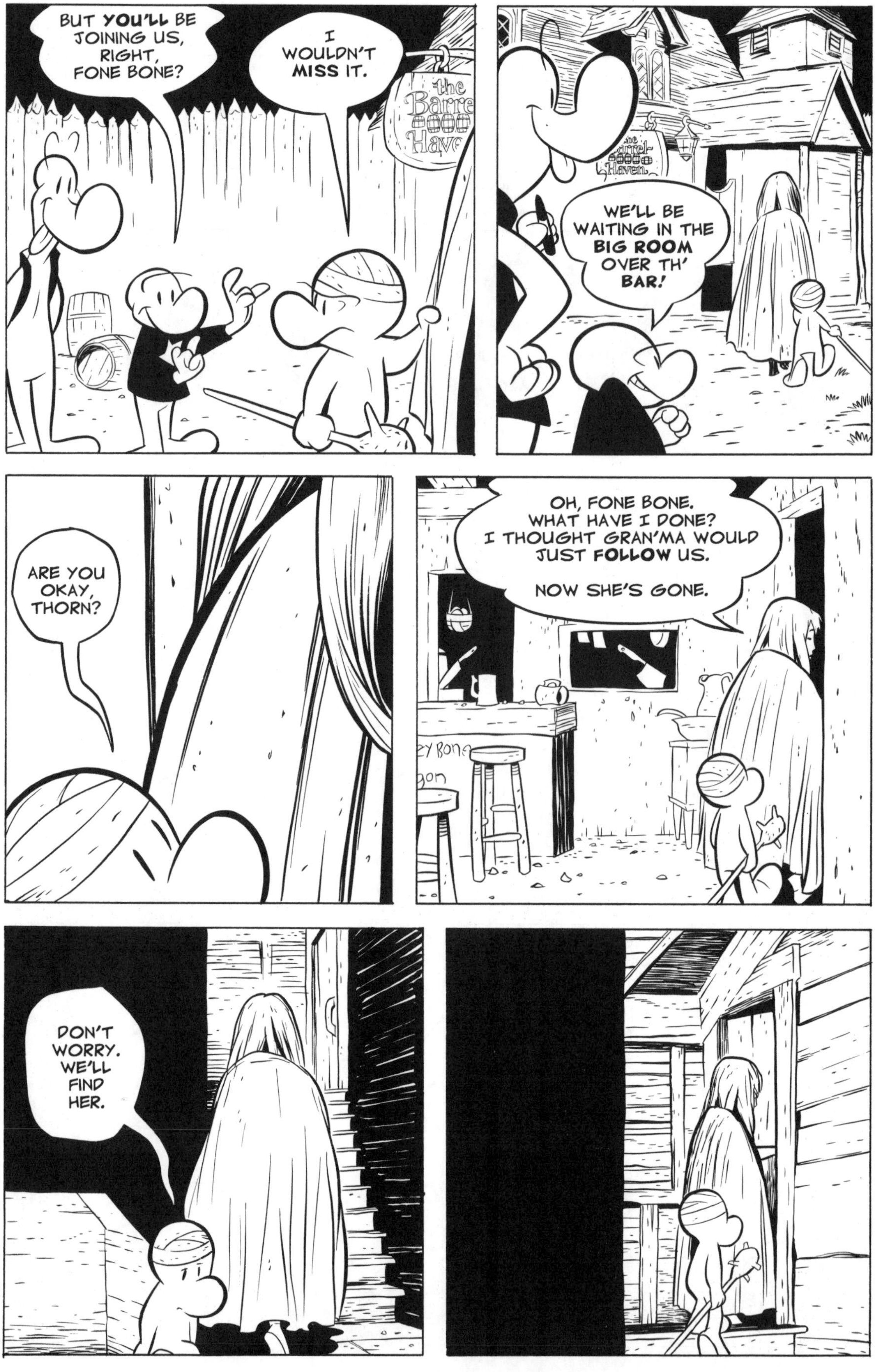
BUT **YOU'LL** BE JOINING US, RIGHT, FONE BONE?
I WOULDN'T **MISS** IT.
the Barrel Haven
WE'LL BE WAITING IN THE **BIG ROOM** OVER TH' **BAR!**
ARE YOU OKAY, THORN?
OH, FONE BONE. WHAT HAVE I DONE? I THOUGHT GRAN'MA WOULD JUST **FOLLOW** US.
NOW SHE'S GONE.
DON'T WORRY. WE'LL FIND HER.

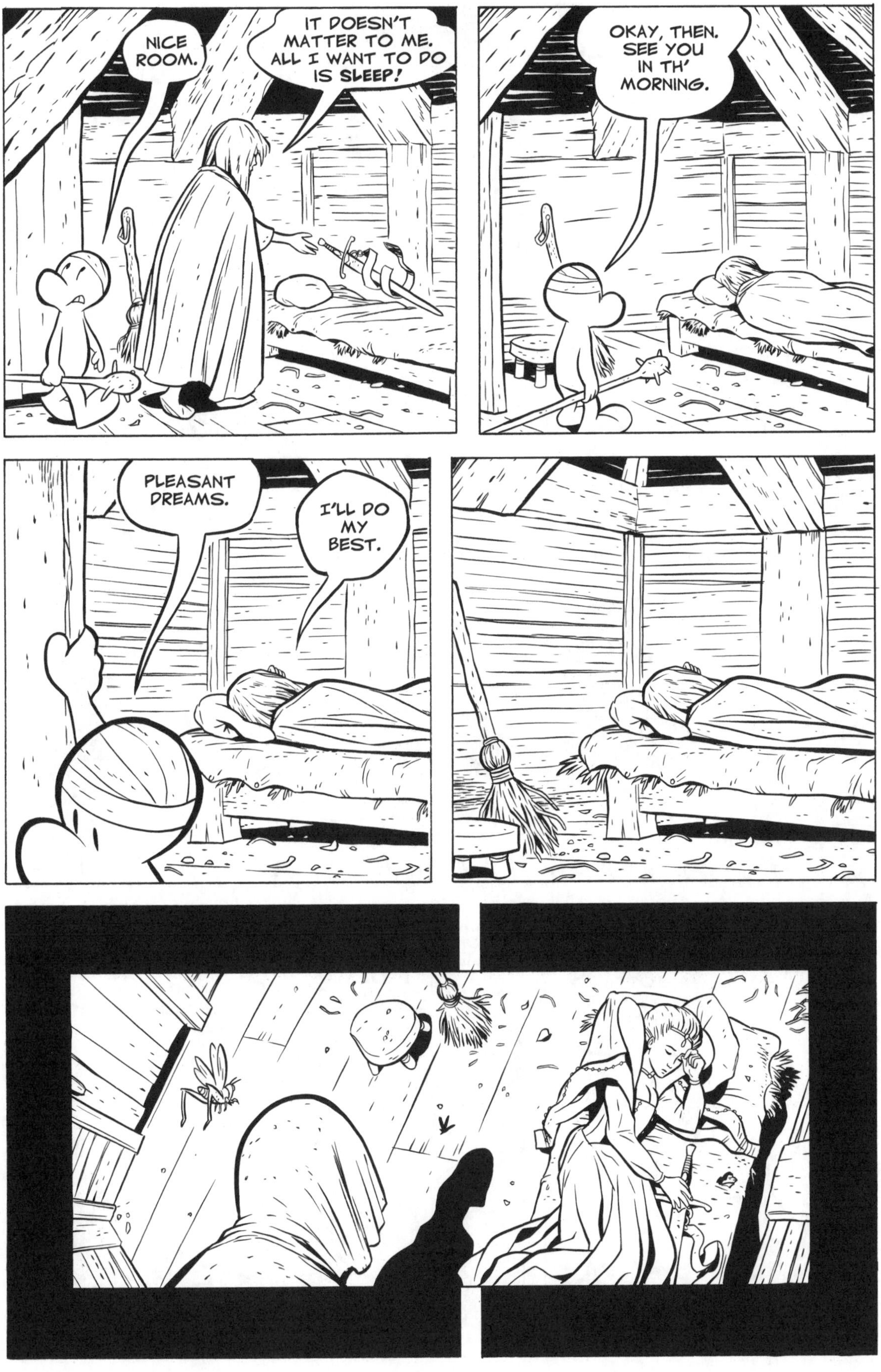
NICE ROOM.
IT DOESN'T MATTER TO ME. ALL I WANT TO DO IS SLEEP!
OKAY, THEN. SEE YOU IN TH' MORNING.
PLEASANT DREAMS.
I'LL DO MY BEST.

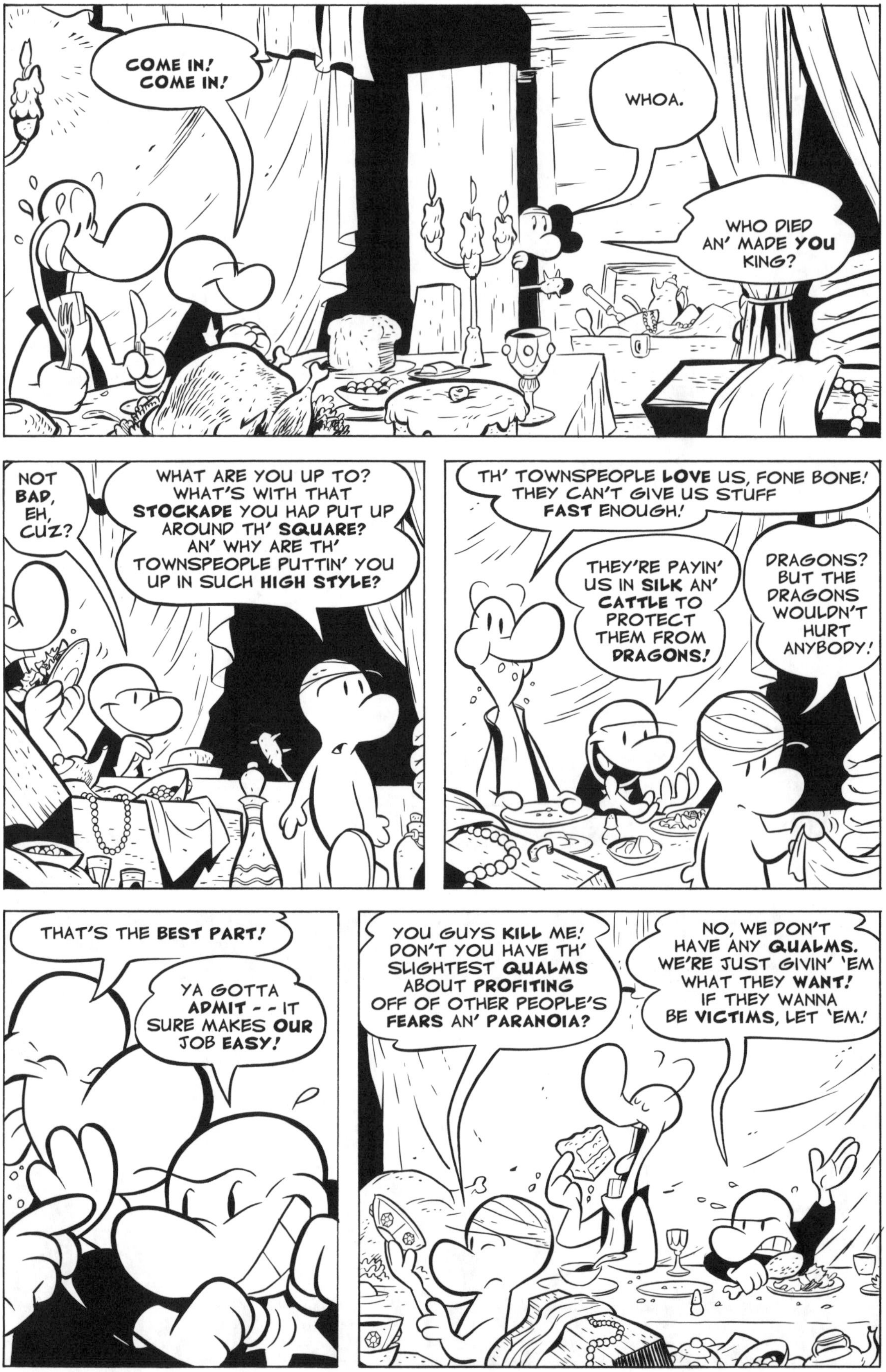
COME IN! COME IN!
WHOA.
WHO DIED AN' MADE YOU KING?
NOT BAD, EH, CUZ?
WHAT ARE YOU UP TO? WHAT'S WITH THAT STOCKADE YOU HAD PUT UP AROUND TH' SQUARE? AN' WHY ARE TH' TOWNSPEOPLE PUTTIN' YOU UP IN SUCH HIGH STYLE?
TH' TOWNSPEOPLE LOVE US, FONE BONE! THEY CAN'T GIVE US STUFF FAST ENOUGH!
THEY'RE PAYIN' US IN SILK AN' CATTLE TO PROTECT THEM FROM DRAGONS!
DRAGONS? BUT THE DRAGONS WOULDN'T HURT ANYBODY!
THAT'S THE BEST PART!
YA GOTTA ADMIT - - IT SURE MAKES OUR JOB EASY!
YOU GUYS KILL ME! DON'T YOU HAVE TH' SLIGHTEST QUALMS ABOUT PROFITING OFF OF OTHER PEOPLE'S FEARS AN' PARANOIA?
NO, WE DON'T HAVE ANY QUALMS. WE'RE JUST GIVIN' 'EM WHAT THEY WANT! IF THEY WANNA BE VICTIMS, LET 'EM!

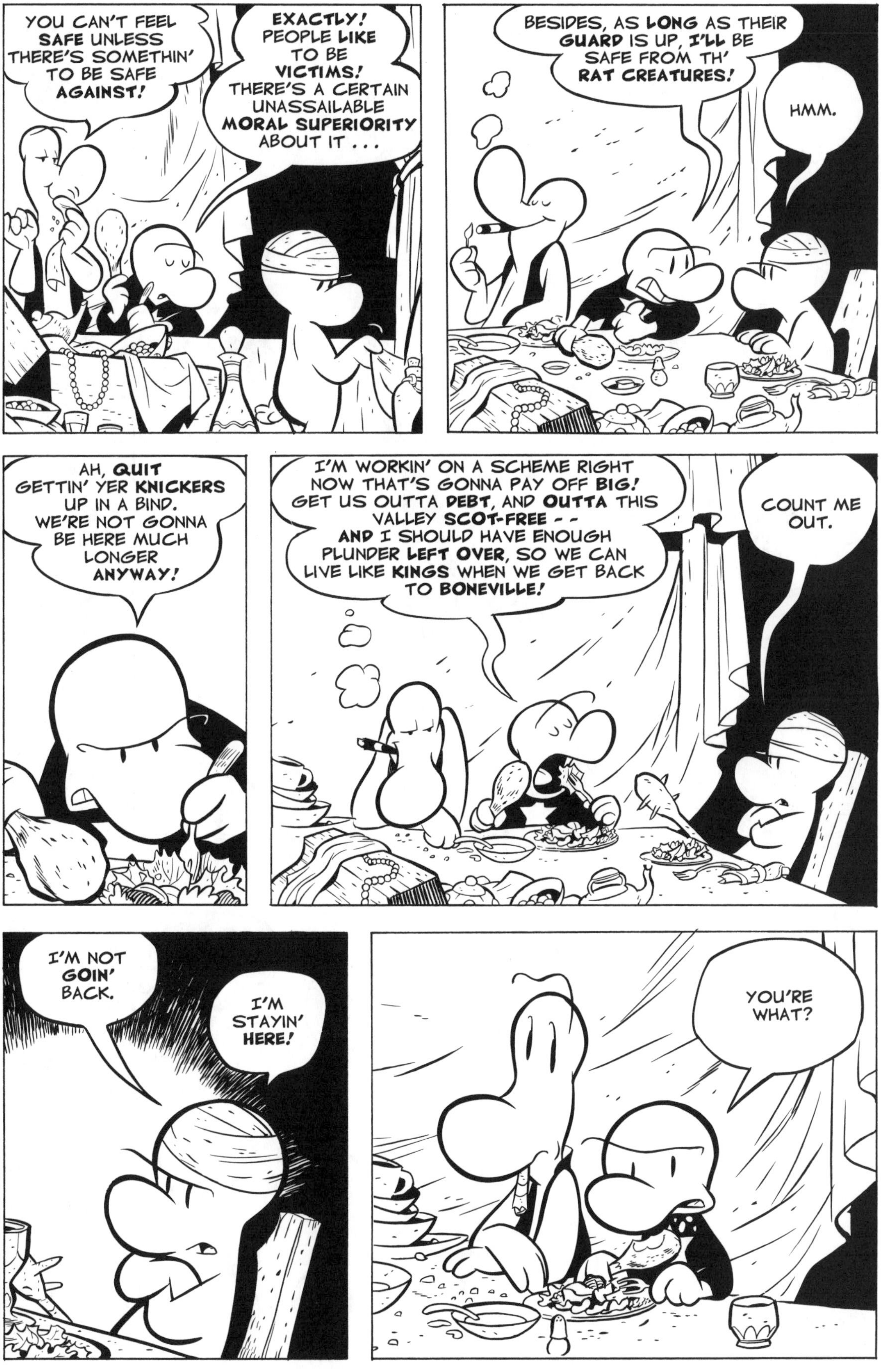
YOU CAN'T FEEL SAFE UNLESS THERE'S SOMETHIN' TO BE SAFE AGAINST!
EXACTLY! PEOPLE LIKE TO BE VICTIMS! THERE'S A CERTAIN UNASSAILABLE MORAL SUPERIORITY ABOUT IT . . .
BESIDES, AS LONG AS THEIR GUARD IS UP, I'LL BE SAFE FROM TH' RAT CREATURES!
HMM.
AH, QUIT GETTIN' YER KNICKERS UP IN A BIND. WE'RE NOT GONNA BE HERE MUCH LONGER ANYWAY!
I'M WORKIN' ON A SCHEME RIGHT NOW THAT'S GONNA PAY OFF BIG! GET US OUTTA DEBT, AND OUTTA THIS VALLEY SCOT-FREE - - AND I SHOULD HAVE ENOUGH PLUNDER LEFT OVER, SO WE CAN LIVE LIKE KINGS WHEN WE GET BACK TO BONEVILLE!
COUNT ME OUT.
I'M NOT GOIN' BACK.
I'M STAYIN' HERE!
YOU'RE WHAT?

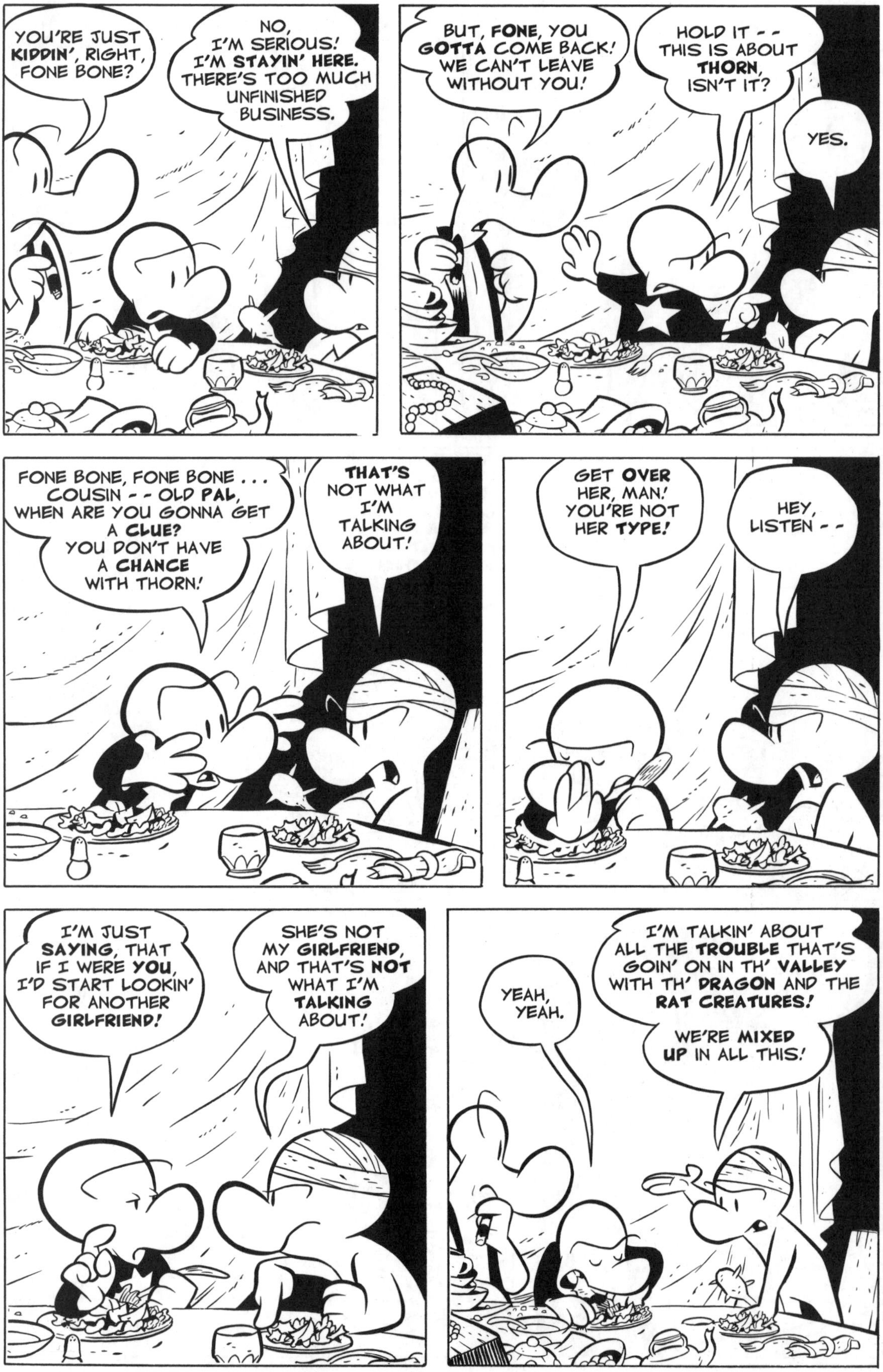

YOU'RE JUST KIDDIN', RIGHT, FONE BONE?
NO, I'M SERIOUS! I'M STAYIN' HERE. THERE'S TOO MUCH UNFINISHED BUSINESS.
BUT, FONE, YOU GOTTA COME BACK! WE CAN'T LEAVE WITHOUT YOU!
HOLD IT - - THIS IS ABOUT THORN, ISN'T IT?
YES.
FONE BONE, FONE BONE . . . COUSIN - - OLD PAL, WHEN ARE YOU GONNA GET A CLUE? YOU DON'T HAVE A CHANCE WITH THORN!
THAT'S NOT WHAT I'M TALKING ABOUT!
GET OVER HER, MAN! YOU'RE NOT HER TYPE!
HEY, LISTEN - -
I'M JUST SAYING, THAT IF I WERE YOU, I'D START LOOKIN' FOR ANOTHER GIRLFRIEND!
SHE'S NOT MY GIRLFRIEND, AND THAT'S NOT WHAT I'M TALKING ABOUT!
YEAH, YEAH.
I'M TALKIN' ABOUT ALL THE TROUBLE THAT'S GOIN' ON IN TH' VALLEY WITH TH' DRAGON AND THE RAT CREATURES!
WE'RE MIXED UP IN ALL THIS!

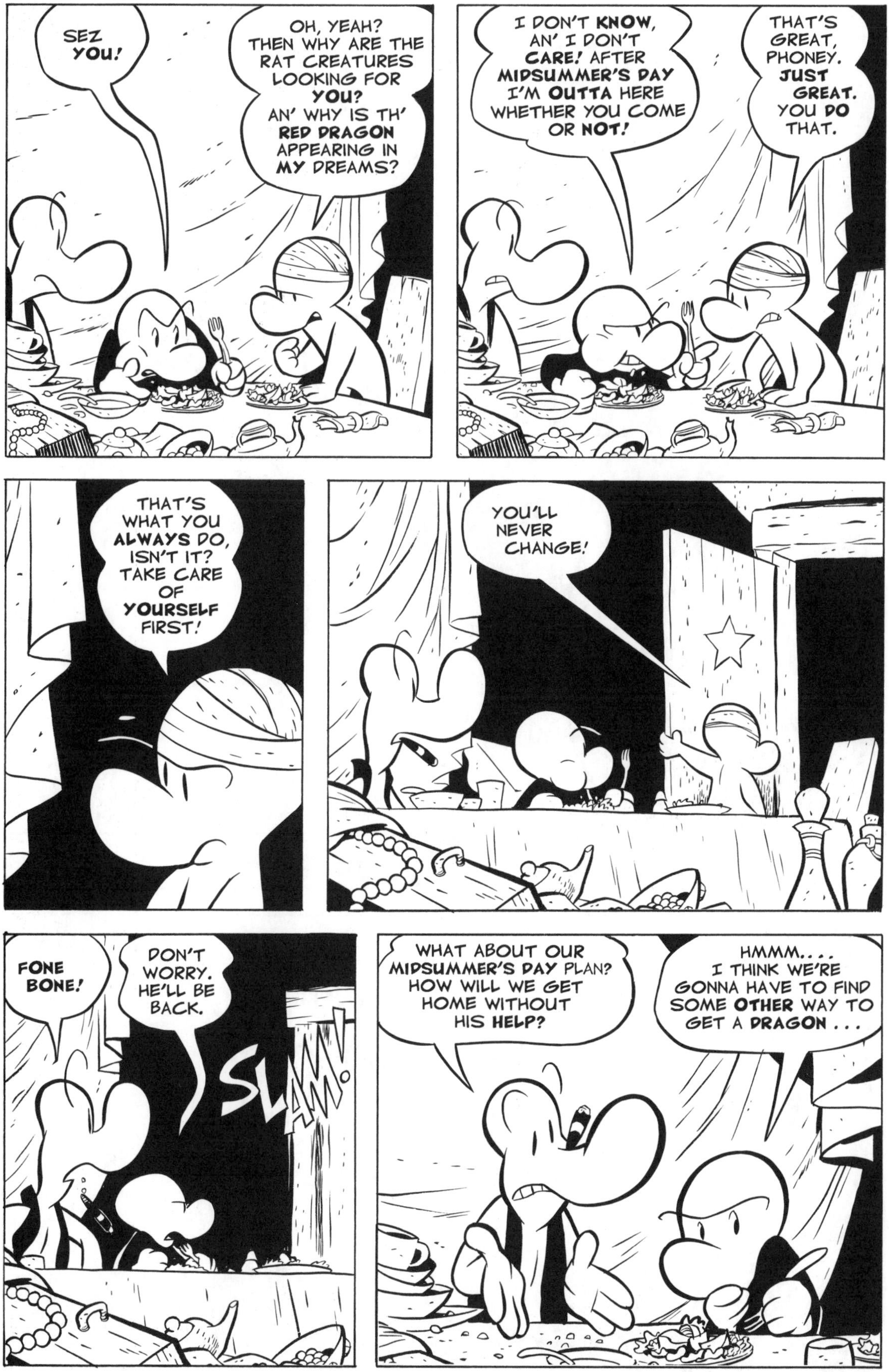
SEZ YOU!
OH, YEAH? THEN WHY ARE THE RAT CREATURES LOOKING FOR YOU? AN' WHY IS TH' RED DRAGON APPEARING IN MY DREAMS?
I DON'T KNOW, AN' I DON'T CARE! AFTER MIDSUMMER'S DAY I'M OUTTA HERE WHETHER YOU COME OR NOT!
THAT'S GREAT, PHONEY. JUST GREAT. YOU DO THAT.
THAT'S WHAT YOU ALWAYS DO, ISN'T IT? TAKE CARE OF YOURSELF FIRST!
YOU'LL NEVER CHANGE!
FONE BONE!
DON'T WORRY. HE'LL BE BACK.
SLAM!
WHAT ABOUT OUR MIDSUMMER'S DAY PLAN? HOW WILL WE GET HOME WITHOUT HIS HELP?
HMMM.... I THINK WE'RE GONNA HAVE TO FIND SOME OTHER WAY TO GET A DRAGON...

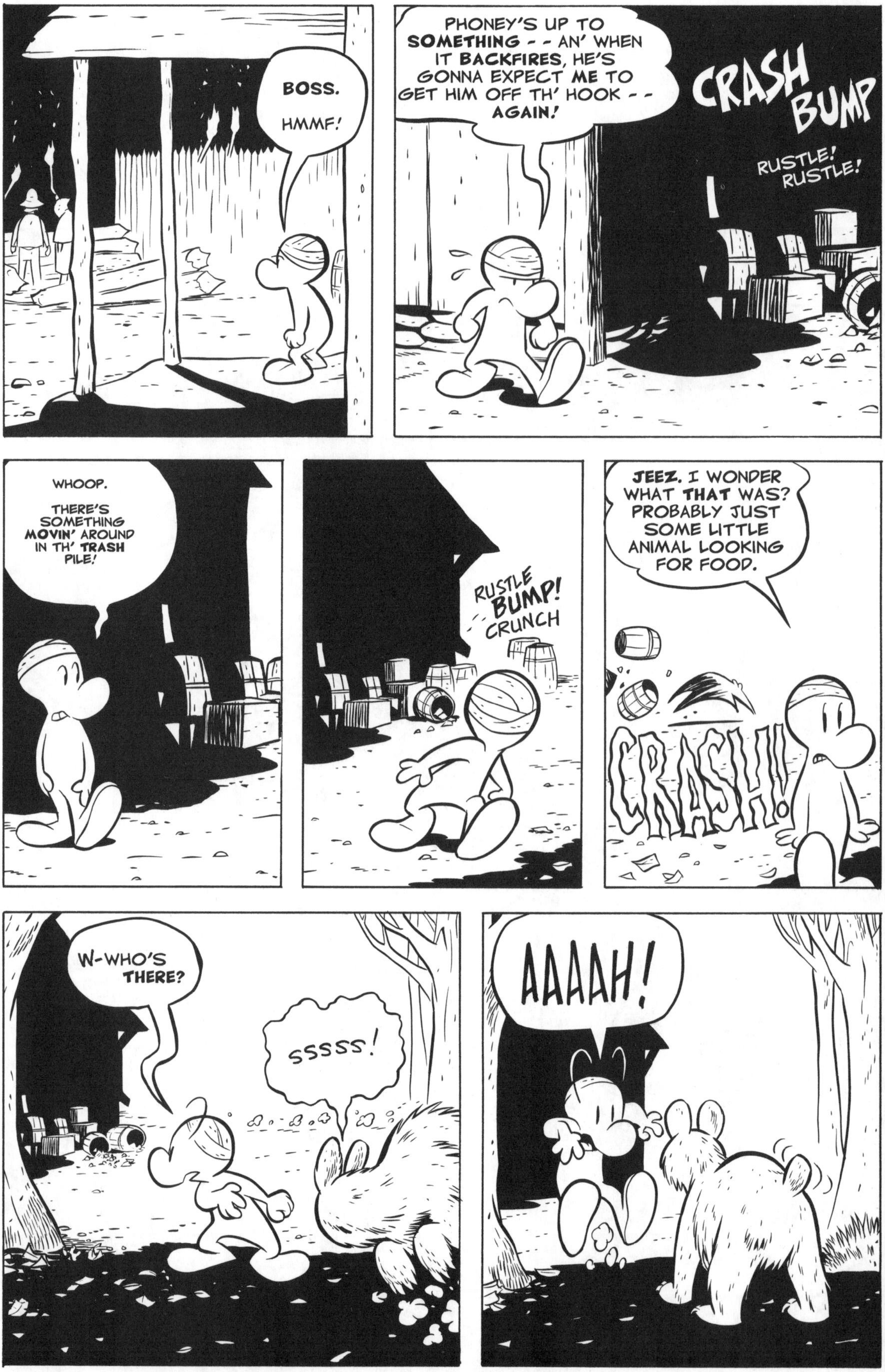

BOSS.
HMMF!
PHONEY'S UP TO SOMETHING - - AN' WHEN IT BACKFIRES, HE'S GONNA EXPECT ME TO GET HIM OFF TH' HOOK - - AGAIN!
CRASH
BUMP
RUSTLE! RUSTLE!
WHOOP.
THERE'S SOMETHING MOVIN' AROUND IN TH' TRASH PILE!
RUSTLE
BUMP!
CRUNCH
JEEZ. I WONDER WHAT THAT WAS? PROBABLY JUST SOME LITTLE ANIMAL LOOKING FOR FOOD.
CRASH!
W-WHO'S THERE?
SSSSS!
AAAAH!

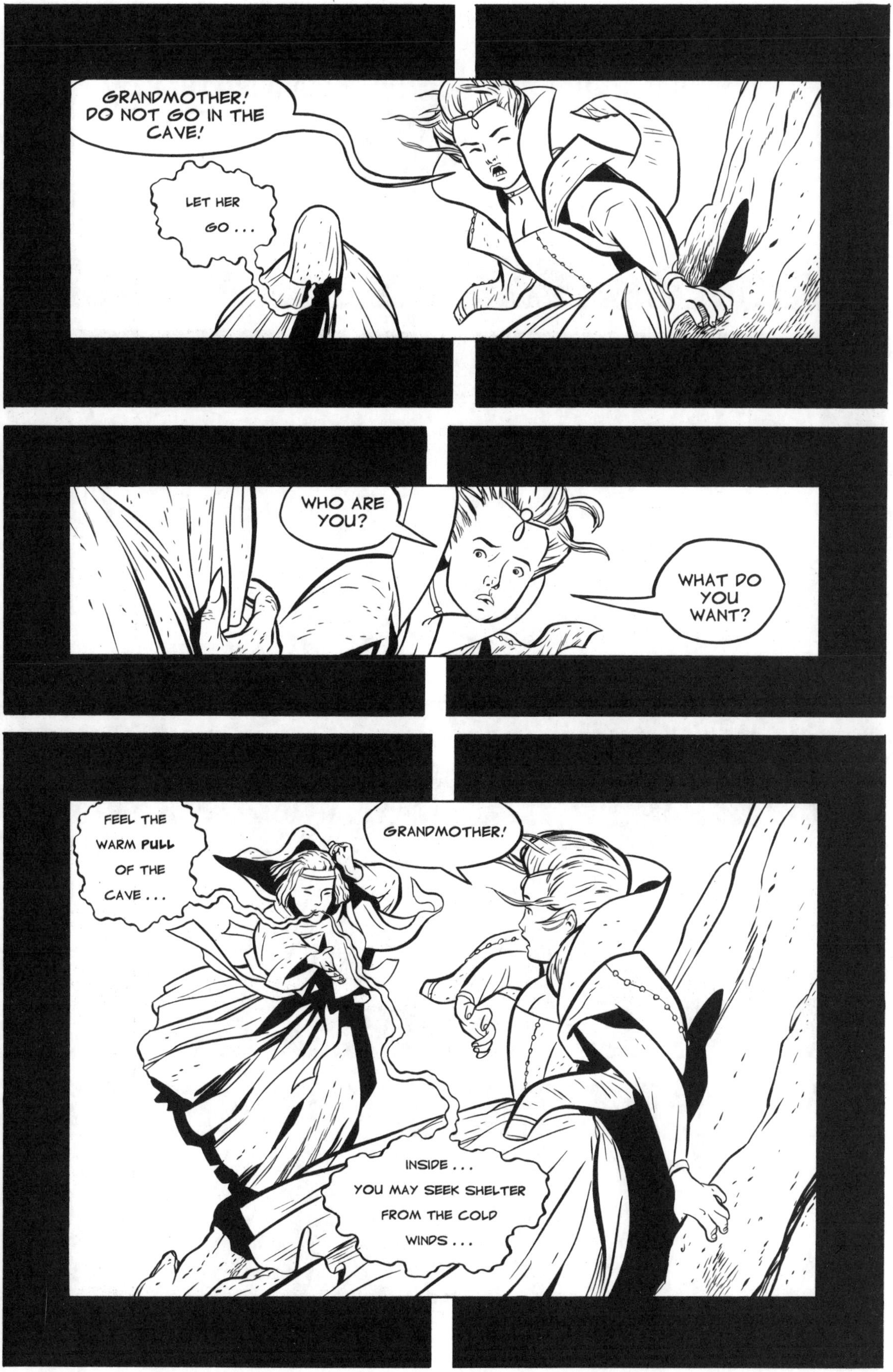
GRANDMOTHER! DO NOT GO IN THE CAVE!
LET HER GO . . .
WHO ARE YOU?
WHAT DO YOU WANT?
FEEL THE WARM **PULL** OF THE CAVE . . .
GRANDMOTHER!
INSIDE . . . YOU MAY SEEK SHELTER FROM THE COLD WINDS . . .

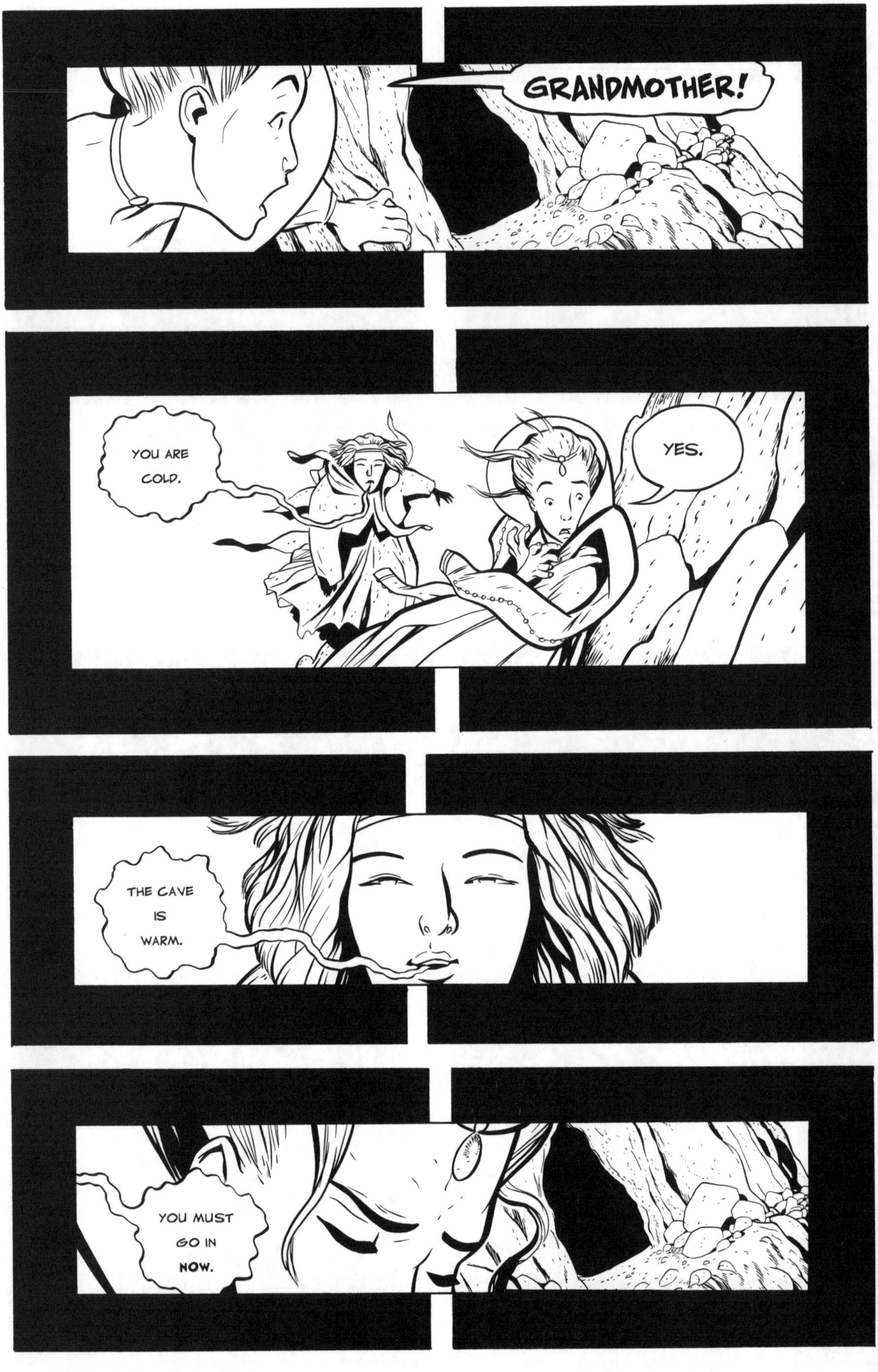
GRANDMOTHER!
YOU ARE COLD.
YES.
THE CAVE IS WARM.
YOU MUST GO IN NOW.

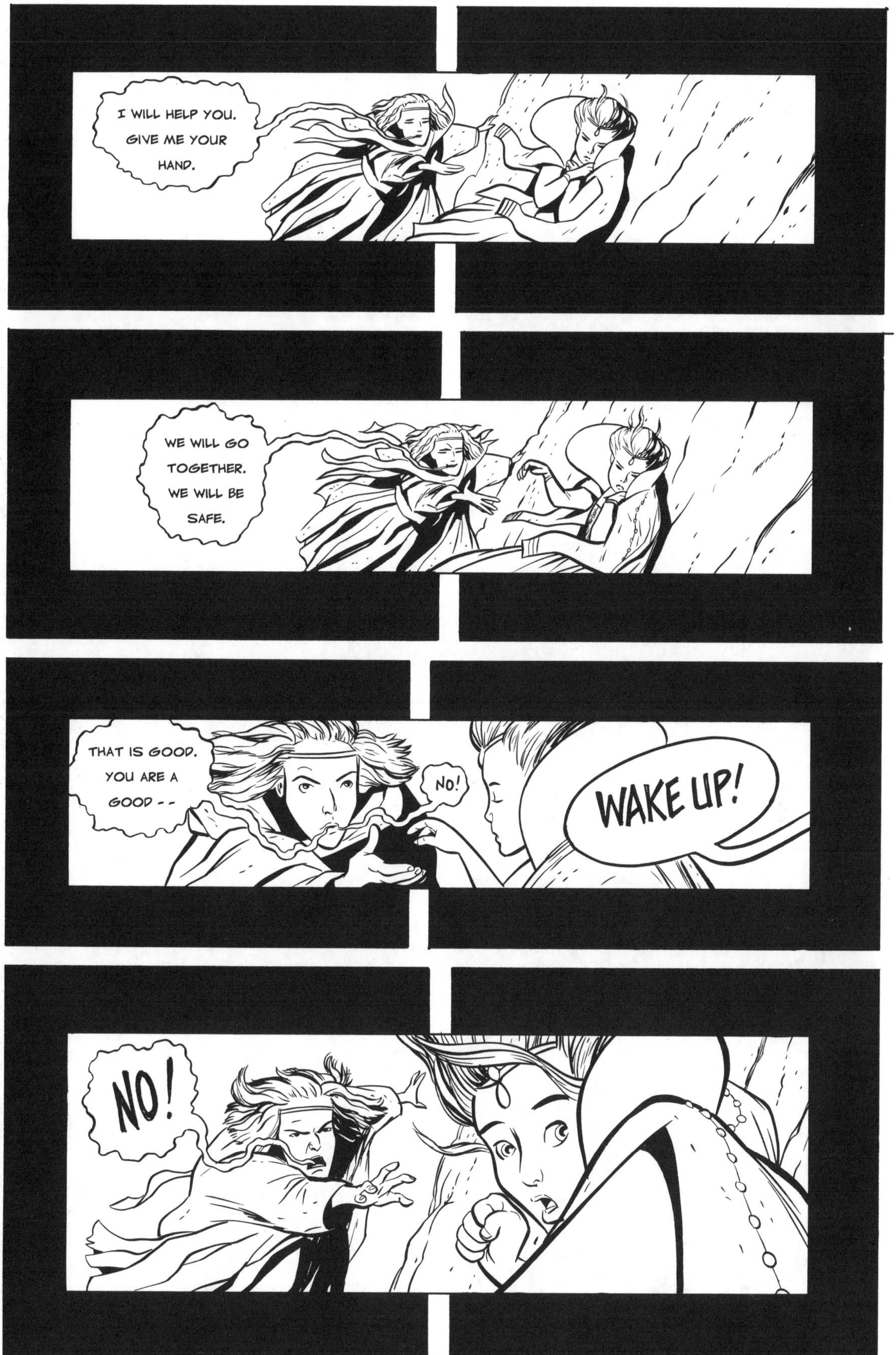
I WILL HELP YOU. GIVE ME YOUR HAND.
WE WILL GO TOGETHER. WE WILL BE SAFE.
THAT IS GOOD. YOU ARE A GOOD - -
NO!
WAKE UP!
NO!

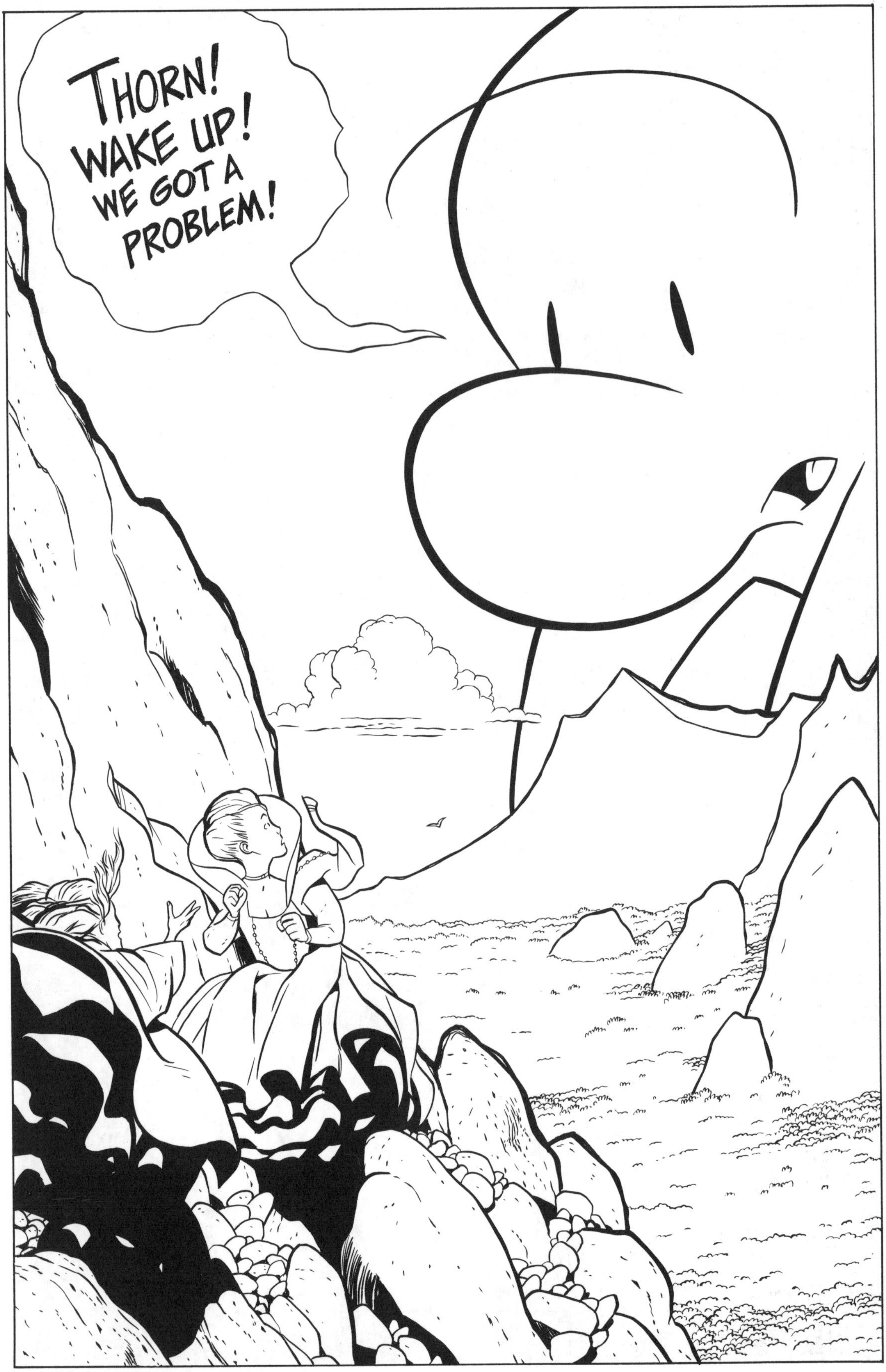
THORN! WAKE UP! WE GOT A PROBLEM!

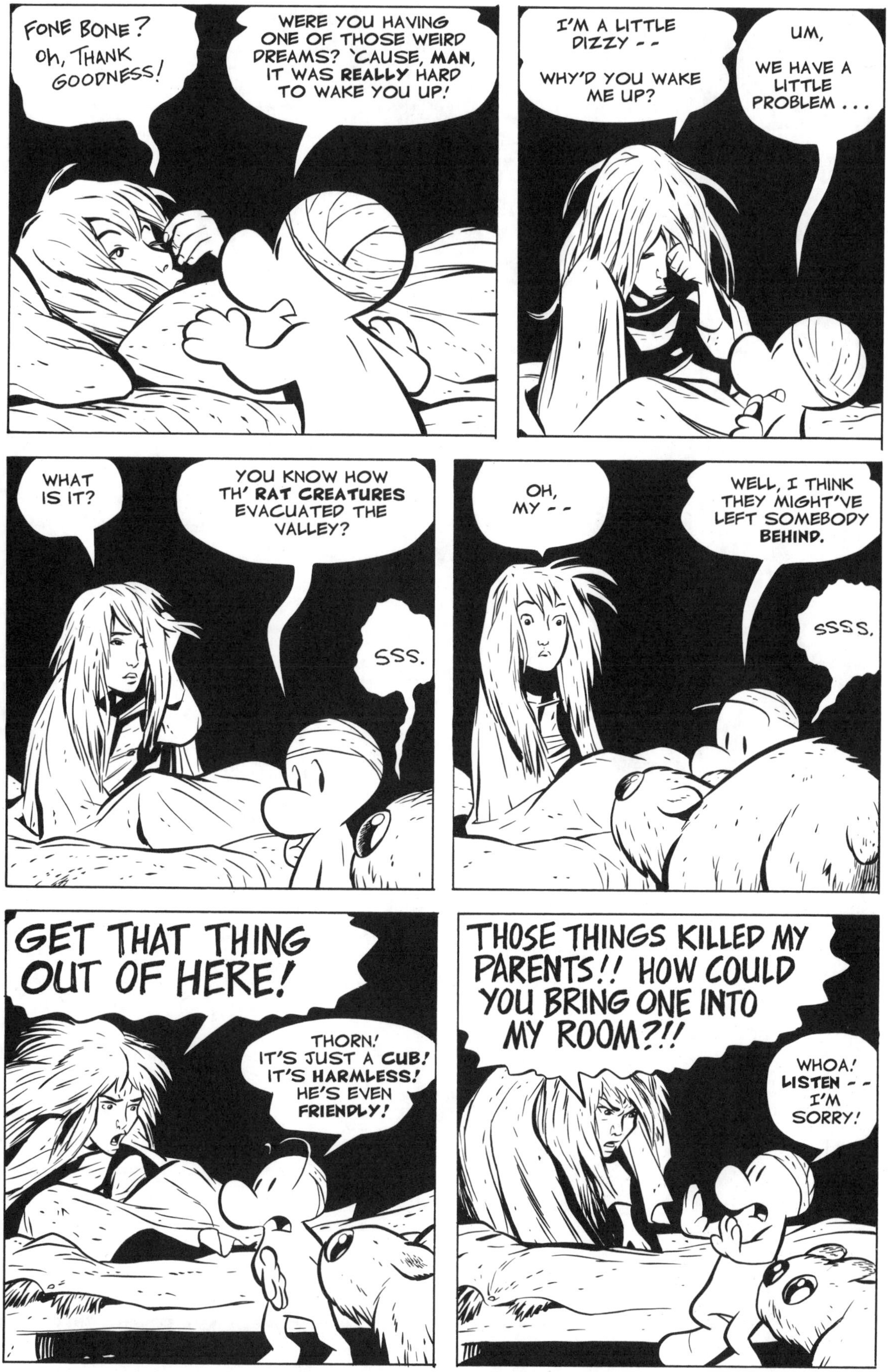
FONE BONE? OH, THANK GOODNESS!
WERE YOU HAVING ONE OF THOSE WEIRD DREAMS? 'CAUSE, **MAN**, IT WAS **REALLY** HARD TO WAKE YOU UP!
I'M A LITTLE DIZZY - -
WHY'D YOU WAKE ME UP?
UM,
WE HAVE A LITTLE PROBLEM . . .
WHAT IS IT?
YOU KNOW HOW TH' **RAT CREATURES** EVACUATED THE VALLEY?
SSS.
OH, MY - -
WELL, I THINK THEY MIGHT'VE LEFT SOMEBODY **BEHIND.**
SSSS.
GET THAT THING OUT OF HERE!
THORN! IT'S JUST A **CUB**! IT'S **HARMLESS**! HE'S EVEN **FRIENDLY**!
THOSE THINGS KILLED MY PARENTS!! HOW COULD YOU BRING ONE INTO MY ROOM?!!
WHOA! **LISTEN** - - I'M SORRY!

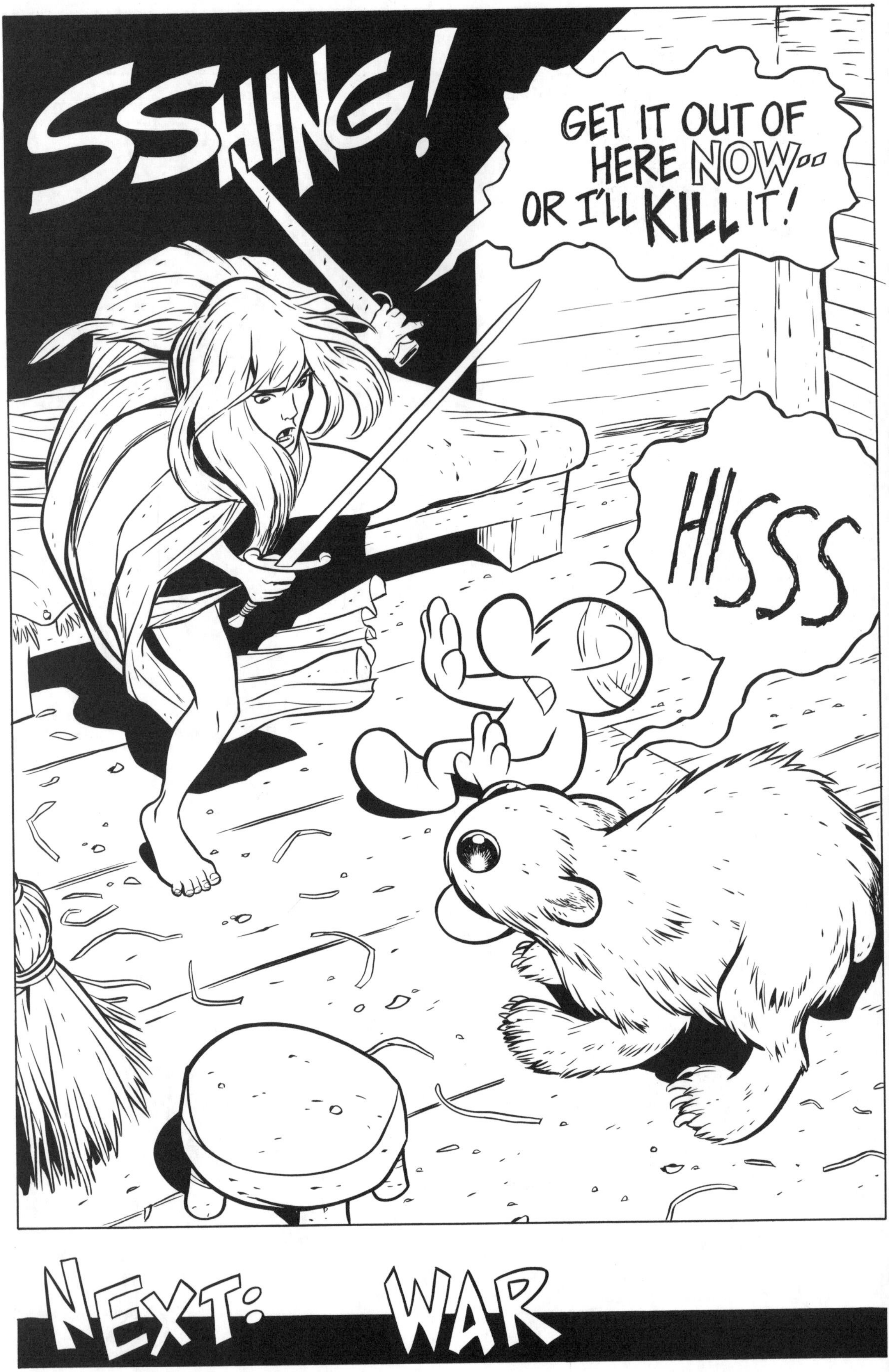
SSHING!
GET IT OUT OF HERE NOW.. OR I'LL KILL IT!
HISSS

NEXT: WAR

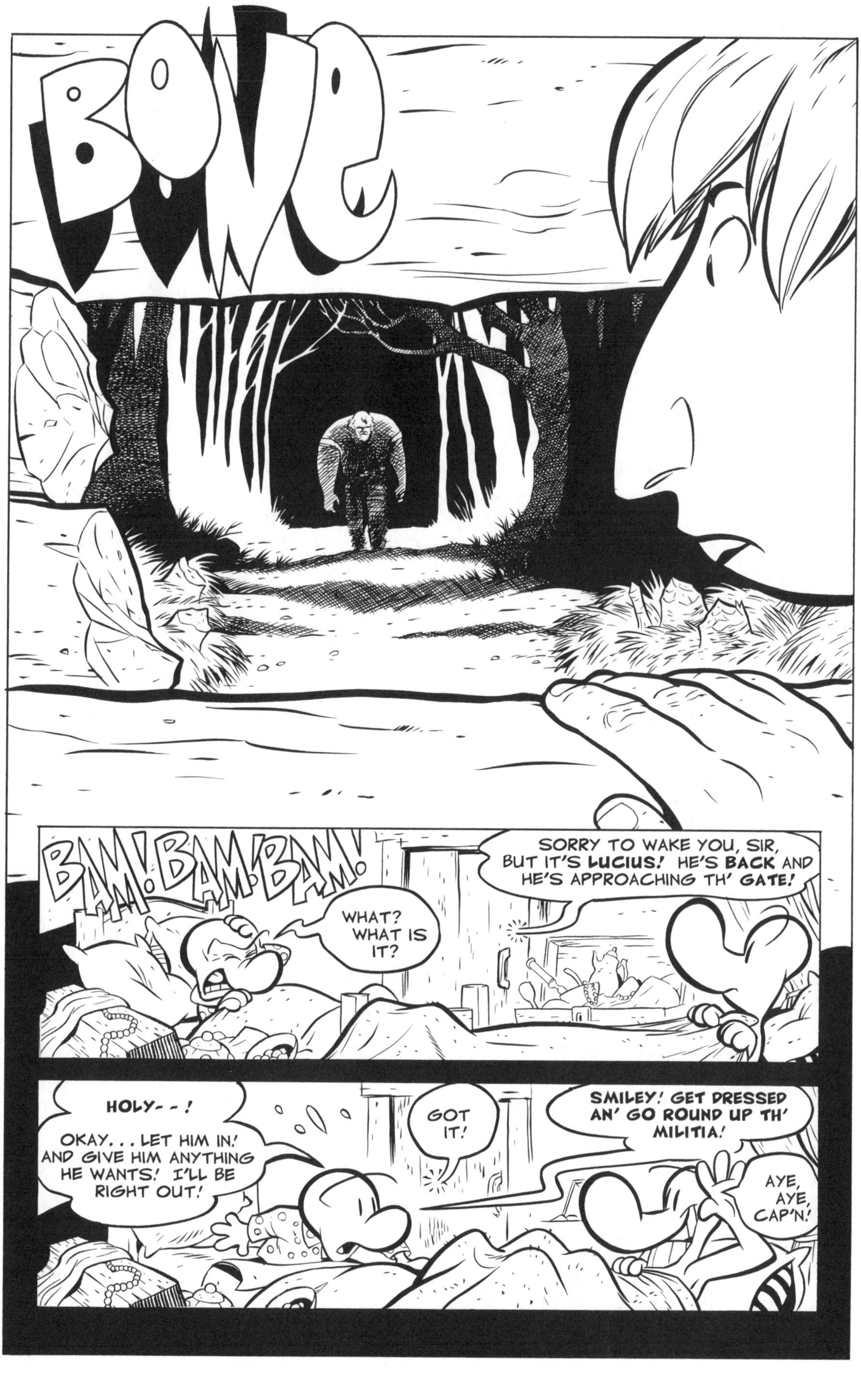
BONE
BAM! BAM! BAM!
SORRY TO WAKE YOU, SIR, BUT IT'S LUCIUS! HE'S BACK AND HE'S APPROACHING TH' GATE!
WHAT? WHAT IS IT?
HOLY- - !
OKAY. . . LET HIM IN! AND GIVE HIM ANYTHING HE WANTS! I'LL BE RIGHT OUT!
GOT IT!
SMILEY! GET DRESSED AN' GO ROUND UP TH' MILITIA!
AYE, AYE, CAP'N!

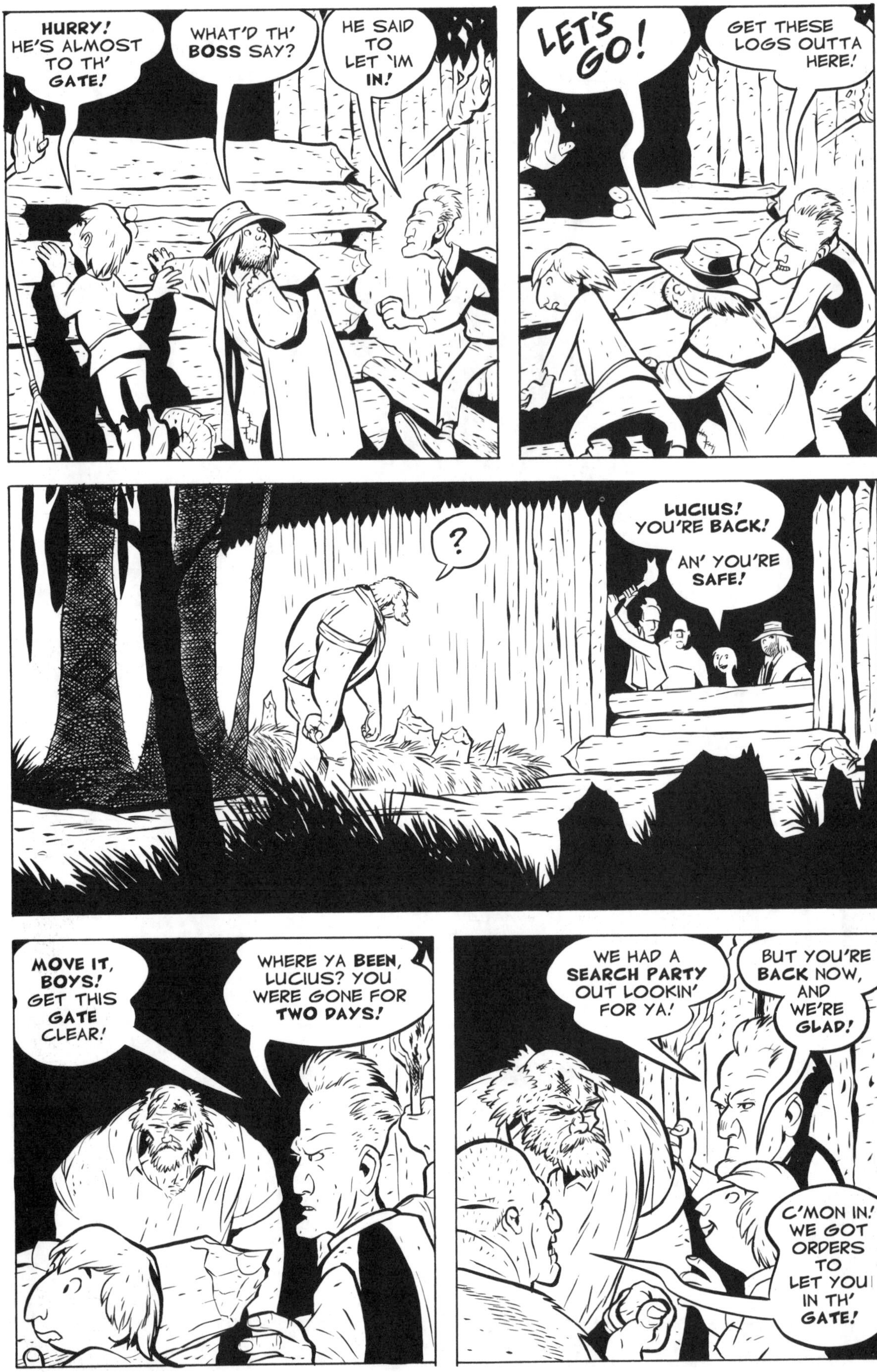
HURRY! HE'S ALMOST TO TH' GATE!
WHAT'D TH' BOSS SAY?
HE SAID TO LET 'IM IN!
LET'S GO!
GET THESE LOGS OUTTA HERE!
?
LUCIUS! YOU'RE BACK!
AN' YOU'RE SAFE!
MOVE IT, BOYS! GET THIS GATE CLEAR!
WHERE YA BEEN, LUCIUS? YOU WERE GONE FOR TWO DAYS!
WE HAD A SEARCH PARTY OUT LOOKIN' FOR YA!
BUT YOU'RE BACK NOW, AND WE'RE GLAD!
C'MON IN! WE GOT ORDERS TO LET YOU IN TH' GATE!

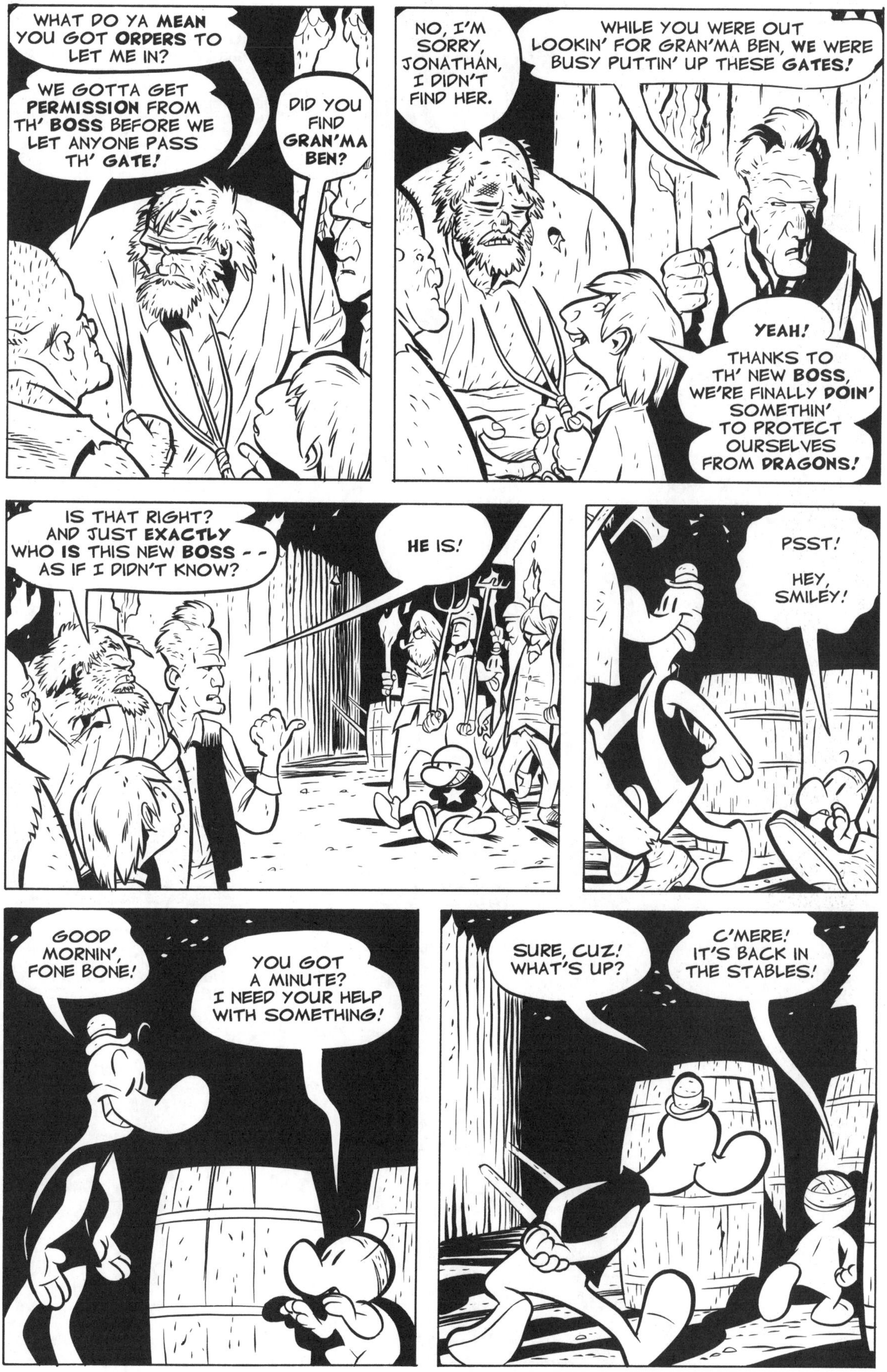
WHAT DO YA MEAN YOU GOT ORDERS TO LET ME IN?
WE GOTTA GET PERMISSION FROM TH' BOSS BEFORE WE LET ANYONE PASS TH' GATE!
DID YOU FIND GRAN'MA BEN?
NO, I'M SORRY, JONATHAN, I DIDN'T FIND HER.
WHILE YOU WERE OUT LOOKIN' FOR GRAN'MA BEN, WE WERE BUSY PUTTIN' UP THESE GATES!
YEAH!
THANKS TO TH' NEW BOSS, WE'RE FINALLY DOIN' SOMETHIN' TO PROTECT OURSELVES FROM DRAGONS!
IS THAT RIGHT? AND JUST EXACTLY WHO IS THIS NEW BOSS - - AS IF I DIDN'T KNOW?
HE IS!
PSST!
HEY, SMILEY!
GOOD MORNIN', FONE BONE!
YOU GOT A MINUTE? I NEED YOUR HELP WITH SOMETHING!
SURE, CUZ! WHAT'S UP?
C'MERE! IT'S BACK IN THE STABLES!

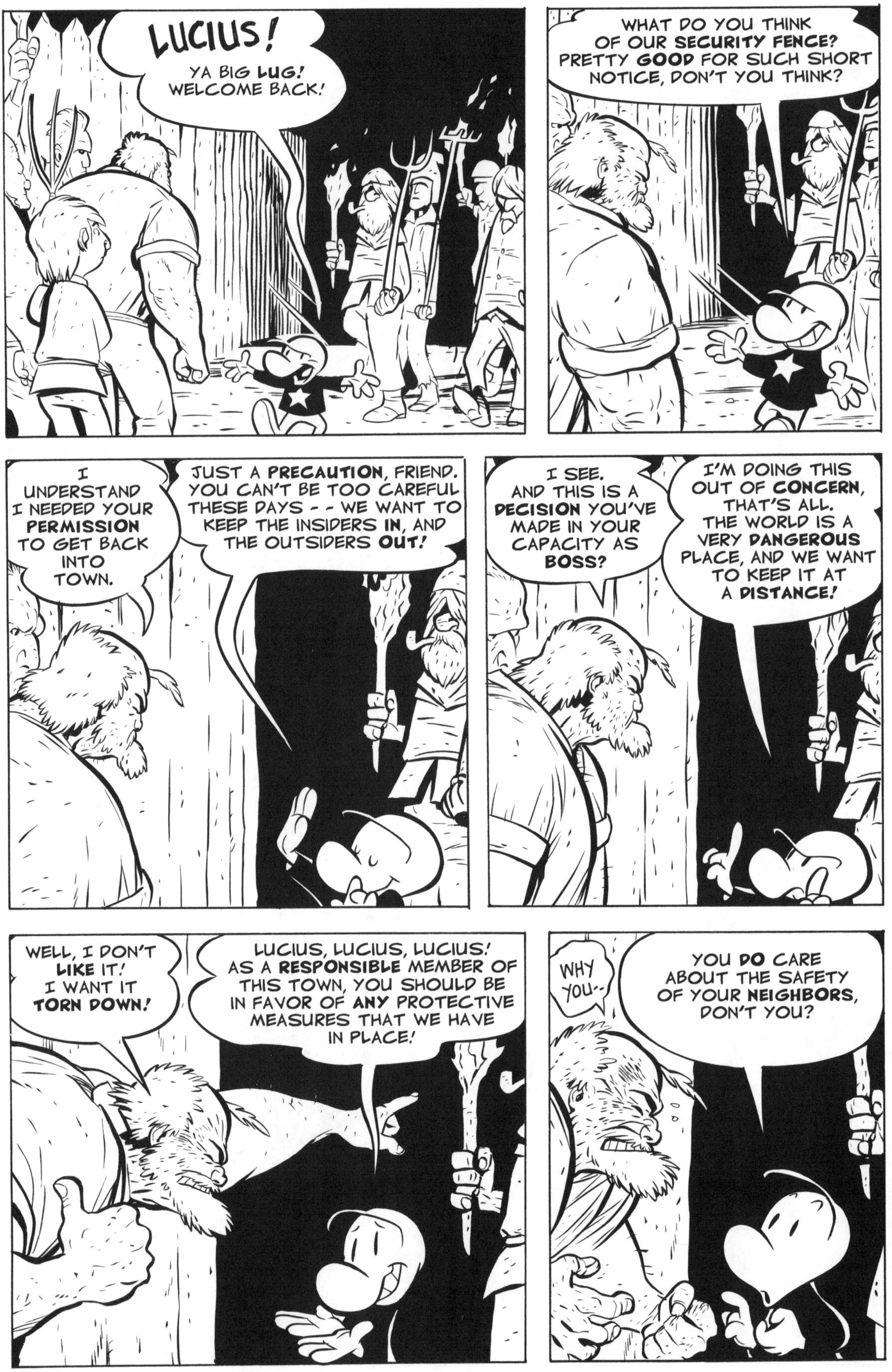
LUCIUS!
YA BIG LUG! WELCOME BACK!
WHAT DO YOU THINK OF OUR SECURITY FENCE? PRETTY GOOD FOR SUCH SHORT NOTICE, DON'T YOU THINK?
I UNDERSTAND I NEEDED YOUR PERMISSION TO GET BACK INTO TOWN.
JUST A PRECAUTION, FRIEND. YOU CAN'T BE TOO CAREFUL THESE DAYS - - WE WANT TO KEEP THE INSIDERS IN, AND THE OUTSIDERS OUT!
I SEE. AND THIS IS A DECISION YOU'VE MADE IN YOUR CAPACITY AS BOSS?
I'M DOING THIS OUT OF CONCERN, THAT'S ALL. THE WORLD IS A VERY DANGEROUS PLACE, AND WE WANT TO KEEP IT AT A DISTANCE!
WELL, I DON'T LIKE IT! I WANT IT TORN DOWN!
LUCIUS, LUCIUS, LUCIUS! AS A RESPONSIBLE MEMBER OF THIS TOWN, YOU SHOULD BE IN FAVOR OF ANY PROTECTIVE MEASURES THAT WE HAVE IN PLACE!
WHY YOU- -
YOU DO CARE ABOUT THE SAFETY OF YOUR NEIGHBORS, DON'T YOU?

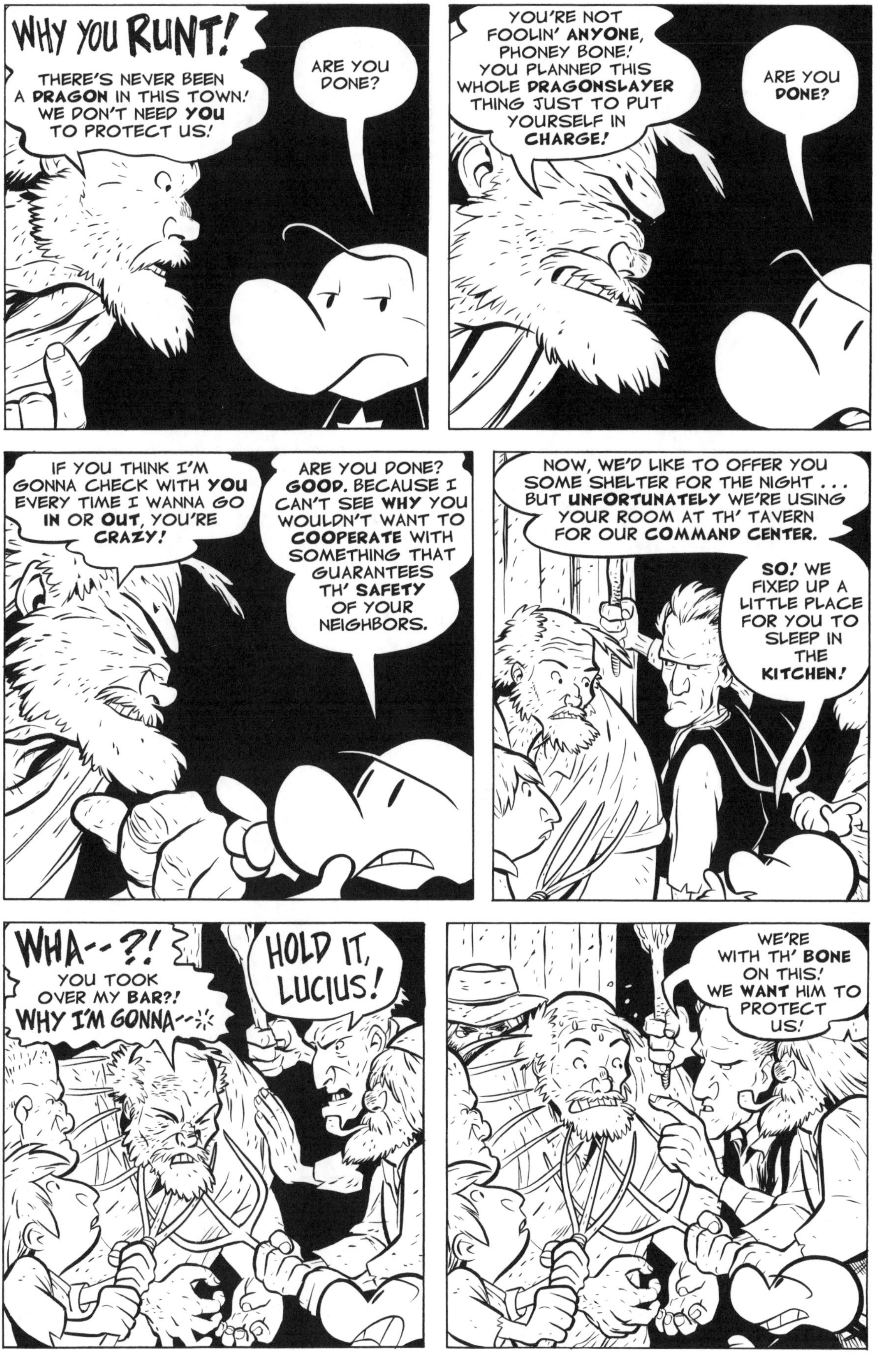
WHY YOU RUNT!
THERE'S NEVER BEEN A DRAGON IN THIS TOWN! WE DON'T NEED YOU TO PROTECT US!
ARE YOU DONE?
YOU'RE NOT FOOLIN' ANYONE, PHONEY BONE! YOU PLANNED THIS WHOLE DRAGONSLAYER THING JUST TO PUT YOURSELF IN CHARGE!
ARE YOU DONE?
IF YOU THINK I'M GONNA CHECK WITH YOU EVERY TIME I WANNA GO IN OR OUT, YOU'RE CRAZY!
ARE YOU DONE? GOOD. BECAUSE I CAN'T SEE WHY YOU WOULDN'T WANT TO COOPERATE WITH SOMETHING THAT GUARANTEES TH' SAFETY OF YOUR NEIGHBORS.
NOW, WE'D LIKE TO OFFER YOU SOME SHELTER FOR THE NIGHT . . . BUT UNFORTUNATELY WE'RE USING YOUR ROOM AT TH' TAVERN FOR OUR COMMAND CENTER.
SO! WE FIXED UP A LITTLE PLACE FOR YOU TO SLEEP IN THE KITCHEN!
WHA--?! YOU TOOK OVER MY BAR?! WHY I'M GONNA--
HOLD IT, LUCIUS!
WE'RE WITH TH' BONE ON THIS! WE WANT HIM TO PROTECT US!

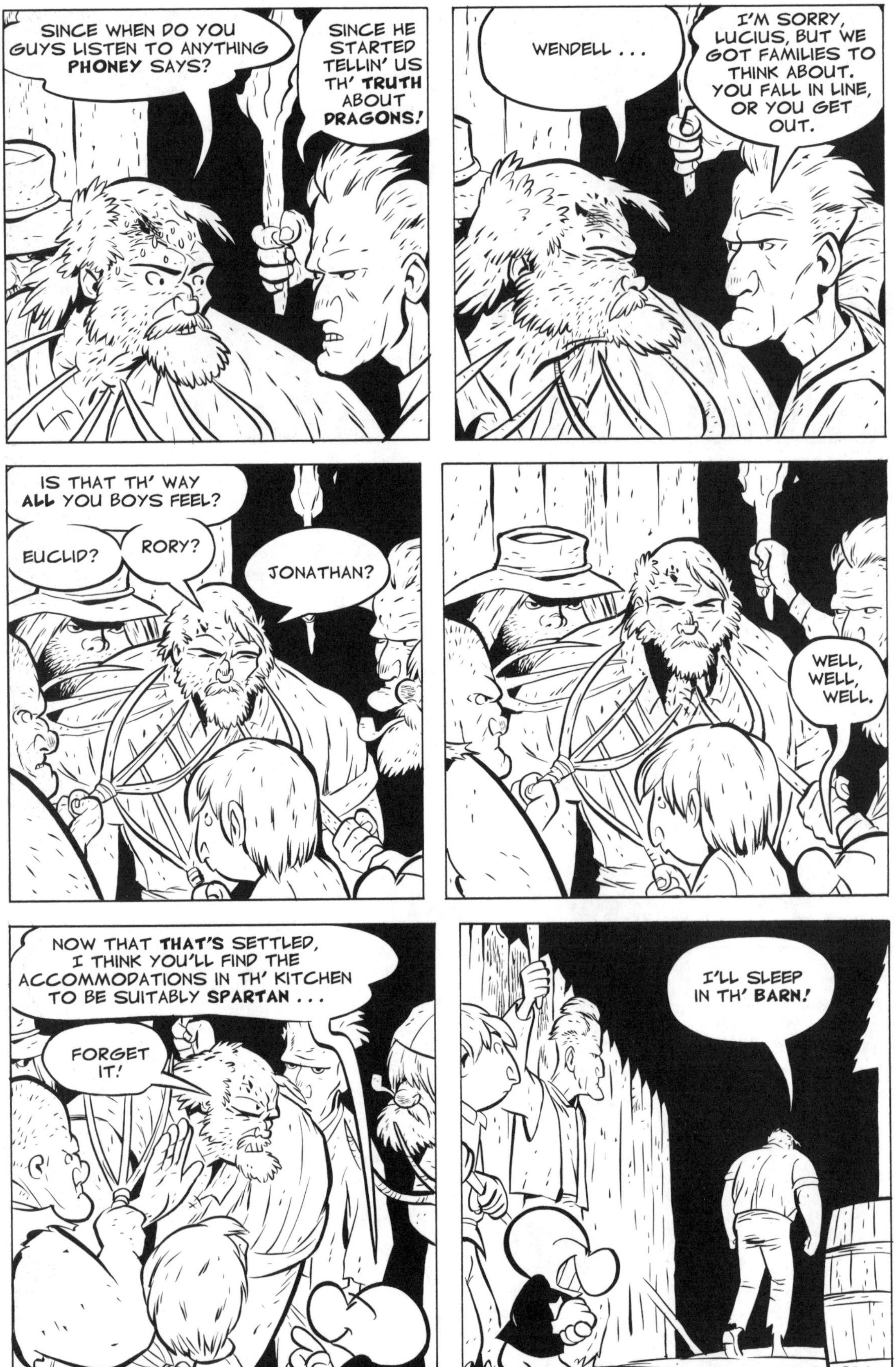
SINCE WHEN DO YOU GUYS LISTEN TO ANYTHING PHONEY SAYS?
SINCE HE STARTED TELLIN' US TH' TRUTH ABOUT DRAGONS!
WENDELL . . .
I'M SORRY, LUCIUS, BUT WE GOT FAMILIES TO THINK ABOUT. YOU FALL IN LINE, OR YOU GET OUT.
IS THAT TH' WAY ALL YOU BOYS FEEL?
EUCLID?
RORY?
JONATHAN?
WELL, WELL, WELL.
NOW THAT THAT'S SETTLED, I THINK YOU'LL FIND THE ACCOMMODATIONS IN TH' KITCHEN TO BE SUITABLY SPARTAN . . .
FORGET IT!
I'LL SLEEP IN TH' BARN!

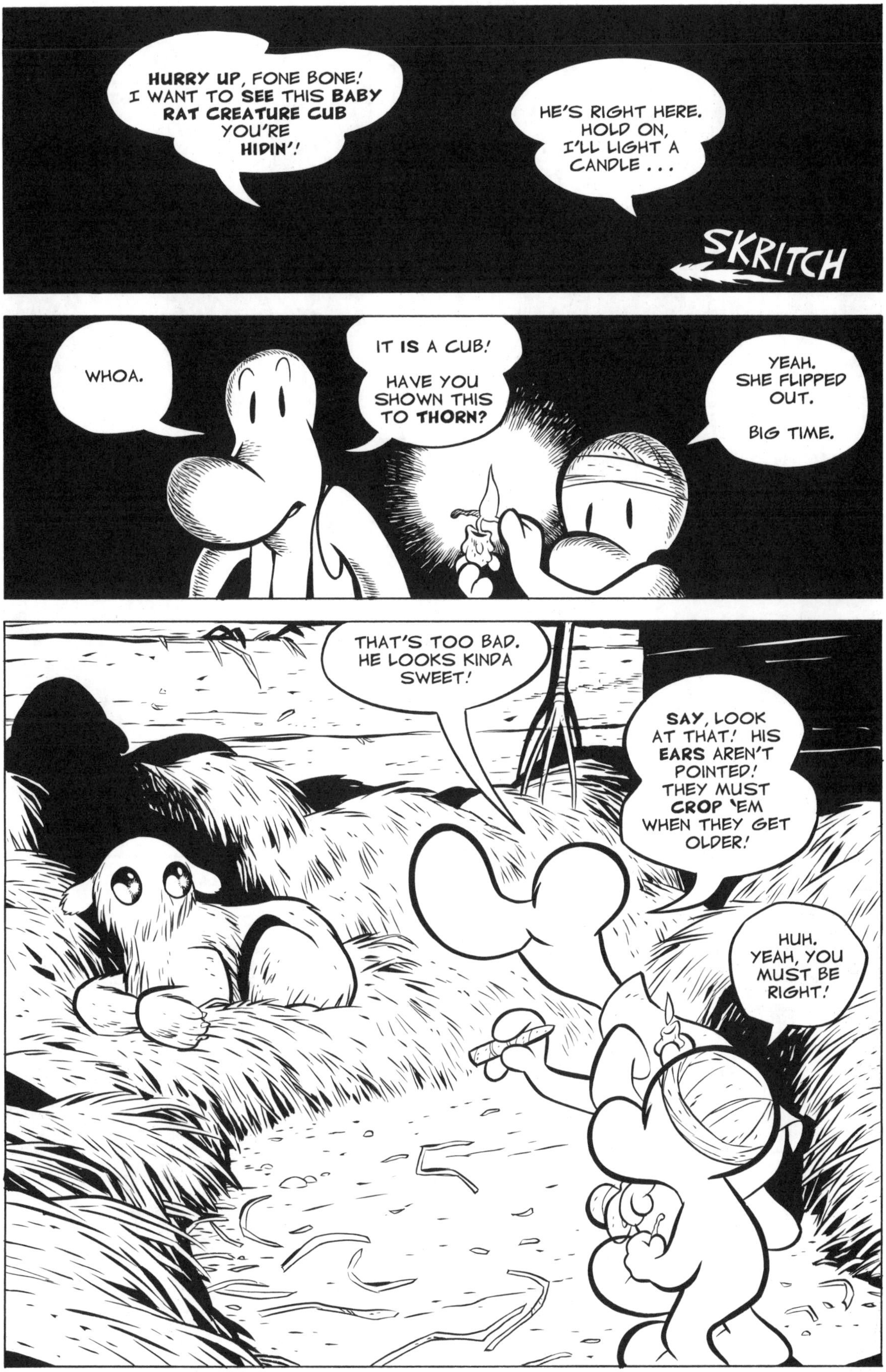
HURRY UP, FONE BONE! I WANT TO SEE THIS BABY RAT CREATURE CUB YOU'RE HIDIN'!
HE'S RIGHT HERE. HOLD ON, I'LL LIGHT A CANDLE . . .
SKRITCH
WHOA.
IT IS A CUB! HAVE YOU SHOWN THIS TO THORN?
YEAH. SHE FLIPPED OUT. BIG TIME.
THAT'S TOO BAD. HE LOOKS KINDA SWEET!
SAY, LOOK AT THAT! HIS EARS AREN'T POINTED! THEY MUST CROP 'EM WHEN THEY GET OLDER!
HUH. YEAH, YOU MUST BE RIGHT!

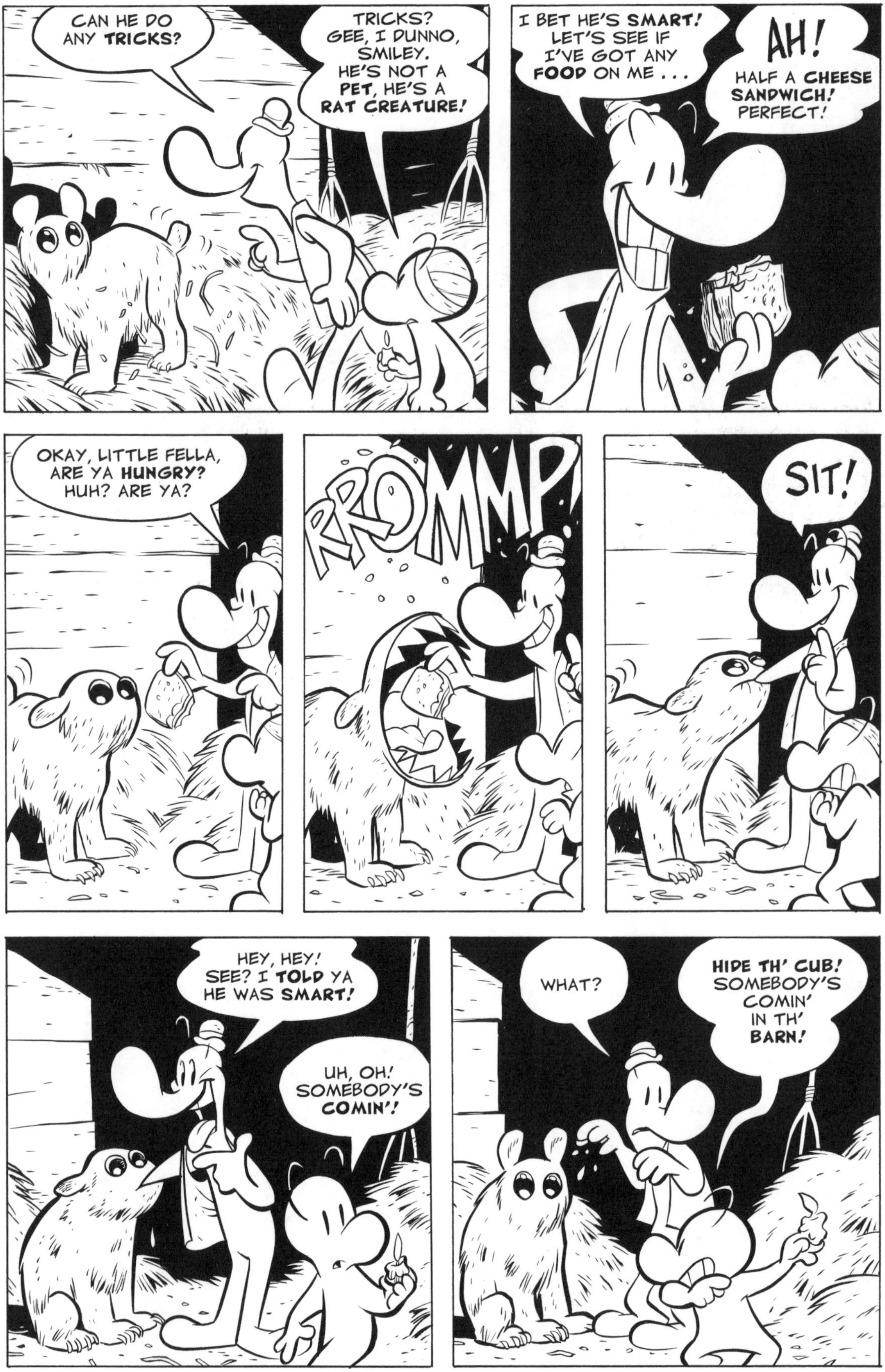
CAN HE DO ANY TRICKS?
TRICKS? GEE, I DUNNO, SMILEY. HE'S NOT A PET, HE'S A RAT CREATURE!
I BET HE'S SMART! LET'S SEE IF I'VE GOT ANY FOOD ON ME . . .
AH! HALF A CHEESE SANDWICH! PERFECT!
OKAY, LITTLE FELLA, ARE YA HUNGRY? HUH? ARE YA?
RROMMP!
SIT!
HEY, HEY! SEE? I TOLD YA HE WAS SMART!
UH, OH! SOMEBODY'S COMIN'!
WHAT?
HIDE TH' CUB! SOMEBODY'S COMIN' IN TH' BARN!

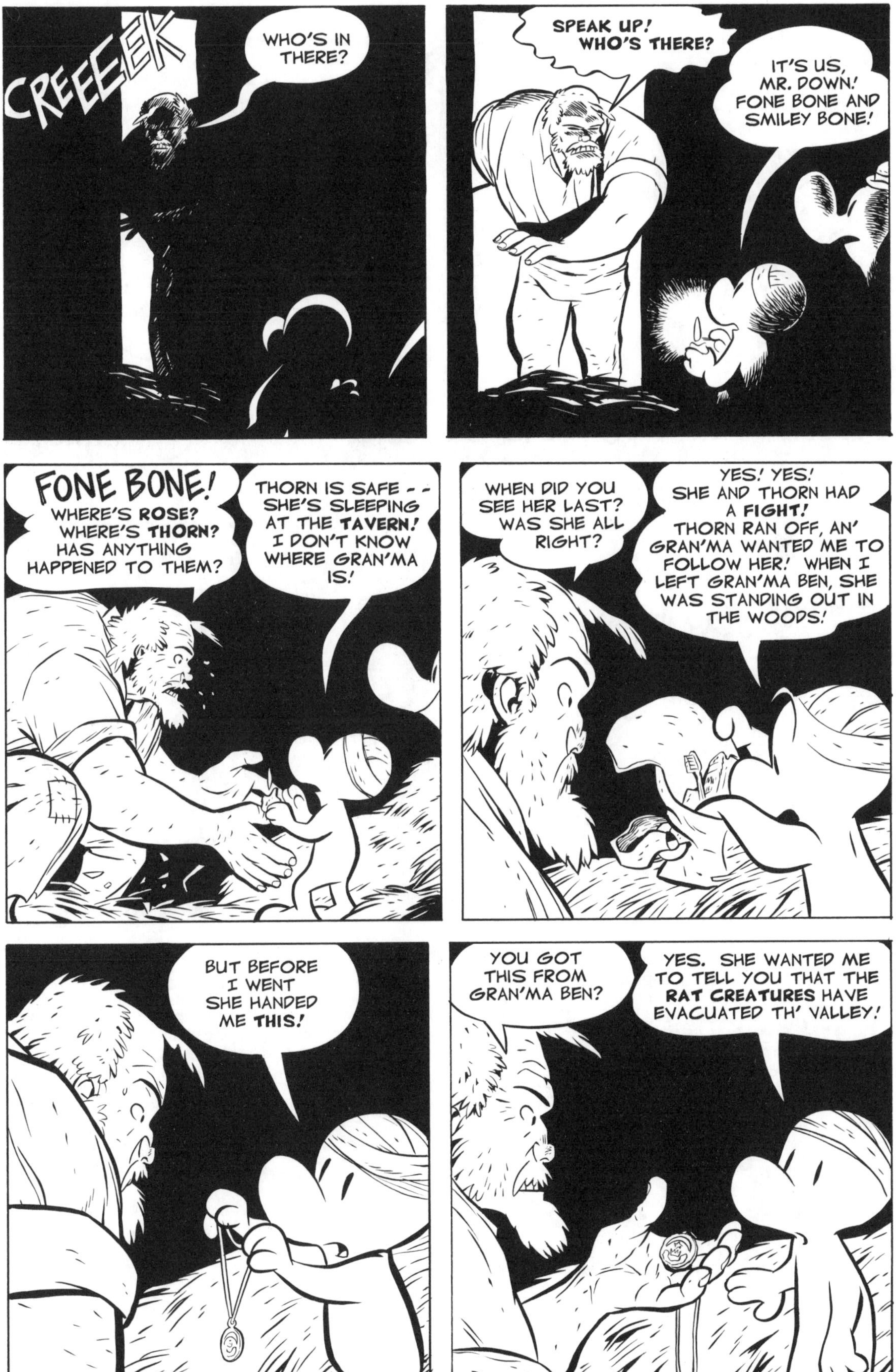
CREEEEK
WHO'S IN THERE?
SPEAK UP! WHO'S THERE?
IT'S US, MR. DOWN! FONE BONE AND SMILEY BONE!
FONE BONE! WHERE'S ROSE? WHERE'S THORN? HAS ANYTHING HAPPENED TO THEM?
THORN IS SAFE -- SHE'S SLEEPING AT THE TAVERN! I DON'T KNOW WHERE GRAN'MA IS!
WHEN DID YOU SEE HER LAST? WAS SHE ALL RIGHT?
YES! YES! SHE AND THORN HAD A FIGHT! THORN RAN OFF, AN' GRAN'MA WANTED ME TO FOLLOW HER! WHEN I LEFT GRAN'MA BEN, SHE WAS STANDING OUT IN THE WOODS!
BUT BEFORE I WENT SHE HANDED ME THIS!
YOU GOT THIS FROM GRAN'MA BEN?
YES. SHE WANTED ME TO TELL YOU THAT THE RAT CREATURES HAVE EVACUATED TH' VALLEY!

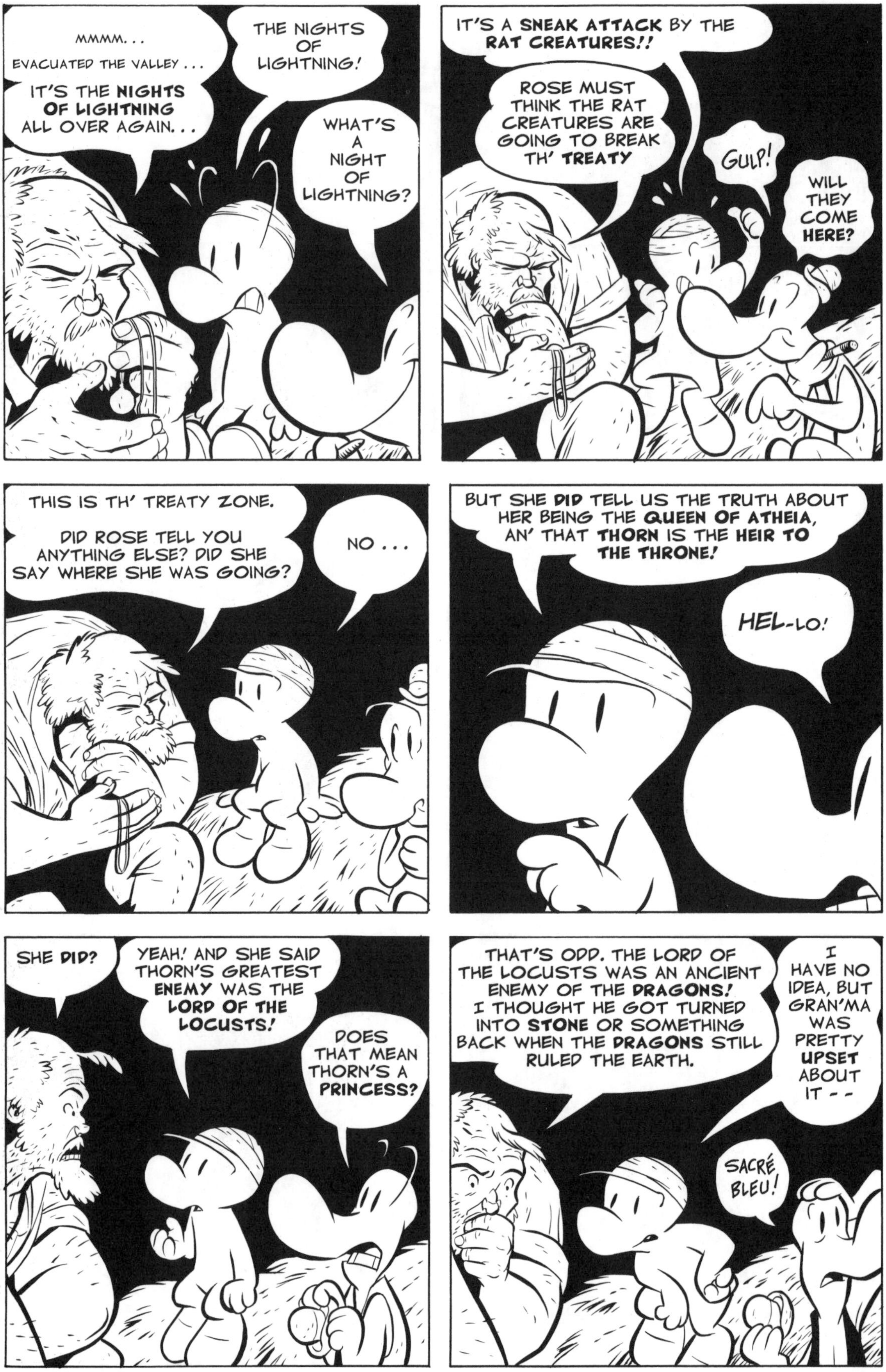
MMMM...
EVACUATED THE VALLEY...
IT'S THE NIGHTS OF LIGHTNING ALL OVER AGAIN...
THE NIGHTS OF LIGHTNING!
WHAT'S A NIGHT OF LIGHTNING?
IT'S A SNEAK ATTACK BY THE RAT CREATURES!!
ROSE MUST THINK THE RAT CREATURES ARE GOING TO BREAK TH' TREATY
GULP!
WILL THEY COME HERE?
THIS IS TH' TREATY ZONE.
DID ROSE TELL YOU ANYTHING ELSE? DID SHE SAY WHERE SHE WAS GOING?
NO...
BUT SHE DID TELL US THE TRUTH ABOUT HER BEING THE QUEEN OF ATHEIA, AN' THAT THORN IS THE HEIR TO THE THRONE!
HEL-LO!
SHE DID?
YEAH! AND SHE SAID THORN'S GREATEST ENEMY WAS THE LORD OF THE LOCUSTS!
DOES THAT MEAN THORN'S A PRINCESS?
THAT'S ODD. THE LORD OF THE LOCUSTS WAS AN ANCIENT ENEMY OF THE DRAGONS! I THOUGHT HE GOT TURNED INTO STONE OR SOMETHING BACK WHEN THE DRAGONS STILL RULED THE EARTH.
I HAVE NO IDEA, BUT GRAN'MA WAS PRETTY UPSET ABOUT IT --
SACRÉ BLEU!

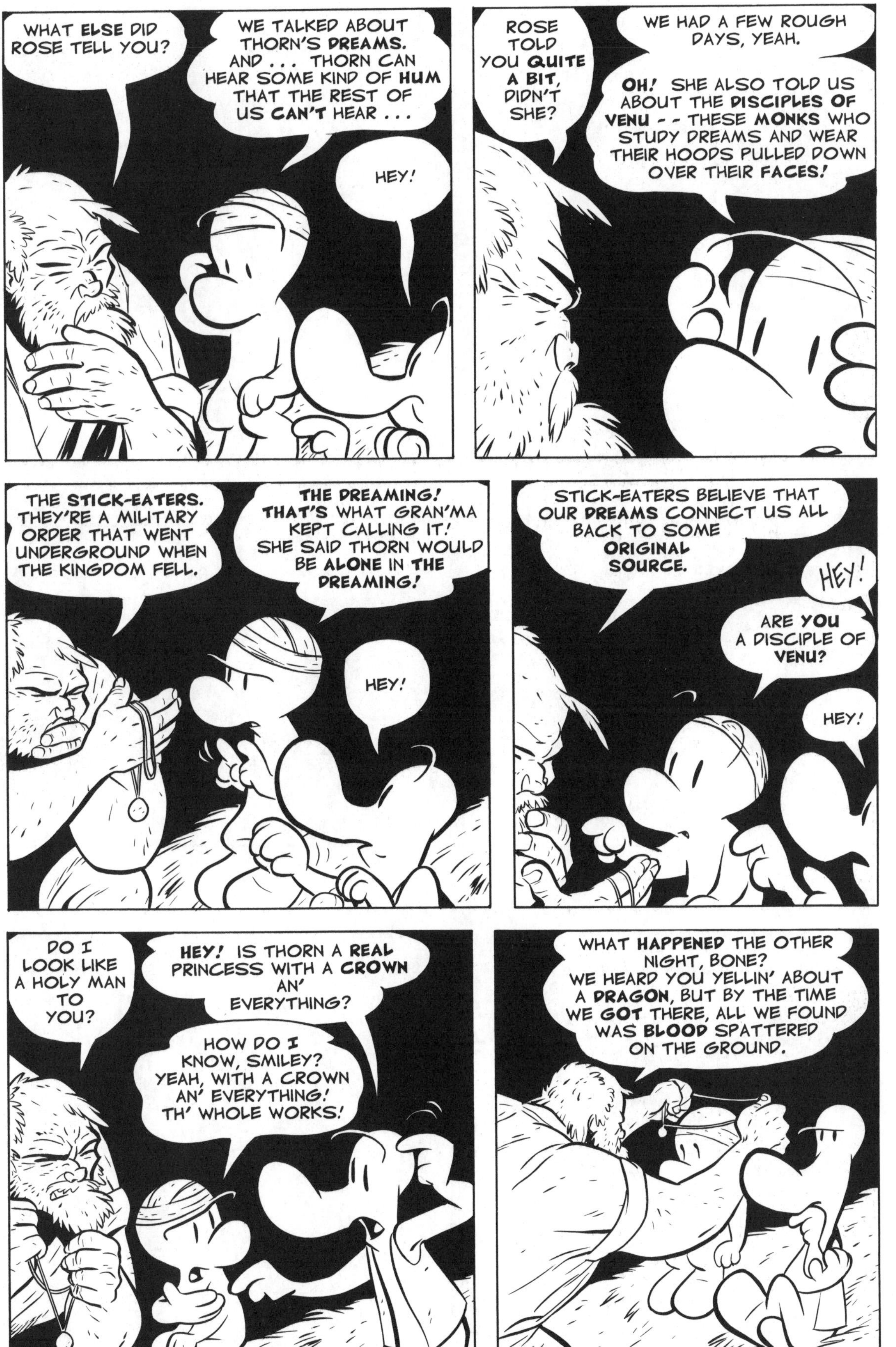
WHAT ELSE DID ROSE TELL YOU?
WE TALKED ABOUT THORN'S DREAMS. AND . . . THORN CAN HEAR SOME KIND OF HUM THAT THE REST OF US CAN'T HEAR . . .
HEY!
ROSE TOLD YOU QUITE A BIT, DIDN'T SHE?
WE HAD A FEW ROUGH DAYS, YEAH.
OH! SHE ALSO TOLD US ABOUT THE DISCIPLES OF VENU -- THESE MONKS WHO STUDY DREAMS AND WEAR THEIR HOODS PULLED DOWN OVER THEIR FACES!
THE STICK-EATERS. THEY'RE A MILITARY ORDER THAT WENT UNDERGROUND WHEN THE KINGDOM FELL.
THE DREAMING! THAT'S WHAT GRAN'MA KEPT CALLING IT! SHE SAID THORN WOULD BE ALONE IN THE DREAMING!
HEY!
STICK-EATERS BELIEVE THAT OUR DREAMS CONNECT US ALL BACK TO SOME ORIGINAL SOURCE.
HEY!
ARE YOU A DISCIPLE OF VENU?
HEY!
DO I LOOK LIKE A HOLY MAN TO YOU?
HEY! IS THORN A REAL PRINCESS WITH A CROWN AN' EVERYTHING?
HOW DO I KNOW, SMILEY? YEAH, WITH A CROWN AN' EVERYTHING! TH' WHOLE WORKS!
WHAT HAPPENED THE OTHER NIGHT, BONE? WE HEARD YOU YELLIN' ABOUT A DRAGON, BUT BY THE TIME WE GOT THERE, ALL WE FOUND WAS BLOOD SPATTERED ON THE GROUND.

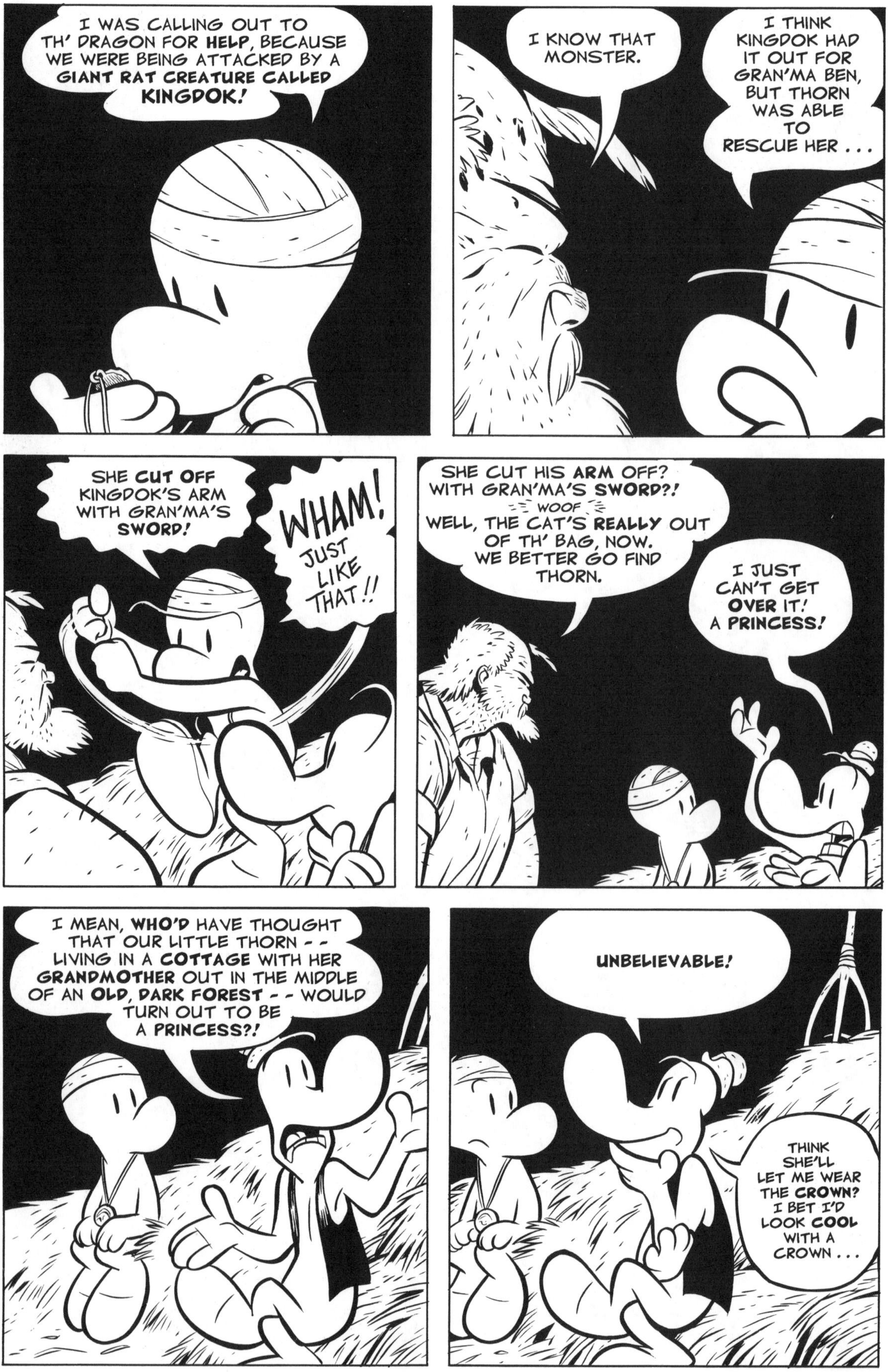

I WAS CALLING OUT TO TH' DRAGON FOR HELP, BECAUSE WE WERE BEING ATTACKED BY A GIANT RAT CREATURE CALLED KINGDOK!
I KNOW THAT MONSTER.
I THINK KINGDOK HAD IT OUT FOR GRAN'MA BEN, BUT THORN WAS ABLE TO RESCUE HER . . .
SHE CUT OFF KINGDOK'S ARM WITH GRAN'MA'S SWORD!
WHAM! JUST LIKE THAT!!
SHE CUT HIS ARM OFF? WITH GRAN'MA'S SWORD?! WOOF WELL, THE CAT'S REALLY OUT OF TH' BAG, NOW. WE BETTER GO FIND THORN.
I JUST CAN'T GET OVER IT! A PRINCESS!
I MEAN, WHO'D HAVE THOUGHT THAT OUR LITTLE THORN - - LIVING IN A COTTAGE WITH HER GRANDMOTHER OUT IN THE MIDDLE OF AN OLD, DARK FOREST - - WOULD TURN OUT TO BE A PRINCESS?!
UNBELIEVABLE!
THINK SHE'LL LET ME WEAR THE CROWN? I BET I'D LOOK COOL WITH A CROWN . . .

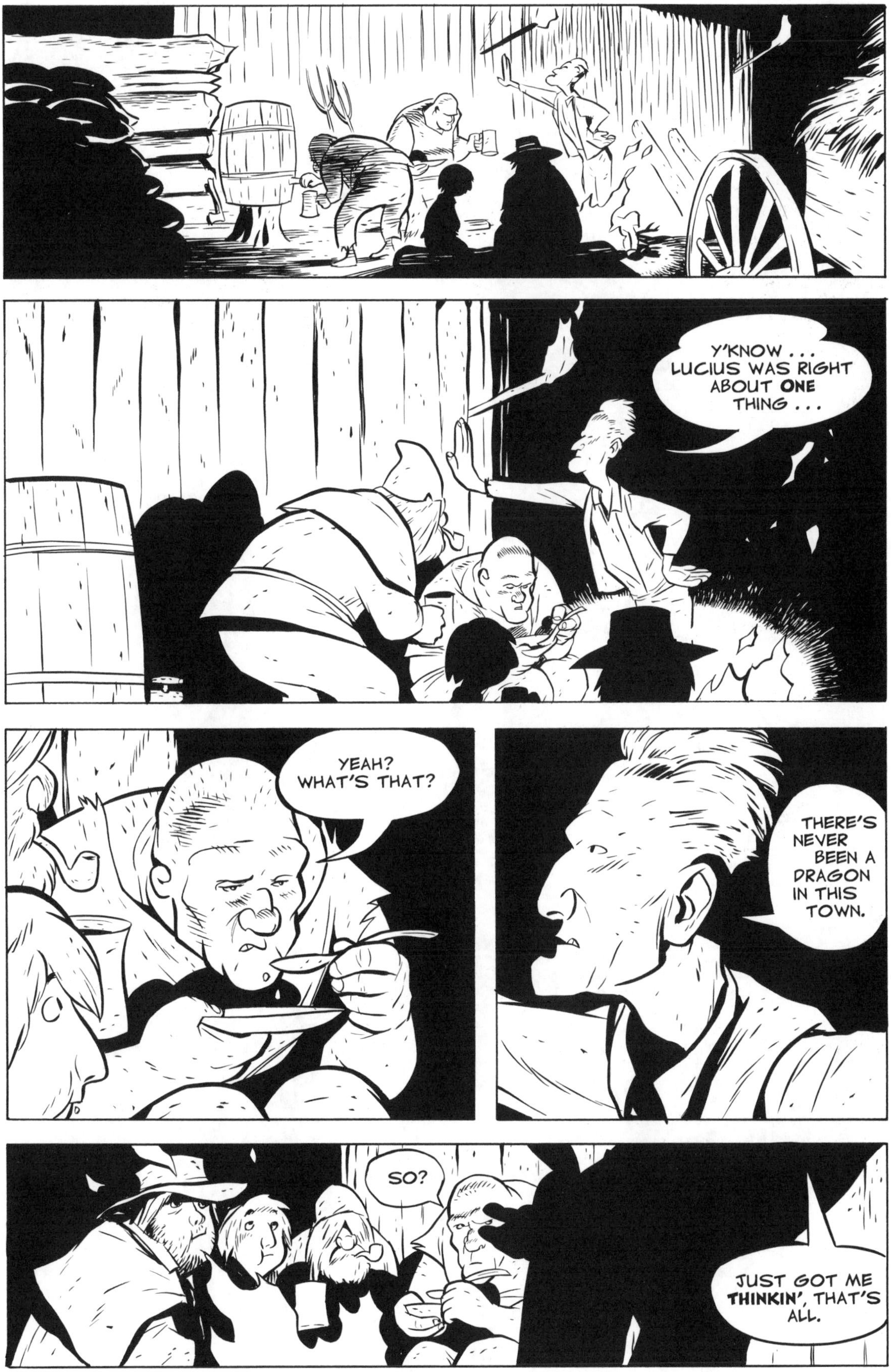
Y'KNOW . . . LUCIUS WAS RIGHT ABOUT ONE THING . . .
YEAH? WHAT'S THAT?
THERE'S NEVER BEEN A DRAGON IN THIS TOWN.
SO?
JUST GOT ME THINKIN', THAT'S ALL.

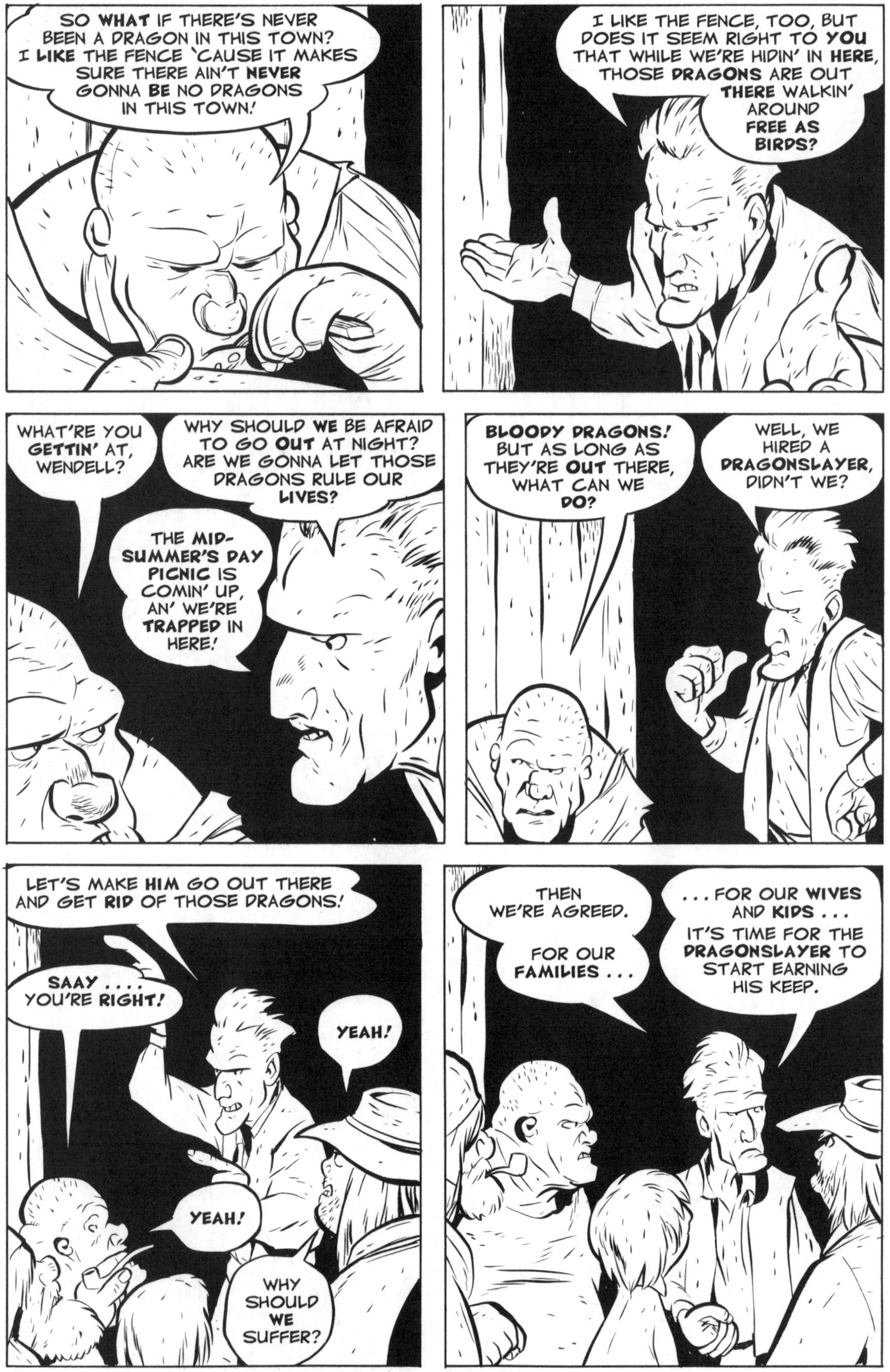
SO WHAT IF THERE'S NEVER BEEN A DRAGON IN THIS TOWN? I LIKE THE FENCE 'CAUSE IT MAKES SURE THERE AIN'T NEVER GONNA BE NO DRAGONS IN THIS TOWN!
I LIKE THE FENCE, TOO, BUT DOES IT SEEM RIGHT TO YOU THAT WHILE WE'RE HIDIN' IN HERE, THOSE DRAGONS ARE OUT THERE WALKIN' AROUND FREE AS BIRDS?
WHAT'RE YOU GETTIN' AT, WENDELL?
WHY SHOULD WE BE AFRAID TO GO OUT AT NIGHT? ARE WE GONNA LET THOSE DRAGONS RULE OUR LIVES?
THE MID-SUMMER'S DAY PICNIC IS COMIN' UP, AN' WE'RE TRAPPED IN HERE!
BLOODY DRAGONS! BUT AS LONG AS THEY'RE OUT THERE, WHAT CAN WE DO?
WELL, WE HIRED A DRAGONSLAYER, DIDN'T WE?
LET'S MAKE HIM GO OUT THERE AND GET RID OF THOSE DRAGONS!
SAAY .... YOU'RE RIGHT!
YEAH!
YEAH!
WHY SHOULD WE SUFFER?
THEN WE'RE AGREED.
FOR OUR FAMILIES ...
... FOR OUR WIVES AND KIDS ...
IT'S TIME FOR THE DRAGONSLAYER TO START EARNING HIS KEEP.

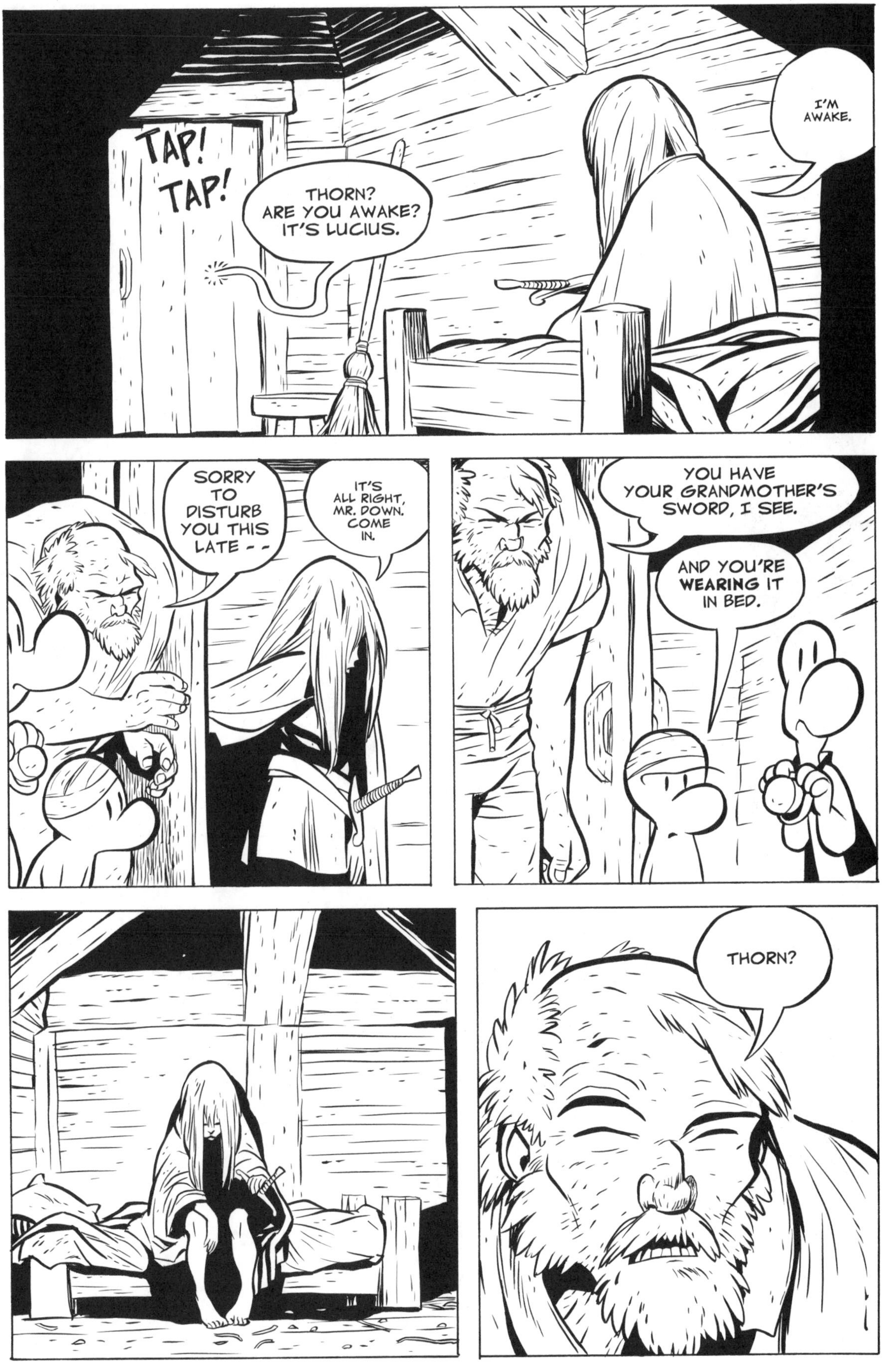
TAP! TAP!
THORN? ARE YOU AWAKE? IT'S LUCIUS.
I'M AWAKE.
SORRY TO DISTURB YOU THIS LATE --
IT'S ALL RIGHT, MR. DOWN. COME IN.
YOU HAVE YOUR GRANDMOTHER'S SWORD, I SEE.
AND YOU'RE **WEARING** IT IN BED.
THORN?

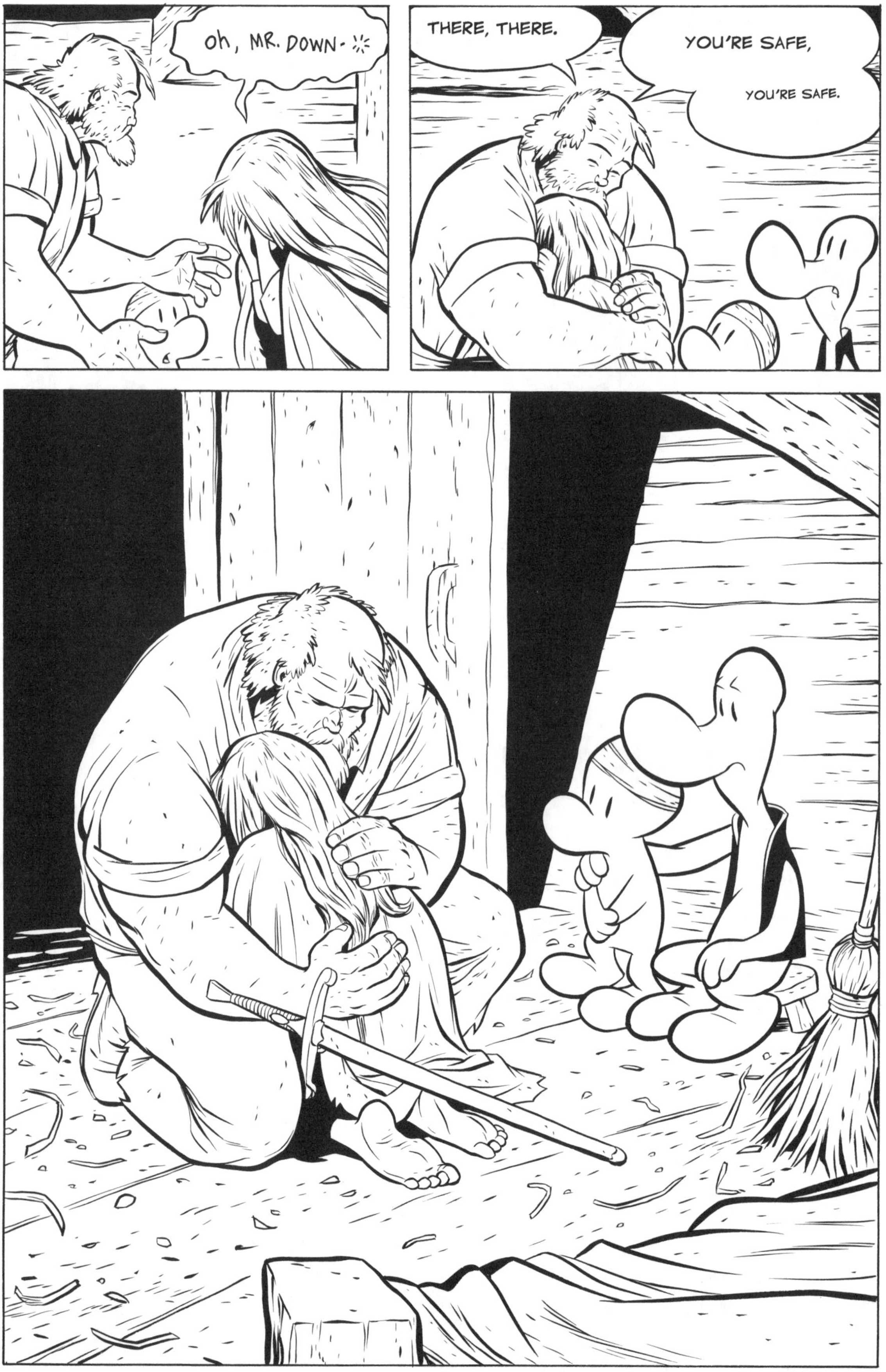
oh, MR. DOWN-
THERE, THERE.
YOU'RE SAFE,
YOU'RE SAFE.

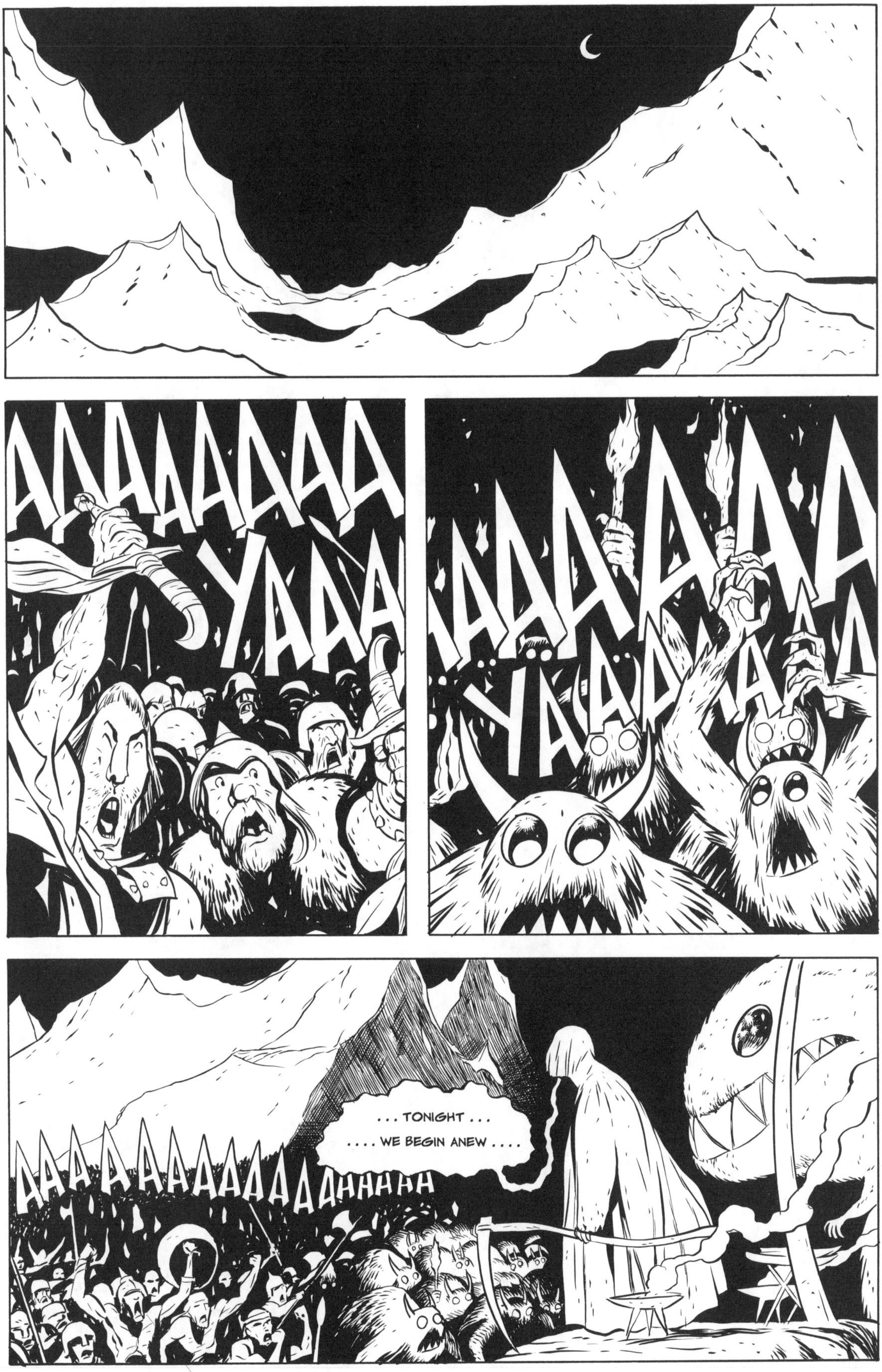
. . . TONIGHT . . .
. . . . WE BEGIN ANEW . . . .

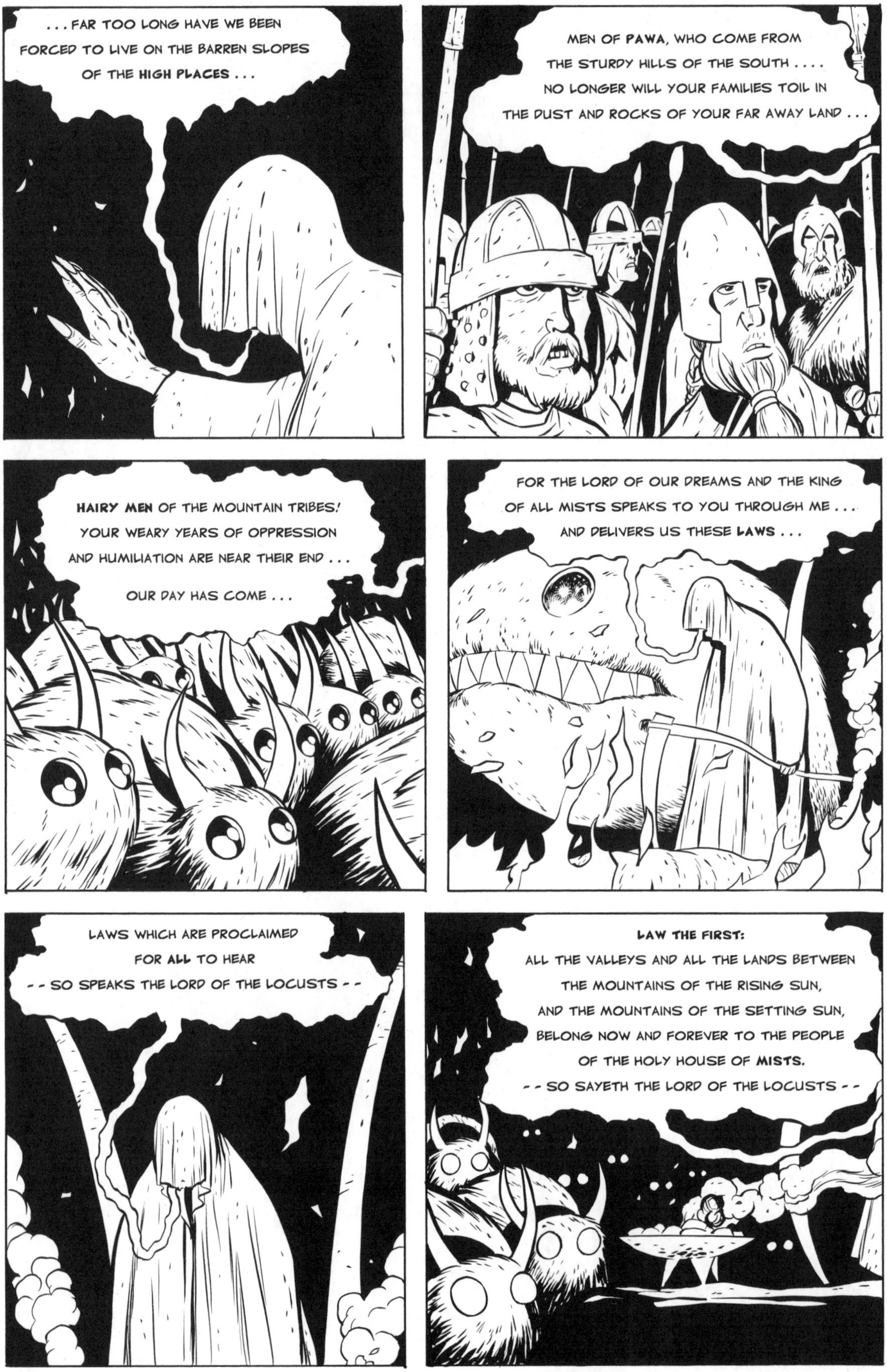
. . . FAR TOO LONG HAVE WE BEEN FORCED TO LIVE ON THE BARREN SLOPES OF THE HIGH PLACES . . .
MEN OF PAWA, WHO COME FROM THE STURDY HILLS OF THE SOUTH . . . . NO LONGER WILL YOUR FAMILIES TOIL IN THE DUST AND ROCKS OF YOUR FAR AWAY LAND . . .
HAIRY MEN OF THE MOUNTAIN TRIBES! YOUR WEARY YEARS OF OPPRESSION AND HUMILIATION ARE NEAR THEIR END . . .
OUR DAY HAS COME . . .
FOR THE LORD OF OUR DREAMS AND THE KING OF ALL MISTS SPEAKS TO YOU THROUGH ME . . . AND DELIVERS US THESE LAWS . . .
LAWS WHICH ARE PROCLAIMED FOR ALL TO HEAR - - SO SPEAKS THE LORD OF THE LOCUSTS - -
LAW THE FIRST:
ALL THE VALLEYS AND ALL THE LANDS BETWEEN THE MOUNTAINS OF THE RISING SUN, AND THE MOUNTAINS OF THE SETTING SUN, BELONG NOW AND FOREVER TO THE PEOPLE OF THE HOLY HOUSE OF MISTS.
- - SO SAYETH THE LORD OF THE LOCUSTS - -

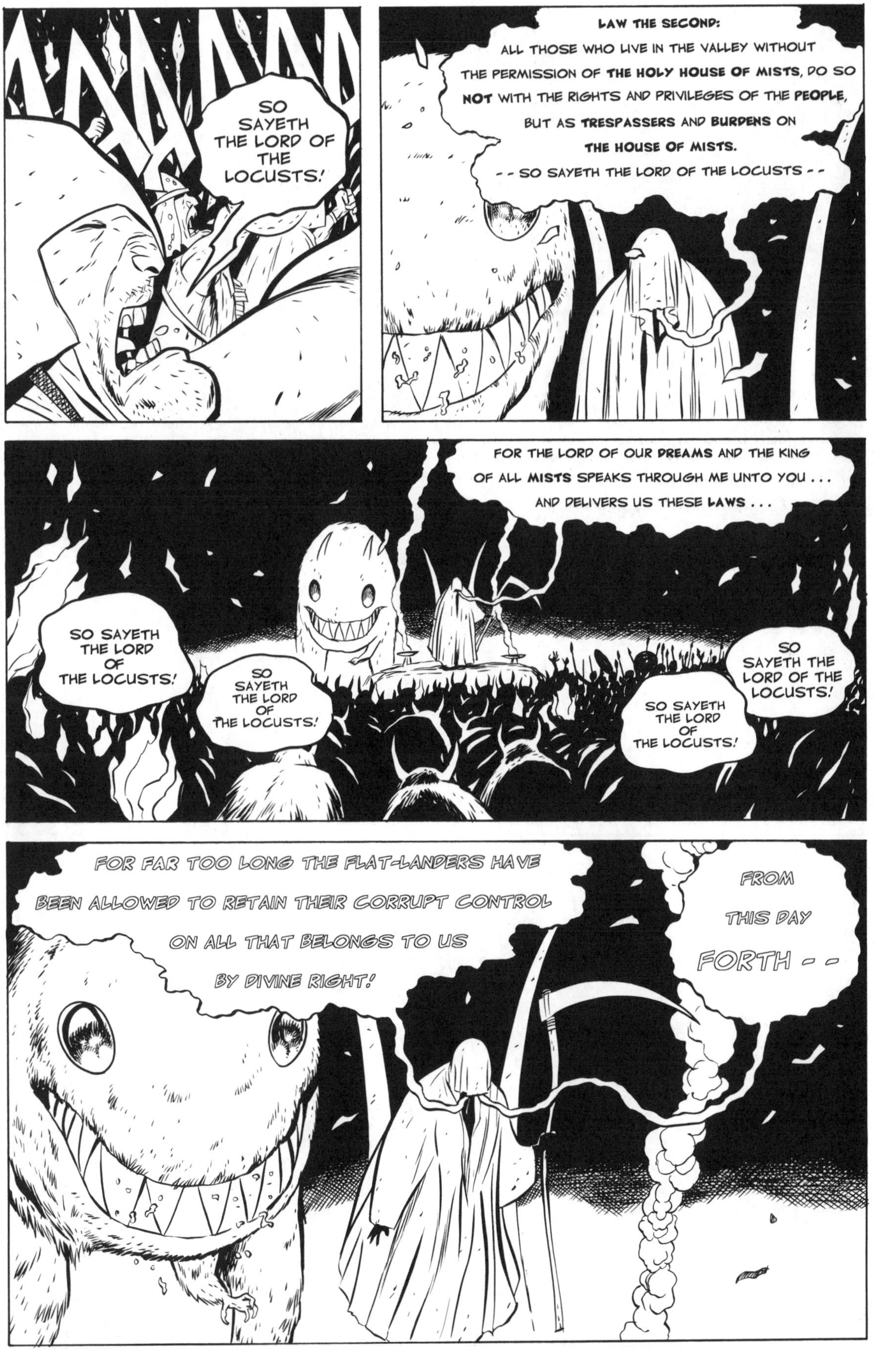
SO SAYETH THE LORD OF THE LOCUSTS!
LAW THE SECOND:
ALL THOSE WHO LIVE IN THE VALLEY WITHOUT THE PERMISSION OF THE HOLY HOUSE OF MISTS, DO SO NOT WITH THE RIGHTS AND PRIVILEGES OF THE PEOPLE, BUT AS TRESPASSERS AND BURDENS ON THE HOUSE OF MISTS.
- - SO SAYETH THE LORD OF THE LOCUSTS - -
FOR THE LORD OF OUR DREAMS AND THE KING OF ALL MISTS SPEAKS THROUGH ME UNTO YOU . . . AND DELIVERS US THESE LAWS . . .
SO SAYETH THE LORD OF THE LOCUSTS!
SO SAYETH THE LORD OF THE LOCUSTS!
SO SAYETH THE LORD OF THE LOCUSTS!
SO SAYETH THE LORD OF THE LOCUSTS!
FOR FAR TOO LONG THE FLAT-LANDERS HAVE BEEN ALLOWED TO RETAIN THEIR CORRUPT CONTROL ON ALL THAT BELONGS TO US BY DIVINE RIGHT!
FROM THIS DAY FORTH - -

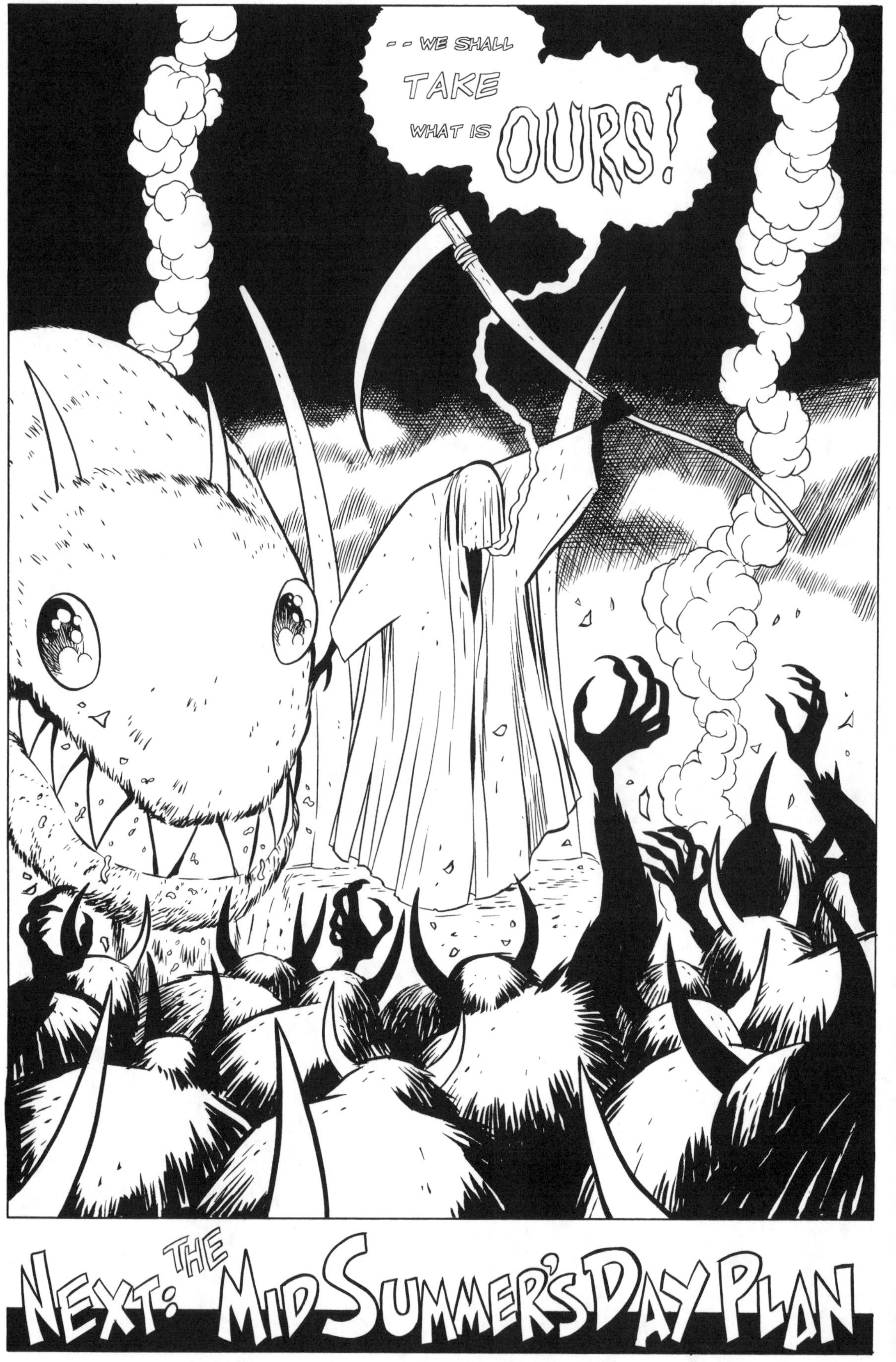
-- WE SHALL TAKE WHAT IS OURS!

NEXT: THE MID SUMMER'S DAY PLAN

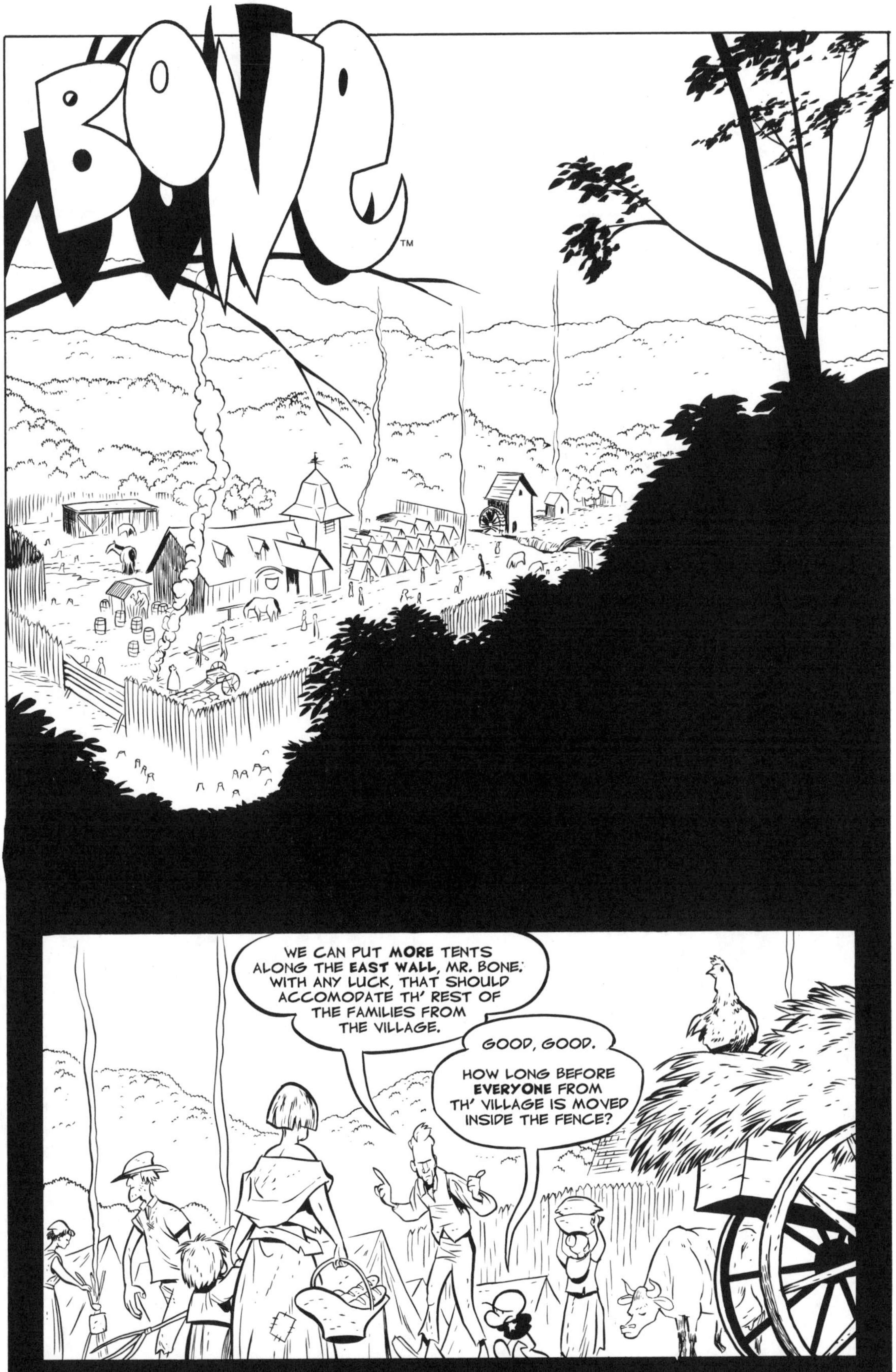
BONE™
WE CAN PUT MORE TENTS ALONG THE EAST WALL, MR. BONE. WITH ANY LUCK, THAT SHOULD ACCOMODATE TH' REST OF THE FAMILIES FROM THE VILLAGE.
GOOD, GOOD.
HOW LONG BEFORE EVERYONE FROM TH' VILLAGE IS MOVED INSIDE THE FENCE?

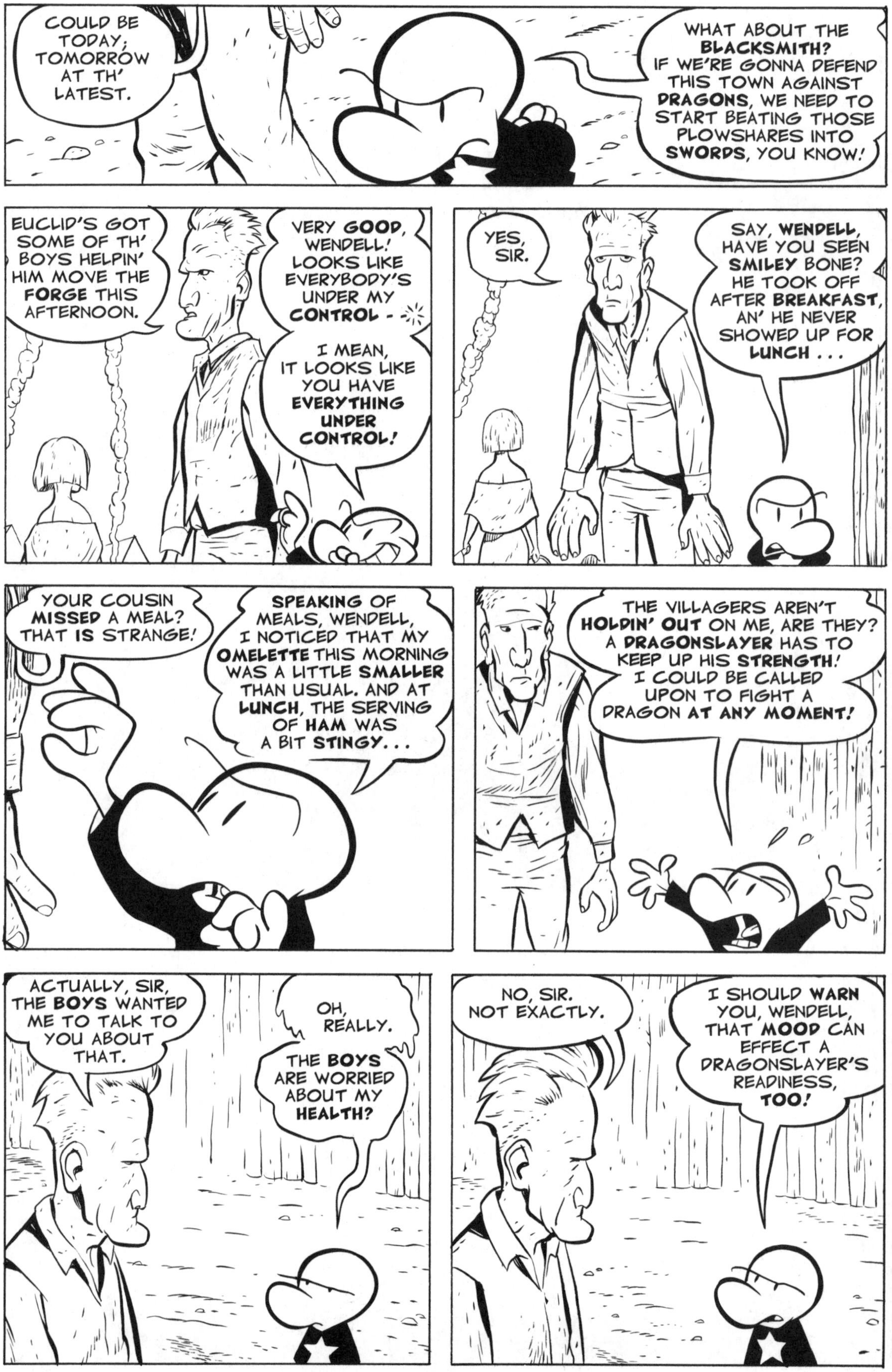
COULD BE TODAY, TOMORROW AT TH' LATEST.
WHAT ABOUT THE BLACKSMITH? IF WE'RE GONNA DEFEND THIS TOWN AGAINST DRAGONS, WE NEED TO START BEATING THOSE PLOWSHARES INTO SWORDS, YOU KNOW!
EUCLID'S GOT SOME OF TH' BOYS HELPIN' HIM MOVE THE FORGE THIS AFTERNOON.
VERY GOOD, WENDELL! LOOKS LIKE EVERYBODY'S UNDER MY CONTROL - -
I MEAN, IT LOOKS LIKE YOU HAVE EVERYTHING UNDER CONTROL!
YES, SIR.
SAY, WENDELL, HAVE YOU SEEN SMILEY BONE? HE TOOK OFF AFTER BREAKFAST, AN' HE NEVER SHOWED UP FOR LUNCH . . .
YOUR COUSIN MISSED A MEAL? THAT IS STRANGE!
SPEAKING OF MEALS, WENDELL, I NOTICED THAT MY OMELETTE THIS MORNING WAS A LITTLE SMALLER THAN USUAL. AND AT LUNCH, THE SERVING OF HAM WAS A BIT STINGY. . .
THE VILLAGERS AREN'T HOLDIN' OUT ON ME, ARE THEY? A DRAGONSLAYER HAS TO KEEP UP HIS STRENGTH! I COULD BE CALLED UPON TO FIGHT A DRAGON AT ANY MOMENT!
ACTUALLY, SIR, THE BOYS WANTED ME TO TALK TO YOU ABOUT THAT.
OH, REALLY.
THE BOYS ARE WORRIED ABOUT MY HEALTH?
NO, SIR. NOT EXACTLY.
I SHOULD WARN YOU, WENDELL, THAT MOOD CAN EFFECT A DRAGONSLAYER'S READINESS, TOO!

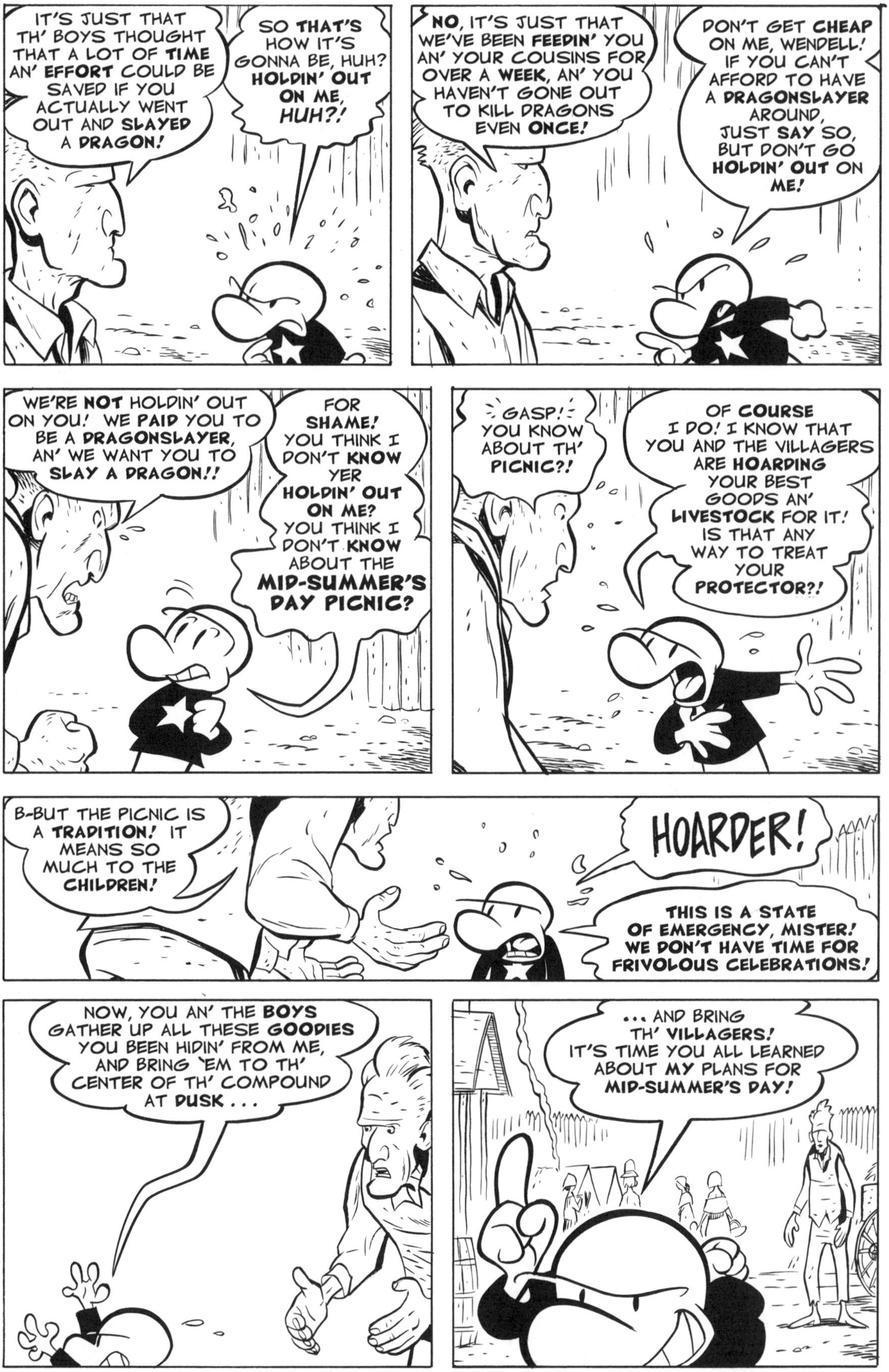
IT'S JUST THAT TH' BOYS THOUGHT THAT A LOT OF TIME AN' EFFORT COULD BE SAVED IF YOU ACTUALLY WENT OUT AND SLAYED A DRAGON!
SO THAT'S HOW IT'S GONNA BE, HUH? HOLDIN' OUT ON ME, HUH?!
NO, IT'S JUST THAT WE'VE BEEN FEEDIN' YOU AN' YOUR COUSINS FOR OVER A WEEK, AN' YOU HAVEN'T GONE OUT TO KILL DRAGONS EVEN ONCE!
DON'T GET CHEAP ON ME, WENDELL! IF YOU CAN'T AFFORD TO HAVE A DRAGONSLAYER AROUND, JUST SAY SO, BUT DON'T GO HOLDIN' OUT ON ME!
WE'RE NOT HOLDIN' OUT ON YOU! WE PAID YOU TO BE A DRAGONSLAYER, AN' WE WANT YOU TO SLAY A DRAGON!!
FOR SHAME! YOU THINK I DON'T KNOW YER HOLDIN' OUT ON ME? YOU THINK I DON'T KNOW ABOUT THE MID-SUMMER'S DAY PICNIC?
GASP! YOU KNOW ABOUT TH' PICNIC?!
OF COURSE I DO! I KNOW THAT YOU AND THE VILLAGERS ARE HOARDING YOUR BEST GOODS AN' LIVESTOCK FOR IT! IS THAT ANY WAY TO TREAT YOUR PROTECTOR?!
B-BUT THE PICNIC IS A TRADITION! IT MEANS SO MUCH TO THE CHILDREN!
HOARDER!
THIS IS A STATE OF EMERGENCY, MISTER! WE DON'T HAVE TIME FOR FRIVOLOUS CELEBRATIONS!
NOW, YOU AN' THE BOYS GATHER UP ALL THESE GOODIES YOU BEEN HIDIN' FROM ME, AND BRING 'EM TO TH' CENTER OF TH' COMPOUND AT DUSK . . .
. . . AND BRING TH' VILLAGERS! IT'S TIME YOU ALL LEARNED ABOUT MY PLANS FOR MID-SUMMER'S DAY!

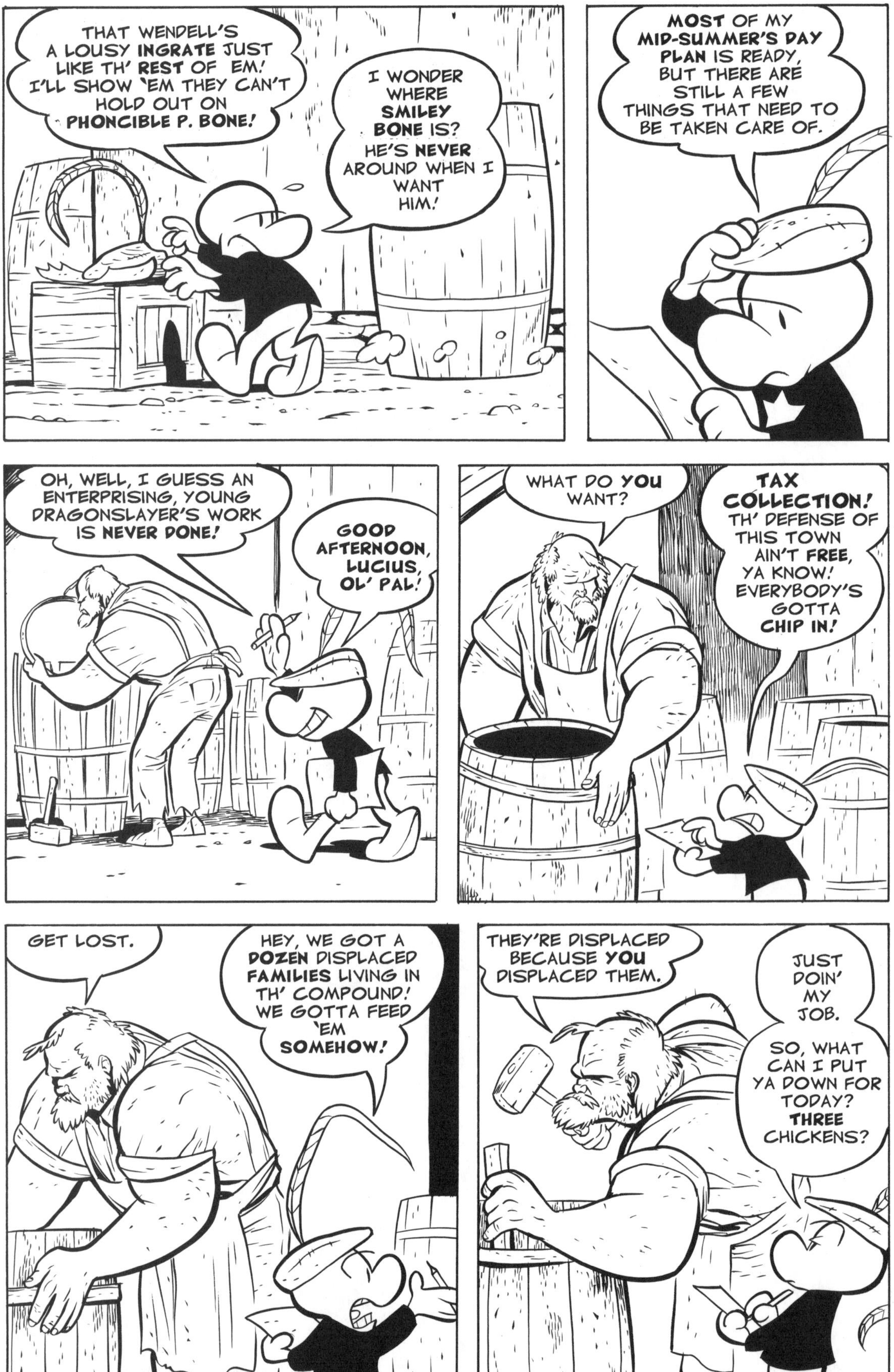
THAT WENDELL'S A LOUSY INGRATE JUST LIKE TH' REST OF 'EM! I'LL SHOW 'EM THEY CAN'T HOLD OUT ON PHONCIBLE P. BONE!
I WONDER WHERE SMILEY BONE IS? HE'S NEVER AROUND WHEN I WANT HIM!
MOST OF MY MID-SUMMER'S DAY PLAN IS READY, BUT THERE ARE STILL A FEW THINGS THAT NEED TO BE TAKEN CARE OF.
OH, WELL, I GUESS AN ENTERPRISING, YOUNG DRAGONSLAYER'S WORK IS NEVER DONE!
GOOD AFTERNOON, LUCIUS, OL' PAL!
WHAT DO YOU WANT?
TAX COLLECTION! TH' DEFENSE OF THIS TOWN AIN'T FREE, YA KNOW! EVERYBODY'S GOTTA CHIP IN!
GET LOST.
HEY, WE GOT A DOZEN DISPLACED FAMILIES LIVING IN TH' COMPOUND! WE GOTTA FEED 'EM SOMEHOW!
THEY'RE DISPLACED BECAUSE YOU DISPLACED THEM.
JUST DOIN' MY JOB.
SO, WHAT CAN I PUT YA DOWN FOR TODAY? THREE CHICKENS?

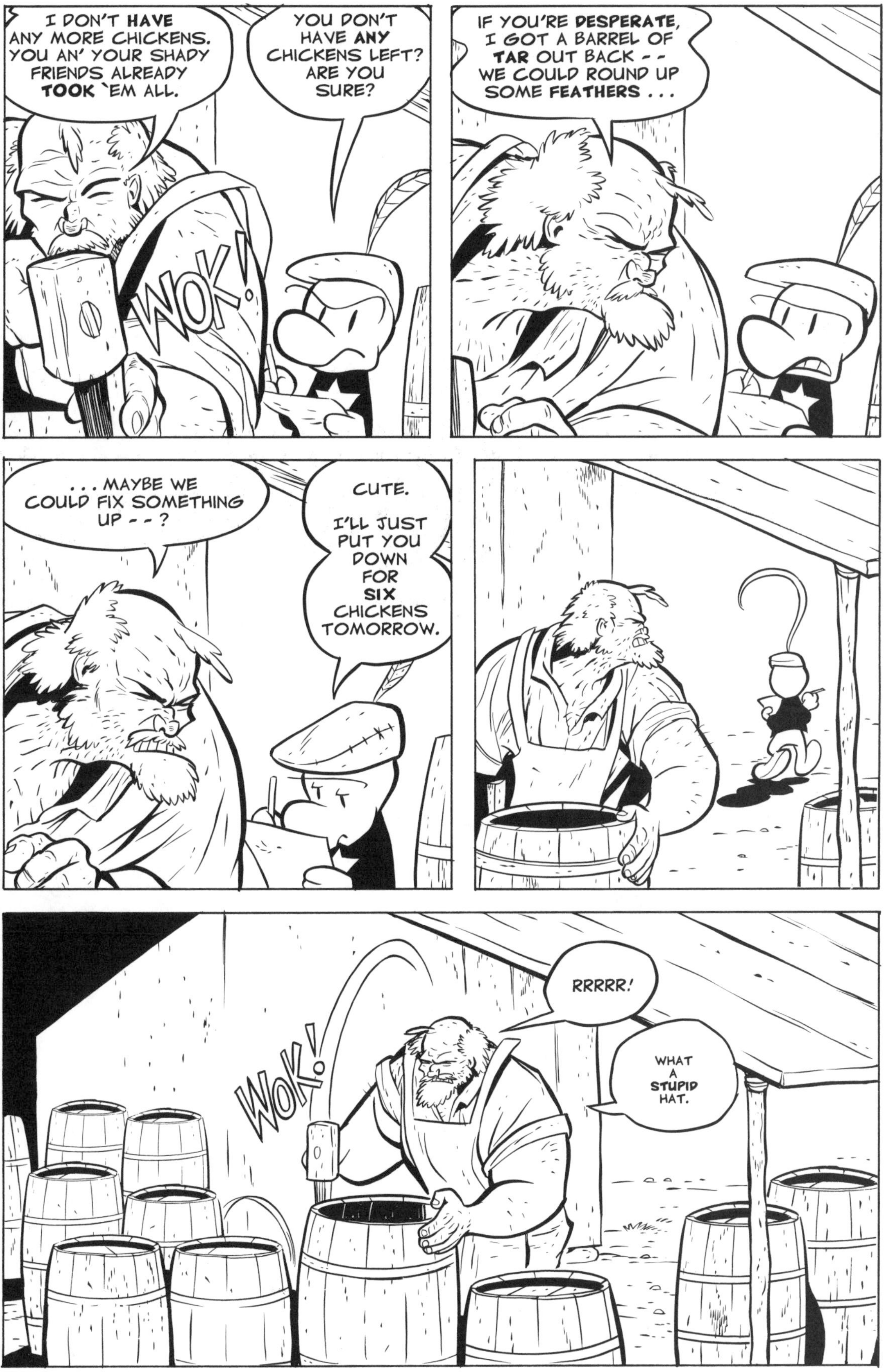

I DON'T HAVE ANY MORE CHICKENS. YOU AN' YOUR SHADY FRIENDS ALREADY TOOK `EM ALL.
WOK!
YOU DON'T HAVE ANY CHICKENS LEFT? ARE YOU SURE?
IF YOU'RE DESPERATE, I GOT A BARREL OF TAR OUT BACK - - WE COULD ROUND UP SOME FEATHERS . . .
. . . MAYBE WE COULD FIX SOMETHING UP - - ?
CUTE.
I'LL JUST PUT YOU DOWN FOR SIX CHICKENS TOMORROW.
RRRRR!
WHAT A STUPID HAT.
WOK!

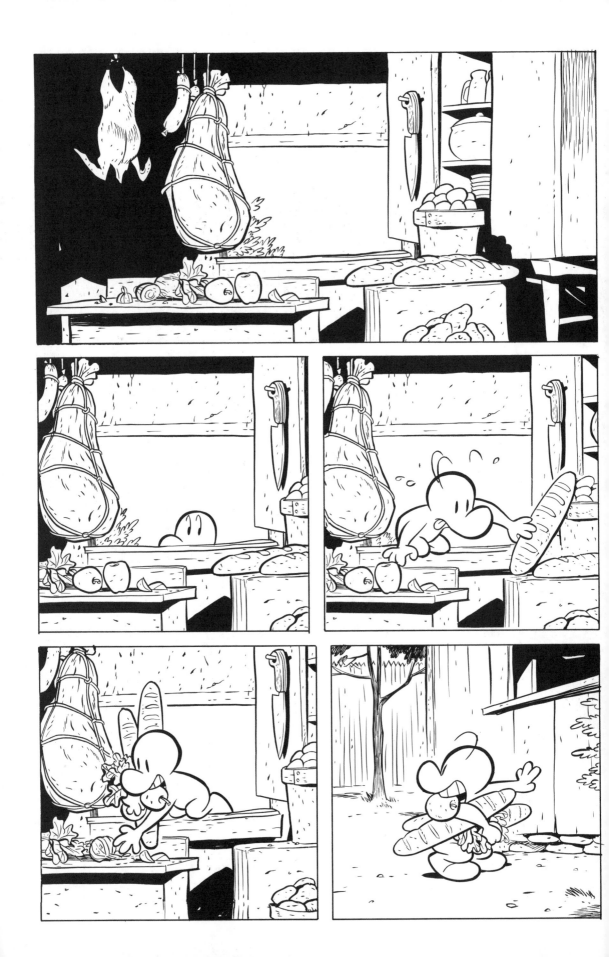

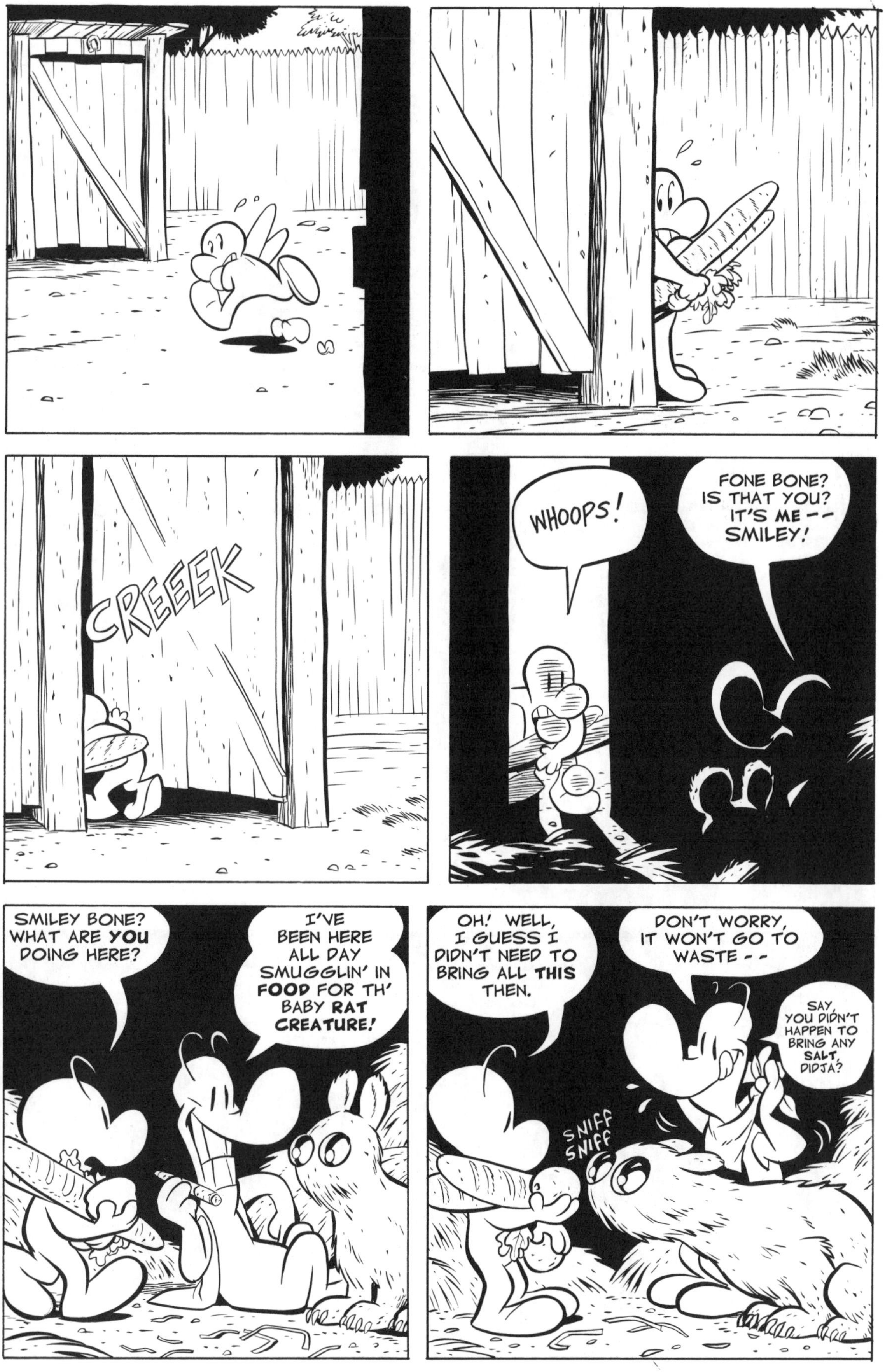
CREEEK
WHOOPS!
FONE BONE? IS THAT YOU? IT'S ME -- SMILEY!
SMILEY BONE? WHAT ARE YOU DOING HERE?
I'VE BEEN HERE ALL DAY SMUGGLIN' IN FOOD FOR TH' BABY RAT CREATURE!
OH! WELL, I GUESS I DIDN'T NEED TO BRING ALL THIS THEN.
DON'T WORRY, IT WON'T GO TO WASTE --
SAY, YOU DIDN'T HAPPEN TO BRING ANY SALT, DIDJA?
SNIFF SNIFF

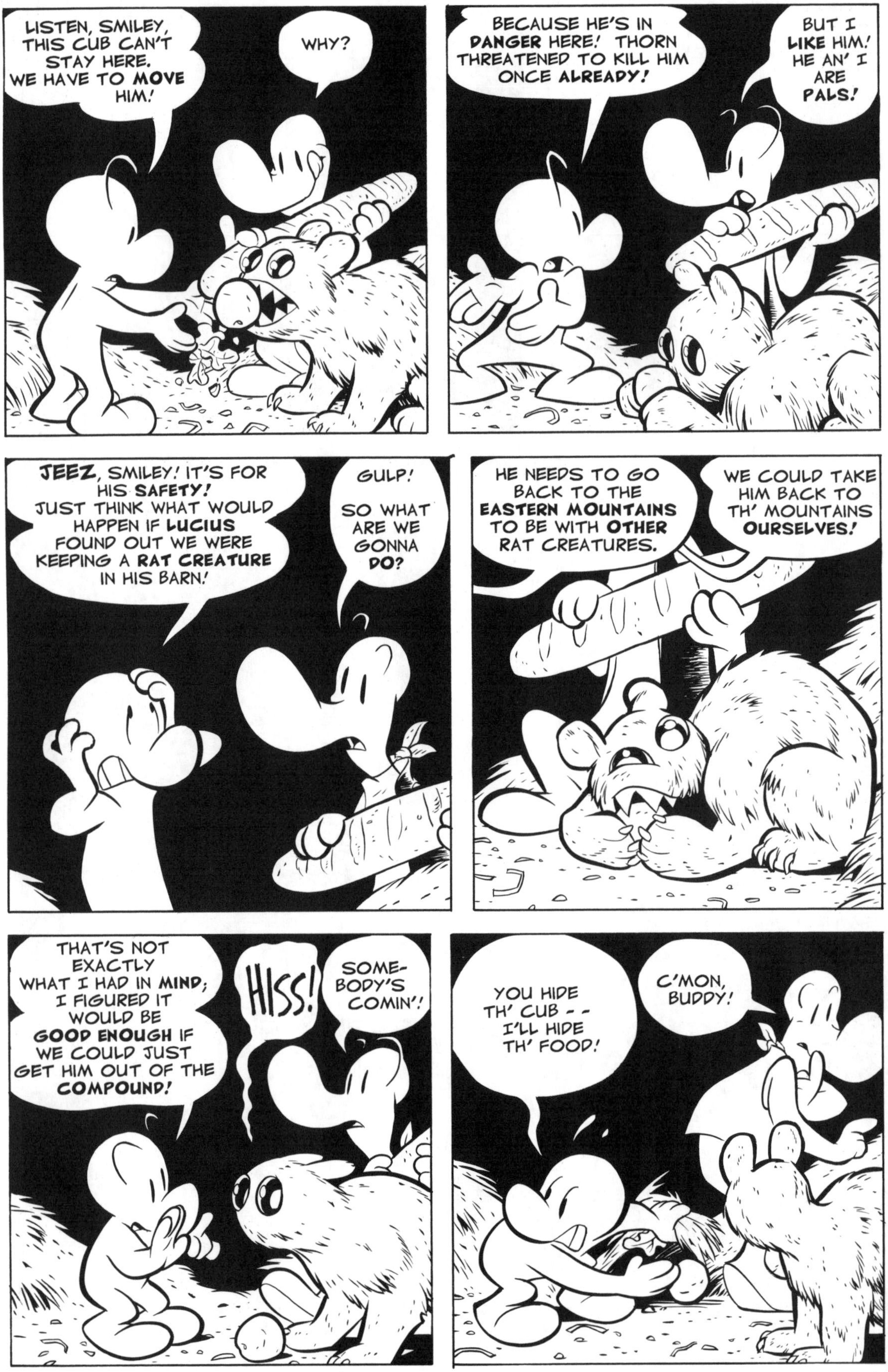
LISTEN, SMILEY, THIS CUB CAN'T STAY HERE. WE HAVE TO **MOVE** HIM!
WHY?
BECAUSE HE'S IN **DANGER** HERE! THORN THREATENED TO KILL HIM ONCE **ALREADY!**
BUT I **LIKE** HIM! HE AN' I ARE **PALS!**
JEEZ, SMILEY! IT'S FOR HIS **SAFETY!** JUST THINK WHAT WOULD HAPPEN IF **LUCIUS** FOUND OUT WE WERE KEEPING A **RAT CREATURE** IN HIS BARN!
GULP!
SO WHAT ARE WE GONNA **DO?**
HE NEEDS TO GO BACK TO THE **EASTERN MOUNTAINS** TO BE WITH **OTHER** RAT CREATURES.
WE COULD TAKE HIM BACK TO TH' MOUNTAINS **OURSELVES!**
THAT'S NOT EXACTLY WHAT I HAD IN **MIND**; I FIGURED IT WOULD BE **GOOD ENOUGH** IF WE COULD JUST GET HIM OUT OF THE **COMPOUND!**
HISS!
SOME-BODY'S COMIN'!
YOU HIDE TH' CUB - - I'LL HIDE TH' FOOD!
C'MON, BUDDY!

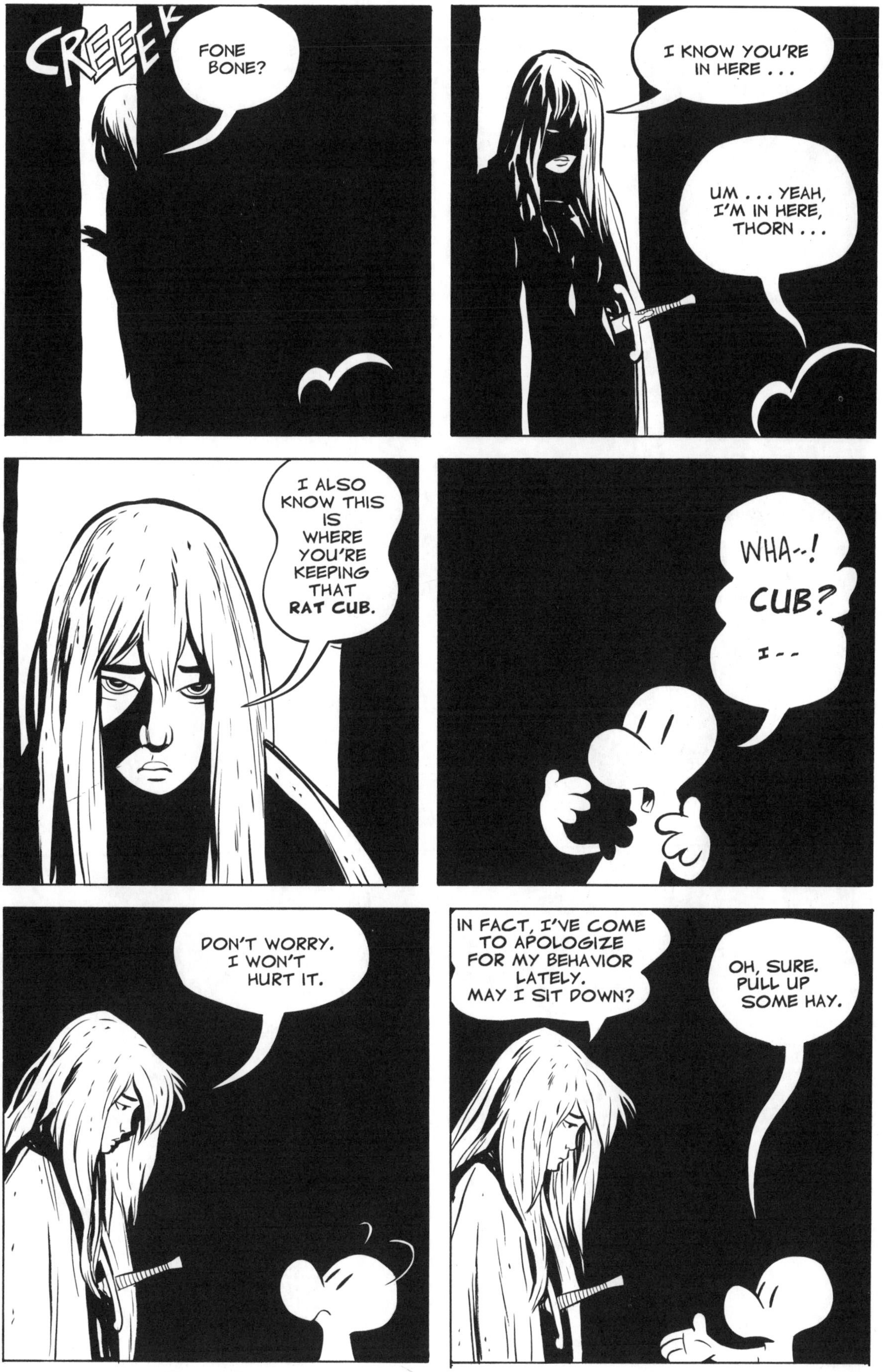
CREEEK
FONE BONE?
I KNOW YOU'RE IN HERE . . .
UM . . . YEAH, I'M IN HERE, THORN . . .
I ALSO KNOW THIS IS WHERE YOU'RE KEEPING THAT **RAT CUB.**
WHA--!
CUB?
I--
DON'T WORRY. I WON'T HURT IT.
IN FACT, I'VE COME TO APOLOGIZE FOR MY BEHAVIOR LATELY. MAY I SIT DOWN?
OH, SURE. PULL UP SOME HAY.

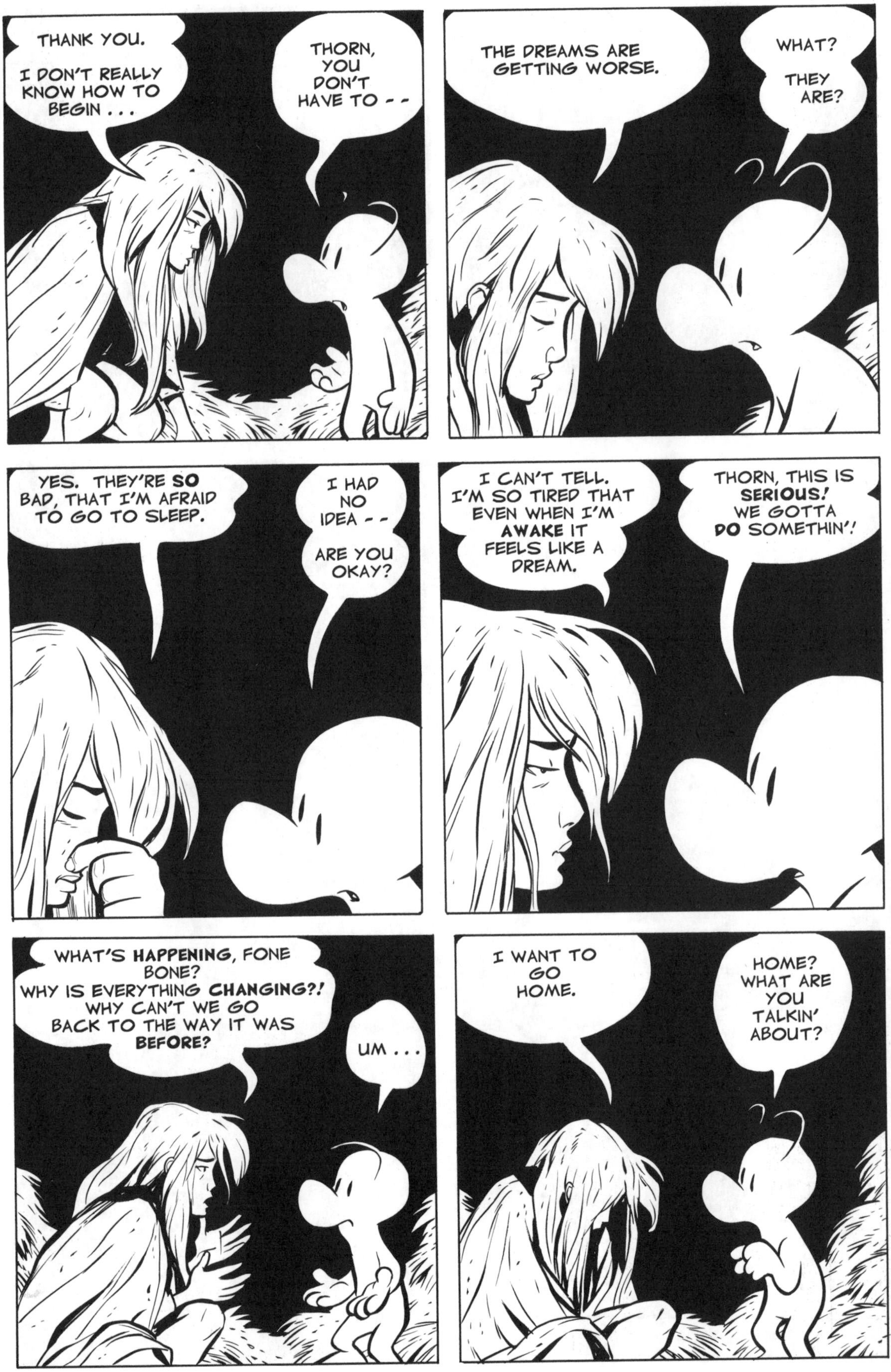
THANK YOU.
I DON'T REALLY KNOW HOW TO BEGIN . . .
THORN, YOU DON'T HAVE TO - -
THE DREAMS ARE GETTING WORSE.
WHAT?
THEY ARE?
YES. THEY'RE **SO** BAD, THAT I'M AFRAID TO GO TO SLEEP.
I HAD NO IDEA - -
ARE YOU OKAY?
I CAN'T TELL. I'M SO TIRED THAT EVEN WHEN I'M **AWAKE** IT FEELS LIKE A DREAM.
THORN, THIS IS **SERIOUS!** WE GOTTA **DO** SOMETHIN'!
WHAT'S **HAPPENING**, FONE BONE? WHY IS EVERYTHING **CHANGING?!** WHY CAN'T WE GO BACK TO THE WAY IT WAS **BEFORE?**
UM . . .
I WANT TO GO HOME.
HOME? WHAT ARE YOU TALKIN' ABOUT?

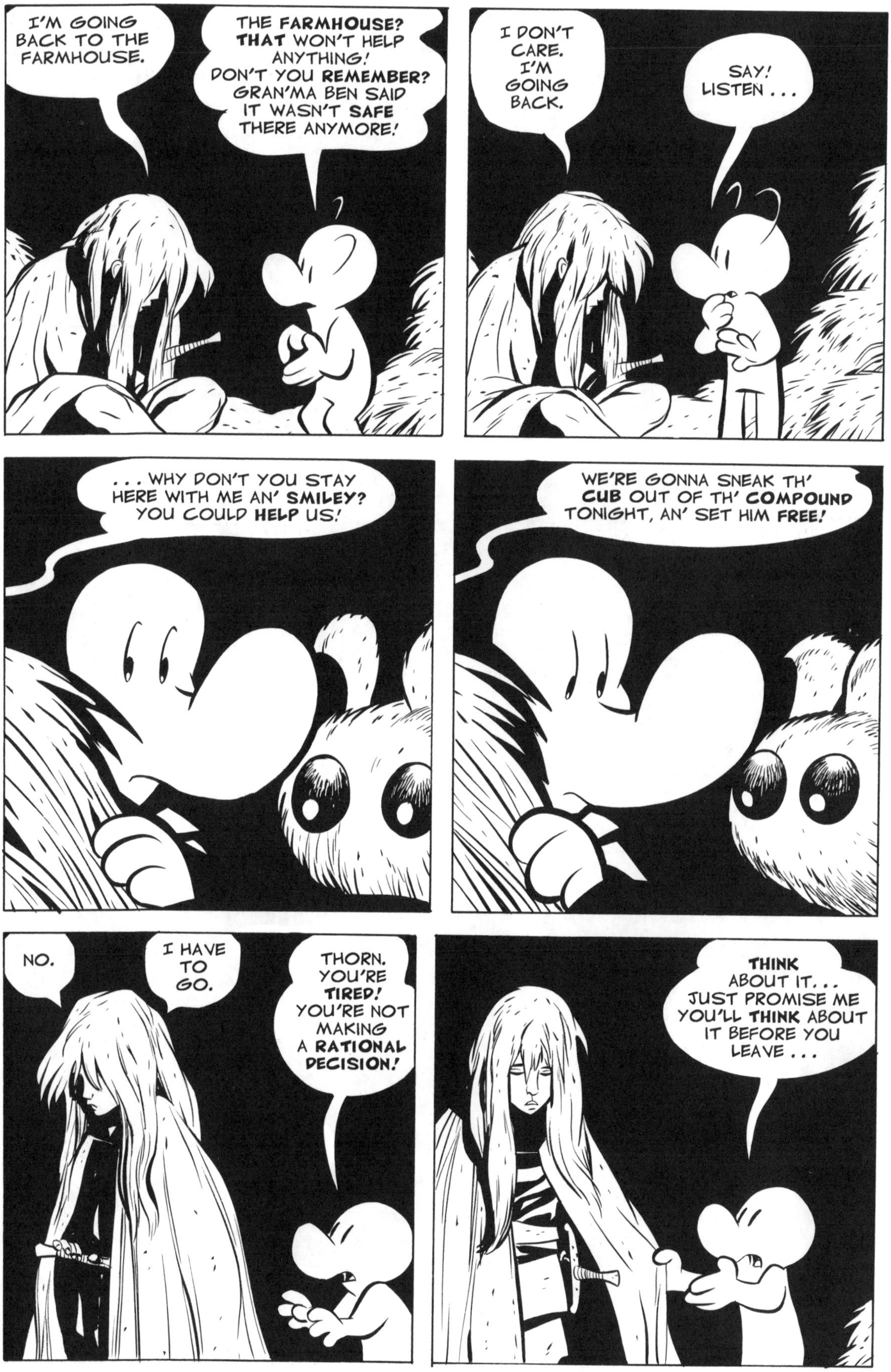
I'M GOING BACK TO THE FARMHOUSE.
THE FARMHOUSE? THAT WON'T HELP ANYTHING! DON'T YOU REMEMBER? GRAN'MA BEN SAID IT WASN'T SAFE THERE ANYMORE!
I DON'T CARE. I'M GOING BACK.
SAY! LISTEN . . .
. . . WHY DON'T YOU STAY HERE WITH ME AN' SMILEY? YOU COULD HELP US!
WE'RE GONNA SNEAK TH' CUB OUT OF TH' COMPOUND TONIGHT, AN' SET HIM FREE!
NO.
I HAVE TO GO.
THORN. YOU'RE TIRED! YOU'RE NOT MAKING A RATIONAL DECISION!
THINK ABOUT IT. . . JUST PROMISE ME YOU'LL THINK ABOUT IT BEFORE YOU LEAVE . . .

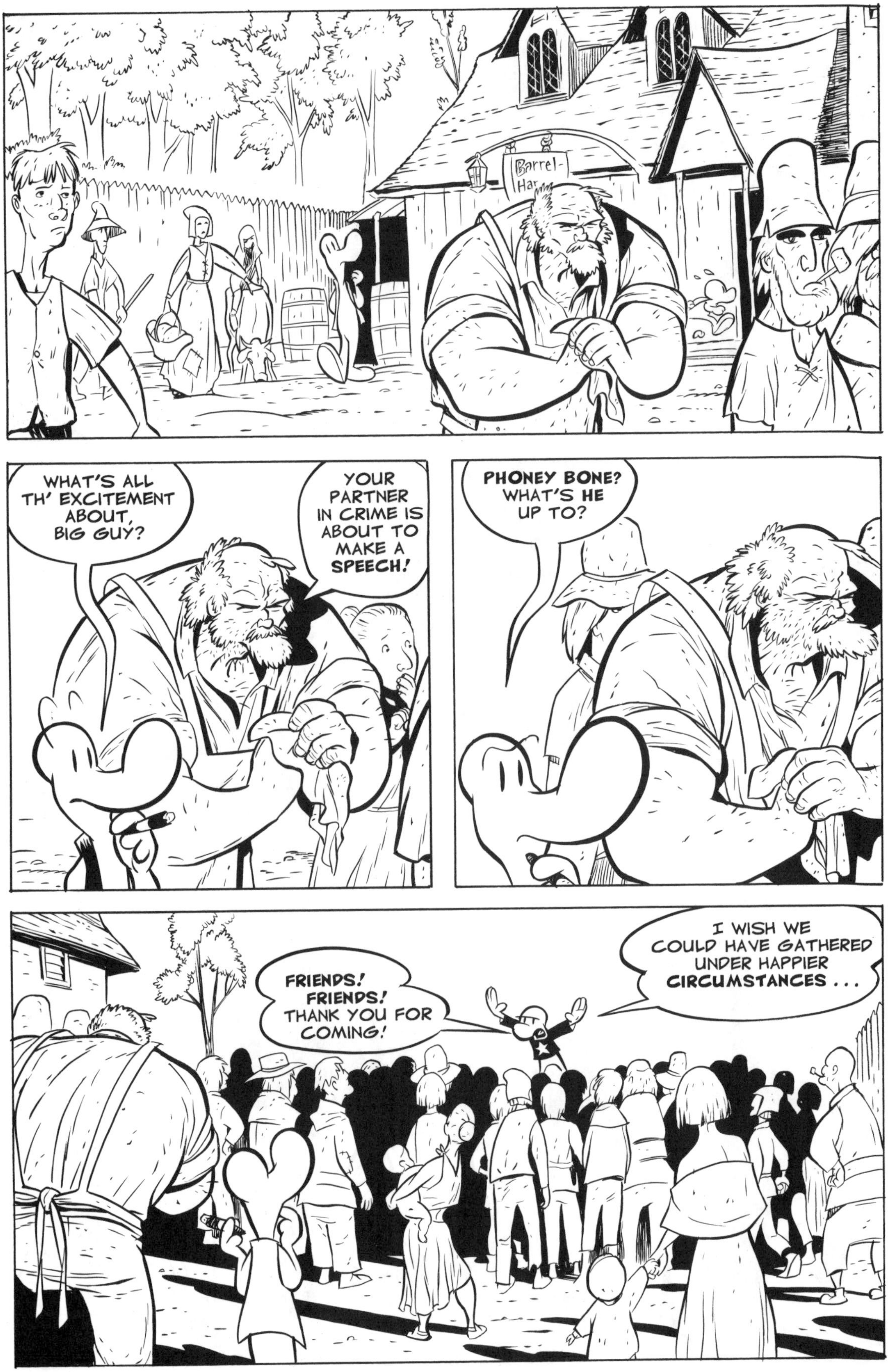
WHAT'S ALL TH' EXCITEMENT ABOUT, BIG GUY?
YOUR PARTNER IN CRIME IS ABOUT TO MAKE A **SPEECH!**
PHONEY BONE? WHAT'S **HE** UP TO?
FRIENDS! FRIENDS! THANK YOU FOR COMING!
I WISH WE COULD HAVE GATHERED UNDER HAPPIER **CIRCUMSTANCES . . .**

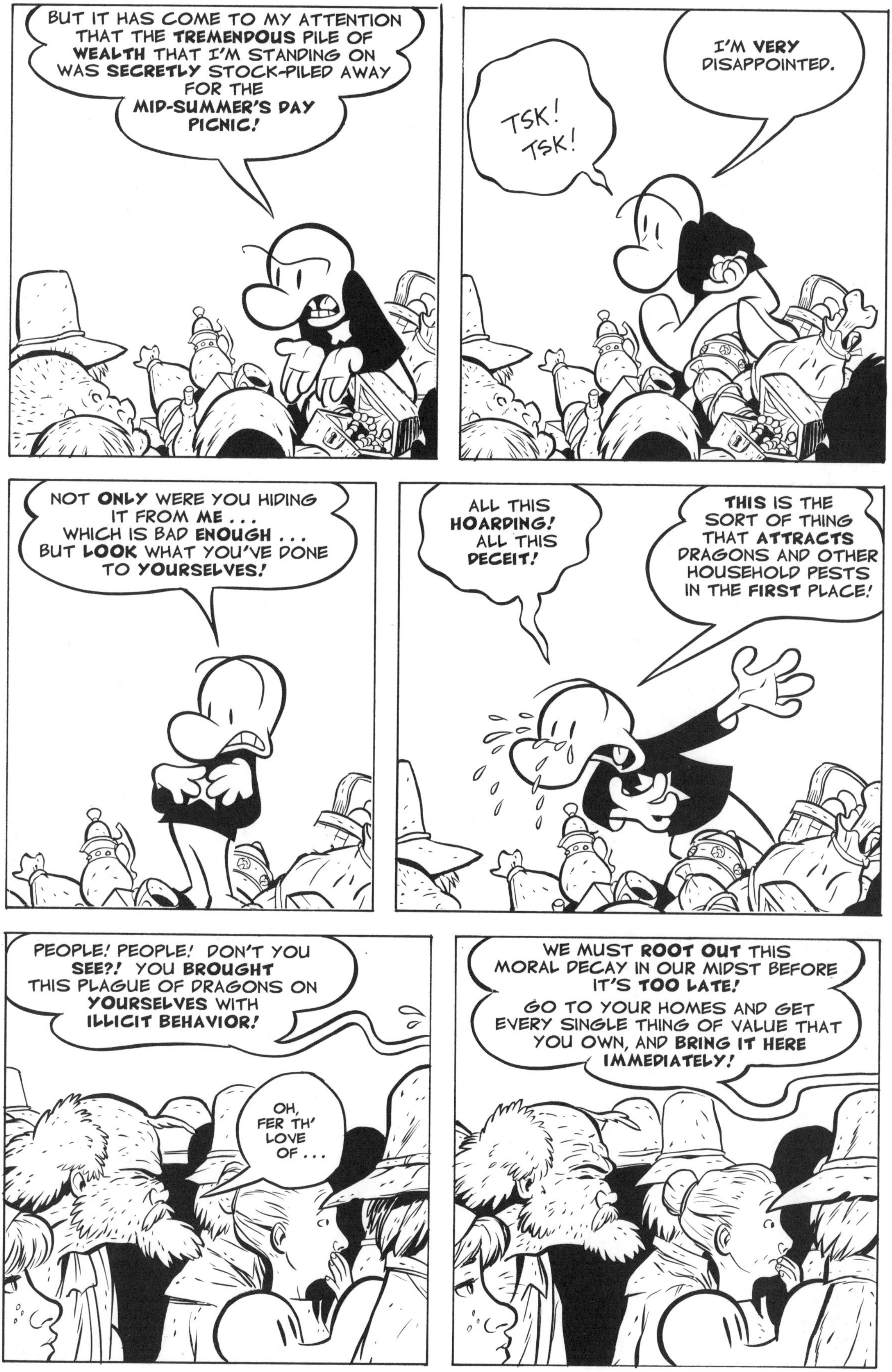
BUT IT HAS COME TO MY ATTENTION THAT THE TREMENDOUS PILE OF WEALTH THAT I'M STANDING ON WAS SECRETLY STOCK-PILED AWAY FOR THE MID-SUMMER'S DAY PICNIC!
TSK! TSK!
I'M VERY DISAPPOINTED.
NOT ONLY WERE YOU HIDING IT FROM ME ... WHICH IS BAD ENOUGH ... BUT LOOK WHAT YOU'VE DONE TO YOURSELVES!
ALL THIS HOARDING! ALL THIS DECEIT!
THIS IS THE SORT OF THING THAT ATTRACTS DRAGONS AND OTHER HOUSEHOLD PESTS IN THE FIRST PLACE!
PEOPLE! PEOPLE! DON'T YOU SEE?! YOU BROUGHT THIS PLAGUE OF DRAGONS ON YOURSELVES WITH ILLICIT BEHAVIOR!
OH, FER TH' LOVE OF ...
WE MUST ROOT OUT THIS MORAL DECAY IN OUR MIDST BEFORE IT'S TOO LATE!
GO TO YOUR HOMES AND GET EVERY SINGLE THING OF VALUE THAT YOU OWN, AND BRING IT HERE IMMEDIATELY!

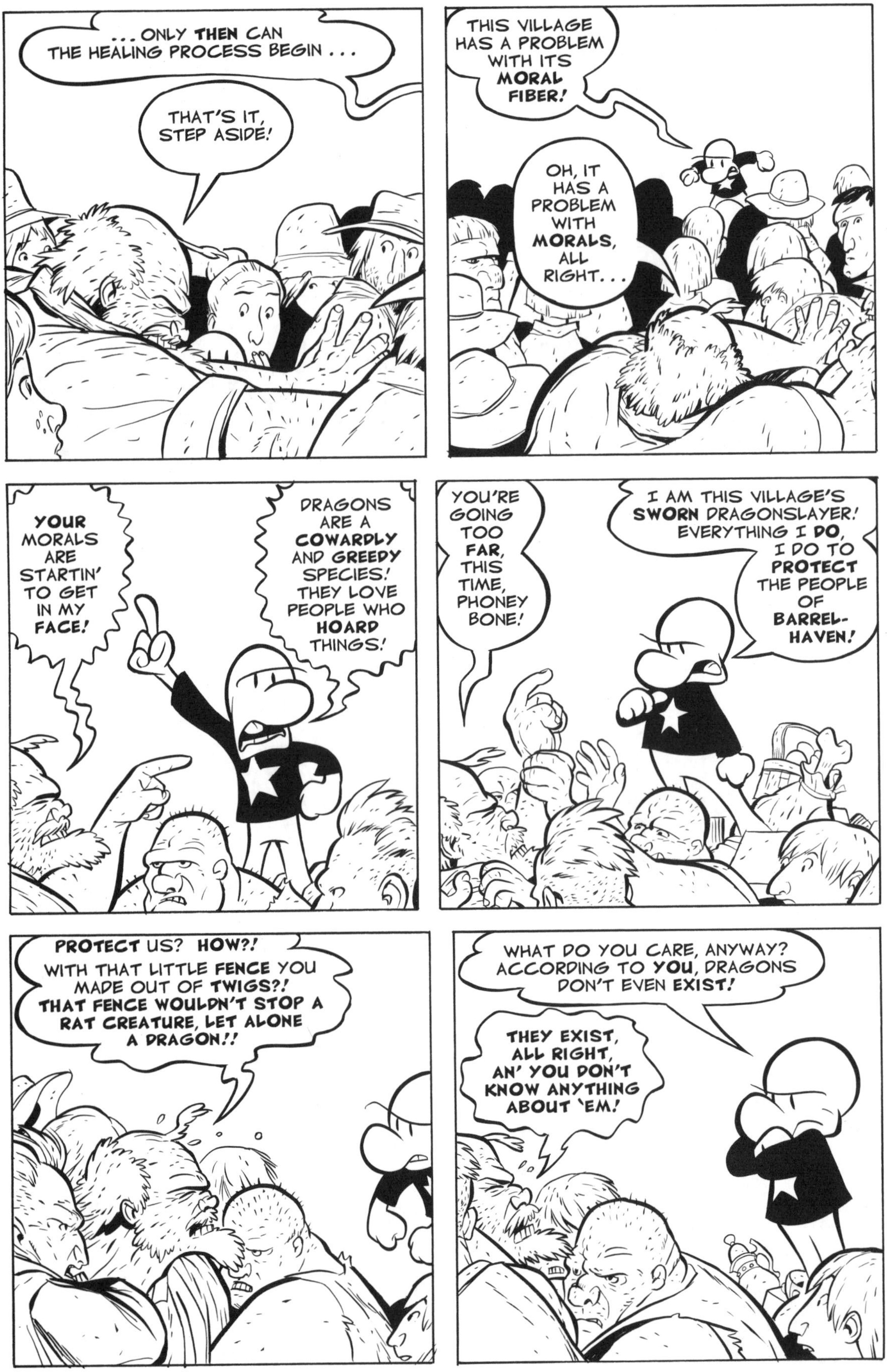
...ONLY THEN CAN THE HEALING PROCESS BEGIN...
THAT'S IT, STEP ASIDE!
THIS VILLAGE HAS A PROBLEM WITH ITS MORAL FIBER!
OH, IT HAS A PROBLEM WITH MORALS, ALL RIGHT...
DRAGONS ARE A COWARDLY AND GREEDY SPECIES! THEY LOVE PEOPLE WHO HOARD THINGS!
YOUR MORALS ARE STARTIN' TO GET IN MY FACE!
YOU'RE GOING TOO FAR, THIS TIME, PHONEY BONE!
I AM THIS VILLAGE'S SWORN DRAGONSLAYER! EVERYTHING I DO, I DO TO PROTECT THE PEOPLE OF BARREL-HAVEN!
PROTECT US? HOW?! WITH THAT LITTLE FENCE YOU MADE OUT OF TWIGS?! THAT FENCE WOULDN'T STOP A RAT CREATURE, LET ALONE A DRAGON!!
WHAT DO YOU CARE, ANYWAY? ACCORDING TO YOU, DRAGONS DON'T EVEN EXIST!
THEY EXIST, ALL RIGHT, AN' YOU DON'T KNOW ANYTHING ABOUT 'EM!

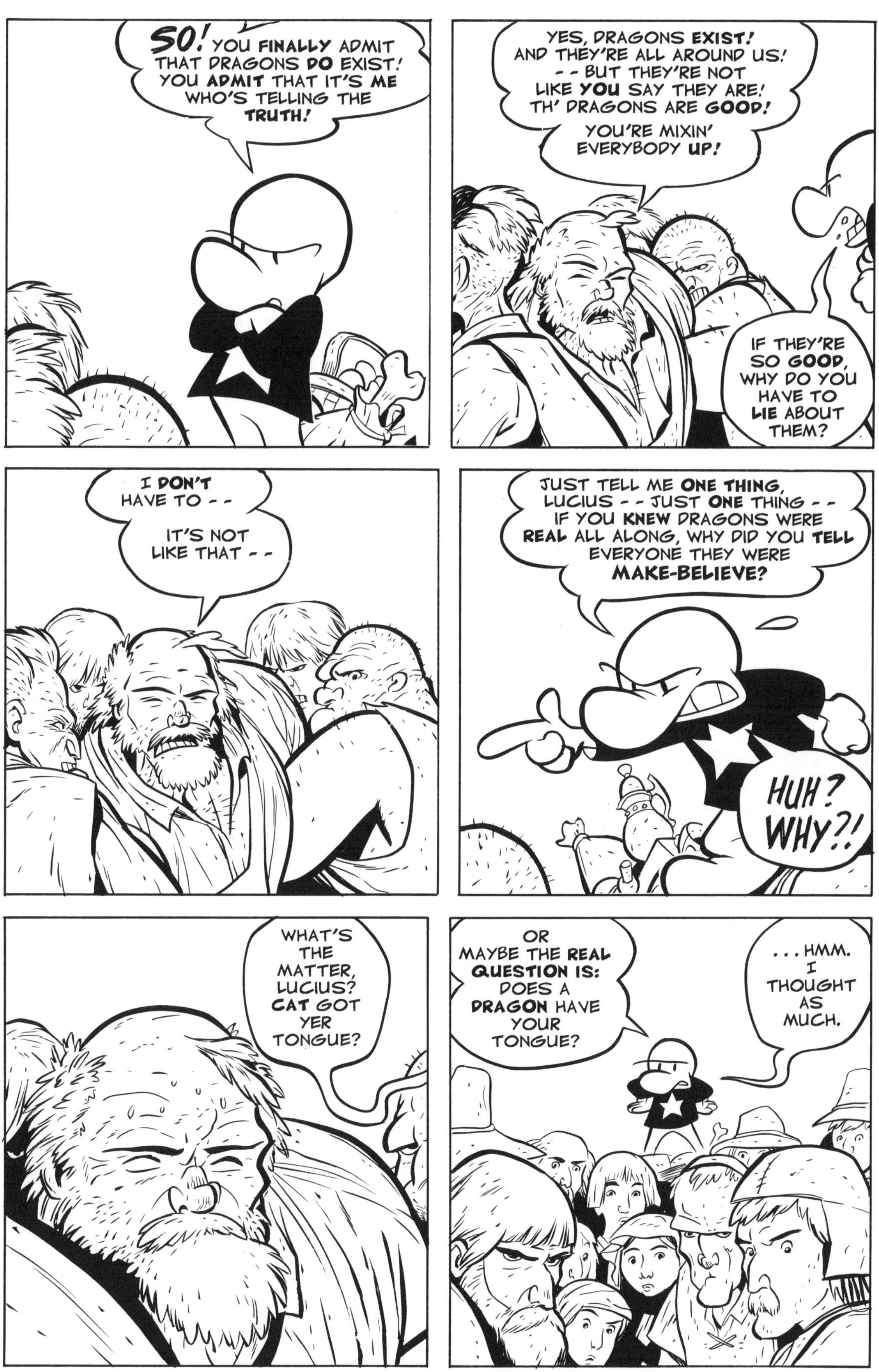

SO! YOU FINALLY ADMIT THAT DRAGONS DO EXIST! YOU ADMIT THAT IT'S ME WHO'S TELLING THE TRUTH!
YES, DRAGONS EXIST! AND THEY'RE ALL AROUND US! - - BUT THEY'RE NOT LIKE YOU SAY THEY ARE! TH' DRAGONS ARE GOOD!
YOU'RE MIXIN' EVERYBODY UP!
IF THEY'RE SO GOOD, WHY DO YOU HAVE TO LIE ABOUT THEM?
I DON'T HAVE TO - -
IT'S NOT LIKE THAT - -
JUST TELL ME ONE THING, LUCIUS - - JUST ONE THING - - IF YOU KNEW DRAGONS WERE REAL ALL ALONG, WHY DID YOU TELL EVERYONE THEY WERE MAKE-BELIEVE?
HUH? WHY?!
WHAT'S THE MATTER, LUCIUS? CAT GOT YER TONGUE?
OR MAYBE THE REAL QUESTION IS: DOES A DRAGON HAVE YOUR TONGUE?
. . . HMM. I THOUGHT AS MUCH.

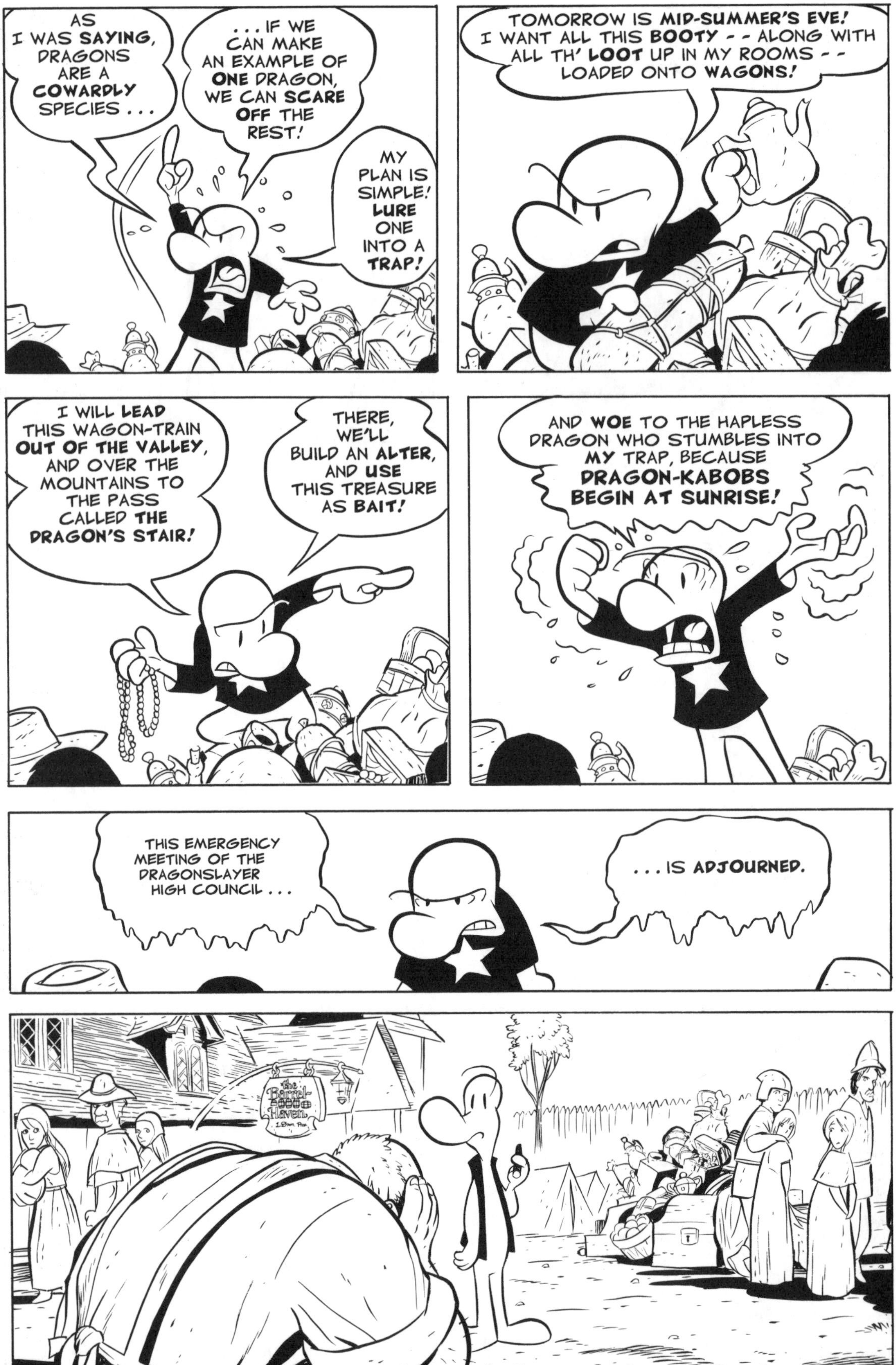
AS I WAS SAYING, DRAGONS ARE A COWARDLY SPECIES . . .
. . . IF WE CAN MAKE AN EXAMPLE OF ONE DRAGON, WE CAN SCARE OFF THE REST!
MY PLAN IS SIMPLE! LURE ONE INTO A TRAP!
TOMORROW IS MID-SUMMER'S EVE! I WANT ALL THIS BOOTY - - ALONG WITH ALL TH' LOOT UP IN MY ROOMS - - LOADED ONTO WAGONS!
I WILL LEAD THIS WAGON-TRAIN OUT OF THE VALLEY, AND OVER THE MOUNTAINS TO THE PASS CALLED THE DRAGON'S STAIR!
THERE, WE'LL BUILD AN ALTER, AND USE THIS TREASURE AS BAIT!
AND WOE TO THE HAPLESS DRAGON WHO STUMBLES INTO MY TRAP, BECAUSE DRAGON-KABOBS BEGIN AT SUNRISE!
THIS EMERGENCY MEETING OF THE DRAGONSLAYER HIGH COUNCIL . . .
. . . IS ADJOURNED.
the Barrel Haven

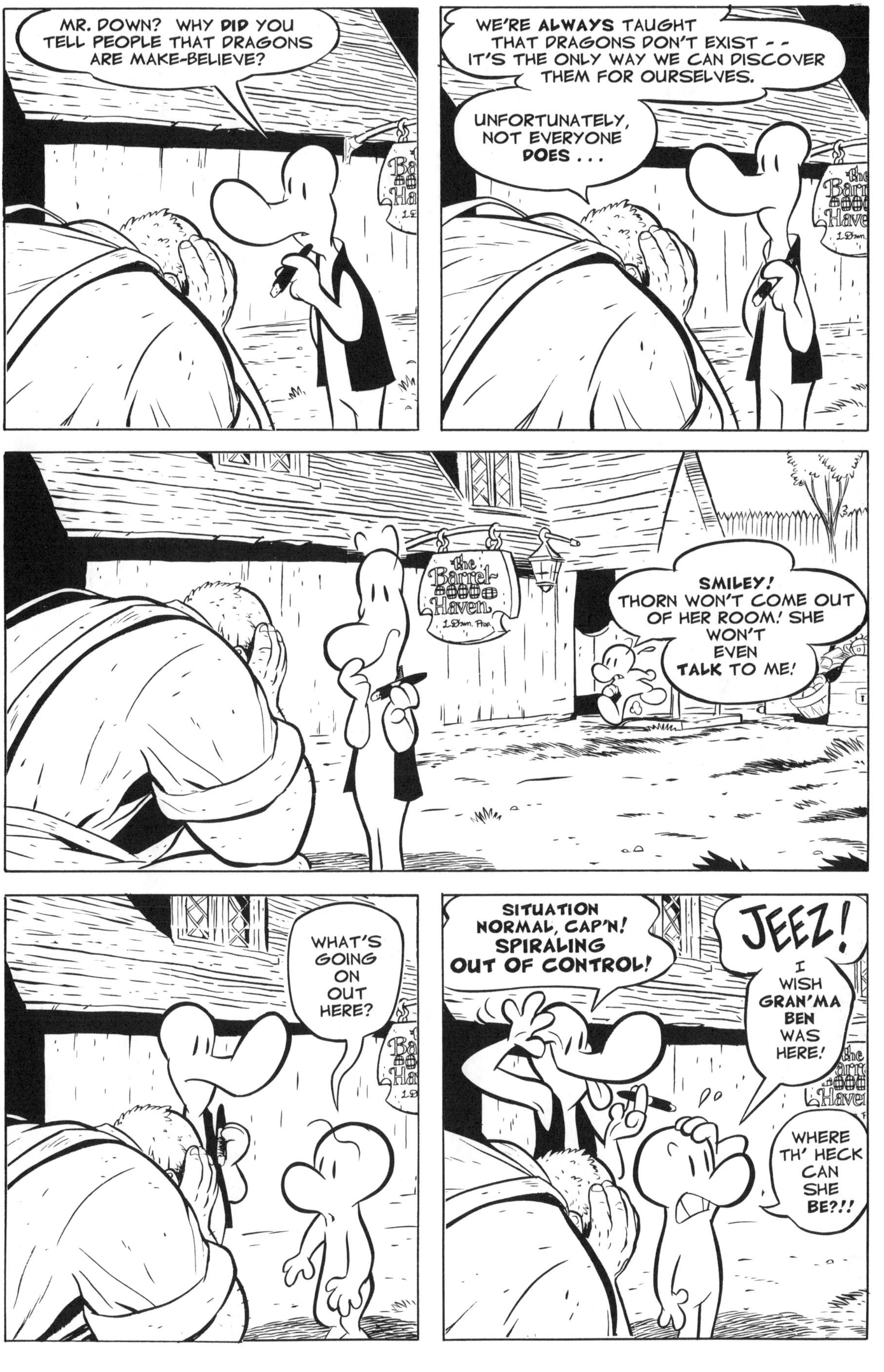
MR. DOWN? WHY DID YOU TELL PEOPLE THAT DRAGONS ARE MAKE-BELIEVE?
WE'RE ALWAYS TAUGHT THAT DRAGONS DON'T EXIST -- IT'S THE ONLY WAY WE CAN DISCOVER THEM FOR OURSELVES.
UNFORTUNATELY, NOT EVERYONE DOES . . .
SMILEY! THORN WON'T COME OUT OF HER ROOM! SHE WON'T EVEN TALK TO ME!
WHAT'S GOING ON OUT HERE?
SITUATION NORMAL, CAP'N! SPIRALING OUT OF CONTROL!
JEEZ! I WISH GRAN'MA BEN WAS HERE!
WHERE TH' HECK CAN SHE BE?!!

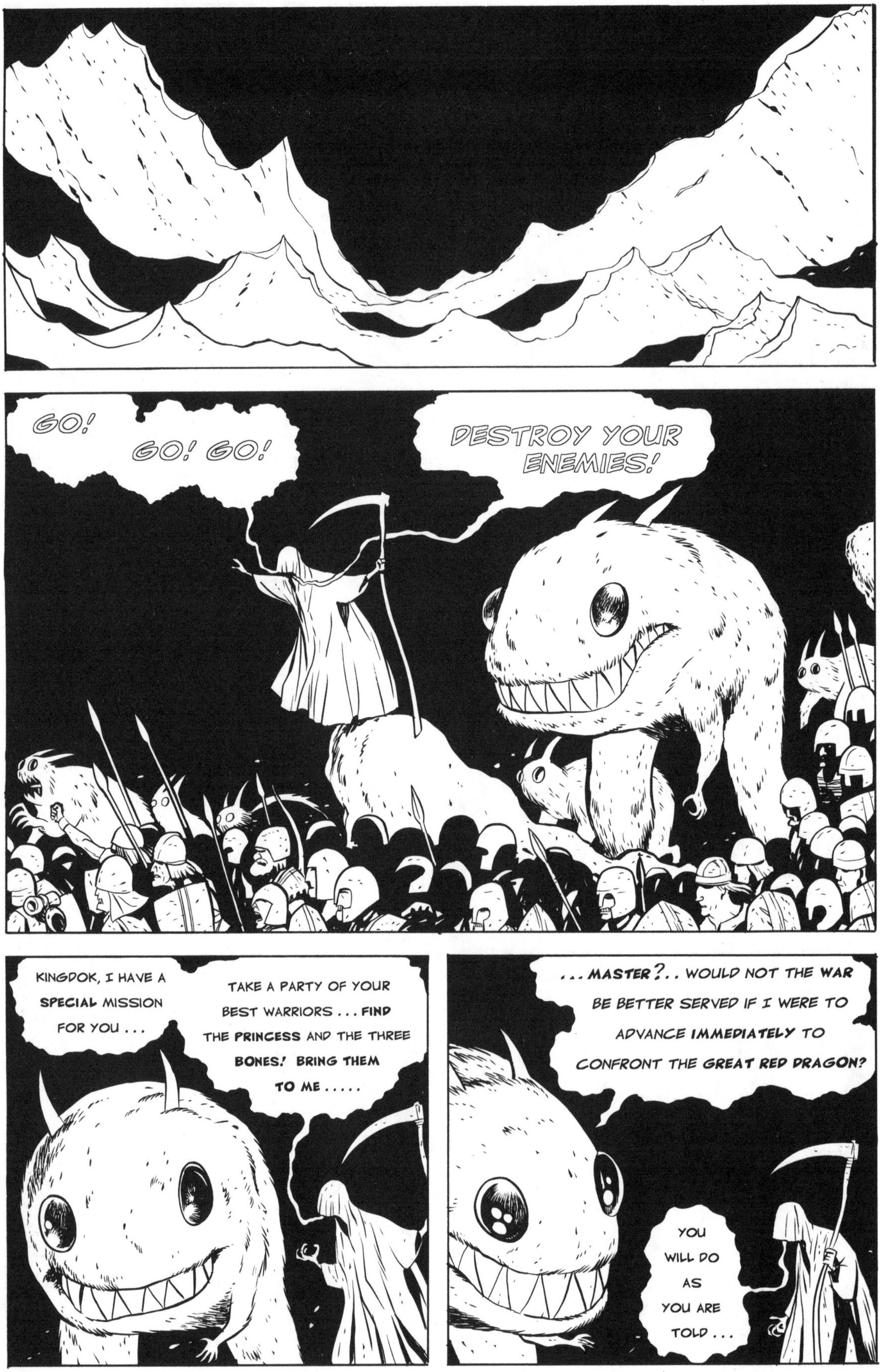
GO!
GO! GO!
DESTROY YOUR ENEMIES!
KINGDOK, I HAVE A SPECIAL MISSION FOR YOU . . .
TAKE A PARTY OF YOUR BEST WARRIORS . . . FIND THE PRINCESS AND THE THREE BONES! BRING THEM TO ME . . . . .
. . . MASTER? . . WOULD NOT THE WAR BE BETTER SERVED IF I WERE TO ADVANCE IMMEDIATELY TO CONFRONT THE GREAT RED DRAGON?
YOU WILL DO AS YOU ARE TOLD . . .

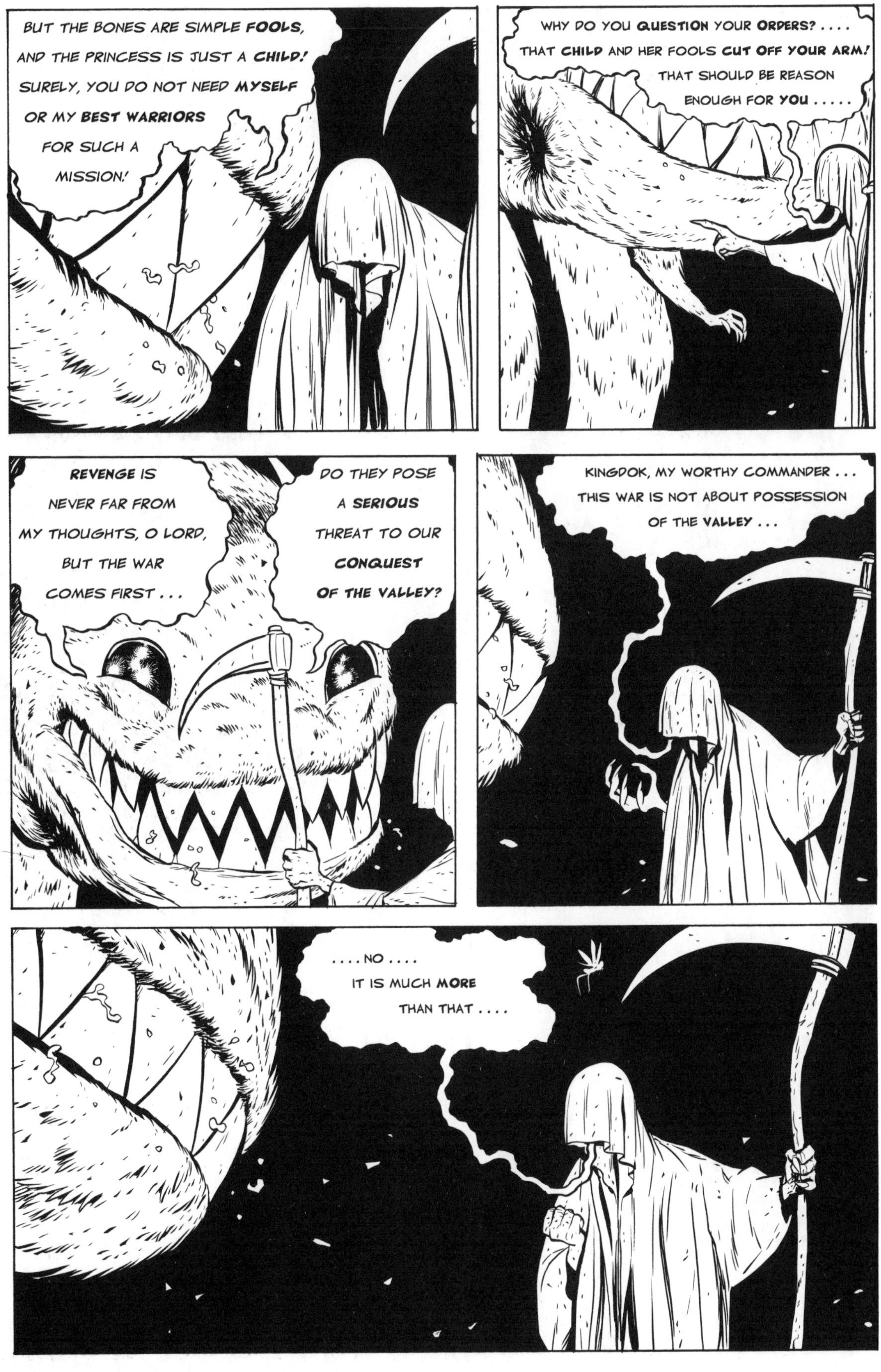
BUT THE BONES ARE SIMPLE FOOLS, AND THE PRINCESS IS JUST A CHILD! SURELY, YOU DO NOT NEED MYSELF OR MY BEST WARRIORS FOR SUCH A MISSION!
WHY DO YOU QUESTION YOUR ORDERS? . . . . THAT CHILD AND HER FOOLS CUT OFF YOUR ARM! THAT SHOULD BE REASON ENOUGH FOR YOU . . . . .
REVENGE IS NEVER FAR FROM MY THOUGHTS, O LORD, BUT THE WAR COMES FIRST . . .
DO THEY POSE A SERIOUS THREAT TO OUR CONQUEST OF THE VALLEY?
KINGDOK, MY WORTHY COMMANDER . . . THIS WAR IS NOT ABOUT POSSESSION OF THE VALLEY . . .
. . . . NO . . . . IT IS MUCH MORE THAN THAT . . . .

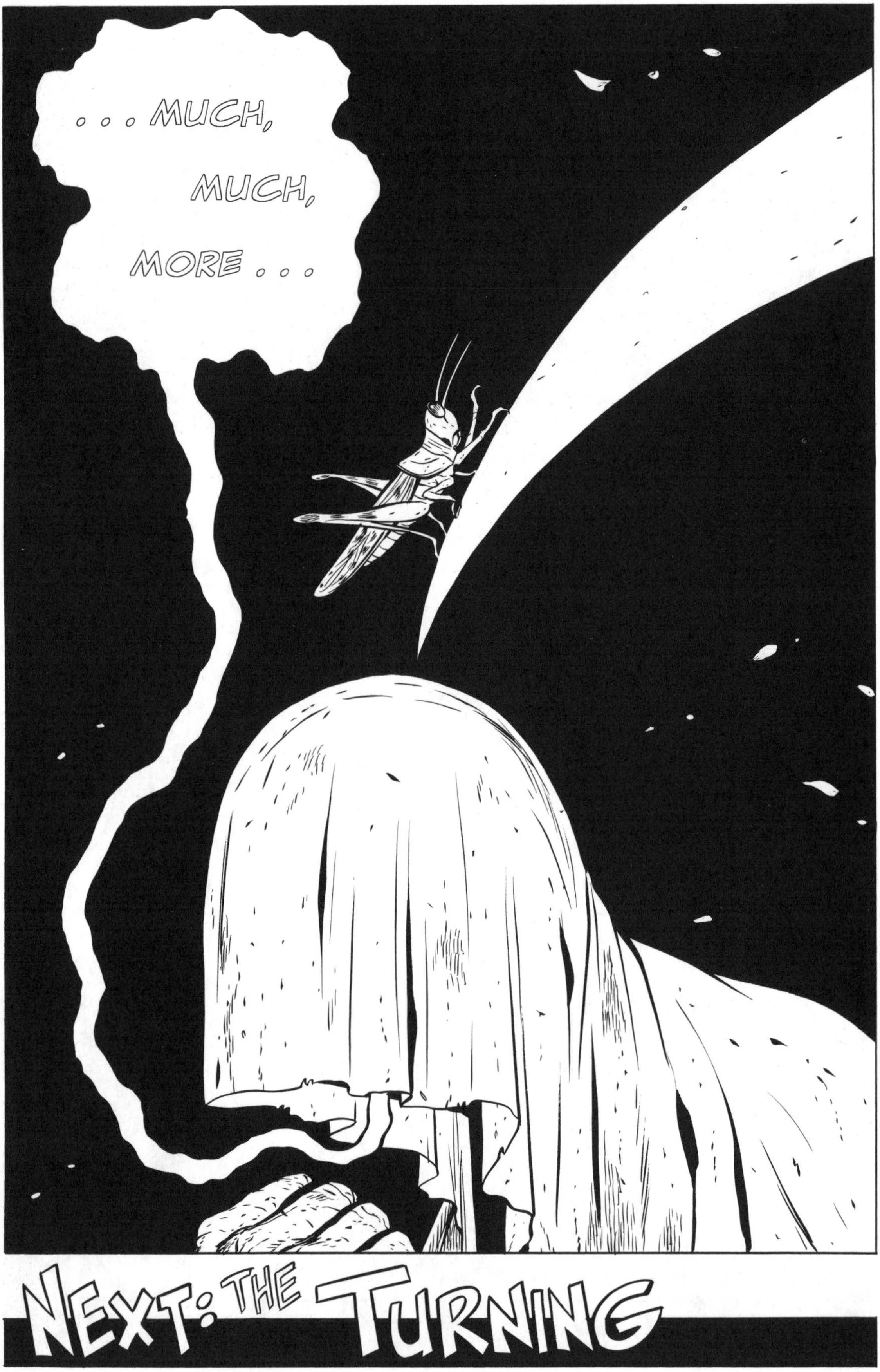
. . . MUCH,
MUCH,
MORE . . .

NEXT: THE TURNING

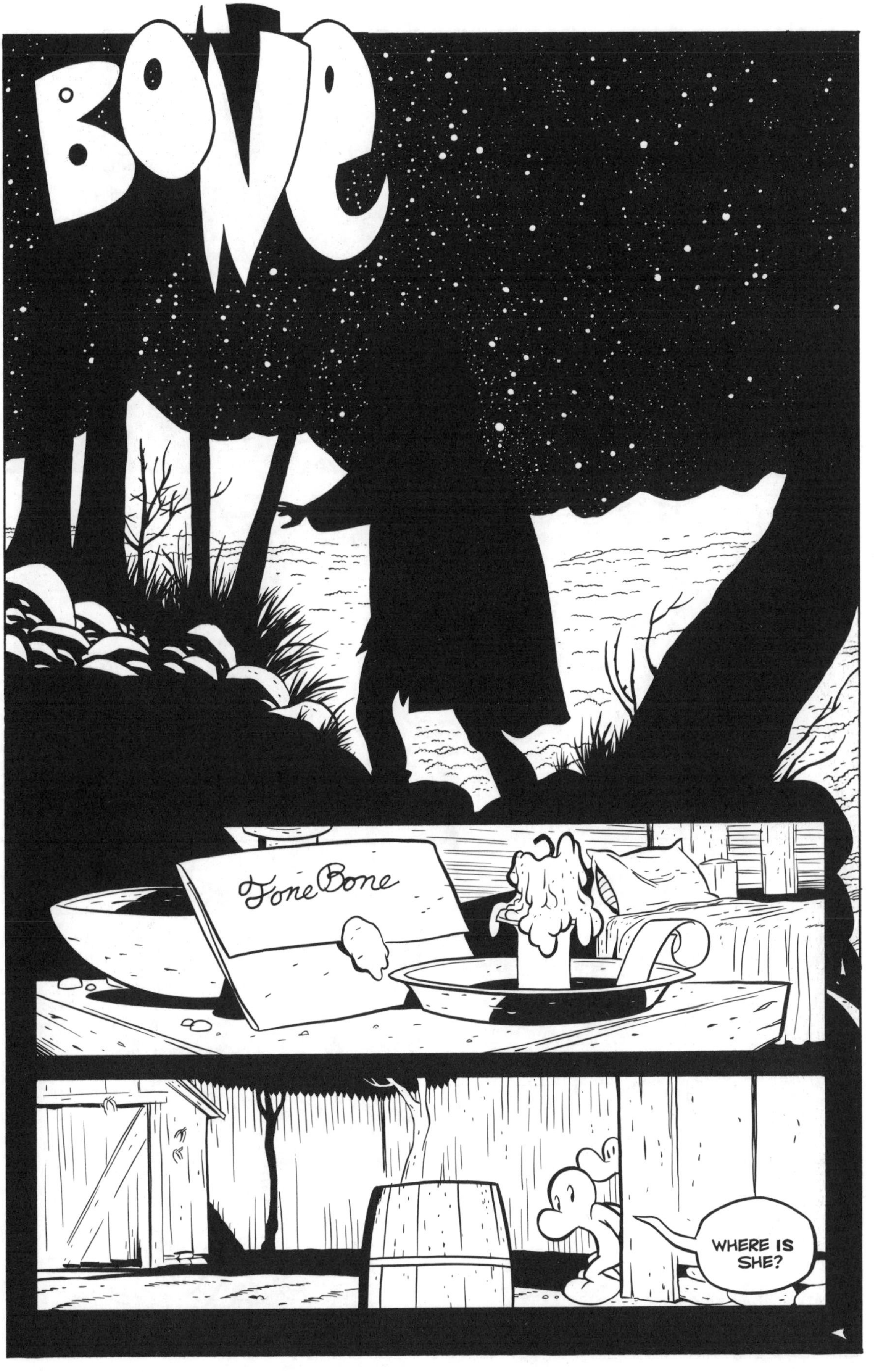
BONE
Fone Bone
WHERE IS SHE?

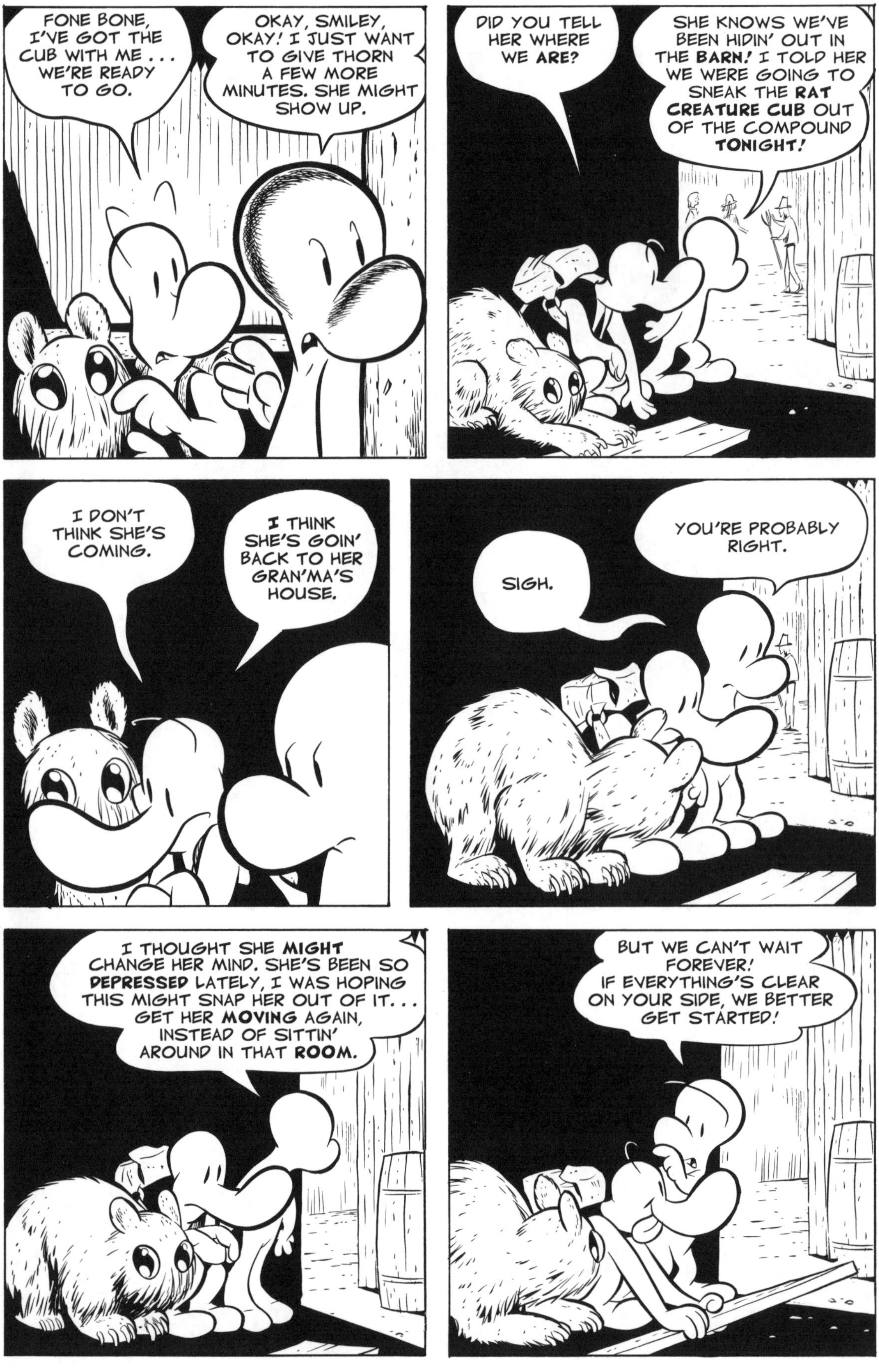
FONE BONE, I'VE GOT THE CUB WITH ME . . . WE'RE READY TO GO.
OKAY, SMILEY, OKAY! I JUST WANT TO GIVE THORN A FEW MORE MINUTES. SHE MIGHT SHOW UP.
DID YOU TELL HER WHERE WE **ARE**?
SHE KNOWS WE'VE BEEN HIDIN' OUT IN THE **BARN**! I TOLD HER WE WERE GOING TO SNEAK THE **RAT CREATURE CUB** OUT OF THE COMPOUND **TONIGHT**!
I DON'T THINK SHE'S COMING.
I THINK SHE'S GOIN' BACK TO HER GRAN'MA'S HOUSE.
SIGH.
YOU'RE PROBABLY RIGHT.
I THOUGHT SHE **MIGHT** CHANGE HER MIND. SHE'S BEEN SO **DEPRESSED** LATELY, I WAS HOPING THIS MIGHT SNAP HER OUT OF IT. . . GET HER **MOVING** AGAIN, INSTEAD OF SITTIN' AROUND IN THAT **ROOM**.
BUT WE CAN'T WAIT FOREVER! IF EVERYTHING'S CLEAR ON YOUR SIDE, WE BETTER GET STARTED!

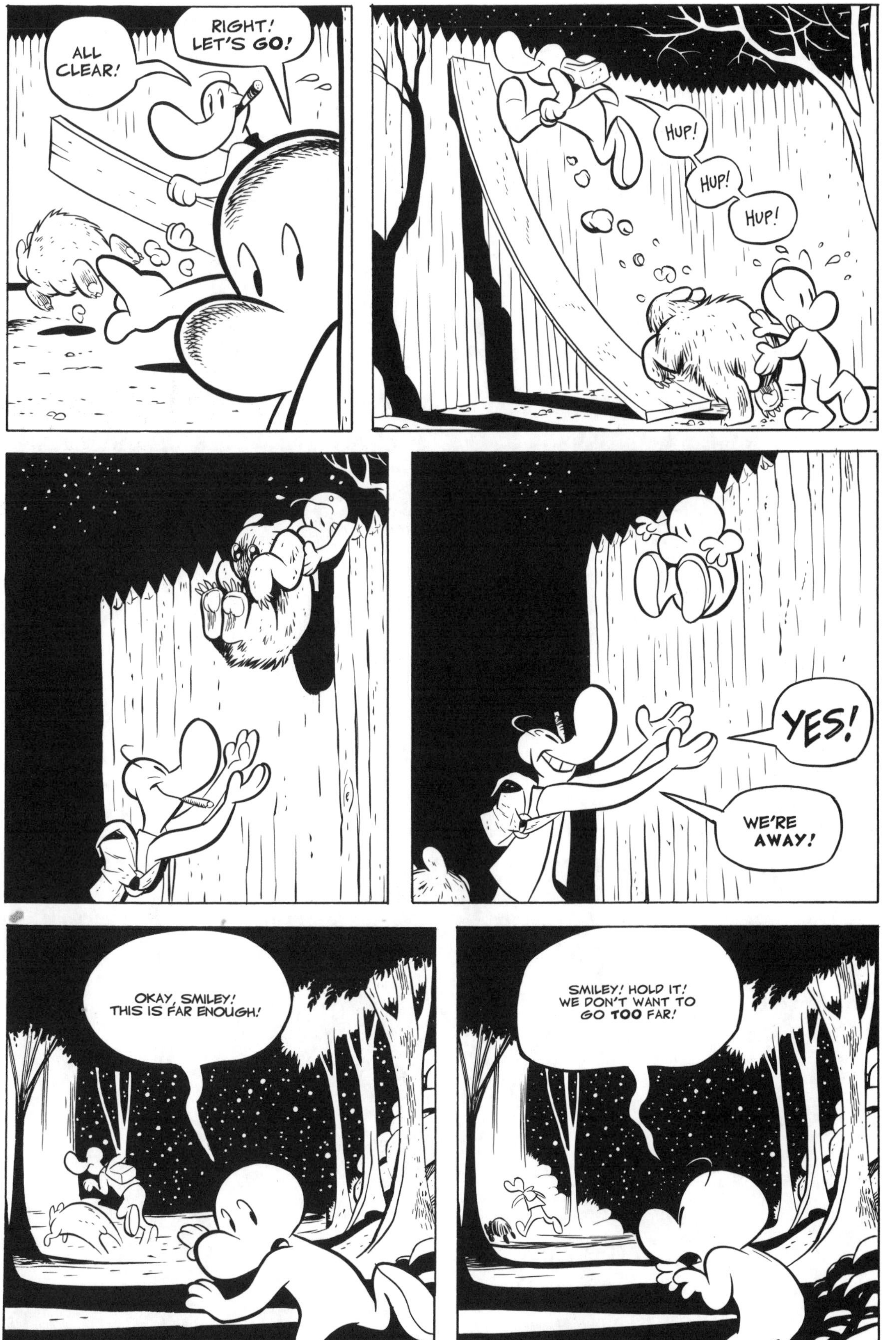
ALL CLEAR!
RIGHT! LET'S GO!
HUP!
HUP!
HUP!
YES!
WE'RE AWAY!
OKAY, SMILEY! THIS IS FAR ENOUGH!
SMILEY! HOLD IT! WE DON'T WANT TO GO TOO FAR!

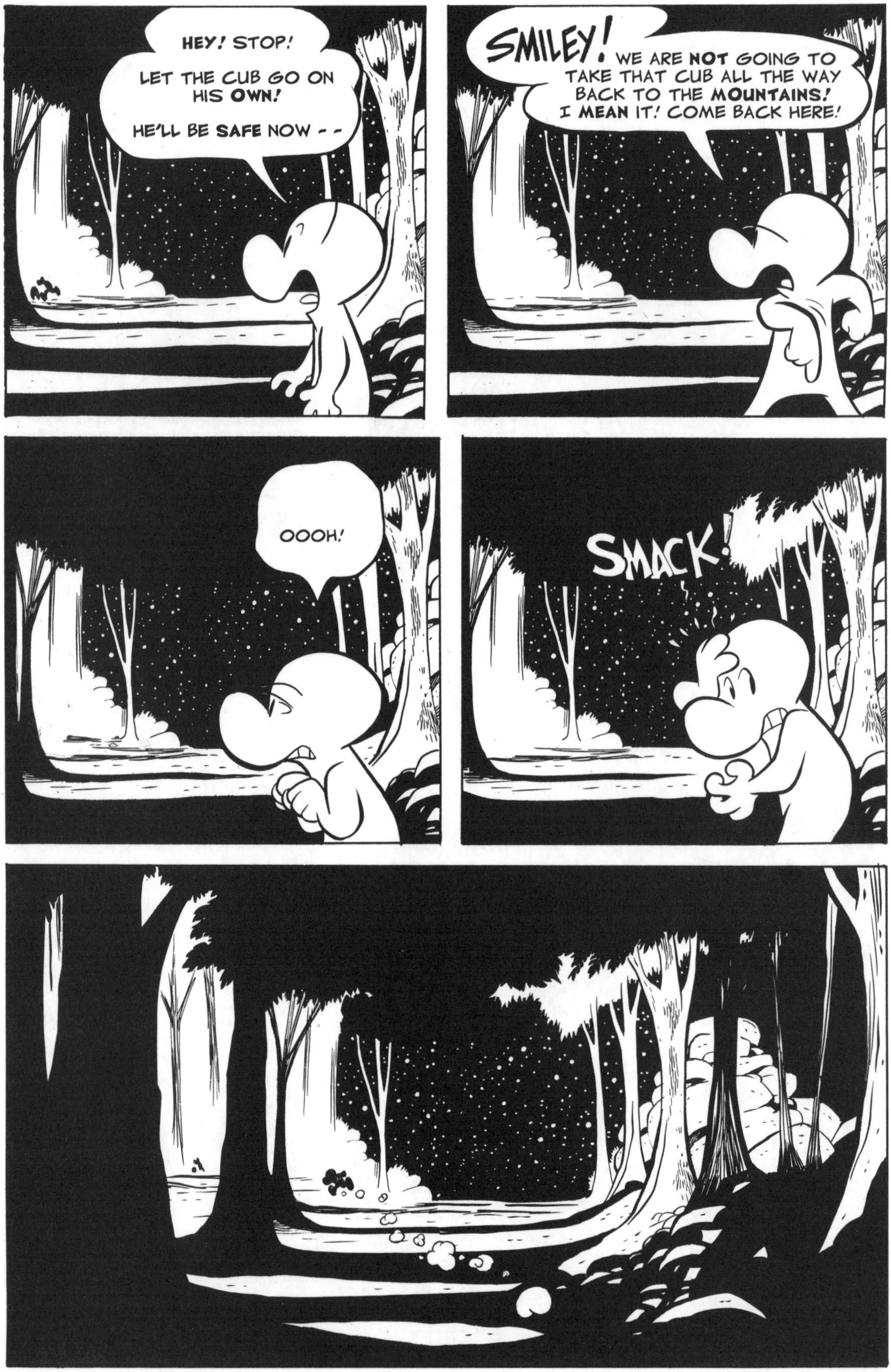
HEY! STOP!
LET THE CUB GO ON HIS OWN!
HE'LL BE SAFE NOW - -
SMILEY! WE ARE NOT GOING TO TAKE THAT CUB ALL THE WAY BACK TO THE MOUNTAINS! I MEAN IT! COME BACK HERE!
OOOH!
SMACK!

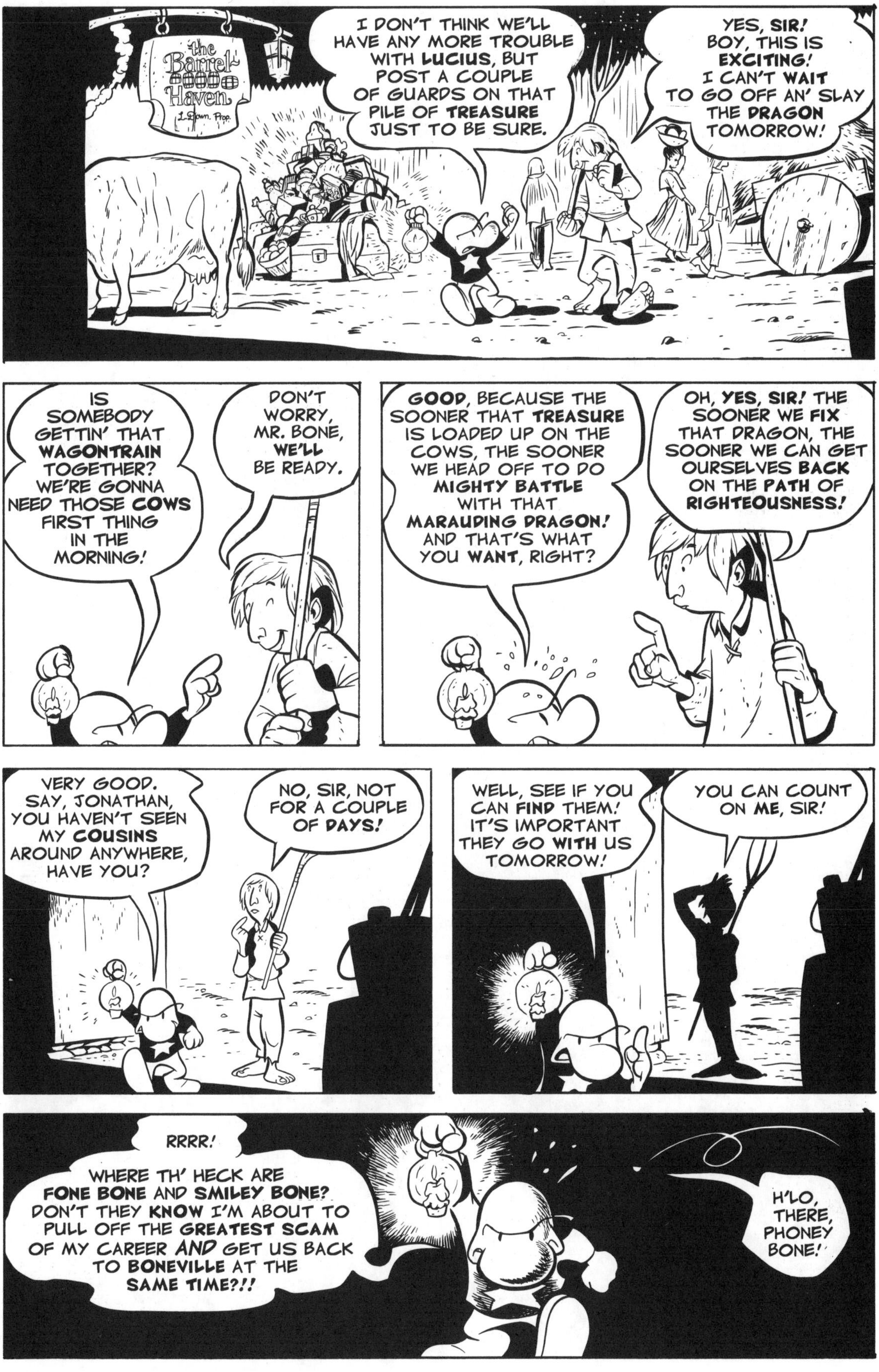
the Barrel Haven L. Down, Prop.
I DON'T THINK WE'LL HAVE ANY MORE TROUBLE WITH LUCIUS, BUT POST A COUPLE OF GUARDS ON THAT PILE OF TREASURE JUST TO BE SURE.
YES, SIR! BOY, THIS IS EXCITING! I CAN'T WAIT TO GO OFF AN' SLAY THE DRAGON TOMORROW!
IS SOMEBODY GETTIN' THAT WAGONTRAIN TOGETHER? WE'RE GONNA NEED THOSE COWS FIRST THING IN THE MORNING!
DON'T WORRY, MR. BONE, WE'LL BE READY.
GOOD, BECAUSE THE SOONER THAT TREASURE IS LOADED UP ON THE COWS, THE SOONER WE HEAD OFF TO DO MIGHTY BATTLE WITH THAT MARAUDING DRAGON! AND THAT'S WHAT YOU WANT, RIGHT?
OH, YES, SIR! THE SOONER WE FIX THAT DRAGON, THE SOONER WE CAN GET OURSELVES BACK ON THE PATH OF RIGHTEOUSNESS!
VERY GOOD. SAY, JONATHAN, YOU HAVEN'T SEEN MY COUSINS AROUND ANYWHERE, HAVE YOU?
NO, SIR, NOT FOR A COUPLE OF DAYS!
WELL, SEE IF YOU CAN FIND THEM! IT'S IMPORTANT THEY GO WITH US TOMORROW!
YOU CAN COUNT ON ME, SIR!
RRRR!
WHERE TH' HECK ARE FONE BONE AND SMILEY BONE? DON'T THEY KNOW I'M ABOUT TO PULL OFF THE GREATEST SCAM OF MY CAREER AND GET US BACK TO BONEVILLE AT THE SAME TIME?!!
H'LO, THERE, PHONEY BONE!

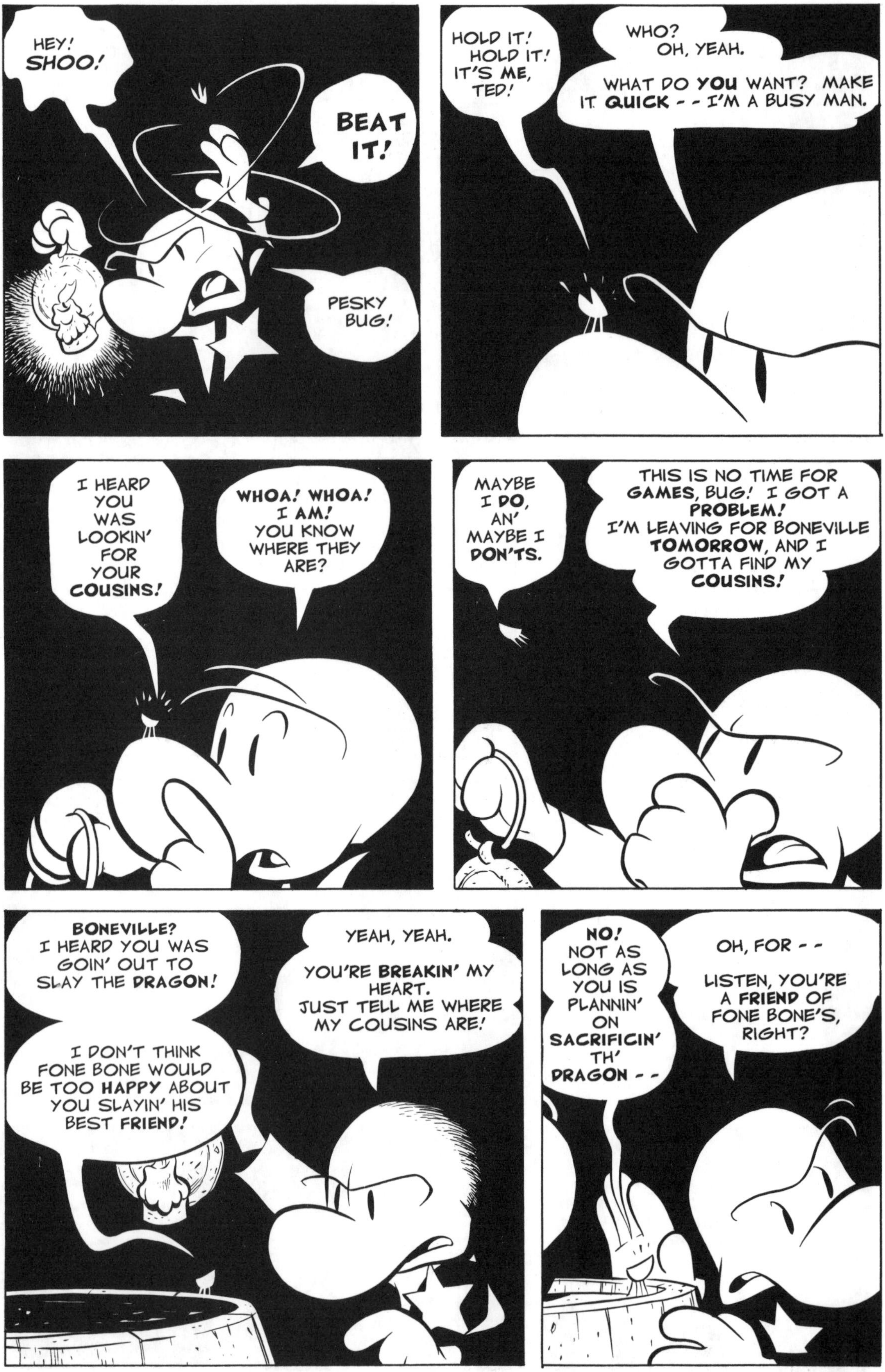

HEY! SHOO!
BEAT IT!
PESKY BUG!
HOLD IT! HOLD IT! IT'S ME, TED!
WHO? OH, YEAH.
WHAT DO YOU WANT? MAKE IT QUICK - - I'M A BUSY MAN.
I HEARD YOU WAS LOOKIN' FOR YOUR COUSINS!
WHOA! WHOA! I AM! YOU KNOW WHERE THEY ARE?
MAYBE I DO, AN' MAYBE I DON'TS.
THIS IS NO TIME FOR GAMES, BUG! I GOT A PROBLEM! I'M LEAVING FOR BONEVILLE TOMORROW, AND I GOTTA FIND MY COUSINS!
BONEVILLE? I HEARD YOU WAS GOIN' OUT TO SLAY THE DRAGON!
I DON'T THINK FONE BONE WOULD BE TOO HAPPY ABOUT YOU SLAYIN' HIS BEST FRIEND!
YEAH, YEAH.
YOU'RE BREAKIN' MY HEART. JUST TELL ME WHERE MY COUSINS ARE!
NO! NOT AS LONG AS YOU IS PLANNIN' ON SACRIFICIN' TH' DRAGON - -
OH, FOR - -
LISTEN, YOU'RE A FRIEND OF FONE BONE'S, RIGHT?

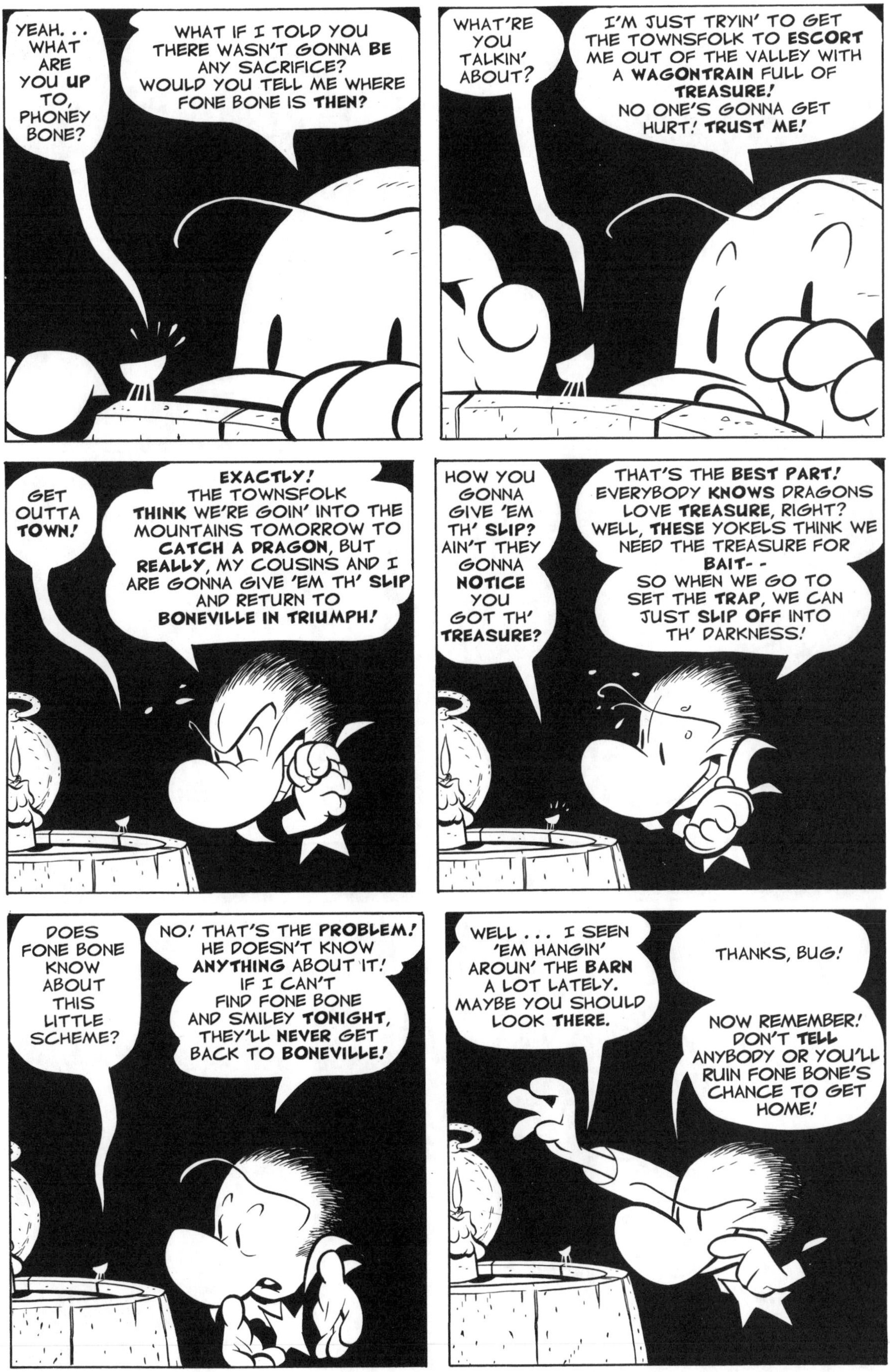
YEAH. . . WHAT ARE YOU **UP** TO, PHONEY BONE?
WHAT IF I TOLD YOU THERE WASN'T GONNA **BE** ANY SACRIFICE? WOULD YOU TELL ME WHERE FONE BONE IS **THEN**?
WHAT'RE YOU TALKIN' ABOUT?
I'M JUST TRYIN' TO GET THE TOWNSFOLK TO **ESCORT** ME OUT OF THE VALLEY WITH A **WAGONTRAIN** FULL OF **TREASURE!** NO ONE'S GONNA GET HURT! **TRUST ME!**
GET OUTTA **TOWN!**
EXACTLY! THE TOWNSFOLK **THINK** WE'RE GOIN' INTO THE MOUNTAINS TOMORROW TO **CATCH A DRAGON**, BUT **REALLY**, MY COUSINS AND I ARE GONNA GIVE 'EM TH' **SLIP** AND RETURN TO **BONEVILLE IN TRIUMPH!**
HOW YOU GONNA GIVE 'EM TH' **SLIP?** AIN'T THEY GONNA **NOTICE** YOU GOT TH' **TREASURE?**
THAT'S THE **BEST PART!** EVERYBODY **KNOWS** DRAGONS LOVE **TREASURE**, RIGHT? WELL, **THESE** YOKELS THINK WE NEED THE TREASURE FOR **BAIT- -** SO WHEN WE GO TO SET THE **TRAP**, WE CAN JUST **SLIP OFF** INTO TH' DARKNESS!
DOES FONE BONE KNOW ABOUT THIS LITTLE SCHEME?
NO! THAT'S THE **PROBLEM!** HE DOESN'T KNOW **ANYTHING** ABOUT IT! IF I CAN'T FIND FONE BONE AND SMILEY **TONIGHT**, THEY'LL **NEVER** GET BACK TO **BONEVILLE!**
WELL . . . I SEEN 'EM HANGIN' AROUN' THE **BARN** A LOT LATELY. MAYBE YOU SHOULD LOOK **THERE.**
THANKS, BUG!
NOW REMEMBER! DON'T **TELL** ANYBODY OR YOU'LL RUIN FONE BONE'S CHANCE TO GET HOME!

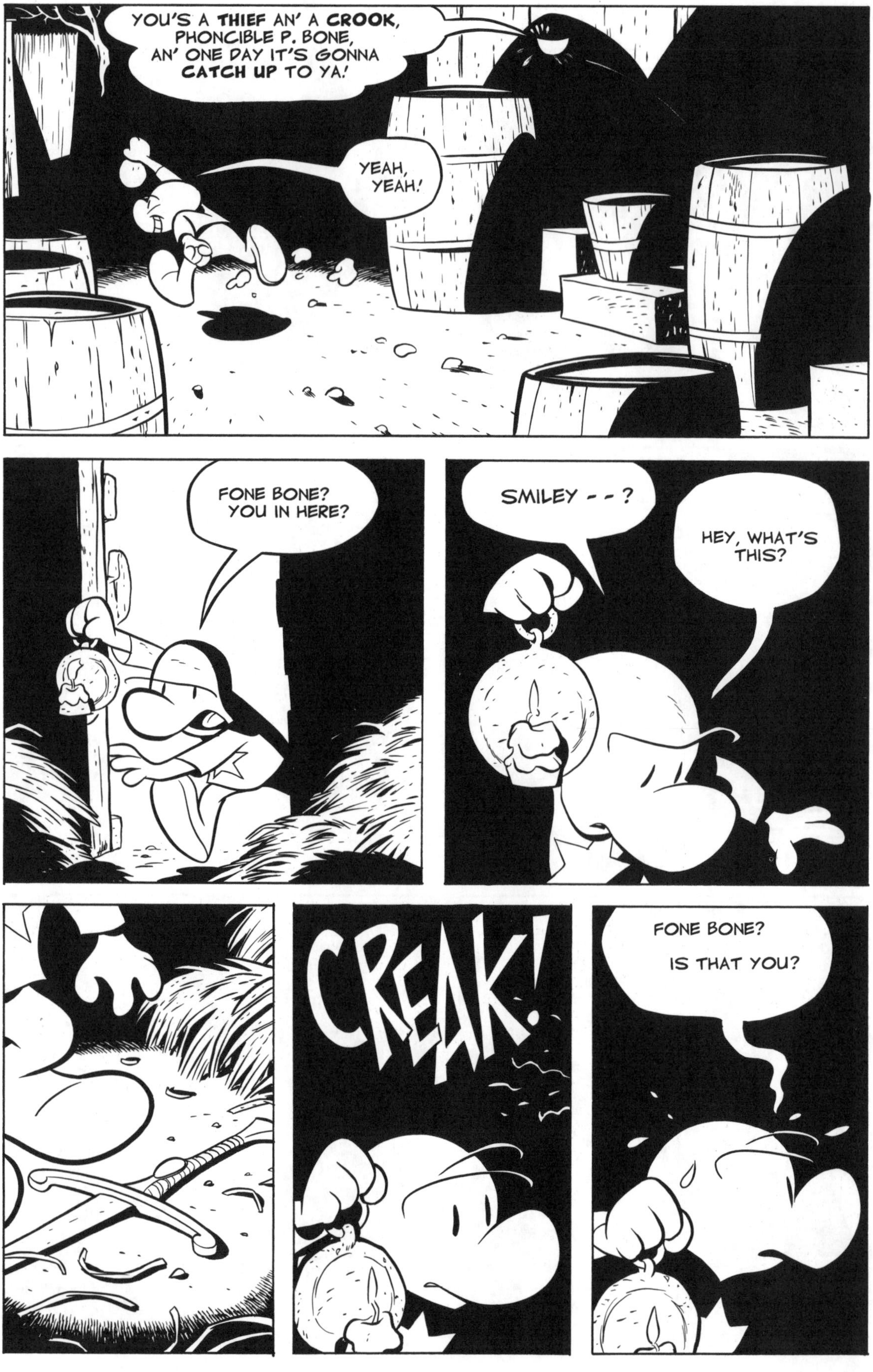
YOU'S A **THIEF** AN' A **CROOK**, PHONCIBLE P. BONE, AN' ONE DAY IT'S GONNA **CATCH UP** TO YA!
YEAH, YEAH!
FONE BONE? YOU IN HERE?
SMILEY - - ?
HEY, WHAT'S THIS?
CREAK!
FONE BONE? IS THAT YOU?

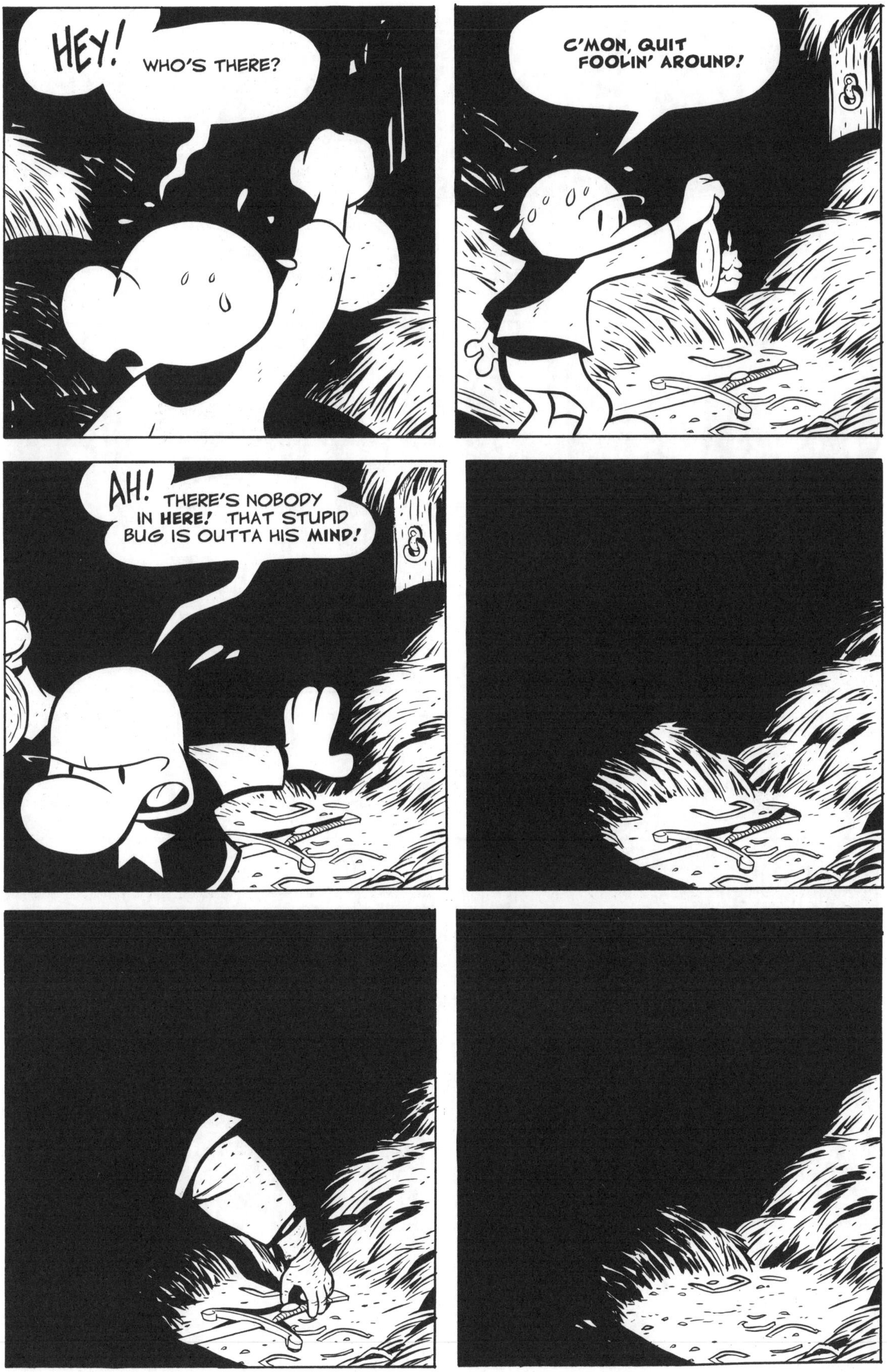
HEY! WHO'S THERE?
C'MON, QUIT FOOLIN' AROUND!
AH! THERE'S NOBODY IN HERE! THAT STUPID BUG IS OUTTA HIS MIND!

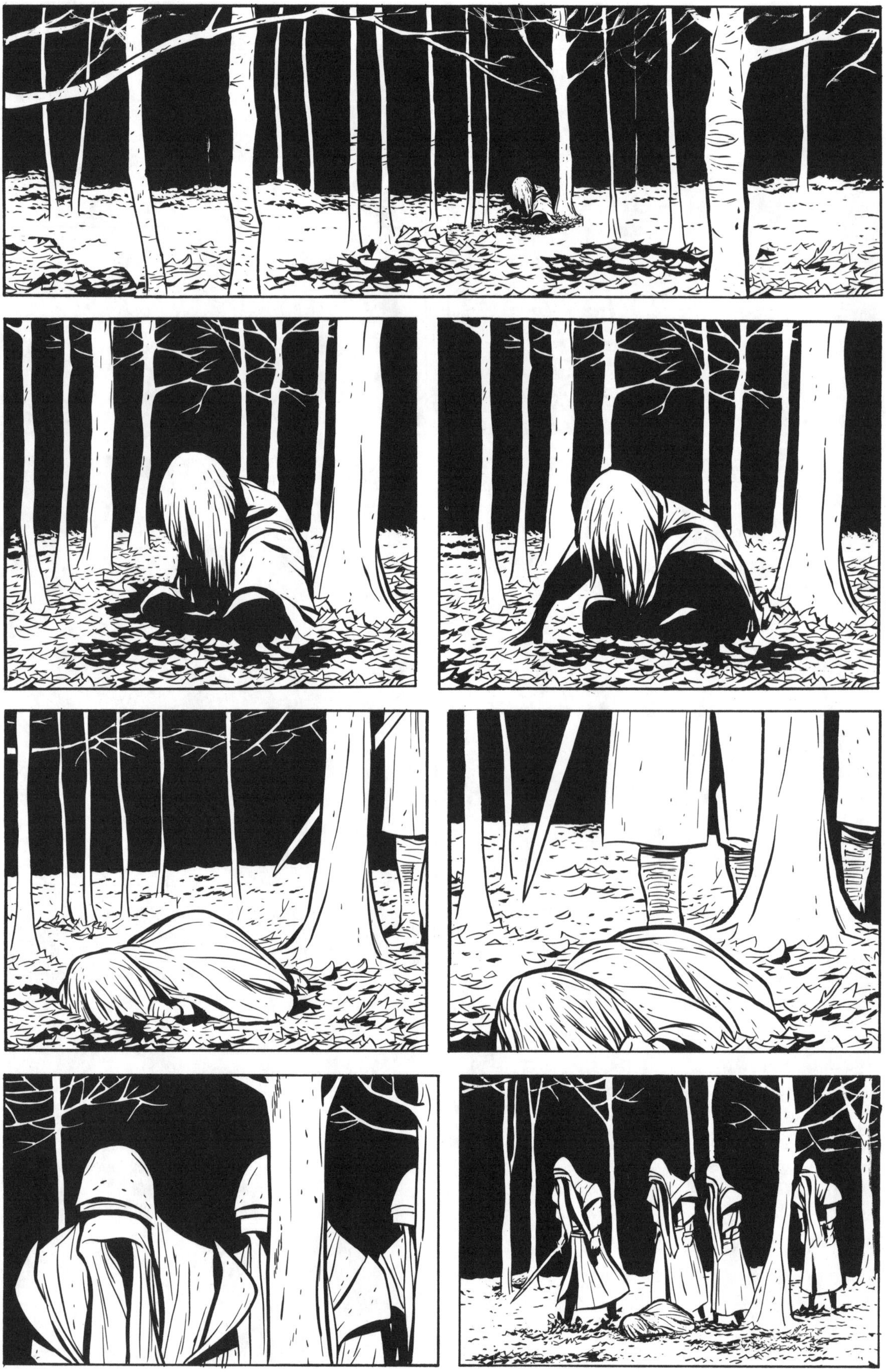

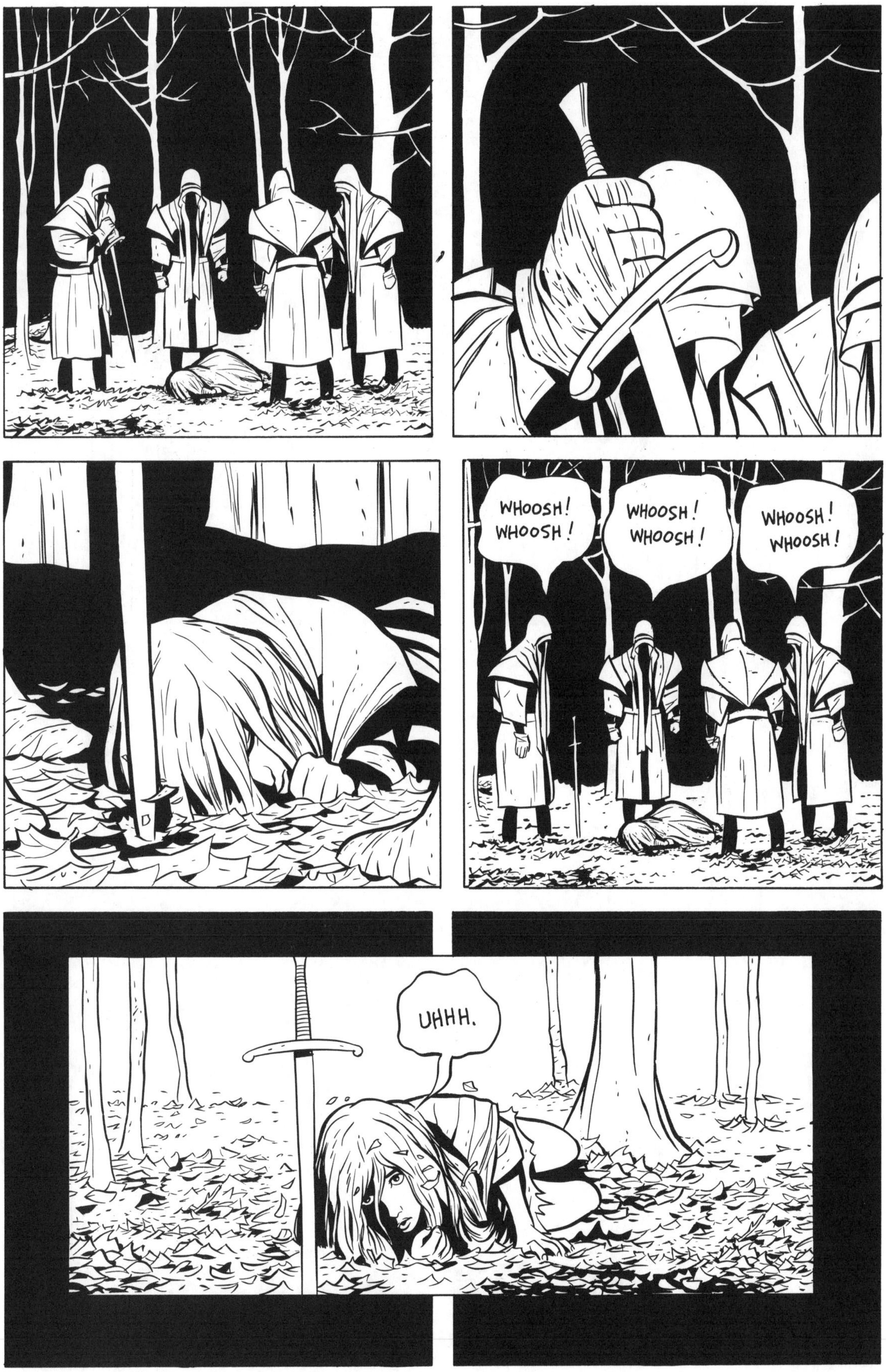
WHOOSH! WHOOSH!
WHOOSH! WHOOSH!
WHOOSH! WHOOSH!
UHHH.

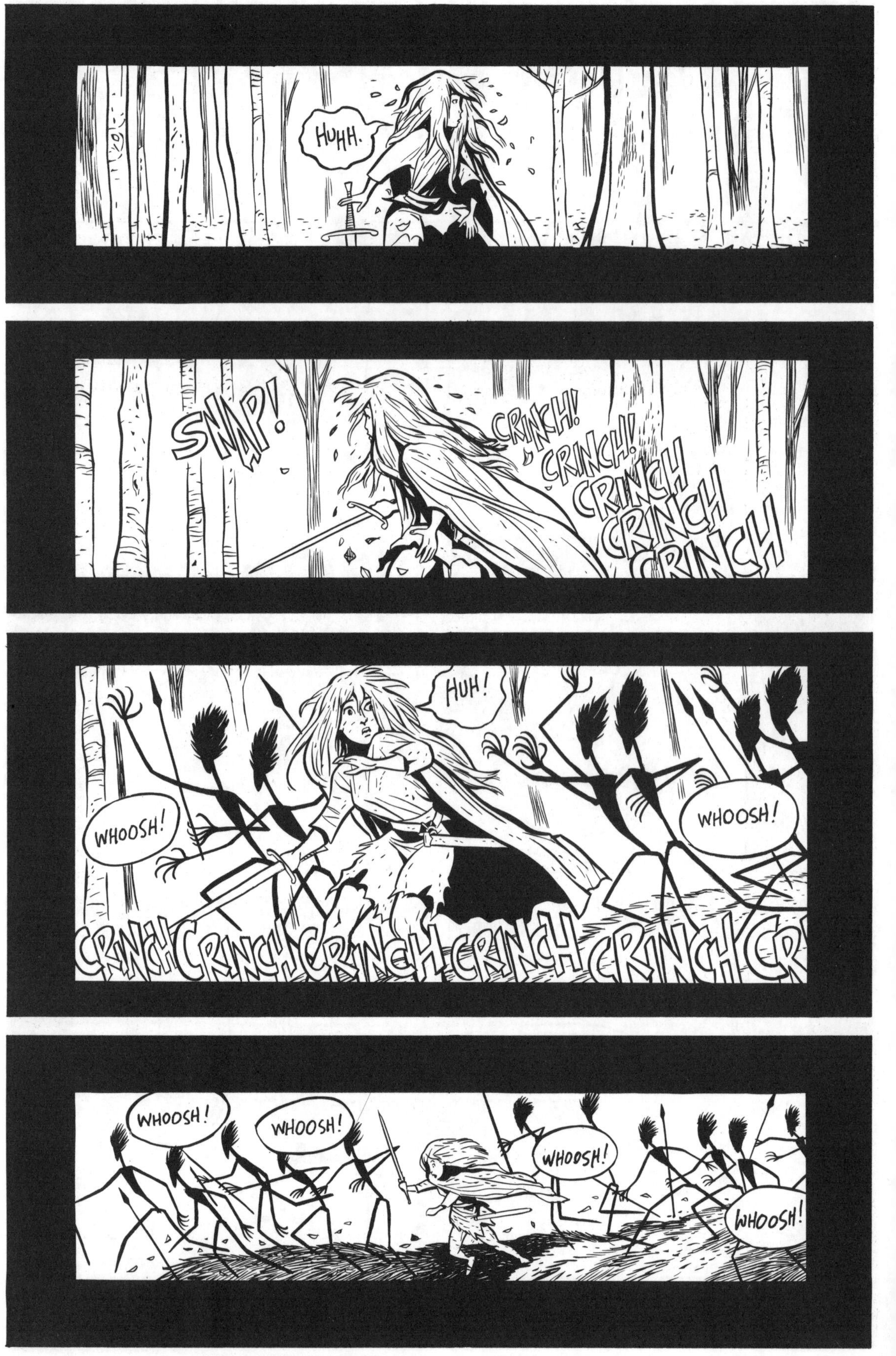
HUHH.
SNAP!
CRINCH!
CRINCH!
CRINCH
CRINCH
CRINCH
HUH!
WHOOSH!
WHOOSH!
CRINCH CRINCH CRINCH CRINCH CRINCH
WHOOSH!
WHOOSH!
WHOOSH!
WHOOSH!

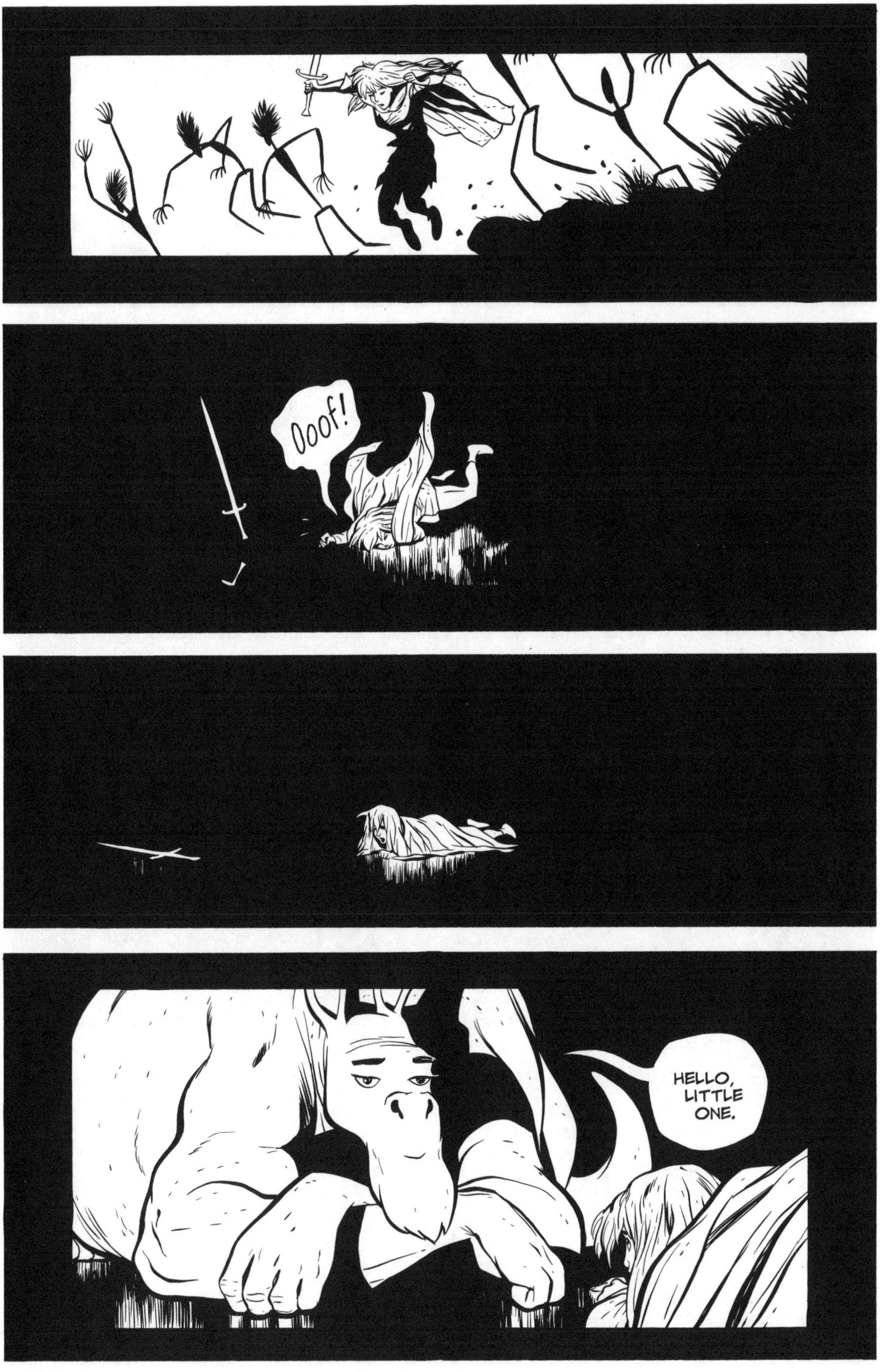
Ooof!
HELLO, LITTLE ONE.

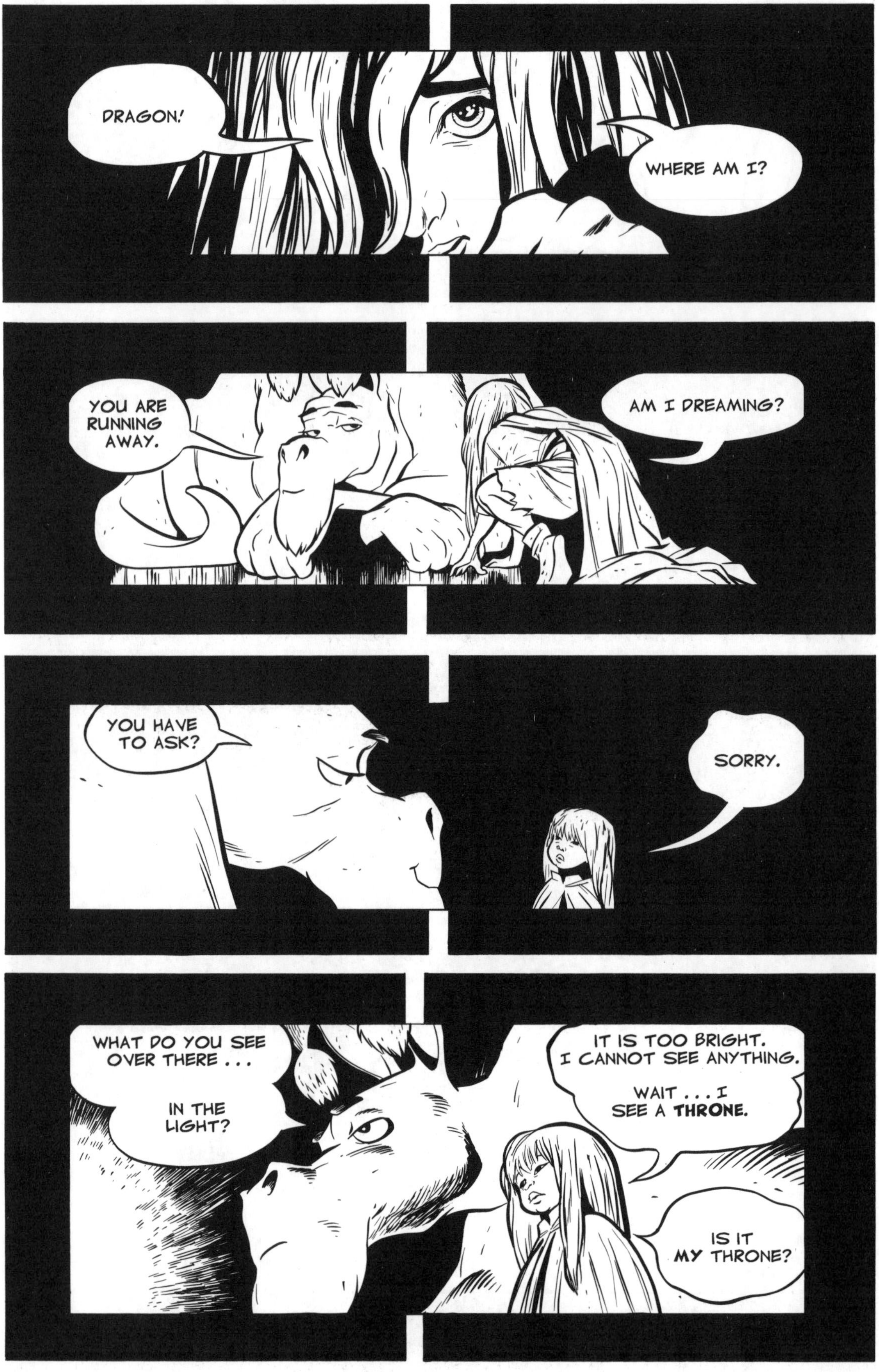
DRAGON!
WHERE AM I?
YOU ARE RUNNING AWAY.
AM I DREAMING?
YOU HAVE TO ASK?
SORRY.
WHAT DO YOU SEE OVER THERE . . .
IN THE LIGHT?
IT IS TOO BRIGHT. I CANNOT SEE ANYTHING.
WAIT . . . I SEE A **THRONE.**
IS IT MY THRONE?

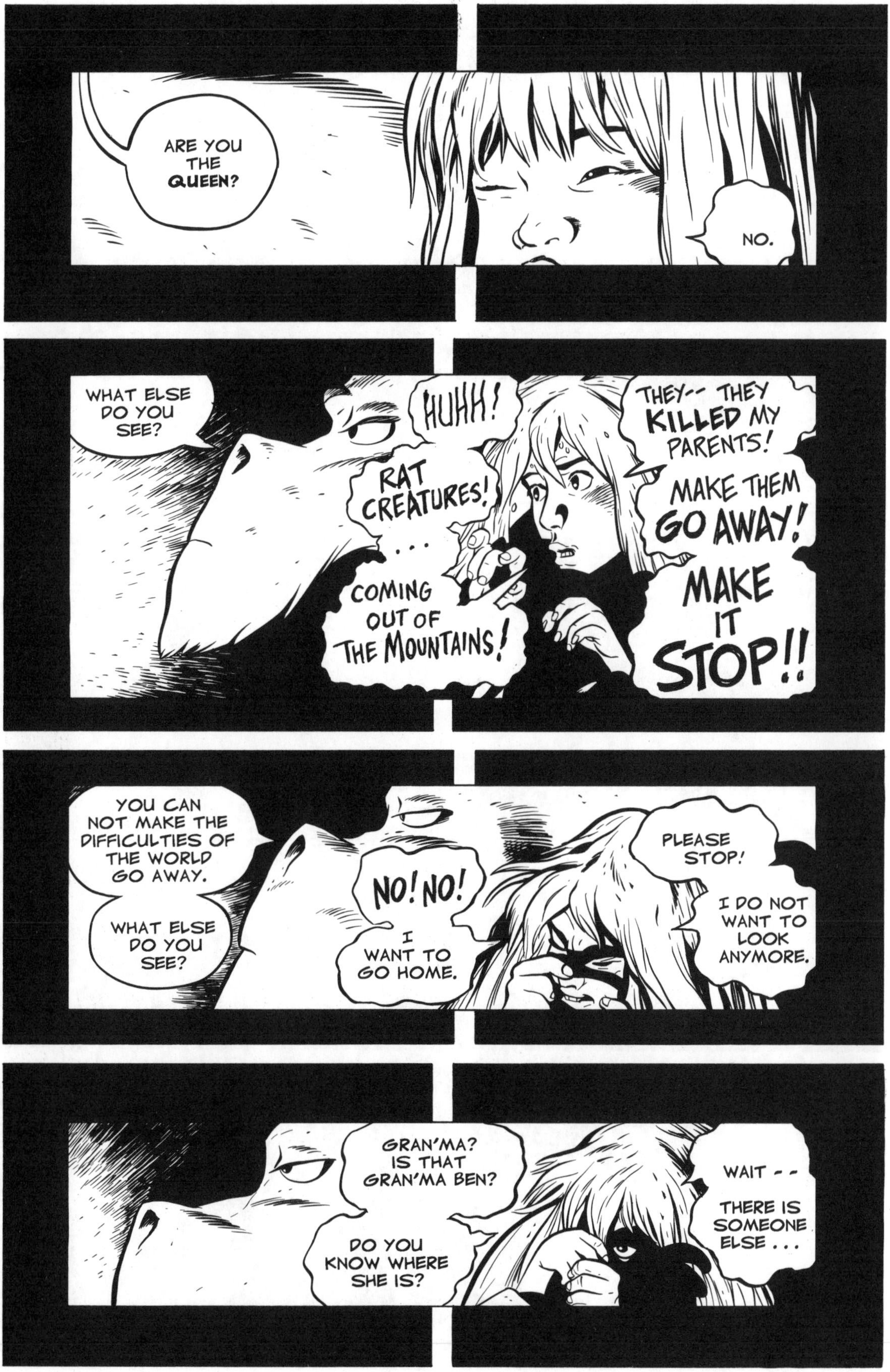
ARE YOU THE QUEEN?
NO.
WHAT ELSE DO YOU SEE?
HUHH!
RAT CREATURES! ... COMING OUT OF THE MOUNTAINS!
THEY-- THEY KILLED MY PARENTS!
MAKE THEM GO AWAY!
MAKE IT STOP!!
YOU CAN NOT MAKE THE DIFFICULTIES OF THE WORLD GO AWAY.
WHAT ELSE DO YOU SEE?
NO! NO!
I WANT TO GO HOME.
PLEASE STOP!
I DO NOT WANT TO LOOK ANYMORE.
GRAN'MA? IS THAT GRAN'MA BEN?
DO YOU KNOW WHERE SHE IS?
WAIT --
THERE IS SOMEONE ELSE ...

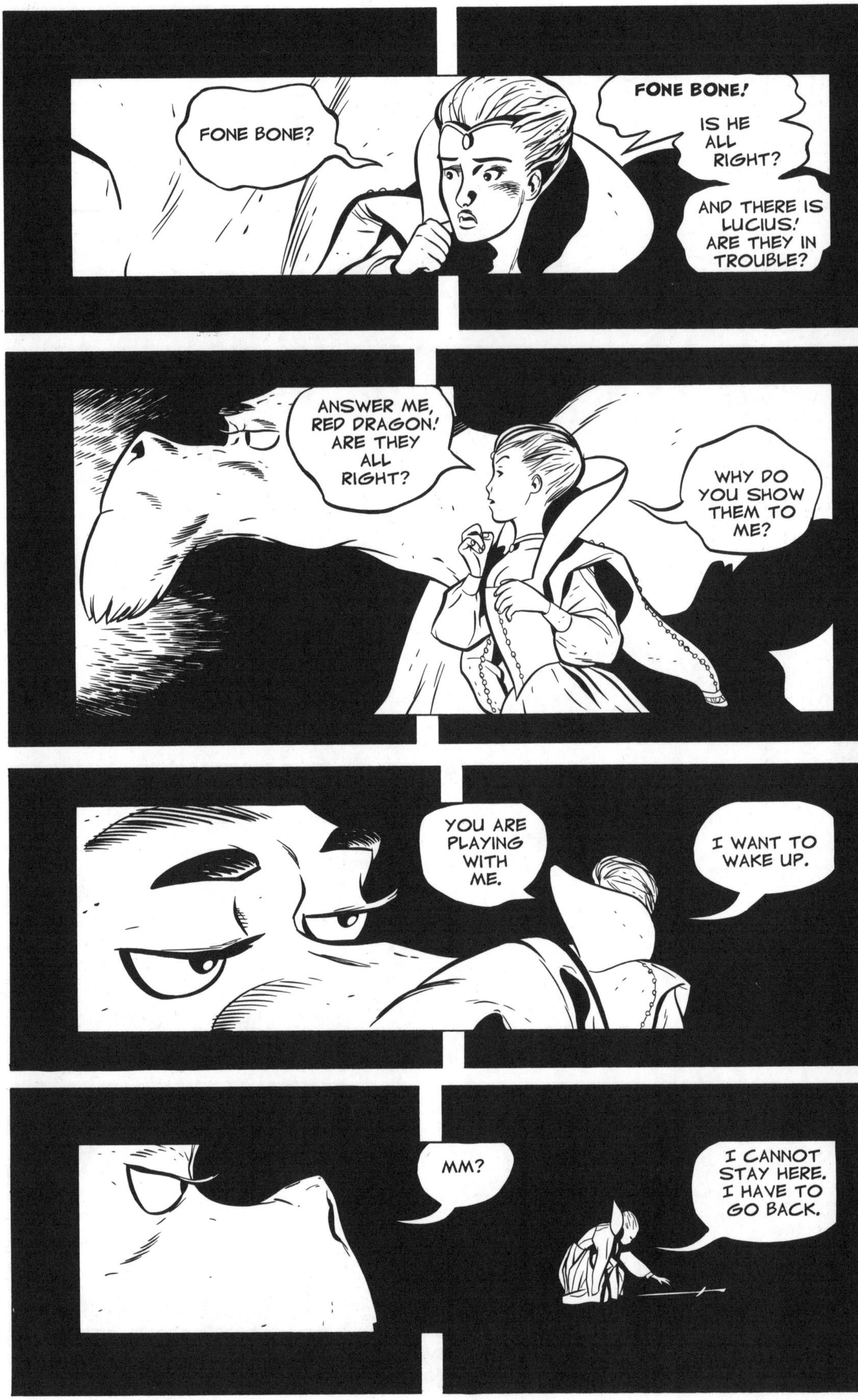
FONE BONE?
FONE BONE! IS HE ALL RIGHT?
AND THERE IS LUCIUS! ARE THEY IN TROUBLE?
ANSWER ME, RED DRAGON! ARE THEY ALL RIGHT?
WHY DO YOU SHOW THEM TO ME?
YOU ARE PLAYING WITH ME.
I WANT TO WAKE UP.
MM?
I CANNOT STAY HERE. I HAVE TO GO BACK.

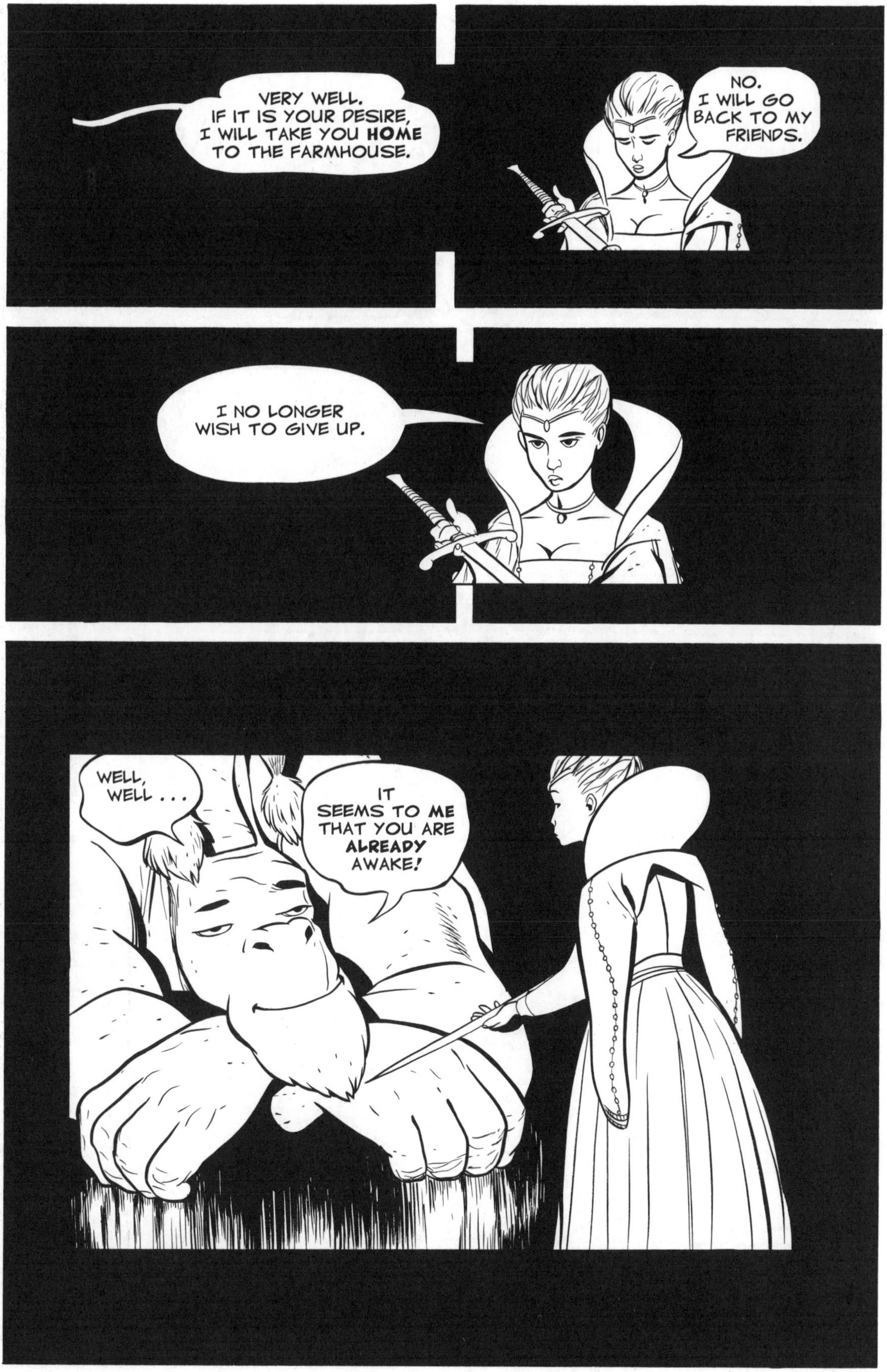
VERY WELL.
IF IT IS YOUR DESIRE, I WILL TAKE YOU **HOME** TO THE FARMHOUSE.
NO. I WILL GO BACK TO MY FRIENDS.
I NO LONGER WISH TO GIVE UP.
WELL, WELL . . .
IT SEEMS TO ME THAT YOU ARE **ALREADY** AWAKE!

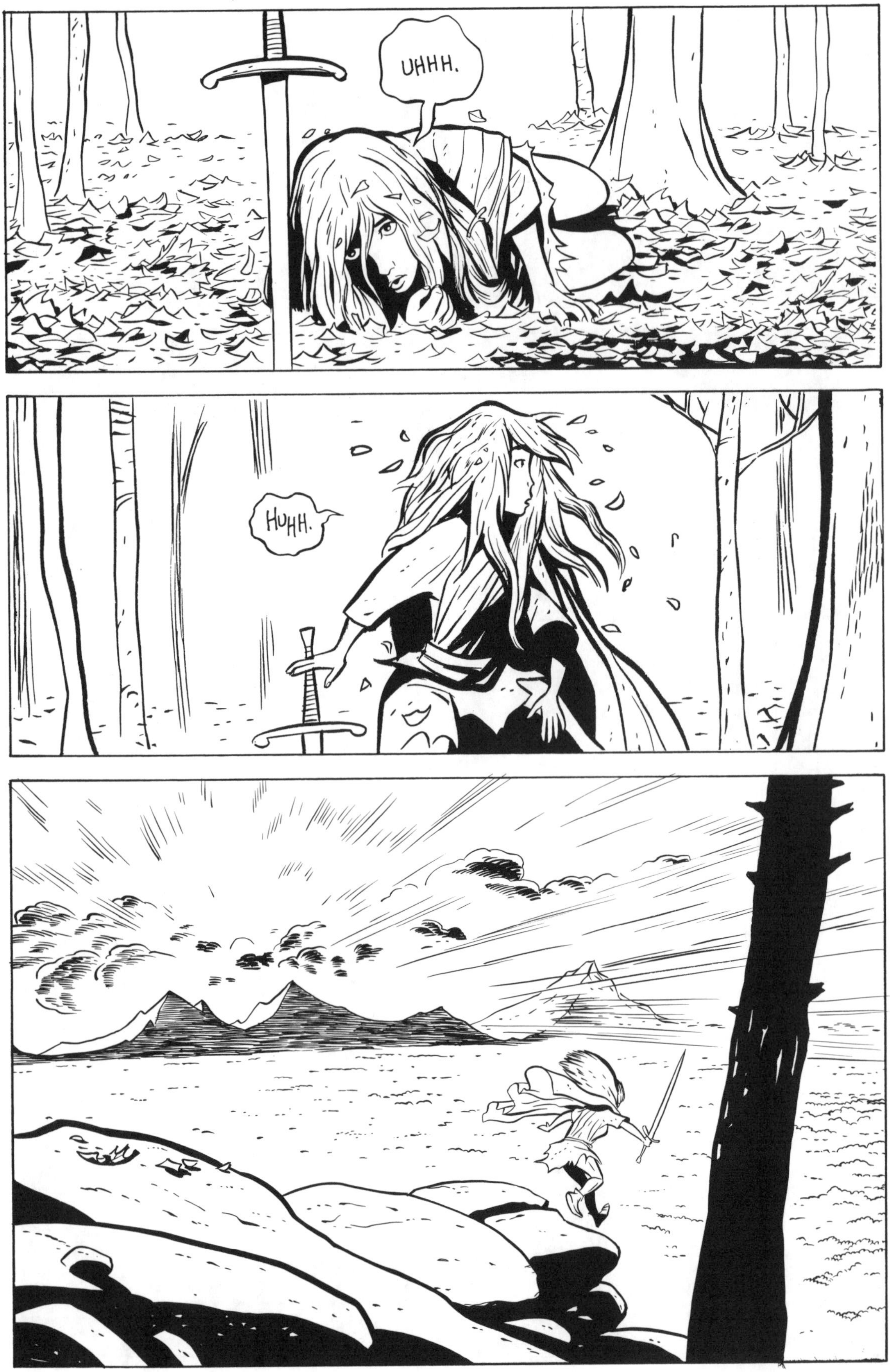
UHHH.
HUHH.

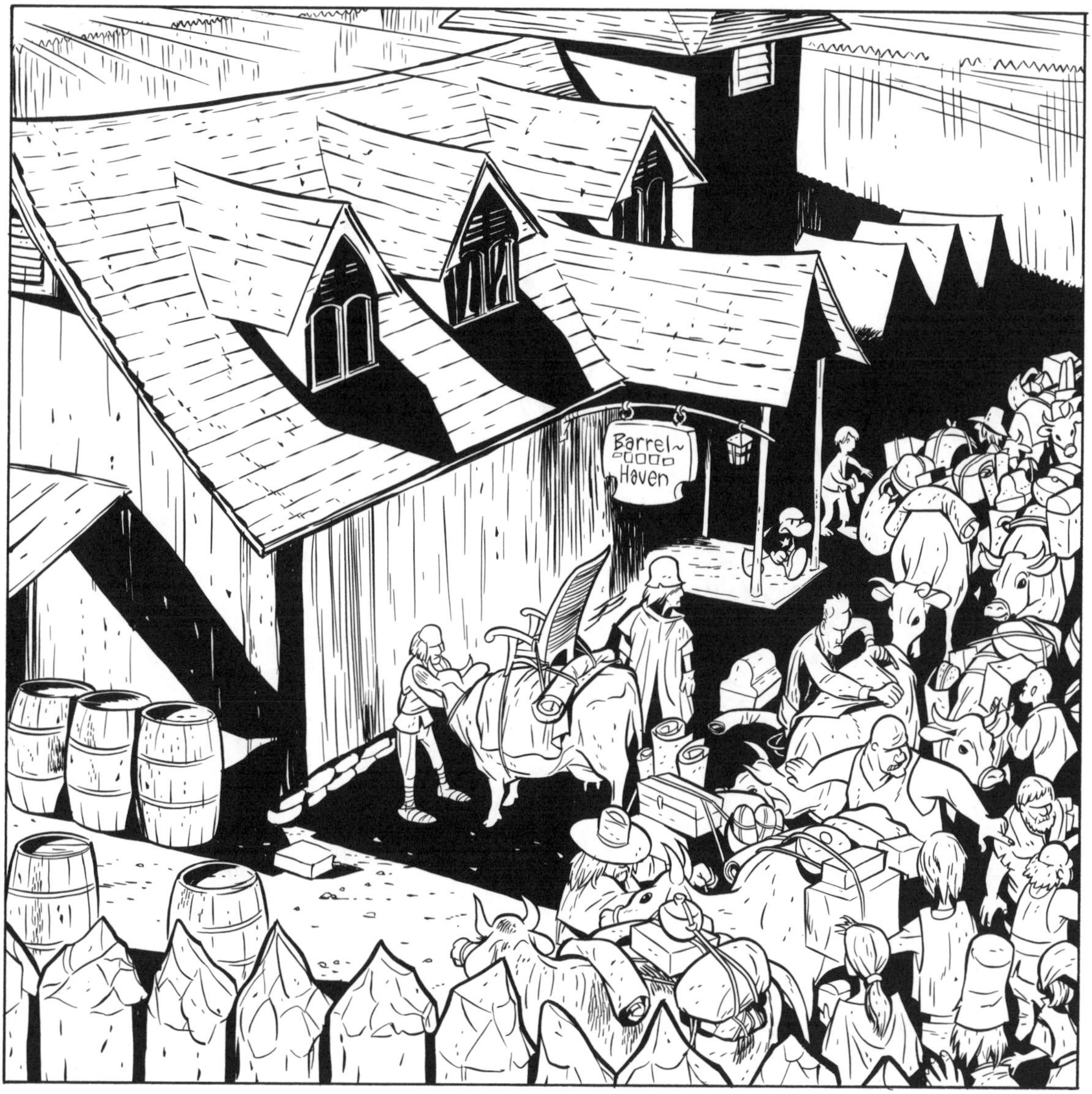
Barrel Haven

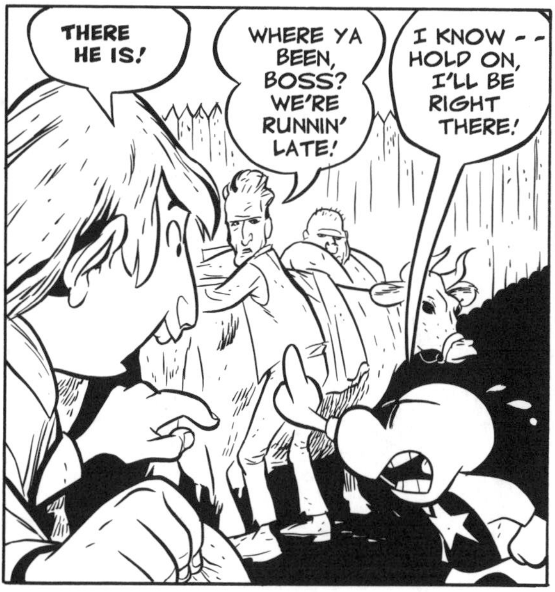
THERE HE IS!
WHERE YA BEEN, BOSS? WE'RE RUNNIN' LATE!
I KNOW - - HOLD ON, I'LL BE RIGHT THERE!

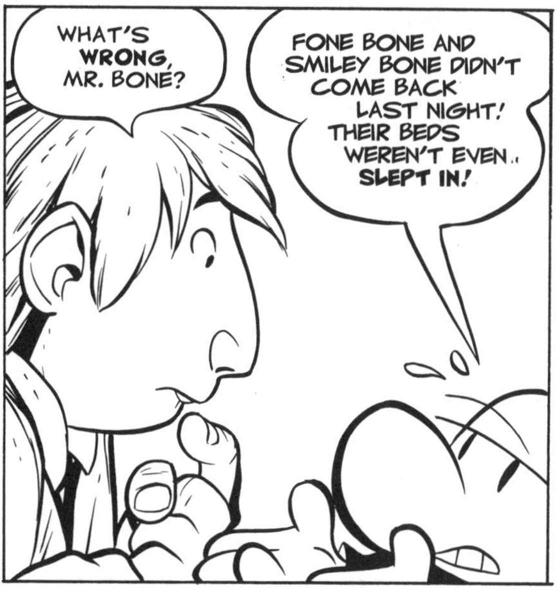
WHAT'S WRONG, MR. BONE?
FONE BONE AND SMILEY BONE DIDN'T COME BACK LAST NIGHT! THEIR BEDS WEREN'T EVEN.. SLEPT IN!

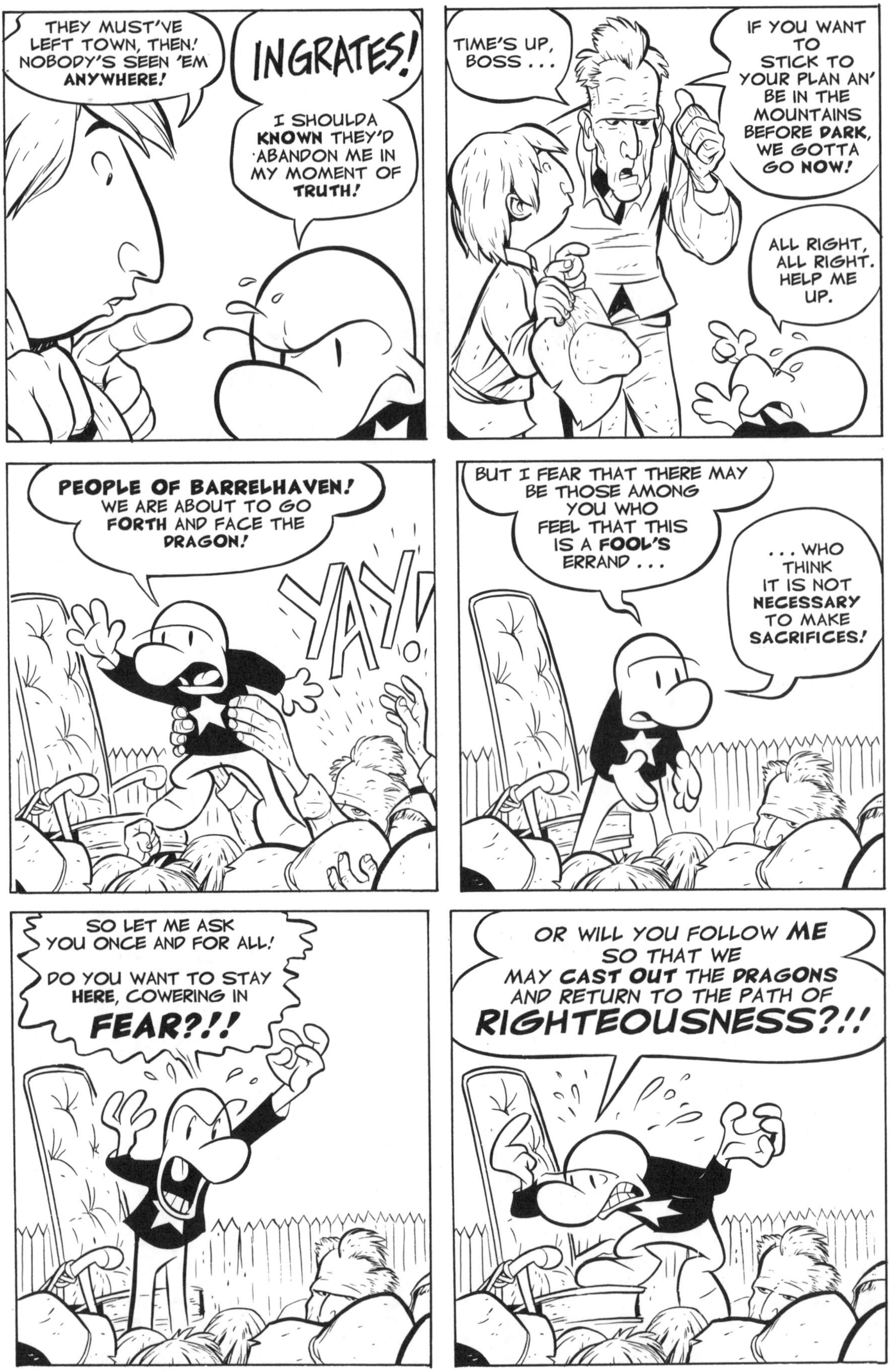
THEY MUST'VE LEFT TOWN, THEN! NOBODY'S SEEN 'EM **ANYWHERE!**
INGRATES!
I SHOULDA **KNOWN** THEY'D ABANDON ME IN MY MOMENT OF **TRUTH!**
TIME'S UP, BOSS . . .
IF YOU WANT TO STICK TO YOUR PLAN AN' BE IN THE MOUNTAINS BEFORE **DARK**, WE GOTTA GO **NOW!**
ALL RIGHT, ALL RIGHT. HELP ME UP.
PEOPLE OF BARRELHAVEN! WE ARE ABOUT TO GO **FORTH** AND FACE THE **DRAGON!**
YAY!
BUT I FEAR THAT THERE MAY BE THOSE AMONG YOU WHO FEEL THAT THIS IS A **FOOL'S** ERRAND . . .
. . . WHO THINK IT IS NOT **NECESSARY** TO MAKE **SACRIFICES!**
SO LET ME ASK YOU ONCE AND FOR ALL!
DO YOU WANT TO STAY **HERE**, COWERING IN **FEAR?!!**
OR WILL YOU FOLLOW **ME** SO THAT WE MAY **CAST OUT** THE **DRAGONS** AND RETURN TO THE PATH OF **RIGHTEOUSNESS?!!**

THE PEOPLE HAVE SPOKEN! IN CASE YOU DIDN'T **CATCH** THAT, **LUCIUS**, OLD PAL, THEY PICKED ME!

-- NOT YOU --

ME!

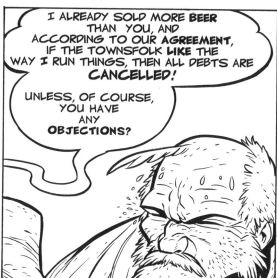

I ALREADY SOLD MORE BEER THAN YOU, AND ACCORDING TO OUR **AGREEMENT**, IF THE TOWNSFOLK **LIKE** THE WAY **I** RUN THINGS, THEN ALL DEBTS ARE **CANCELLED!**

UNLESS, OF COURSE, YOU HAVE ANY **OBJECTIONS?**

DIDN'T THINK SO.

SEE YA AROUND, LUCIUS!

ALL RIGHT, PEOPLE, **MOVE 'EM OUT!!**

Moo!

Moo!

THREE CHEERS FOR THE DRAGONSLAYER!

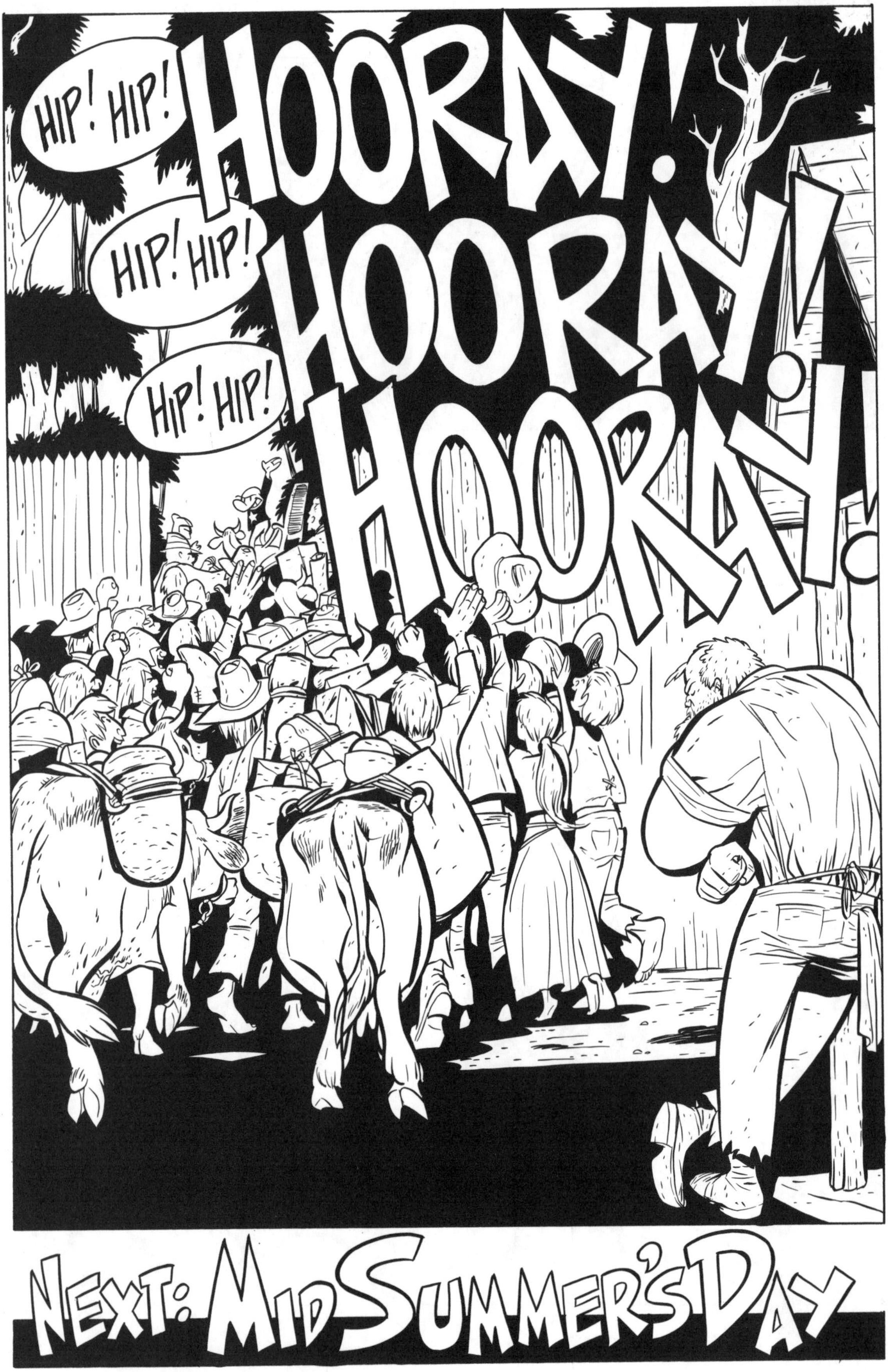
HIP! HIP! HOORAY!
HIP! HIP! HOORAY!
HIP! HIP! HOORAY!

NEXT: MIDSUMMER'S DAY

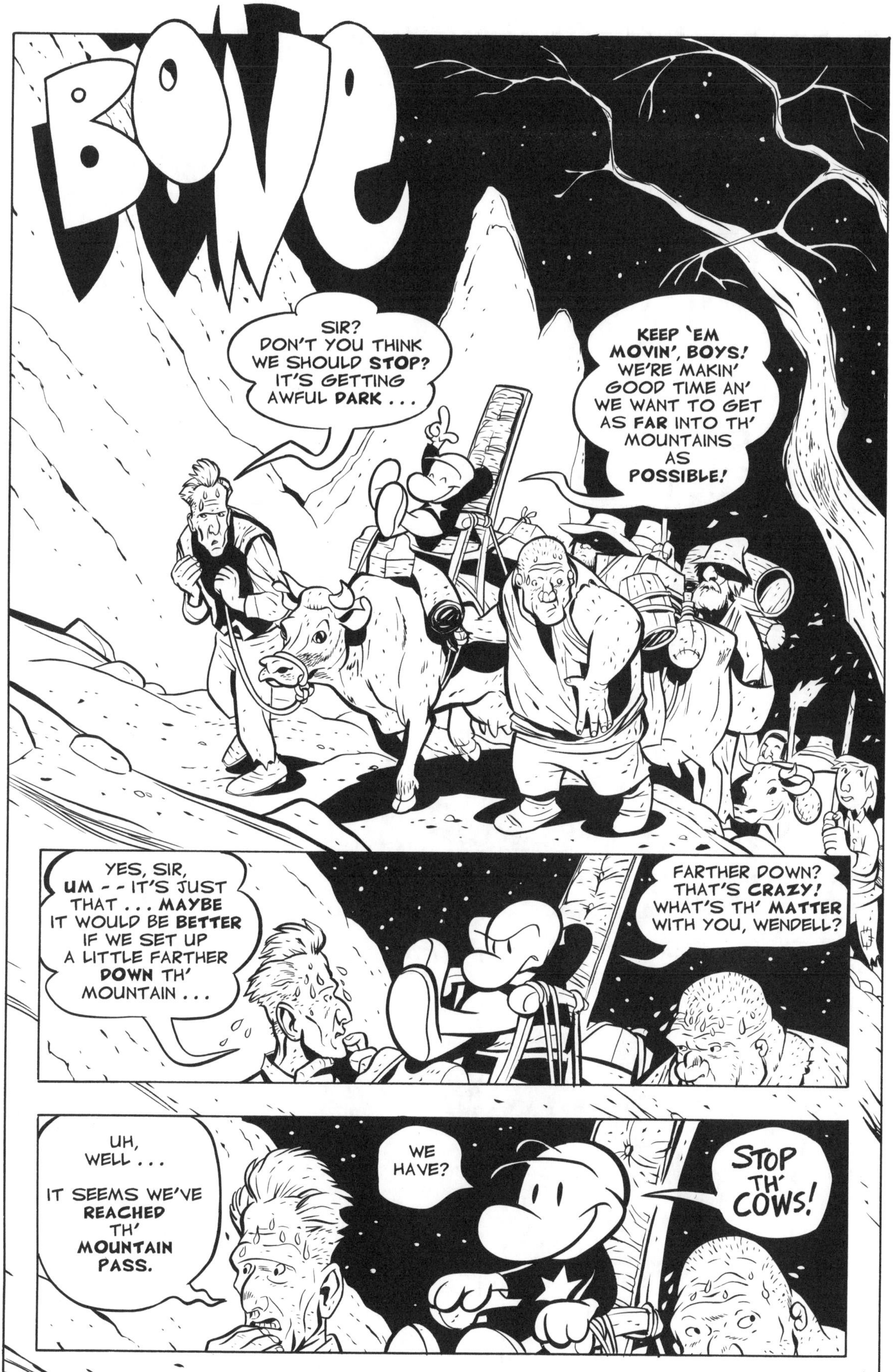
BONE
SIR? DON'T YOU THINK WE SHOULD STOP? IT'S GETTING AWFUL DARK . . .
KEEP 'EM MOVIN', BOYS! WE'RE MAKIN' GOOD TIME AN' WE WANT TO GET AS FAR INTO TH' MOUNTAINS AS POSSIBLE!
YES, SIR, UM - - IT'S JUST THAT . . . MAYBE IT WOULD BE BETTER IF WE SET UP A LITTLE FARTHER DOWN TH' MOUNTAIN . . .
FARTHER DOWN? THAT'S CRAZY! WHAT'S TH' MATTER WITH YOU, WENDELL?
UH, WELL . . .
IT SEEMS WE'VE REACHED TH' MOUNTAIN PASS.
WE HAVE?
STOP TH' COWS!

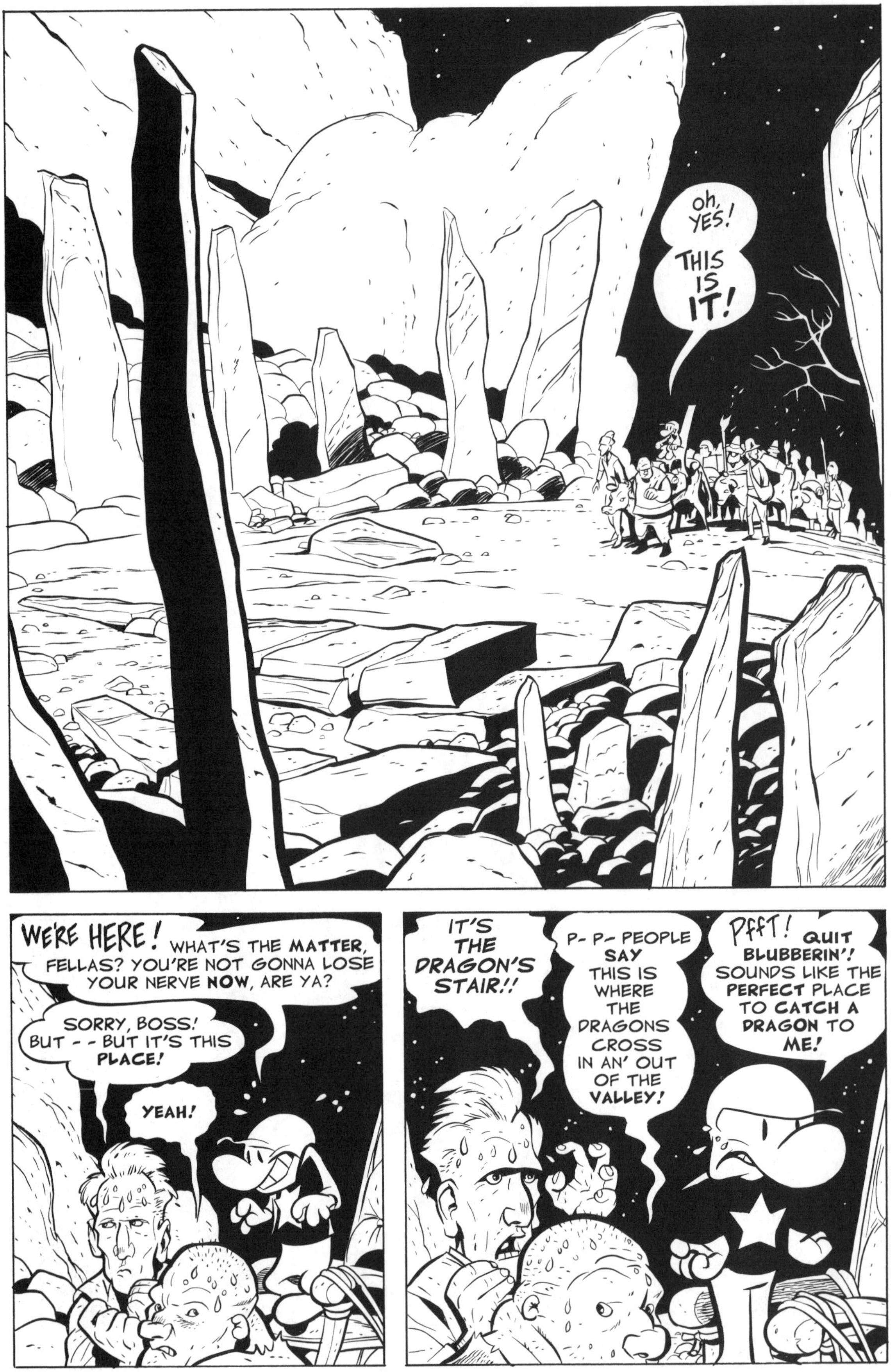
Oh, YES!
THIS IS IT!
WE'RE HERE! WHAT'S THE MATTER, FELLAS? YOU'RE NOT GONNA LOSE YOUR NERVE NOW, ARE YA?
SORRY, BOSS! BUT - - BUT IT'S THIS PLACE!
YEAH!
IT'S THE DRAGON'S STAIR!!
P- P- PEOPLE SAY THIS IS WHERE THE DRAGONS CROSS IN AN' OUT OF THE VALLEY!
PFFT! QUIT BLUBBERIN'! SOUNDS LIKE THE PERFECT PLACE TO CATCH A DRAGON TO ME!

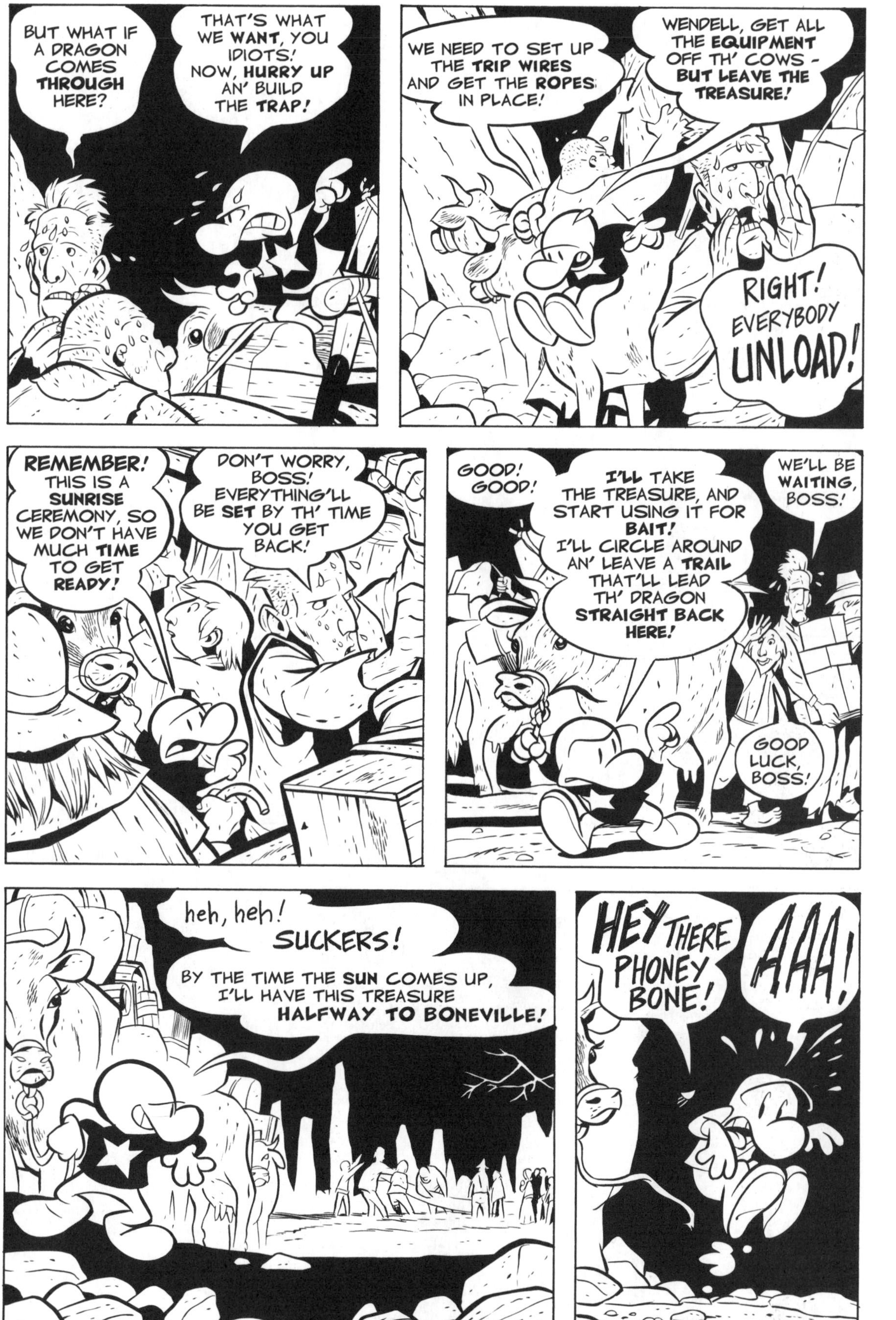
BUT WHAT IF A DRAGON COMES THROUGH HERE?
THAT'S WHAT WE WANT, YOU IDIOTS! NOW, HURRY UP AN' BUILD THE TRAP!
WE NEED TO SET UP THE TRIP WIRES AND GET THE ROPES IN PLACE!
WENDELL, GET ALL THE EQUIPMENT OFF TH' COWS - BUT LEAVE THE TREASURE!
RIGHT! EVERYBODY UNLOAD!
REMEMBER! THIS IS A SUNRISE CEREMONY, SO WE DON'T HAVE MUCH TIME TO GET READY!
DON'T WORRY, BOSS! EVERYTHING'LL BE SET BY TH' TIME YOU GET BACK!
GOOD! GOOD!
I'LL TAKE THE TREASURE, AND START USING IT FOR BAIT! I'LL CIRCLE AROUND AN' LEAVE A TRAIL THAT'LL LEAD TH' DRAGON STRAIGHT BACK HERE!
WE'LL BE WAITING, BOSS!
GOOD LUCK, BOSS!
heh, heh! SUCKERS!
BY THE TIME THE SUN COMES UP, I'LL HAVE THIS TREASURE HALFWAY TO BONEVILLE!
HEY THERE PHONEY BONE!
AAA!

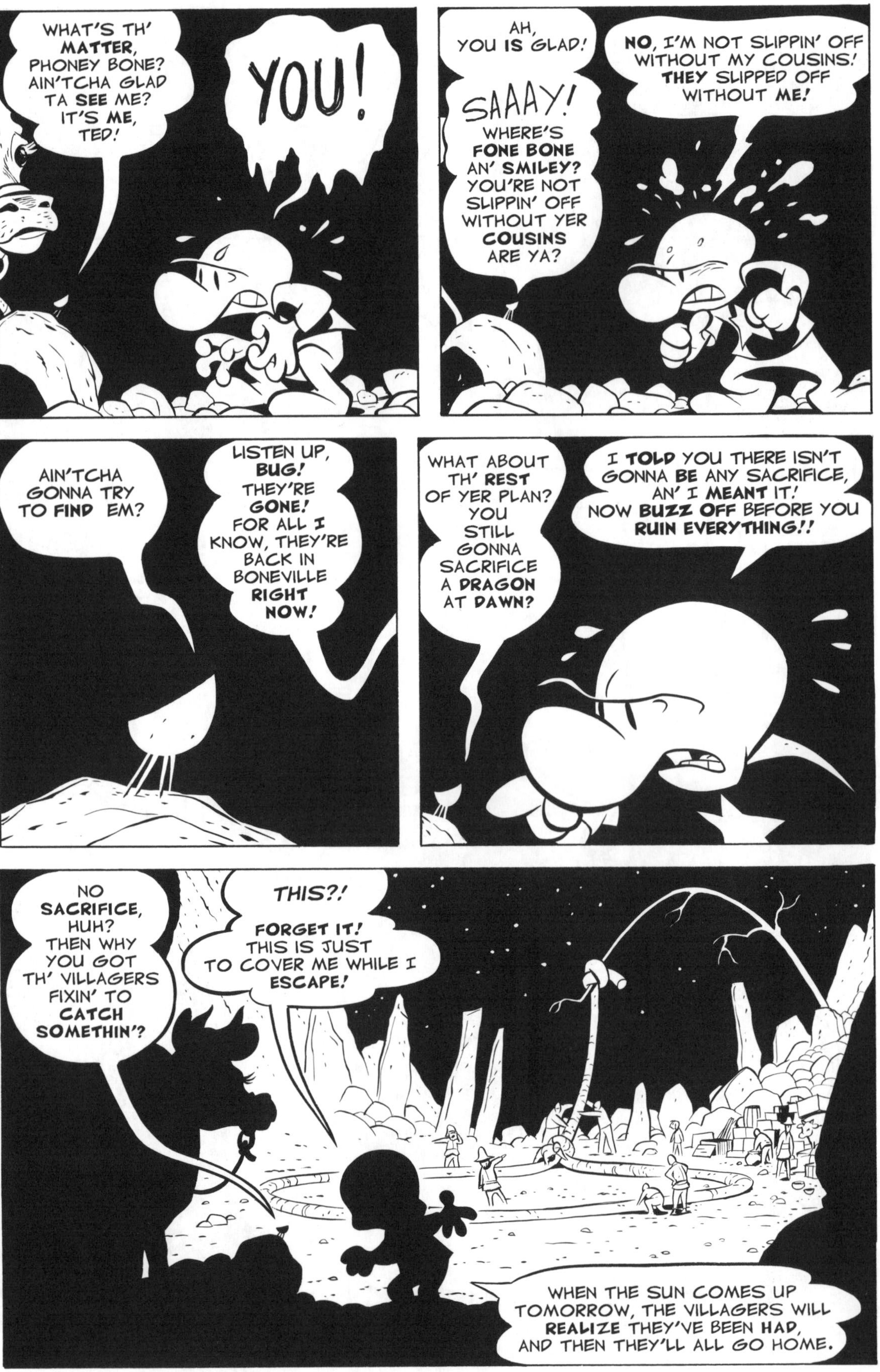
WHAT'S TH' MATTER, PHONEY BONE? AIN'TCHA GLAD TA SEE ME? IT'S ME, TED!
YOU!
AH, YOU IS GLAD!
SAAAY! WHERE'S FONE BONE AN' SMILEY? YOU'RE NOT SLIPPIN' OFF WITHOUT YER COUSINS ARE YA?
NO, I'M NOT SLIPPIN' OFF WITHOUT MY COUSINS! THEY SLIPPED OFF WITHOUT ME!
AIN'TCHA GONNA TRY TO FIND EM?
LISTEN UP, BUG! THEY'RE GONE! FOR ALL I KNOW, THEY'RE BACK IN BONEVILLE RIGHT NOW!
WHAT ABOUT TH' REST OF YER PLAN? YOU STILL GONNA SACRIFICE A DRAGON AT DAWN?
I TOLD YOU THERE ISN'T GONNA BE ANY SACRIFICE, AN' I MEANT IT! NOW BUZZ OFF BEFORE YOU RUIN EVERYTHING!!
NO SACRIFICE, HUH? THEN WHY YOU GOT TH' VILLAGERS FIXIN' TO CATCH SOMETHIN'?
THIS?!
FORGET IT! THIS IS JUST TO COVER ME WHILE I ESCAPE!
WHEN THE SUN COMES UP TOMORROW, THE VILLAGERS WILL REALIZE THEY'VE BEEN HAD, AND THEN THEY'LL ALL GO HOME.

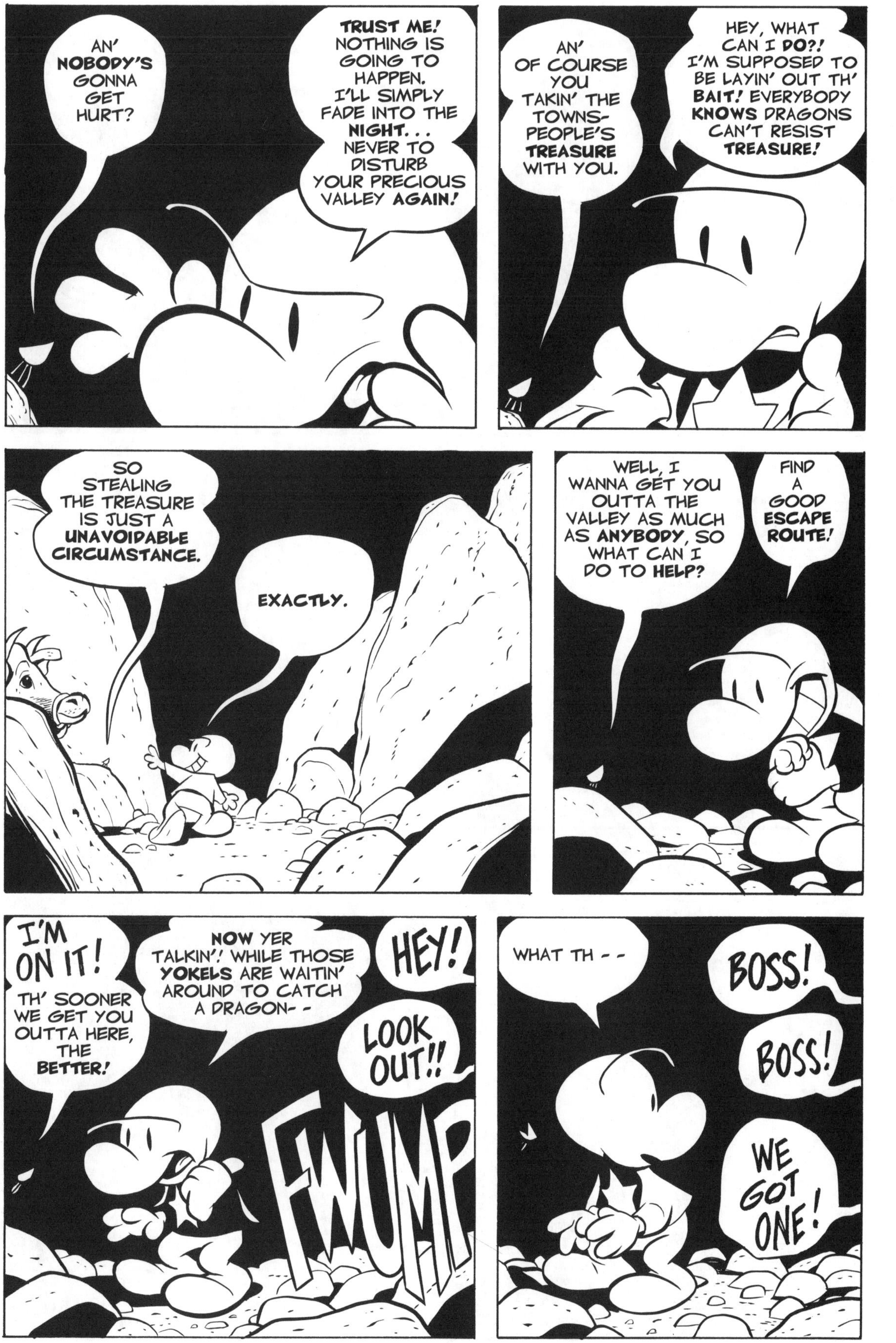
AN' NOBODY'S GONNA GET HURT?
TRUST ME! NOTHING IS GOING TO HAPPEN. I'LL SIMPLY FADE INTO THE NIGHT... NEVER TO DISTURB YOUR PRECIOUS VALLEY AGAIN!
AN' OF COURSE YOU TAKIN' THE TOWNS-PEOPLE'S TREASURE WITH YOU.
HEY, WHAT CAN I DO?! I'M SUPPOSED TO BE LAYIN' OUT TH' BAIT! EVERYBODY KNOWS DRAGONS CAN'T RESIST TREASURE!
SO STEALING THE TREASURE IS JUST A UNAVOIDABLE CIRCUMSTANCE.
EXACTLY.
WELL, I WANNA GET YOU OUTTA THE VALLEY AS MUCH AS ANYBODY, SO WHAT CAN I DO TO HELP?
FIND A GOOD ESCAPE ROUTE!
I'M ON IT!
TH' SOONER WE GET YOU OUTTA HERE, THE BETTER!
NOW YER TALKIN'! WHILE THOSE YOKELS ARE WAITIN' AROUND TO CATCH A DRAGON- -
HEY!
LOOK OUT!!
FWUMP
WHAT TH - -
BOSS!
BOSS!
WE GOT ONE!

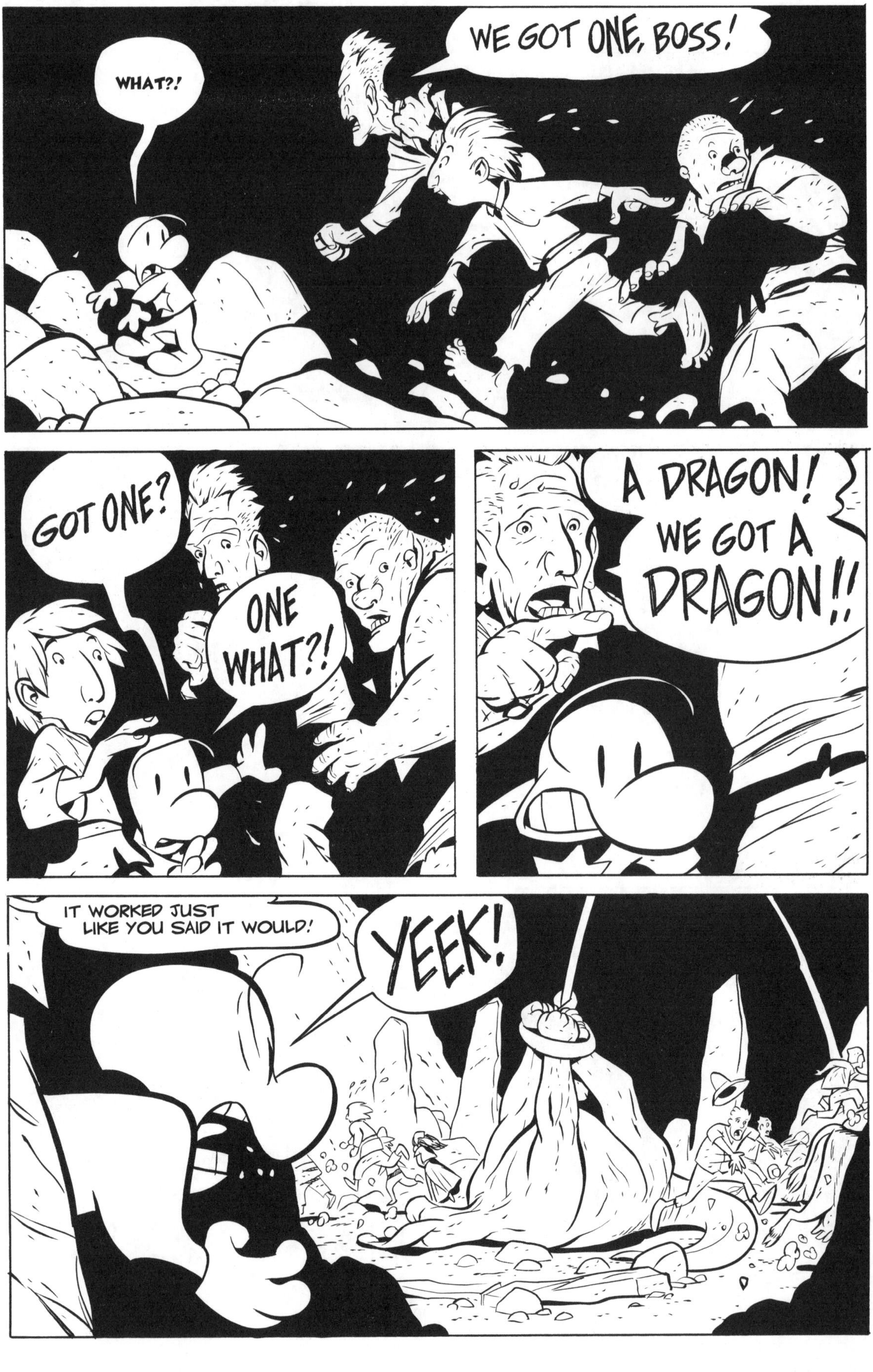
WHAT?!
WE GOT ONE, BOSS!
GOT ONE?
ONE WHAT?!
A DRAGON! WE GOT A DRAGON!!
IT WORKED JUST LIKE YOU SAID IT WOULD!
YEEK!

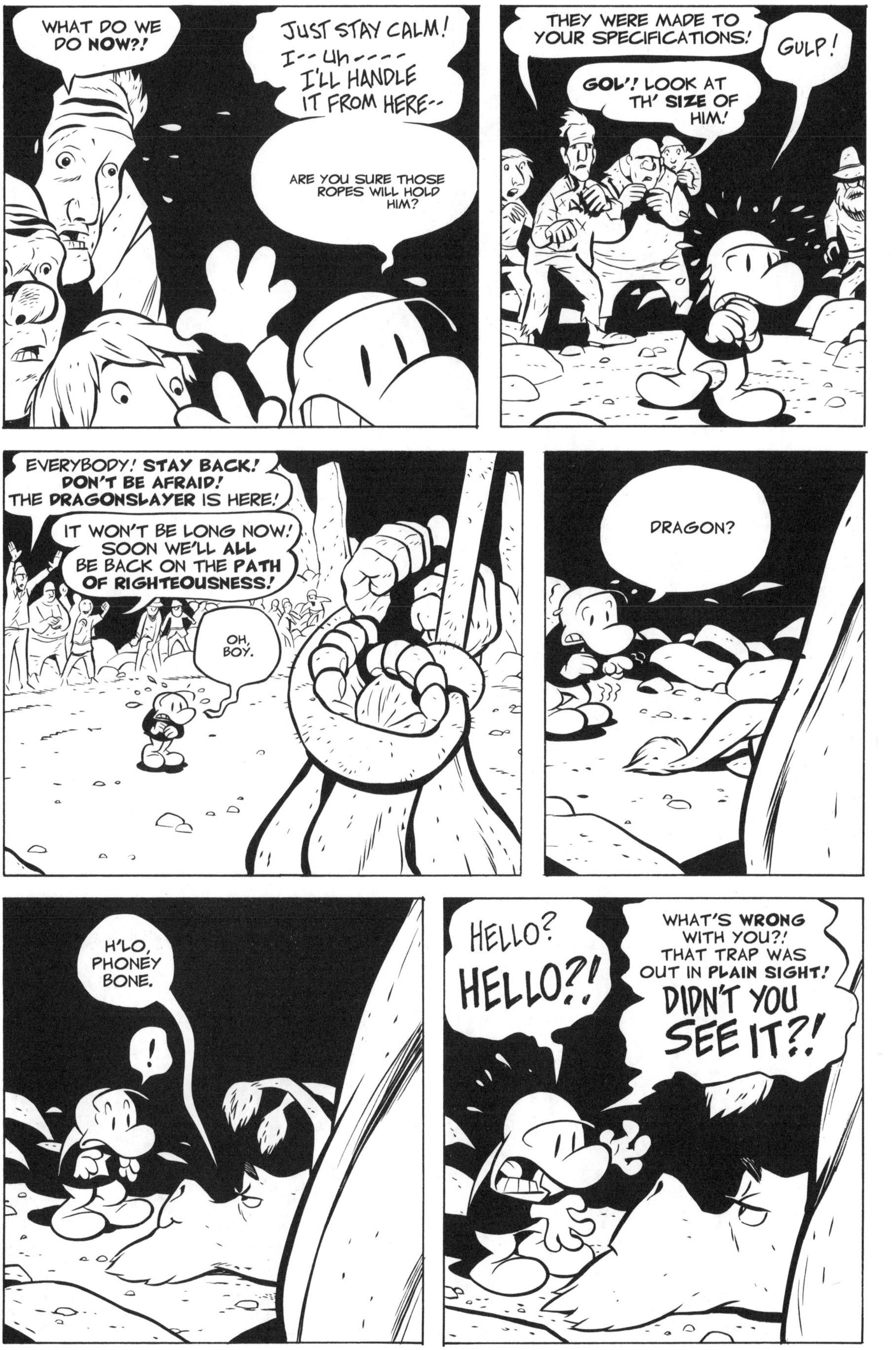
WHAT DO WE DO NOW?!
JUST STAY CALM! I-- Uh---- I'LL HANDLE IT FROM HERE--
ARE YOU SURE THOSE ROPES WILL HOLD HIM?
THEY WERE MADE TO YOUR SPECIFICATIONS!
GOL'! LOOK AT TH' SIZE OF HIM!
GULP!
EVERYBODY! STAY BACK! DON'T BE AFRAID! THE DRAGONSLAYER IS HERE!
IT WON'T BE LONG NOW! SOON WE'LL ALL BE BACK ON THE PATH OF RIGHTEOUSNESS!
OH, BOY.
DRAGON?
H'LO, PHONEY BONE.
!
HELLO? HELLO?!
WHAT'S WRONG WITH YOU?! THAT TRAP WAS OUT IN PLAIN SIGHT! DIDN'T YOU SEE IT?!

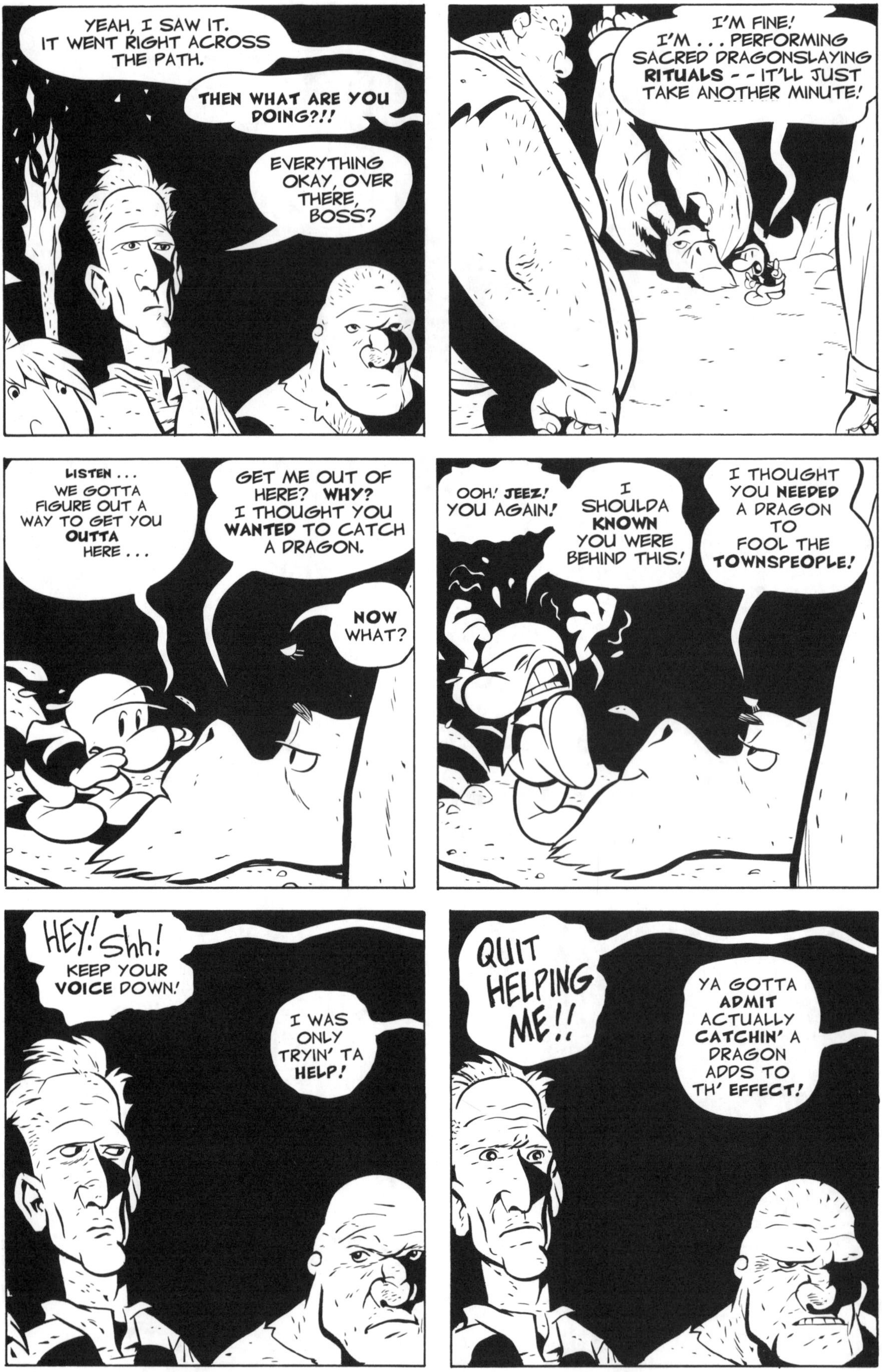
YEAH, I SAW IT. IT WENT RIGHT ACROSS THE PATH.
THEN WHAT ARE YOU DOING?!!
EVERYTHING OKAY, OVER THERE, BOSS?
I'M FINE! I'M . . . PERFORMING SACRED DRAGONSLAYING RITUALS - - IT'LL JUST TAKE ANOTHER MINUTE!
LISTEN . . . WE GOTTA FIGURE OUT A WAY TO GET YOU OUTTA HERE . . .
GET ME OUT OF HERE? WHY? I THOUGHT YOU WANTED TO CATCH A DRAGON.
NOW WHAT?
OOH! JEEZ! YOU AGAIN!
I SHOULDA KNOWN YOU WERE BEHIND THIS!
I THOUGHT YOU NEEDED A DRAGON TO FOOL THE TOWNSPEOPLE!
HEY! Shh! KEEP YOUR VOICE DOWN!
I WAS ONLY TRYIN' TA HELP!
QUIT HELPING ME!!
YA GOTTA ADMIT ACTUALLY CATCHIN' A DRAGON ADDS TO TH' EFFECT!

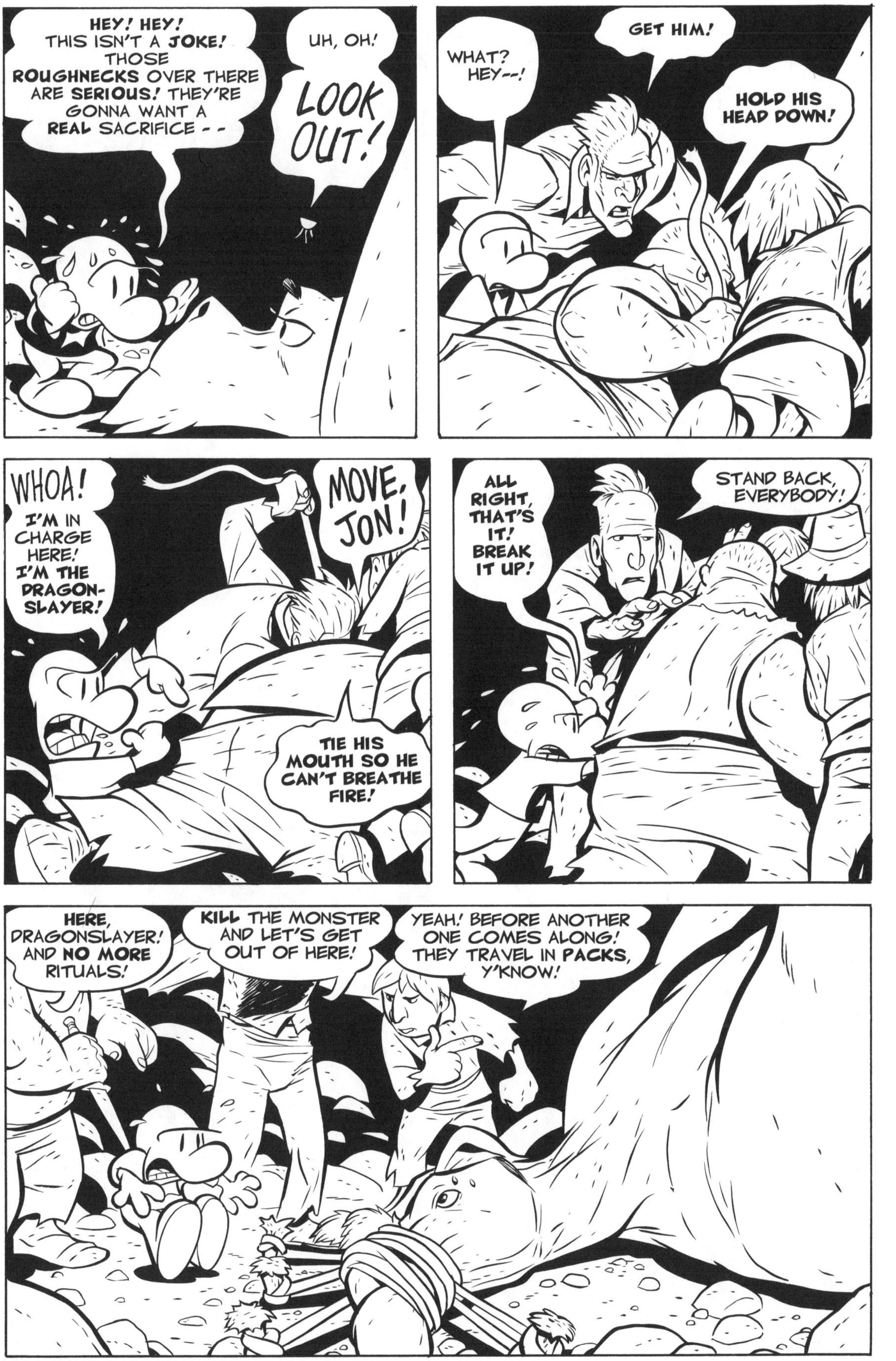
HEY! HEY! THIS ISN'T A JOKE! THOSE ROUGHNECKS OVER THERE ARE SERIOUS! THEY'RE GONNA WANT A REAL SACRIFICE - -
UH, OH!
LOOK OUT!
WHAT? HEY--!
GET HIM!
HOLD HIS HEAD DOWN!
WHOA!
I'M IN CHARGE HERE! I'M THE DRAGON-SLAYER!
MOVE, JON!
TIE HIS MOUTH SO HE CAN'T BREATHE FIRE!
ALL RIGHT, THAT'S IT! BREAK IT UP!
STAND BACK, EVERYBODY!
HERE, DRAGONSLAYER! AND NO MORE RITUALS!
KILL THE MONSTER AND LET'S GET OUT OF HERE!
YEAH! BEFORE ANOTHER ONE COMES ALONG! THEY TRAVEL IN PACKS, Y'KNOW!

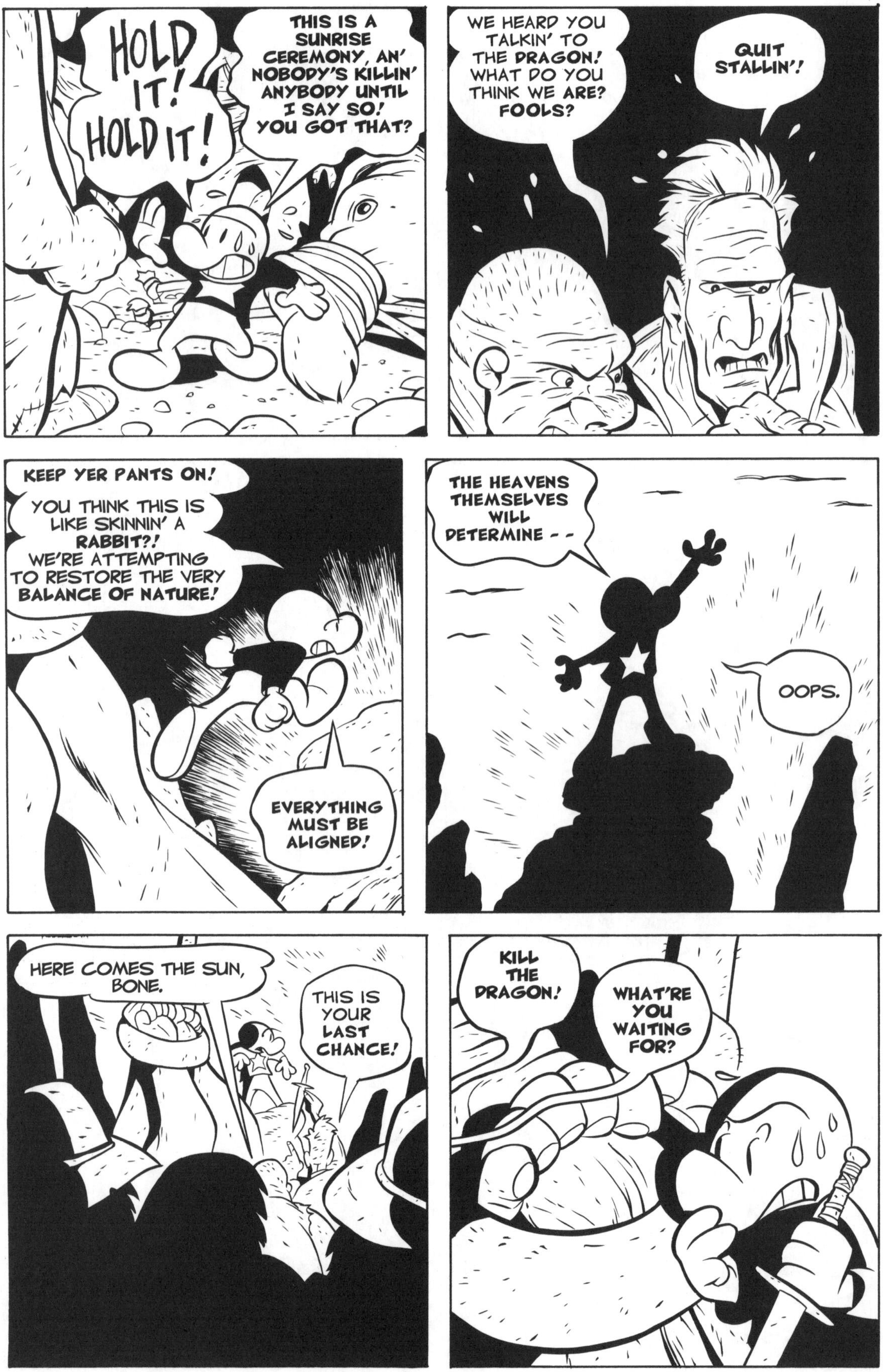
HOLD IT! HOLD IT!
THIS IS A SUNRISE CEREMONY, AN' NOBODY'S KILLIN' ANYBODY UNTIL I SAY SO! YOU GOT THAT?
WE HEARD YOU TALKIN' TO THE DRAGON! WHAT DO YOU THINK WE ARE? FOOLS?
QUIT STALLIN'!
KEEP YER PANTS ON!
YOU THINK THIS IS LIKE SKINNIN' A RABBIT?! WE'RE ATTEMPTING TO RESTORE THE VERY BALANCE OF NATURE!
EVERYTHING MUST BE ALIGNED!
THE HEAVENS THEMSELVES WILL DETERMINE --
OOPS.
HERE COMES THE SUN, BONE.
THIS IS YOUR LAST CHANCE!
KILL THE DRAGON!
WHAT'RE YOU WAITING FOR?

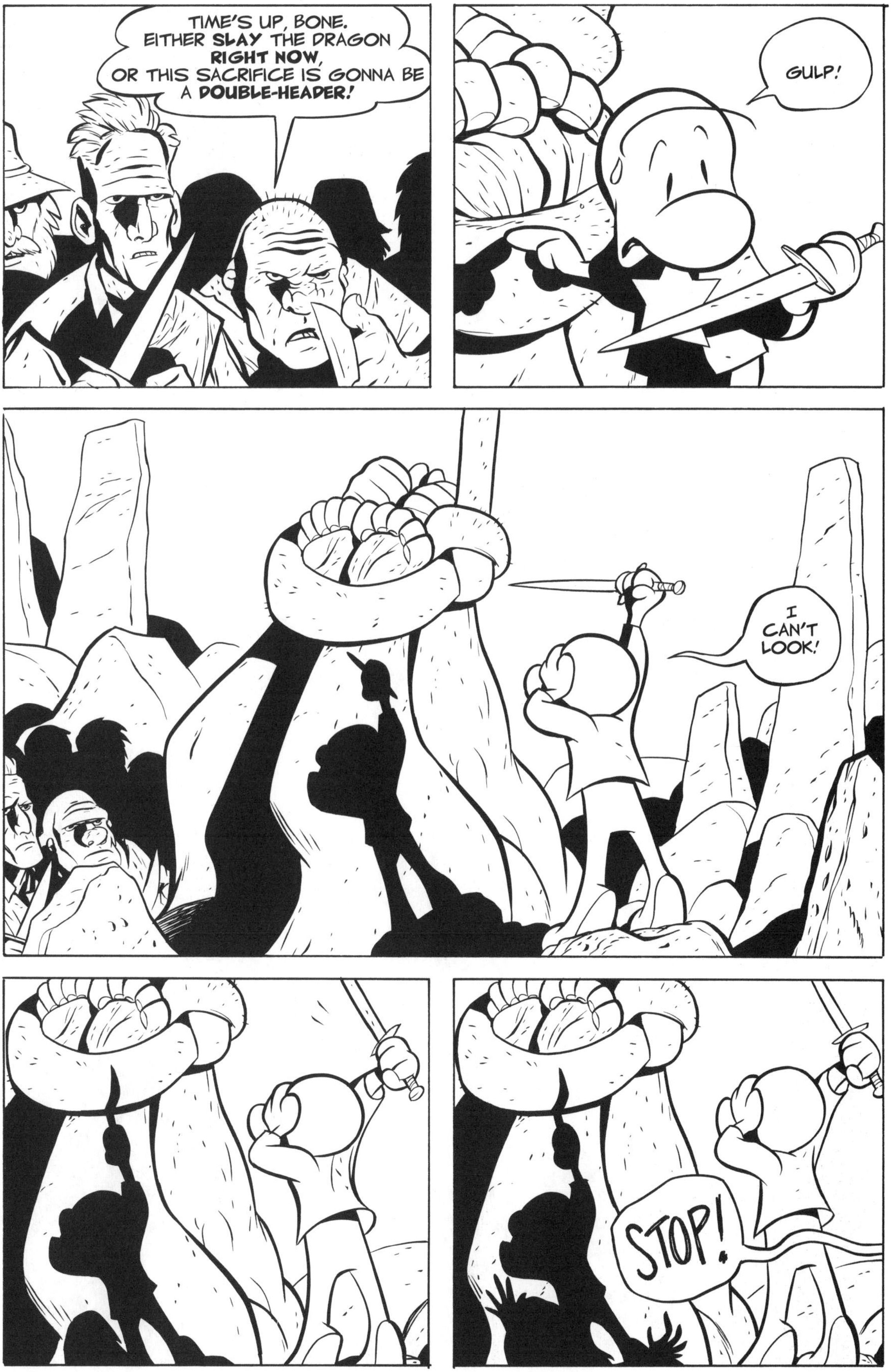
TIME'S UP, BONE. EITHER **SLAY** THE DRAGON **RIGHT NOW**, OR THIS SACRIFICE IS GONNA BE A **DOUBLE-HEADER!**
GULP!
I CAN'T LOOK!
STOP!

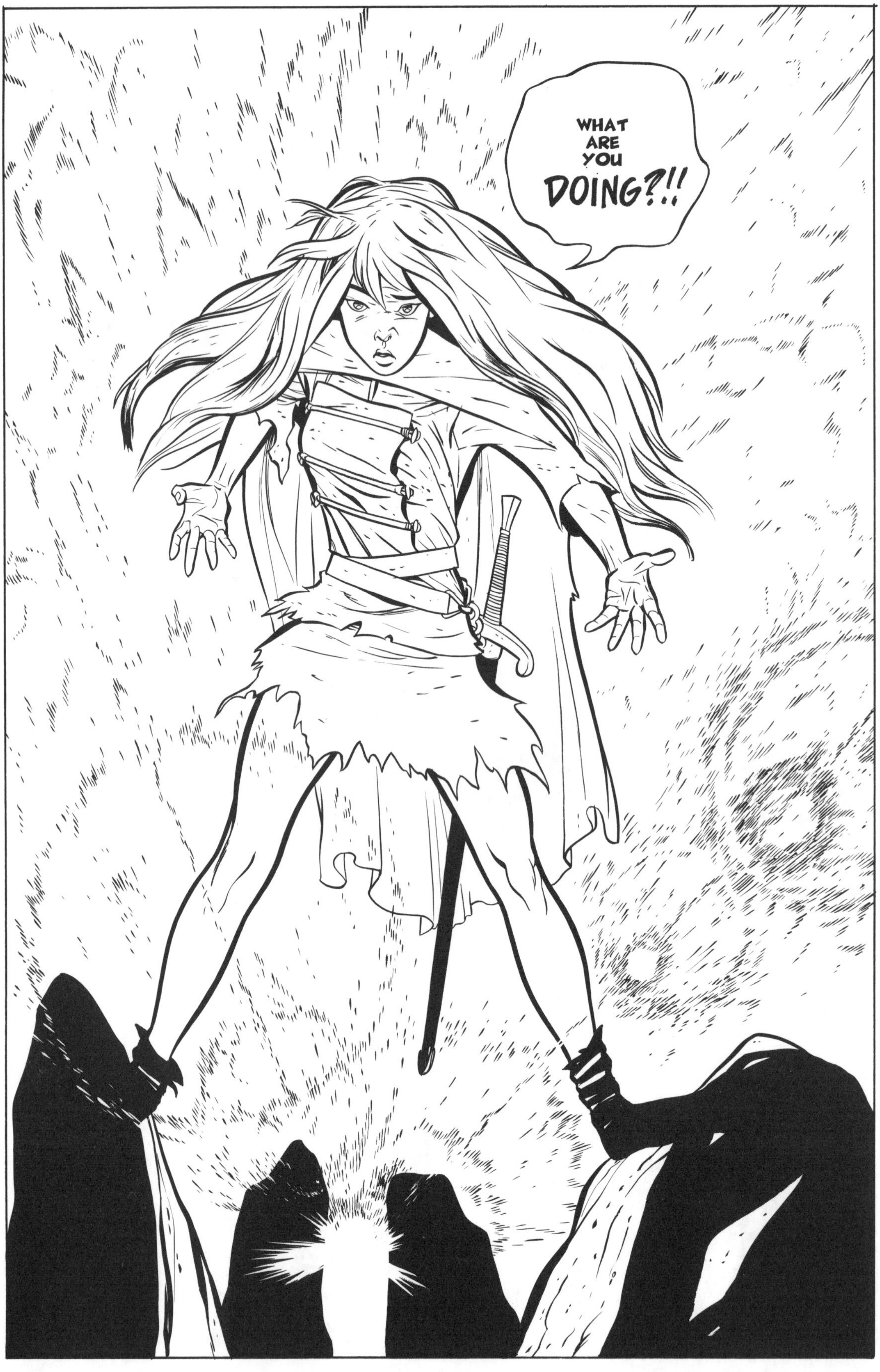
WHAT ARE YOU DOING?!!

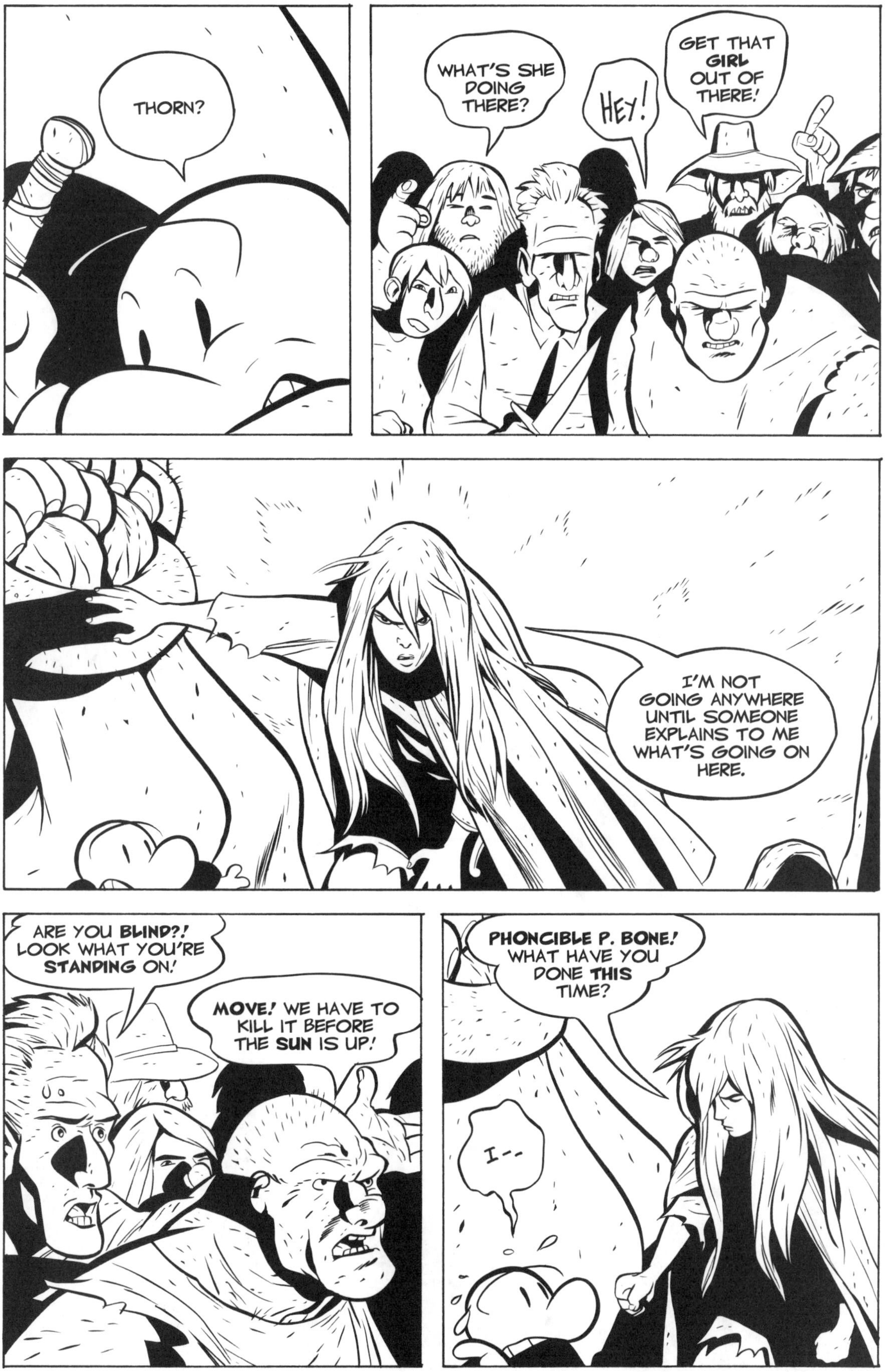
THORN?
WHAT'S SHE DOING THERE?
HEY!
GET THAT GIRL OUT OF THERE!
I'M NOT GOING ANYWHERE UNTIL SOMEONE EXPLAINS TO ME WHAT'S GOING ON HERE.
ARE YOU BLIND?! LOOK WHAT YOU'RE STANDING ON!
MOVE! WE HAVE TO KILL IT BEFORE THE SUN IS UP!
PHONCIBLE P. BONE! WHAT HAVE YOU DONE THIS TIME?
I--

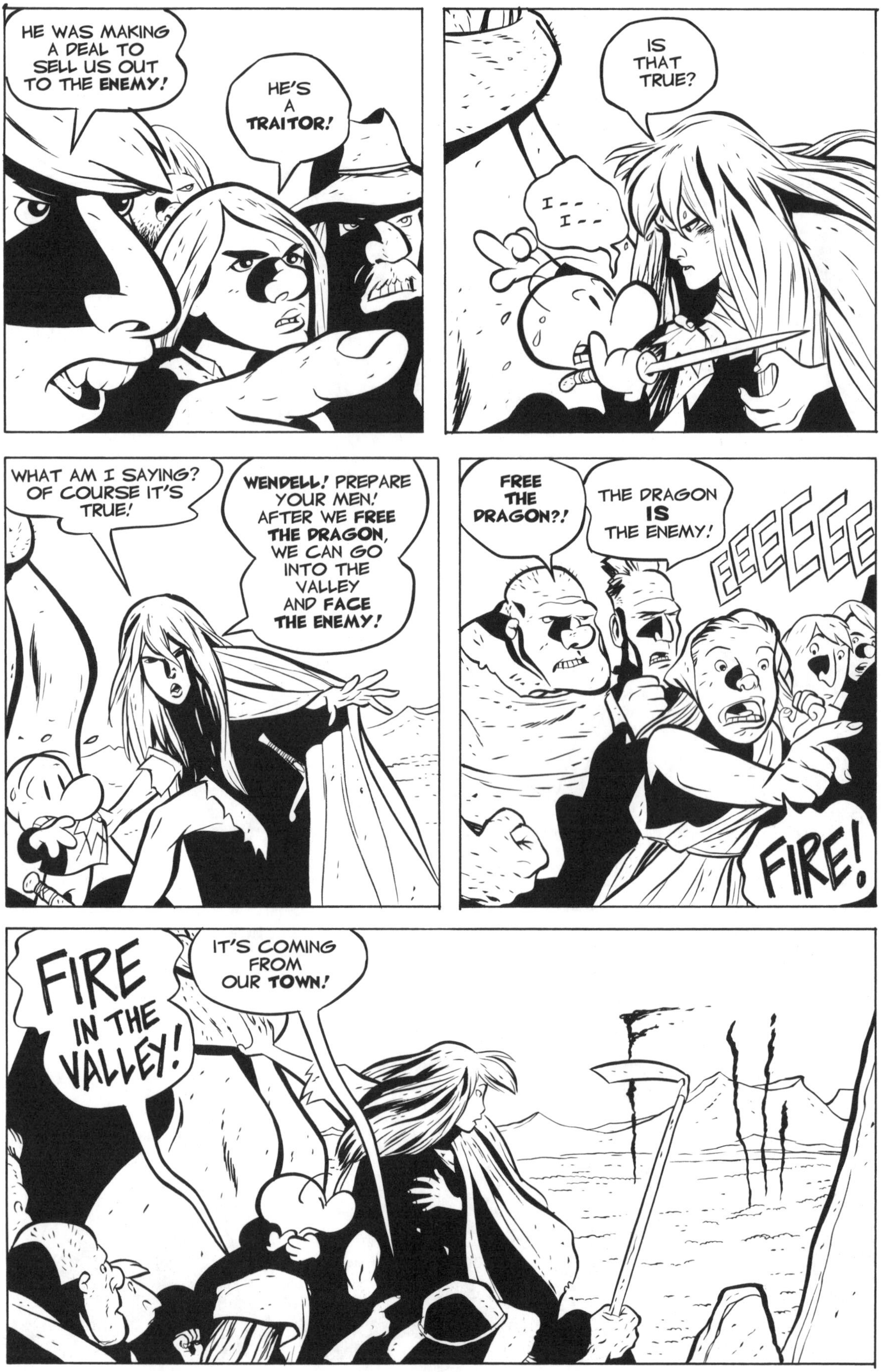
HE WAS MAKING A DEAL TO SELL US OUT TO THE ENEMY!
HE'S A TRAITOR!
IS THAT TRUE?
I-- I--
WHAT AM I SAYING? OF COURSE IT'S TRUE!
WENDELL! PREPARE YOUR MEN! AFTER WE FREE THE DRAGON, WE CAN GO INTO THE VALLEY AND FACE THE ENEMY!
FREE THE DRAGON?!
THE DRAGON IS THE ENEMY!
EEEEEEE
FIRE!
FIRE IN THE VALLEY!
IT'S COMING FROM OUR TOWN!

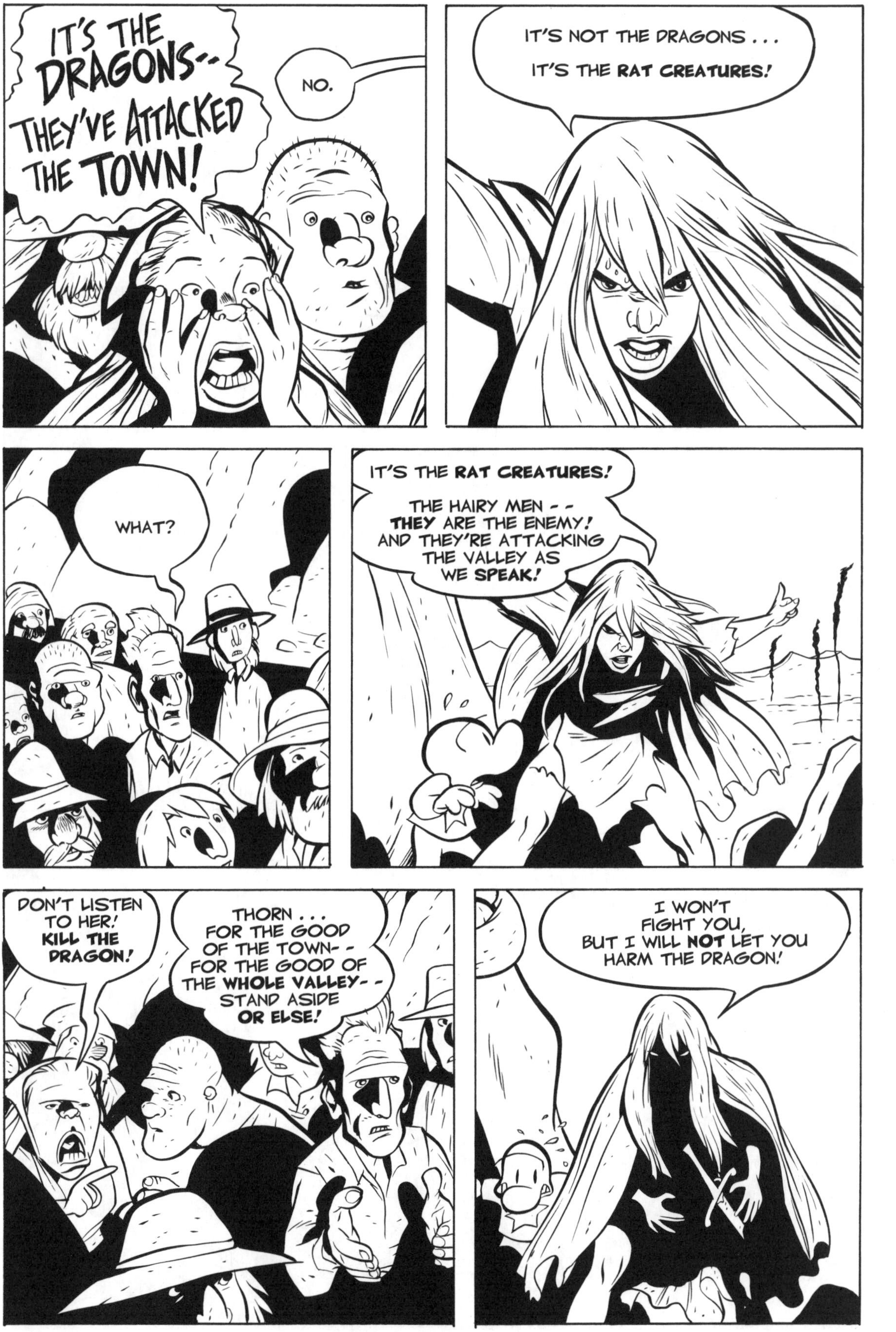
IT'S THE DRAGONS-- THEY'VE ATTACKED THE TOWN!
NO.
IT'S NOT THE DRAGONS . . .
IT'S THE RAT CREATURES!
WHAT?
IT'S THE RAT CREATURES!
THE HAIRY MEN - - THEY ARE THE ENEMY! AND THEY'RE ATTACKING THE VALLEY AS WE SPEAK!
DON'T LISTEN TO HER! KILL THE DRAGON!
THORN . . . FOR THE GOOD OF THE TOWN- - FOR THE GOOD OF THE WHOLE VALLEY- - STAND ASIDE OR ELSE!
I WON'T FIGHT YOU, BUT I WILL NOT LET YOU HARM THE DRAGON!

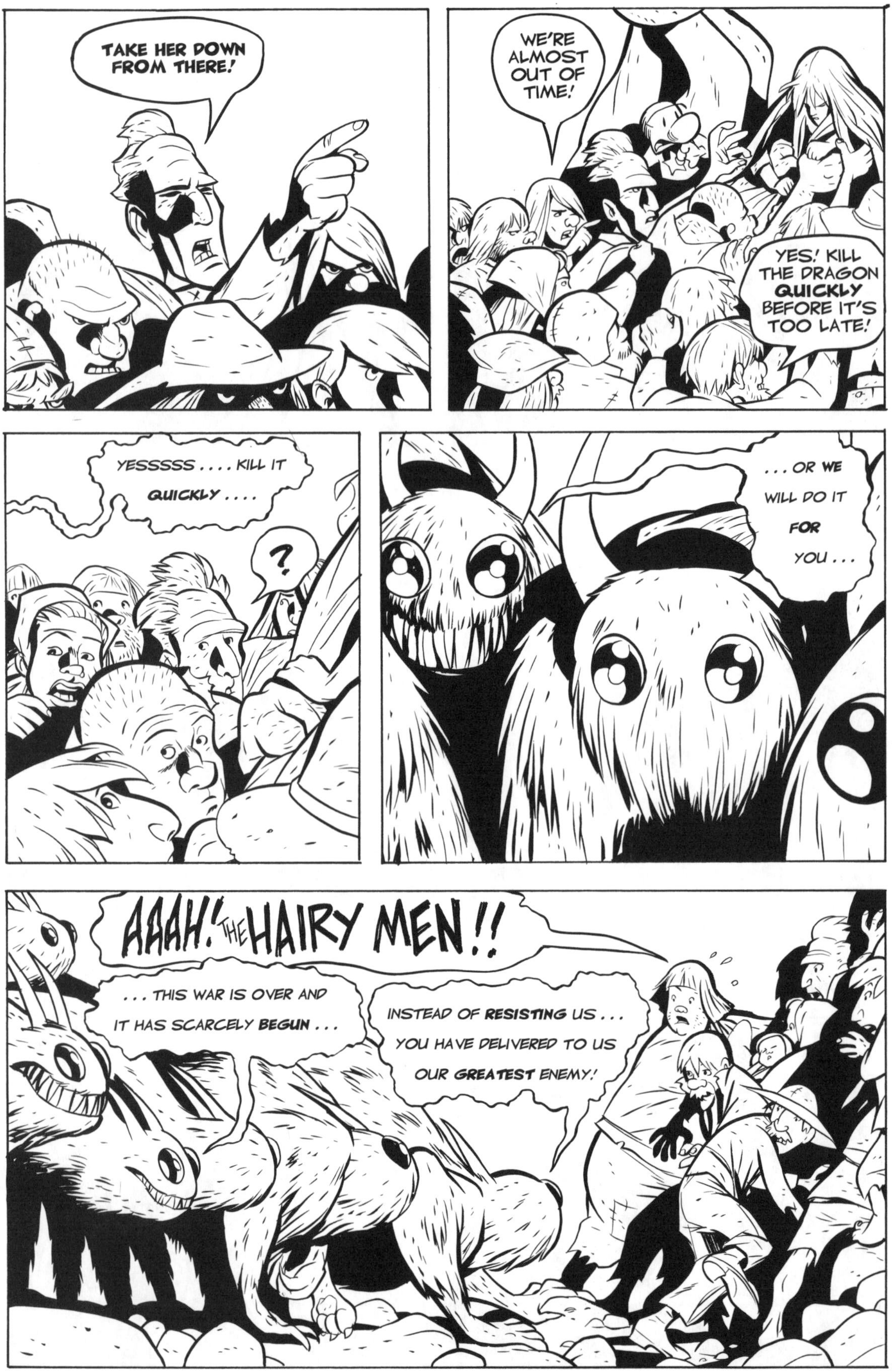
TAKE HER DOWN FROM THERE!
WE'RE ALMOST OUT OF TIME!
YES! KILL THE DRAGON QUICKLY BEFORE IT'S TOO LATE!
YESSSSS . . . . KILL IT QUICKLY . . . .
?
. . . OR WE WILL DO IT FOR YOU . . .
AAAH! THE HAIRY MEN!!
. . . THIS WAR IS OVER AND IT HAS SCARCELY BEGUN . . .
INSTEAD OF RESISTING US . . . YOU HAVE DELIVERED TO US OUR GREATEST ENEMY!

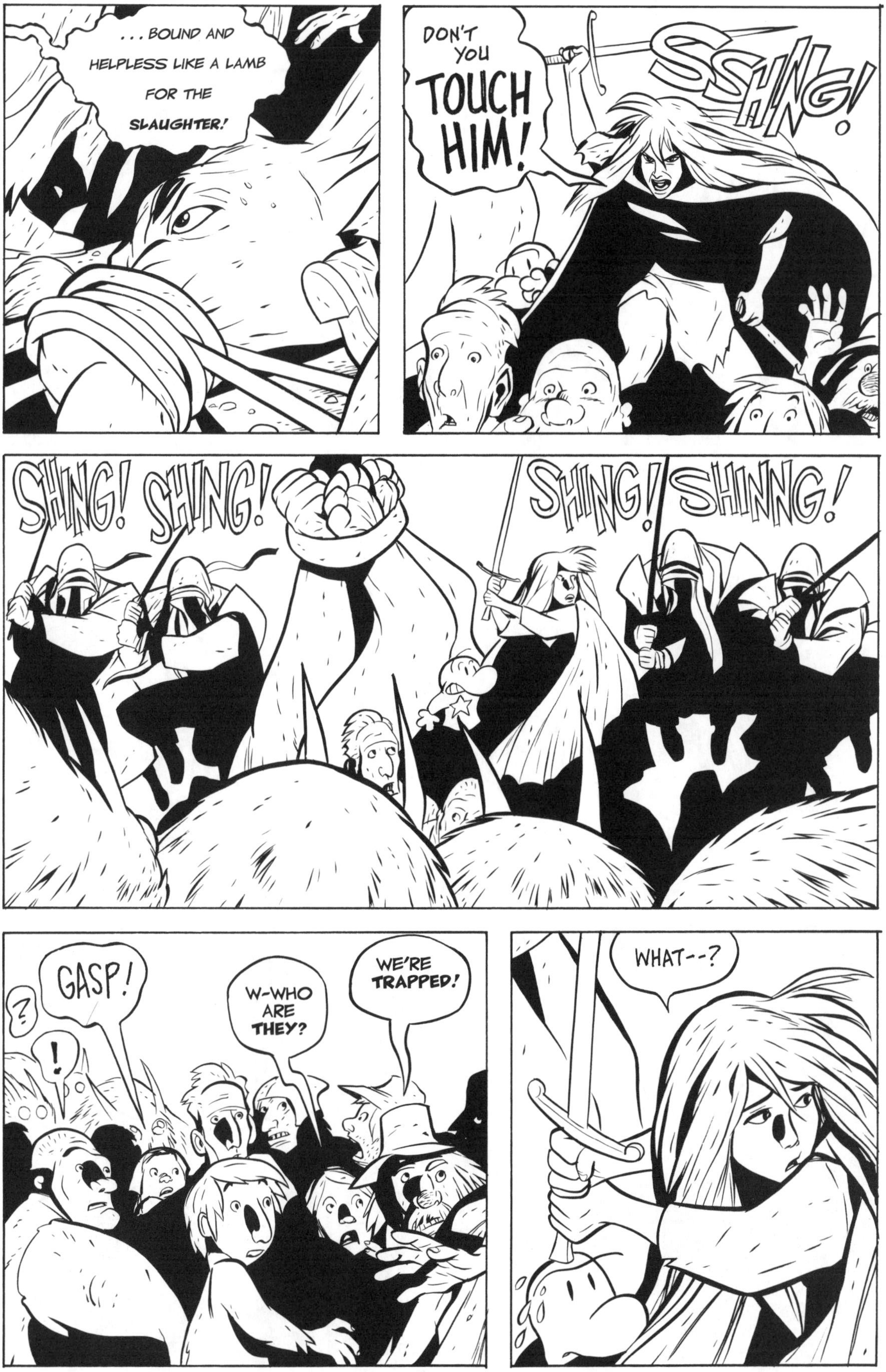

. . . BOUND AND HELPLESS LIKE A LAMB FOR THE SLAUGHTER!
DON'T YOU TOUCH HIM!
SSHING!
SHING!
SHING!
SHING!
SHINNG!
?
!
GASP!
W-WHO ARE THEY?
WE'RE TRAPPED!
WHAT--?

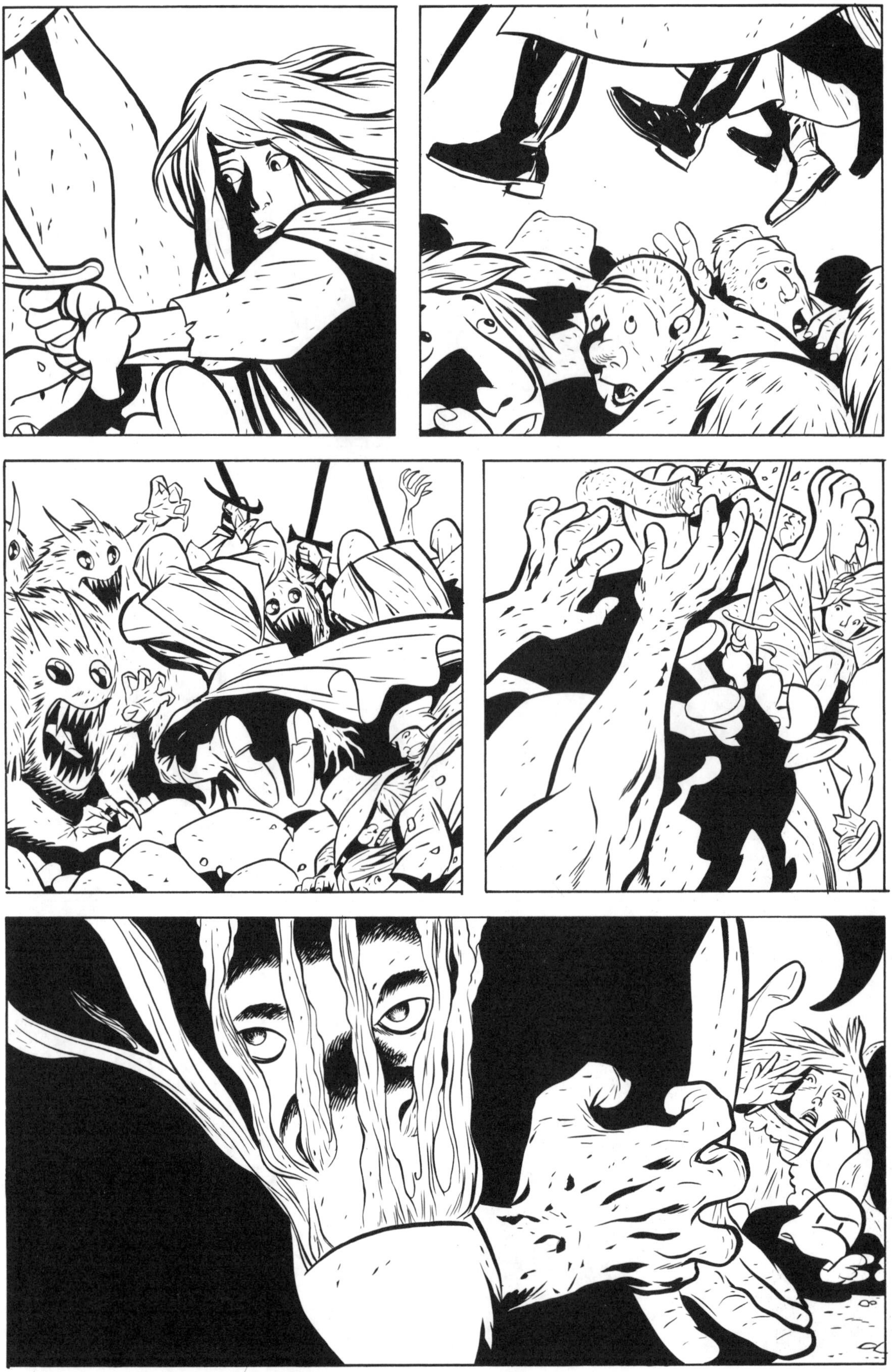

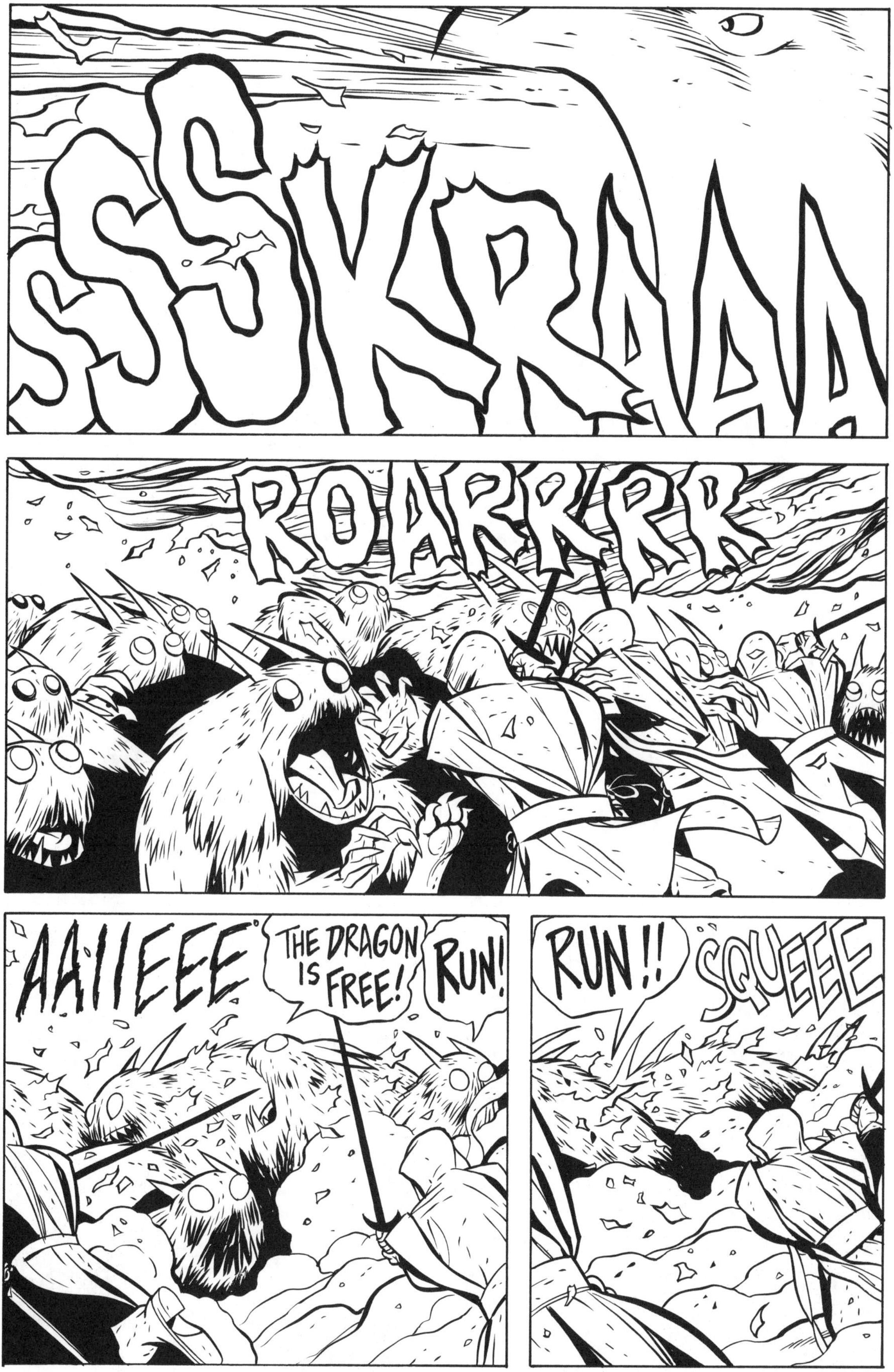
SSSKRAAA
ROARRRR
AAIIEEE
THE DRAGON IS FREE!
RUN!
RUN!!
SQUEEE

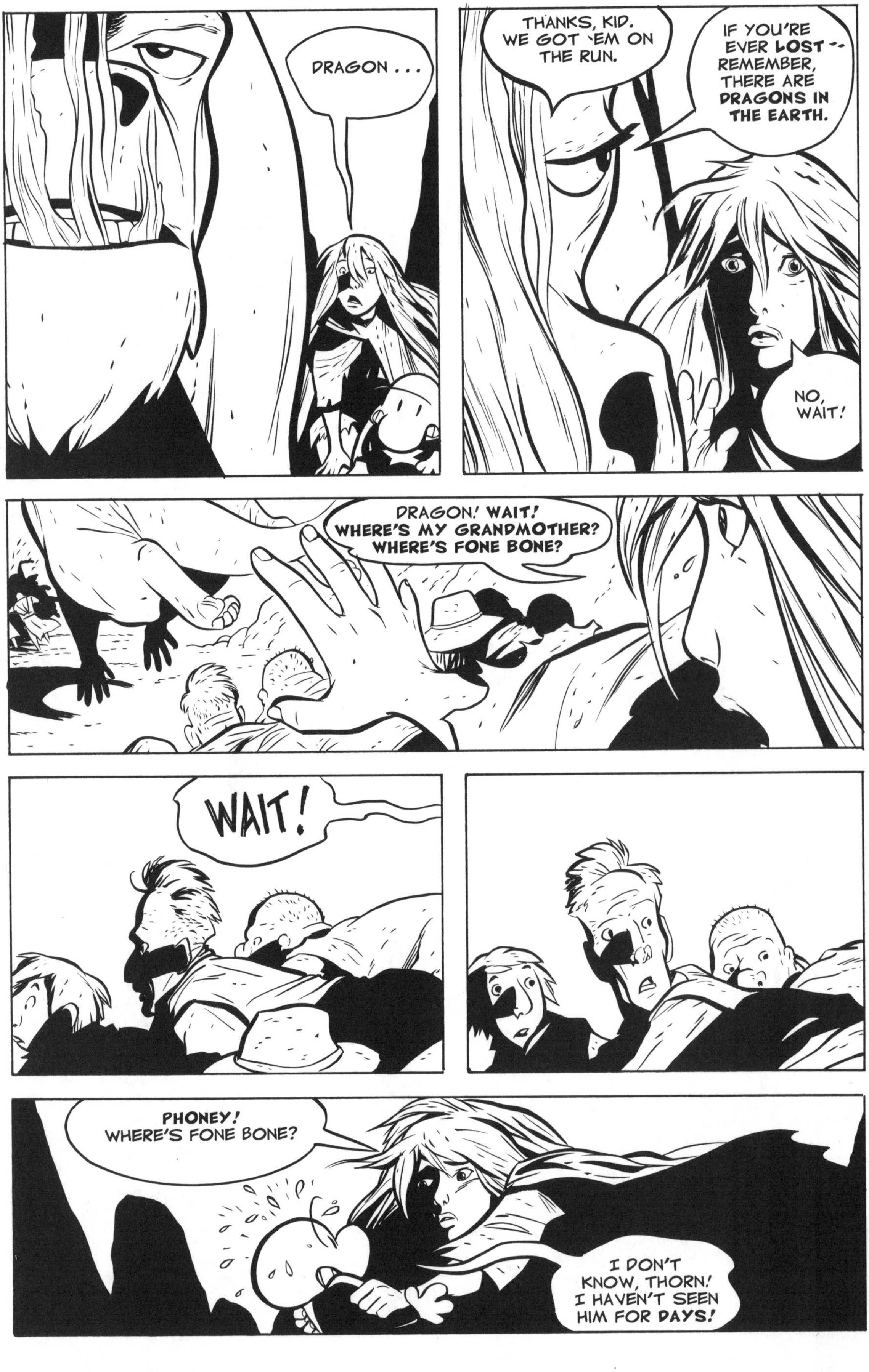
DRAGON . . .
THANKS, KID. WE GOT 'EM ON THE RUN.
IF YOU'RE EVER LOST -- REMEMBER, THERE ARE DRAGONS IN THE EARTH.
NO, WAIT!
DRAGON! WAIT! WHERE'S MY GRANDMOTHER? WHERE'S FONE BONE?
WAIT!
PHONEY! WHERE'S FONE BONE?
I DON'T KNOW, THORN! I HAVEN'T SEEN HIM FOR DAYS!

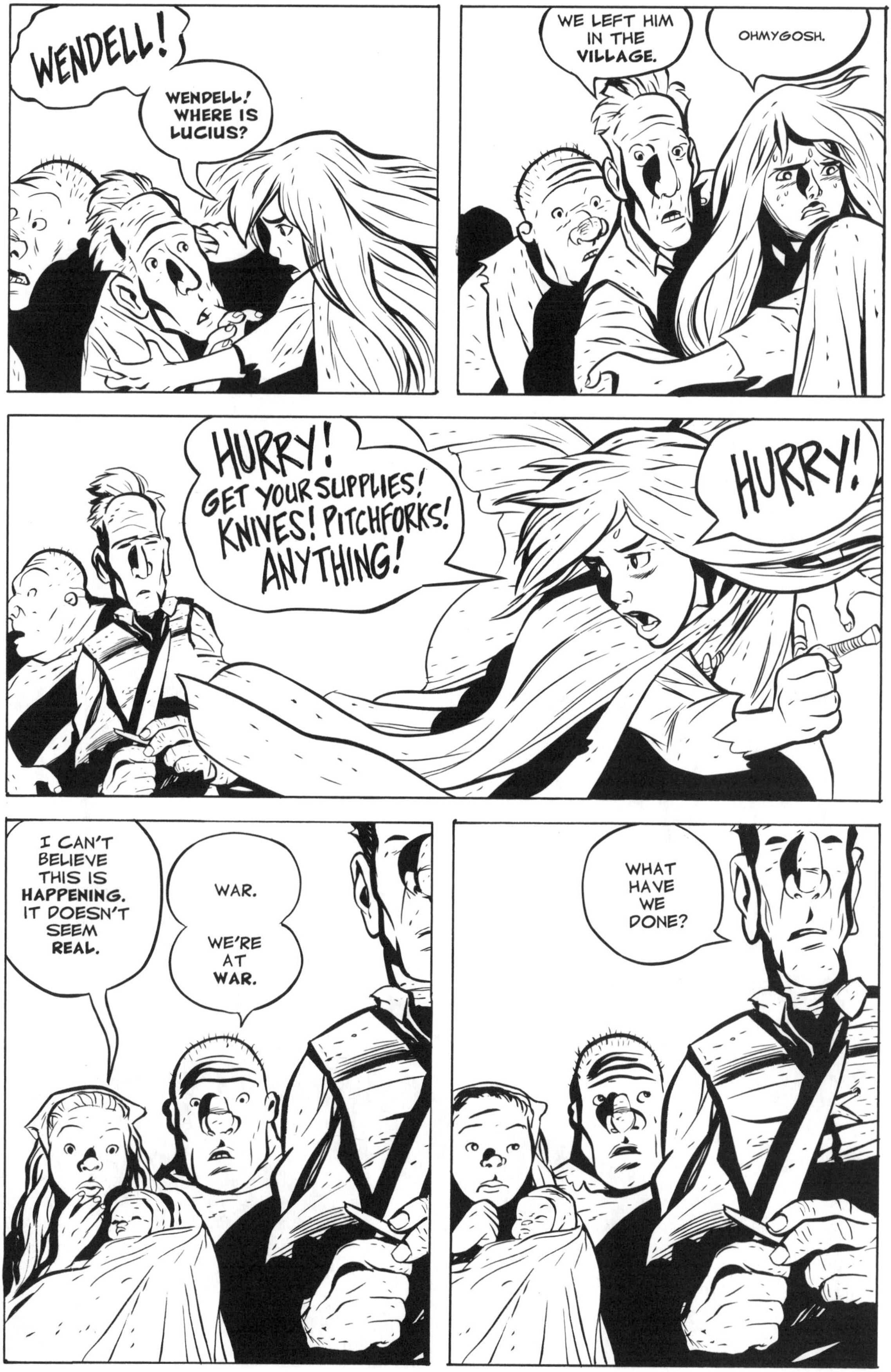
WENDELL!
WENDELL! WHERE IS LUCIUS?
WE LEFT HIM IN THE VILLAGE.
OHMYGOSH.
HURRY! GET YOUR SUPPLIES! KNIVES! PITCHFORKS! ANYTHING!
HURRY!
I CAN'T BELIEVE THIS IS HAPPENING. IT DOESN'T SEEM REAL.
WAR.
WE'RE AT WAR.
WHAT HAVE WE DONE?

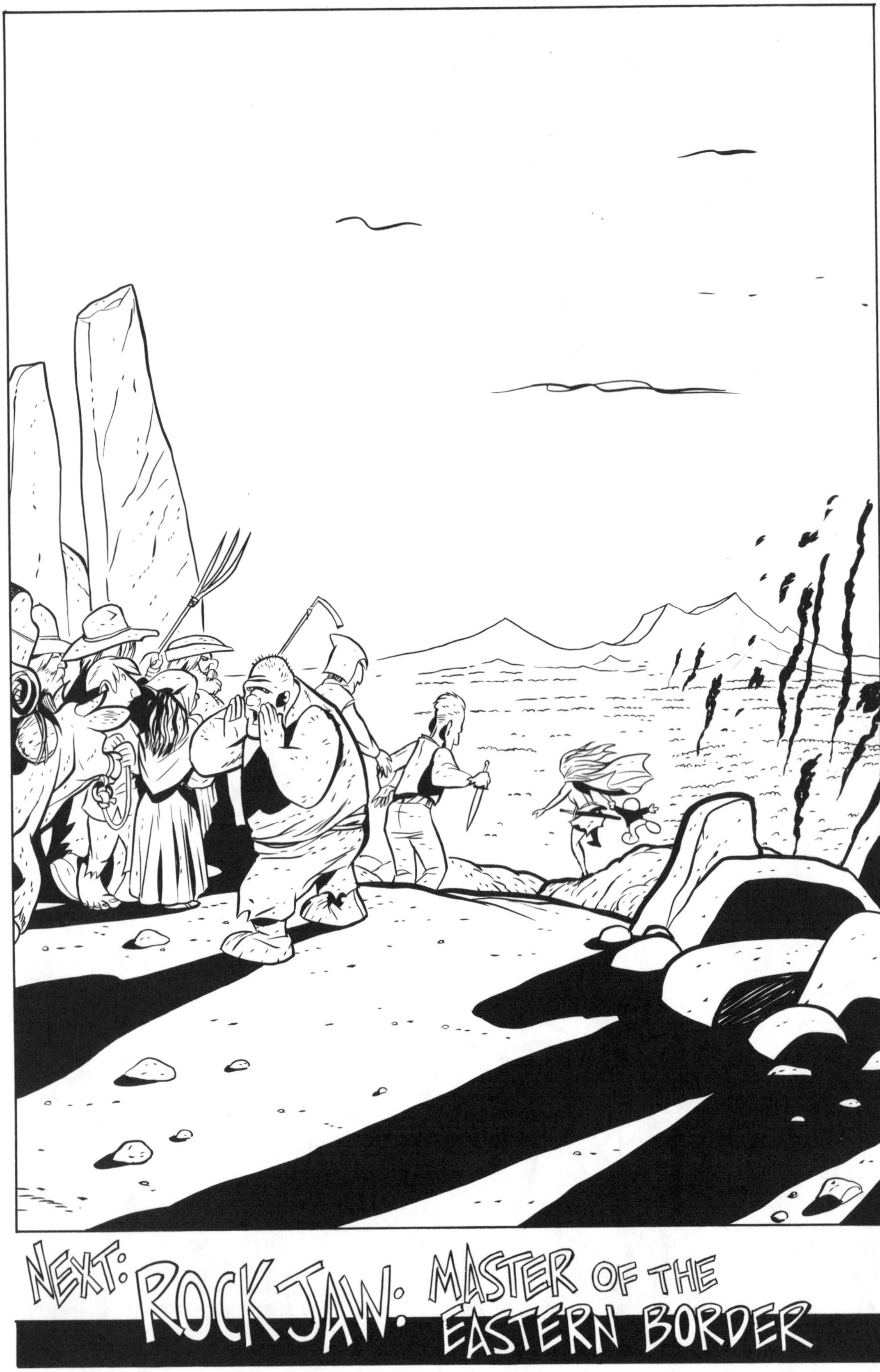

NEXT: ROCK JAW: MASTER OF THE EASTERN BORDER

OTHER BOOKS BY JEFF SMITH

THE FIRST TRILOGY

BONE VOLUME ONE: OUT FROM BONEVILLE

BONE VOLUME TWO: THE GREAT COW RACE

BONE VOLUME THREE: EYES OF THE STORM

THE SECOND TRILOGY

BONE VOLUME FOUR: THE DRAGONSLAYER

BONE VOLUME FIVE: ROCKJAW, MASTER OF THE EASTERN BORDER

BONE VOLUME SIX: OLD MAN'S CAVE

THE THIRD TRILOGY

BONE VOLUME SEVEN: GHOST CIRCLES

BONE VOLUME EIGHT: TREASURE HUNTERS

PREQUELS

STUPID, STUPID RAT TAILS: THE ADVENTURES OF BIG JOHNSON BONE,
FRONTIER HERO
(WRITTEN BY TOM SNIEGOSKI, DRAWN BY JEFF SMITH)

ROSE
(WRITTEN BY JEFF SMITH, PAINTED BY CHARLES VESS)

Available in fine bookstores and comic shops everywhere
For more information or to order online visit us at
www.boneville.com